W9-CLB-667

Poor Law to Poverty Program

Poor Law to Poverty Program

Economic Security Policy
in Britain and the United States

Samuel Mencher

University of Pittsburgh Press

CARNEGIE LIBRARY
LIVINGSTONE COLLEGE
SALISBURY, N. C. 28144

Library of Congress Catalog Card Number 67-13926
ISBN 0-8229-5243-2
Copyright © 1967, University of Pittsburgh Press
All Rights Reserved
Second Printing 1970
Paperback reissue 1974
Media Directions Inc., London
Manufactured in the United States of America

360
M536
c. 2

In the completion of this volume, I should like to acknowledge my indebtedness to Dr. Eveline Burns, who, as teacher and friend, continuously stimulated my interest in social policy, to the University of Pittsburgh, which provided the kind of balanced academic diet permitting research and writing, and to my wife, who persevered with me over the long and dusty trail.

100771

Foreword

THE PREPARATION of a Foreword to a posthumous book is inevitably a saddening task, and never more so than when the author was a valued colleague as well as a close friend, for to the sense of personal loss is added the regret at the loss suffered by the profession.

Sam Mencher, as he was always known, died suddenly at the early age of 49. He belonged to that all-too-small group of contemporary social workers who have made the study of social policy their central concern. Trained in the social sciences at the City College of New York and holding a Master's degree in sociology from Columbia University, he decided, at the age of 27, to enter social work and received his professional Master's degree in 1947. After a brief period of social work practice, as a children's worker, and as a casework consultant in Maine, he taught in the Sociology Department at Bowdoin College, before returning to the Columbia University School of Social Work to study for his doctorate. It seems likely that he selected the Columbia School because it was offering a degree in Social *Welfare* rather than Social *Work,* and because of the opportunity offered by the then new doctoral program for specialization in social policy. In any event, he quickly made his mark through his intellectual abilities and his sharp critical capacities.

Because of his interest, even then, in trends in the respective roles of government action and voluntarism, I urged him to apply for a Fulbright Fellowship (which he received), so that he could study the role of voluntary welfare in a society where the state had accepted very extensive responsibilities for the welfare of its citizens. His fellowship was held at the London School of Economics where he worked under Professor Richard Titmuss, who quickly recognized his qualities and arranged for him to deliver a number of lectures, including the distinguished Loch Memorial Lecture.

Sam Mencher concentrated for his doctoral research on the public-voluntary relationships in the child welfare field and produced a valuable study of the varying adjustments made by the voluntary agencies to the expanding role of the state, and a judicious evaluation of the effects and viability of the various policies. Parts of his study subsequently appeared as articles in the *Social Service Review* in March and June 1958.

A year after receiving his doctorate in 1957, Mencher left the faculty of the School of Social Work at New York University to join the faculty of Social Work at Pittsburgh and had been a full professor there for several years at the time of his death. The intervening years were richly productive. He held a full-time teaching appointment, in the course of which he took major responsibility for the teaching in research and social policy and developed a new curriculum in social administration which involved lengthy negotiations with the social work educational establishment. He served for a period on the Editorial Board of *Social Work*. He conducted a study for the State and Local Welfare Commission of Pennsylvania on the basis of which he made some interesting proposals for the organization of community welfare services, and he returned to England in 1965–66, this time under a Public Health Service grant, holding office at the University of Manchester. But above all he wrote. These nine years saw the publication of three books and at least fifteen significant articles or monographs. A fourth book, the product of his recent work in England, is scheduled for early publication.

Three major concerns occupied him. He was eager to strengthen the research component of social work education and to raise the level of social work scholarship. A number of his publications are directed to this end (in particular, his book on *The Research Method in Social Work Education*, and his contributions to the volumes edited by Edward E. Schwartz on *Manpower in Social Welfare: Research Perspectives*, and by

Henry Maas entitled *Five Fields of Social Service: Reviews of Research*).
On occasion his concern took the form of sharply critical reports on
current pieces of research, but his comments though sharp were always
fair and unemotional (as, for instance, his "Critique of the Conceptual
Foundation of Community Research Associates," with Irving Lukoff,
or his earlier critique of efforts to evaluate productivity in casework).

In the second place, he was disturbed by social work's preoccupation with the clinical method and its neglect of social and institutional
factors viewed either as causes or as possible solutions of some of the
major contemporary social problems. He strove to bring about a change
of emphasis in social work education by his own teaching and curriculum
development, by the publication of articles on various social policy issues,
notably in the field of public assistance, and by his membership on a
variety of committees dealing with graduate education for social work.

Finally, to an increasing degree he had become fascinated by the
development of policies and programs and the historical forces which
explained contemporary developments. A series of articles beginning in
1961, and a book of readings, which he edited jointly with Roy Lubove
and John Duffy, entitled *Social Welfare in Transition,* culminated in the
present work. Already in 1961, at the time of publication of his first
"historical" article, "The Changing Balance of Status and Contract in
Assistance Policy," he wrote me that he intended to write a major study
of the development of social policy in regard to the economic security of
the able-bodied, utilizing these concepts as the organizing principles.

Poor Law to Poverty Program was clearly regarded by Mencher as
his most ambitious work. In it he seeks to provide "a frame of reference
for understanding the complex system of modern economic security programs" by surveying the economic environment, the ideologies and issues
prevalent at different periods from the sixteenth century onwards. It is a
bold undertaking, and probably only one whose reading was as extensive
as Mencher's would have dared to attempt to cover so broad a canvass and
to weave together so many different threads. For Mencher was a prodigious reader, especially in the history of ideas, and everything was grist
to his mill. The book does not make easy reading; it is almost too dense
with information, but the attentive reader will emerge with a much
widened perspective, and a better understanding of the historical roots of
many of the ideas, especially those concerning human behavior and motivation, that influence economic security policy even today.

The fourth part of the book differs somewhat from the rest: it is less tightly organized. Mencher no longer follows the earlier plan, whereby he describes the nature of the social and economic order of the period he is concerned with, explores prevailing ideologies regarding the nature of man and of society, and then analyses the economic security policies of that period, relating them to their context. This change of approach is undoubtedly due, in part, to the fact that in the modern period the concepts of status and contract are no longer so helpful as organizing principles. Indeed, Mencher himself in his Introduction intimated that there were limits to their usefulness. But one cannot help suspecting also that Part IV reflects the fact that Mencher had some kind of premonition that he would not be granted time to complete the work according to his original scheme, let alone to write that second volume to which he occasionally referred. It is as if he was so eager to set on paper his ideas about the nature of contemporary policies and the problems to which they give rise that he could not stop to consider whether they were all relevant to a study of the historical development of policies. Surely, too, had time been given him, he would have produced a more comprehensive concluding chapter than the brief comments which here appear. Its inadequacy in relation to the richness of the body of the book serves only to underline the loss the field of social work has suffered in Mencher's early death.

But this dry recital of Sam Mencher's all-too-short professional life gives little picture of the human side of the man. He had a great sense of humor and of the ridiculous, and an evening spent with him "talking shop" was always memorable. His critical comments were bracing and he was always great fun to argue with. One gained new insights and learned of new developments, for he seemed to have access to a very effective "grapevine." And there was always the release of laughter at his wit. He was tough-minded and did not suffer fools gladly, and some of the shoddy work published under the guise of "scholarship" or "research" in social work journals, or the "woolly-mindedness" and time-consuming professional platitudes of some of his colleagues in committee meetings provoked the lash of his sharp tongue. But he was always good-humored; there was nothing personal about his criticism, and the standards he applied to others he applied to himself. He was a good friend, a challenging teacher, and a stimulating colleague, and the gap he has left will be hard to fill.

June 1967   Eveline M. Burns

Contents

Introduction

PLANNING for economic security has been one of the most pressing problems of modern society. Although the nature of social welfare has, in many respects, been greatly altered over the centuries, current economic security programs represent a gradual accretion of new approaches rather than a radical change from the philosophies and practices of the past. The evolution of economic security policy has been marked not so much by the abandonment of previous practices as by their incorporation within the changing pattern of welfare institutions. The persistence of policies and procedures for dealing with economic need and their survival in different periods and under different circumstances frequently make economic welfare programs appear to follow the maxim of "Le plus ça change, le plus ça reste même." This is often deceptive, as it is the form rather than the function that tends to be static. The study of the development of any social phenomenon is useful for better understanding its current state, and this is particularly true in the field of economic security, where so many segments of the past are imbedded in the present.

It is difficult to select any arbitrary point in the history of western society as the start of modern economic security policy. The roots of contemporary social welfare may be traced to the many sources that have provided the background for the growth of western culture. However, modern policy may be conceived of as commencing with the shift in the sixteenth century from the economic assistance programs of a declining feudal society to those of a rising commercial and secular world. Both in England and in the countries of western Europe there arose a series of reforms in the traditional practices of assistance to the poor. These reforms were the first realistic attempts to deal with the problem of economic insecurity in accord with the changing religious, social, and economic ideologies of the period. Earlier approaches to the needs of those unable to provide for their own welfare were motivated by a desire to reinforce the fixed relationships of a feudal economy, to conform to the medieval religious principles of charity, or to lessen the threat to society of an unattached and frequently idle population.

Reforms at the beginning of the sixteenth century strengthened the deterrent practices of the feudal period, but they also included constructive measures designed to lessen the need for dependence on either private or public sources of charitable support. It might be said that the modern era of welfare policy began with the reaction against economic dependency, a reaction that resulted in the great series of sixteenth-century poor laws throughout both Catholic and Protestant western Europe. These measures indicated that dependency on the part of those capable of earning a living would no longer be tolerated. As John Major, a distinguished Scottish scholar of the period, remarked, "If the Prince or Community should decree that there should be no beggar in the country, and should provide for the impotent, the action would be praiseworthy and lawful."[1]

The focal issue for all economic security policy since the sixteenth century has been the treatment of the able-bodied or potentially productive individual. While provision for those incapable of employment has varied and the definition of the impotent class has changed, there has been continuous acceptance of some social responsibility for the impotent poor. Basic issues of policy affecting responsibility for this group have arisen only as members of the employable group have become involved. For example, to what extent should the employable group be held responsible for impotent individuals dependent on them? To what extent should all individuals be expected to provide from their previous earnings for their incapacity or lack of employment?

The treatment of the able-bodied or employable has thus been the most continuous and controversial concern of economic security policy. This book will consider the issues, trends, ideas, and ideologies influencing the development of policies related to the economic welfare of the employable population. The approach has been influenced by the continuing conflict between "status" and "contract" relationships since the period of the Reformation. The concepts of status and contract are broadly derived from Sir Henry Maine, but a similar framework is present in a wide variety of conceptual schemes. Perhaps the best known in the field of sociology is Ferdinand Tonnies' classic dichotomy, Gemeinschaft and Gesellschaft, which, like Maine's and Hegel's a generation before, tried to clarify the differing relationships and values in simple and complex societies.[2]

Status here will refer to relationships essentially determined by informal membership in the group, whether it be the family, community, society as a whole, or any particular institution or association. In a status society rights and responsibilities are inherent in the relationship of the individual to his social unity. The term *contract* will refer to a formal system of relationships specifically and purposefully entered into, with rights and responsibilities determined by their willful acceptance.

The concepts should not, of course, be confused with reality. They are ideal types or logical constructs devised as the poles at the opposite ends of an imaginary continuum. Between these two points, and mixing to varying degrees the qualities incorporated in each, fall the actual social forms encountered in human society. Overlapping and transitional types are characteristic rather than pure and static entities.

It should be emphasized that status and contract, like other concepts, are merely tools for analysis, and if they prove to obstruct rather than clarify, they should be avoided by the reader as useless scholarly baggage. It is hoped that they will be helpful in ordering the development of economic security policy, but at the same time they should not be viewed as final or definitive sieves through which all must be strained. Like all sieves, much of quality may be lost through too complete reliance on mechanical sifting, and frequently more than one type is necessary to obtain the finest results.

The distinction between the impotent and the employable alluded to above illustrates well the difference between status and contract. The continued assistance to the impotent has been on a status basis. No matter what the pressures toward a contract society, extenuating circumstances have resulted in the protection of children and the handicapped, members of society held incapable of autonomously managing their own affairs and therefore not held responsible according to the contract code of society. The definition of capacity will, of course, vary according to the complexity and demands of society, and the kinds of protection will be determined largely by the humanitarian ideas and resources present. It is the employable person, however, whose assistance has been most sensitively affected by the attitudes of society toward dependency and by the dominance of status or contract relationships in particular periods.

From the point of view of status and contract, economic security policy since the Reformation may be roughly divided into three periods: the growth of a contract society between the Reformation and the early nineteenth century, the revival of status influences in the nineteenth century, and the mixture of status and contract relationships in the twentieth century. Naturally, as suggested, sharp distinctions tend to be more abstract than real. In the three periods overlappings occur particularly in the continuance of traditional practices concomitant with the development of new policies, but the mere outward resemblance of institutions should not be interpreted as similarity of function. As with other social phenomena, changes are often disguised by the maintenance of formal conformity to accepted values.

Because of the close connections of American with English ideas and practices, it is necessary to follow English development to understand fully American policy. In addition, a comparative analysis of economic security programs in both England and the United States is useful for appreciating the unique aspects of each. It should not, however, be assumed that the English and American systems were isolated from developments in other countries. This analysis attempts to counteract an insular interpretation by pointing to the common foundation of English and western European policies in the sixteenth century. A full-scale treatment of the cross-fertilization of ideas beyond the borders of England and the United States is needed but is the subject of another volume.

The goal here is to provide a frame of reference for understanding the complex system of modern economic security programs. A variety of issues, trends, ideas, and ideologies considered relevant for contemporary policy have been explored. The frame of reference and the material discussed are significant for the total field of social welfare and social policy of which economic security is an important and integral part. There has been a paucity of scholarship in social policy, and hopefully this work, through its sins of omission and commission, will stimulate further research.

Part I

THE MERCANTILIST ERA

1

The Rise of Mercantilism

Background

THE origins of modern economic security policy may most accurately be identified with the rise of mercantilism. The goals and measures generally descriptive of the mercantilist era in England became prevalent in the latter half of the sixteenth century. Mercantilism, however, did not represent a sharp and dramatic shift from earlier social and economic policies.[1] It is better understood as a gradual change from a feudal to a laissez-faire economy. It was well toward the end of the seventeenth century before clear distinctions between feudalism and mercantilism occurred, and by that time, at least as concerns English domestic policies, the movement toward laissez-faire concepts had already begun.

The mercantilist era, even at its height, did not present a uniform pattern of thought and policy.[2] It was a period of transition between the medieval and the modern and contained the inherent conflicts between the new and the old. It grew out of the static ideal of the medieval world and pointed toward the fluidity of modern social and economic life. Perhaps mercantilism's unique characteristic was its faith in the government's capacity to arrange satisfactorily the affairs of men. This faith was rooted in the need for order on the rapidly moving scene caused by the disintegration of the established social system. The sixteenth century was

3

characterized less by any positive theory of state responsibility than by a naive belief in the ability of centralized government to realize whatever purposes it set out to accomplish. Everything seemed within the range of a government powerful enough to dominate the nation.[3]

The nationalist emphasis of mercantilist policies has resulted in greater attention being given to their foreign than to their domestic implications. In England internal social and economic policies were less consistent and more short-lived than those governing relationships with the colonies and other states. The waning of governmental interference in domestic affairs occurred almost a century before laissez-faire was applied to the foreign scene. Mercantilist measures made a significant impression on local matters, however, and had lasting consequences, particularly in the development of economic security policy.

The interests of the state were the dominant focus of all mercantilist policy. The state, through an elaborate complex of governmental bodies, concerned itself with all phases of the social and economic life of its subjects and assumed a guiding role in directing their behavior. In both national and international affairs the mercantilist state acted on the assumption that there was a fixed and limited amount of available wealth and that active intervention was necessary to control its distribution. As a corollary, the state did not accept, as did laissez-faire society later, the premise that the free play of individual interests would enhance the welfare of all. It acted on the assumption that the welfare of the state and society could be achieved only through the active, paternalistic guidance of the state. In contrast to later socialist doctrine, however, the control of the state was exercised in restricting or encouraging the activities of its members rather than in directly managing the productive institutions of society.

Despite its emphasis on state control, the mercantilist state did much to provide the foundation for the laissez-faire era to follow. Primarily concerned with national interests and national self-sufficiency, mercantilist governments overrode the separatist and local influences that had obstructed the free movement of trade. As distinguished from earlier eras, the concept of private property and private profit became fully accepted, and the reliance on industry and commerce to enrich the national wealth developed and strengthened those elements of society interested in a free market system.[4]

The aims of the mercantilist state involved the expansion of governmental power and the increase of national wealth, closely connected objectives. To achieve those objectives mercantilist policy stressed the maintenance of stability within the country and the growth of agricultural, industrial, and commercial pursuits that would provide the foundation of a favorable balance of foreign trade. These goals were not entirely compatible and account for some of the inconsistencies in mercantilist policy.[5] There was an attempt to support the traditional modes of the earlier medieval status society and at the same time exploit the advantages of the new contract relationships of the growing commercial economy. English mercantilist governments at first tried valiantly to maintain the status quo of the medieval period. They opposed enclosure, limited the growth of industry, controlled the supply of agricultural laborers, and generally acted to solidify the existing class system. It was not long, however, before the state's interest in expanding national wealth prompted support of the commercial sections of society. The restrictive policies of the early Stuarts were opposed and defeated, and major changes occurred in the earlier, more status-oriented view of society.

The paternalism of the mercantilist state has led some to emphasize its role as the protector of the underdog. What protection it afforded, however, may be viewed more accurately as a means of enhancing the position of the state than of benefiting any particular group. Yet there was much in early mercantilist policy more favorable to the poor and labor generally than was to be found in the periods immediately before and after. Whatever its motivations, the mercantilist state more actively pursued positive measures for the welfare of the poor than was true in the medieval era, and less was left to the vagaries of individual action than in the laissez-faire period. The doctrines of individual responsibility and natural harmony of interests had not yet become predominant. Mercantilism inherited the medieval notion of causation being beyond individual control. In moving from a religious to a secular emphasis mercantilist society attributed some of the responsibility for such phenomena as poverty to social conditions and intervened to correct these conditions.

As a whole, however, mercantilist policy cannot be considered as consciously favoring the welfare of the poor. More enlightened than earlier eras and less avowedly harsh than later periods, mercantilist policy toward the poor was organized in the interests of the state and whatever groups were identified with the power and wealth of the state. The goal of mercantilism was at best to supply the poor with minimum subsistence. In the beginning the state, still influenced by medieval values and threatened by the potential anarchy of the emerging commercial society, tended to carry out its obligation to the poor. With the rise of the merchant and industrial interests this minimal concern for the welfare of the poor gradually dissolved. An increasing share of wealth for the poor and the laboring class was never a goal of mercantilist policy, and when the welfare of the lower classes conflicted with commercial interests of the state, it was the former that was sacrificed.

Attitudes Toward
Work and the Laboring Class

The importance of work and effort, so essential to the development of western industrial society, received its first major impetus during the mercantilist period. This emphasis on productivity represented a radical departure from earlier societies. The mounting attention to work reflected in all the institutions of society after the Reformation was perhaps the most significant psychological change since the Middle Ages.[6] While concern with the importance of work did not originate in mercantilist society, it was during this period that the ideology of work and productivity assumed its central position in the life of western society.

The state and all the major forces of mercantilist life combined in their support of labor and effort. Work was the duty of man before God. Work was the source of national wealth and state power. Work was important for the stability of the nation, for idleness led to dissatisfaction, crime, and social disturbance. Work was the basis of economic value and the rationale for the ownership of property. Finally, work was the responsibility of man to his neighbor and the foundation of all moral and socially useful conduct. Work was an end in itself, not merely a means of obtaining satisfactions. Thomas More, the celebrated sixteenth-century humanist philosopher, although antagonized by the materialism of his day, made work the core value of his *Utopia*. All must contribute to the ideal of work, and it was recommended that even leisure be given over to work as that was "beneficial to the commonwealth."[7]

It was the dominance of economic values in sixteenth-century thought that provided an integrating force for the variety of emphases on the importance of work. The moral and social attributes of work became integrated with economic considerations.[8] If the moral and economic aspects were separated at the beginning of mercantilism, as, for example, in More's writings, they coalesced by the time of the Puritan era. The mercantilist period inherited the medieval concept of labor value. Natural resources were important to a country, but it was labor that converted these resources into economic value, and it was upon labor that national wealth depended. Holland was held up as the model of a country with poor natural resources which had achieved great wealth through the exemplary industry of its inhabitants.

Both Petty and Locke in the latter half of the seventeenth century expanded the theoretical rationale of labor value. Petty recognized labor and land as contributing to production but attempted to reduce exchange value to the cost of the subsistence of the labor required in production.[9] Locke maintained that the only worthwhile measure of value was the labor expended. The value of land he considered negligible, and capital represented labor incorporated in the past. Labor was the foundation of all ownership or property, according to Locke. It was the labor applied to what was formerly common property that justified the existence of private property. Locke's social contract theory assumed that the right of property preceded the social contract and was inviolate regardless of other modifications that might occur in the contract.[10]

Labor played the critical role with respect to the most important aspect of mercantilist policy, foreign trade. Since the labor forming the raw into the finished product was considered the basis of its increased value, a favorable balance of trade depended on the relatively greater amount of labor a country invested in the preparation of articles for export. The exportation of raw materials was a loss to the exporting country because it provided an opportunity for other nations to exploit the increase in value through their own labor of manufacture.

The encouragement of labor was thus of primary concern to the state. Apart from the political and social consequences of an idle and poorly cared for population, the state could not afford to see labor, its major source of wealth, not engaged in wealth-producing activities. By the middle of the seventeenth century the constructive employment of all labor was advocated as national policy. Work was suggested as the socially useful punishment for all criminals, an idea that More had proposed a century before.[11] This period was especially rich in schemes for organizing the unemployed into productive enterprises.

Despite the singular importance of work, the effort of work was not looked upon by the laboring population as a particularly pleasurable activity. The new entrepreneur classes, who proclaimed the importance of work as the only acceptable way of life and the way to attain God's grace, did not foster an appreciation of work as an agreeable activity in itself. Work was a task and a duty, and its very unpleasantness assured its sacredness. Work was a discipline, not a satisfaction. The classical economists of the eighteenth and nineteenth centuries were to equate work with the renunciation of leisure and freedom of choice, but this was already recognized in the mercantilist era. While the entrepreneur classes found sufficient incentive directly from their material gains and ultimately from being among God's chosen, there was little to motivate the laboring classes beyond the pressure of starvation and the legal strictures of government policy.

The laboring classes saw little advantage in the freedom of trade espoused by the mercantile interests. Freedom from restraint or freedom to make the best bargain was an important right for the entrepreneurs, but workers were not given equal opportunities. Though the influential industrial and commercial groups impatiently strove to divest themselves of restrictive government policies, they did not favor similar freedom for workers. In fact, the state and its judicial machinery was regarded as an instrument for enforcing the duty of labor under the most advantageous conditions to the employer.[12]

Even if they had been totally unrestricted, it is doubtful that the laboring classes would have viewed the new society as optimistically as the merchants and manufacturers. The transition from a status society of established relationships to a contract society of fluid agreements offered few advantages to the lower classes. The latter arrangement gradually stripped the agricultural and industrial laborer of the security formerly provided by the status system and forced them to rely solely on the irregular employment patterns of the economic market. The development of an open economy was vitally important to the rising commercial leadership, and the possibility of the lower classes depending on the previous guarantees of support of manorial or religious communities would have seriously hindered the advance of the new economy.

The reluctance of the laborers to adapt to the new ideologies was a cause of much friction. The lower classes had not absorbed the new view of the importance of work but continued to regard work merely as a means of meeting subsistence needs. Frequent complaints were voiced by employers about the delinquent habits of workers. If workers earned enough in a short time, according to employers, they would refuse to continue, and if they earned a surplus, they would not work again until necessity required more earnings. These as well as other reasons provided the rationale for low wages.

Workers found little in the religious and economic ideologies of the sixteenth and seventeenth centuries to motivate them to extra exertion. There was little room in the class structure for upward mobility. In fact, attempts to live beyond their station were strongly discouraged. Education and other measures for improving the conditions of the lower classes were considered superfluous and wasteful. Employers insisted on the subsistence doctrine as wage policy and thus prevented any possible accumulation of enterprise capital by workers. While employers envisioned a new commercial world, their workers still thought in terms of the old system of mutual relationships of classes. It was some time before the lower classes accepted and became adjusted to the ideology of economic independence, and when they did, they were faced with the organized opposition of employers. In the mercantilist era, however, it was the employers who wished to free themselves of the traditional patterns of interdependence of the classes. The paternalism of the state and the upper classes was still clearly evident on many sides, and the resolution of the conflict between work and dependency was one of the major issues of mercantilist society.

The attitude of the dominant elements in society toward the lower classes underwent some fundamental changes between the sixteenth and the eighteenth centuries although the position of the lower classes remained extremely poor throughout this period. At the beginning the paternalistic attitudes of the upper classes and the policies of the government were more sympathetic and placed less stress on the shortcomings of the laborers as the cause of their condition. By the close of the seventeenth century the laziness and immorality of the lower classes were constantly referred to and alleged to account for their inferior standard of living. At no stage were the lower classes considered full members of society with rights in any way comparable to other classes. They were looked upon as a rough, ignorant, and dangerous element who must be controlled. Their lot was assumed to be harsh, and the virtue of poverty in keeping the lower classes industrious was elaborated upon in the second half of the seventeenth century after the Puritan Commonwealth. Even in the prior period, however, those attitudes were prevalent, although not so clearly formulated.

While mercantilist policy favored the indirect arranging or guiding of individual interests so that they would be compatible with the interests of the state, this was not true of the treatment of the lower classes. Despite the sentiment against direct control of economic behavior, the host of regulations dealing with the laboring classes indicated no assumption that the laborer, like others in society, was a rational being whose interests might be "provoked, encouraged and allured" to conform to those of the state.[13] A few reformers during the Commonwealth suggested the possibility of the poor rising through their own efforts to achieve the position of their superiors. Somewhat later, Defoe, although generally unsympathetic to the laboring classes, considered the advantages of a high wage policy as an incentive in contrast to the contemporary insistence on minimal subsistence. The prevailing attitude was represented by such cryptic statements as Mun's in the 1660s that "penury and want do make a people wise and industrious" and Young's in the following century that "everyone but an idiot knows that the lower classes must be kept poor or they will never be industrious."[14] These views of the lower classes were accentuated when unemployment or dependency was the subject of concern. Poverty came to be looked upon more and more unsympathetically during the mercantilist era. As one writer of the Commonwealth period remarked, "Better it is to die than to be poore."[15]

Causes of Poverty

Attitudes toward the laboring classes and the poor were reflected in contemporary views of the causes of poverty. Up to the end of the seventeenth century, despite the increasingly harsh feelings about the poor, poverty continued to be recognized as socially rather than individually caused. Mercantilist policy assumed social responsibility where earlier philosophies looked to divine determination of events. The provisions for employment in the Elizabethan poor laws indicated one of the prevailing sixteenth- and seventeenth-century beliefs—that unemployment and its consequent poverty were due to insufficiency of available employment. In 1622 the first English commission for the study of unemployment gave its major attention to problems of trade and methods of improving and stabilizing the market for manufactured goods. Factors affecting the economic market, such as foreign competition, wars, and domestic manufacturing practices, rather than the habits of English labor were stressed. The irregularities of commerce and the enclosure of agricultural properties made sixteenth- and seventeenth-century England conscious of the external forces influencing the livelihood of the laboring classes.

Some recognized that the prevalent low wages kept the laboring population so close to the edge of poverty that the moral failings of the poor could hardly be held totally responsible for their condition. In the second part of the seventeenth century Petty stated: "It is unjust to let any starve when we think it just to limit the wages of the poor, so as they can lay up nothing against the time of their impotency and want of work."[16]

By the time of the Commonwealth, a noticeable change in emphasis on the causes of poverty could be observed. Though continued attention was given to social factors, the impression was gaining ground that the causes of poverty were in the poor themselves. At the end of the century the view was widely held that it was not lack of employment but the laziness of workers and their profligate habits that led to poverty. Defoe and others were convinced that the poor preferred idleness and would pursue any course but work to satisfy their needs.

The poor laws themselves were considered to have an important influence on the extent of poverty. By the beginning of the sixteenth century any assistance to the poor was viewed as an encouragement of begging and vagrancy. Voluntary charity was held particularly responsible, and efforts were made both in England and on the continent to control charitable giving. In time, the growing numbers of the poor despite the poor laws led to the belief that the poor laws themselves rather than economic conditions were responsible for the increase.

During the seventeenth century a variety of new schemes for dealing with the poor were tried. These schemes attempted to accomplish the dual purpose of relieving the poor and adding to the wealth of the nation. There were efforts to reform earlier poor law policy, with which there was so much dissatisfaction. The increasing emphasis on the shortcomings of the poor and the disillusionment with previous policies were reflected in the harsher deterrent policies of the eighteenth century. Thus the workhouse changed from a place of employment to a punitive measure for the discouragement of any reliance on public aid.

Class Relationships

The shift toward a commercial society already indicated by the changing attitudes toward work and the laboring classes and the nature of poverty was closely identified with the relationships between the laboring and the privileged classes. As early as the beginning of the sixteenth century Thomas More condemned the tendency of the landed gentry and even "holy men and abbotts" to unify their estates at the expense of the small landholders and tenants. "The tenants," he wrote, "are turned out, and by trickery or main force, or by being worn out through ill usage, are compelled to sell their possessions."[17]

More laid much of the social problems of the time at the door of private greed:

For when every man gets as much as he can for himself by one device or another, the few divide the whole wealth among themselves and leave want to the rest. The result generally is that there will be two sorts of people, and their fortunes ought to be interchanged; one sort are useless, but ravenous and wicked, while the other sort are unassuming, modest men who serve the public more than themselves by their daily work.[18]

The developing concept of private property was of primary importance to the relationship of the classes in the post-medieval world. Although influential leaders in government under the Tudors and early Stuarts struggled to maintain the previous system, they were overwhelmed by the emerging social and economic forces. Ownership no longer indicated merely the privilege of stewardship but signified the free use of possessions unencumbered by any sense of mutual dependency or communal responsibility. The efforts of the government to force responsibility upon employers or to limit enclosures showed that the previous bonds between the wealthy and their dependents were rapidly dissolving. The national government through formal paternalistic policies tried to withstand the tide of disintegrating local relationships.

The laboring classes were being transformed into a wage-earning group, and although the worker continued to hold the employer responsible for his subsistence, the employer began to interpret wages as the price paid for a commodity of labor. The full impact of this change occurred in the eighteenth century, but the beginnings were felt in the seventeenth century. By the Commonwealth, it was said, "What does the merchant care, so that he be rich, how poor the public is? that the Commonwealth sink, so that he gets his profit?"[19] There were those who bitterly opposed the prevailing tendencies and tried to maintain the traditional standards of morality and social responsibility against the pressures of economic self-interest.

The new entrepreneur class, with the support of a rigorously individualistic Protestantism, had little tolerance for a system of interdependent relationships. Their critics complained that the new religion had not been accompanied by the charitable tendencies that might be expected from a spiritual reawakening. In this regard Richardson remarked in 1653, "The Papists may rise up against many of this generation: It is a sad thing that they should be more foreward upon a bad principal than a Christian upon a good one."[20] There were no strong countervailing forces. Before the Commonwealth the state had recognized the potential conflict of public and private interests and had exerted its influence in accommodating them. The state's intervention in internal economic affairs, however, had greatly waned by the second half of the seventeenth century, and the absence of any traditional social code of responsibility resulted in the practice of crude individualism.

Mercantilist Labor Policy

Economic policy affecting the low-income groups in the mercantilist era was focused on wages and population. The belief was prevalent that the nation's welfare was dependent on a system of low wages and the presence of a large laboring population. These two principles were, of course, opposite sides of the same coin. The major emphasis of mercantilist policy was on production; through increased production national wealth and power would be enhanced. The production of large quantities of goods at low cost guaranteed success in foreign commerce. Since the mercantilists were not concerned with domestic consumption, they had little interest in maintaining purchasing power through adequate wages. In fact, all their thinking influenced the propagation of a low-wage policy.

The theory of low wages was supported by the assumption that only continual need would motivate laborers to work. Any increase in wages, it was believed, would result in lowering productivity. After satisfying their basic necessities, laborers would sink into idleness and immorality. Any desire for comfort or pleasure was frowned upon by the Puritans. This was particularly true for the lower classes, whose station made them unfit for any of the relaxations permitted the more select.

Low wages thus kept up the national productive power, gave the English manufacturer an advantage over his foreign competitors, and preserved the morality of the nation. They also had the advantage of limiting imports into England. The lower the purchasing power of the population, the less the demand for foreign wares. It was preferable for domestic products to be consumed by foreign than by native purchasers. From all points of view, the lowest possible subsistence level for the lower classes seemed logical. William Petty, one of the major economic spokesmen of the period, believed that if any surplus were produced, it should be stored in granaries rather than "abused by the vile and brutish part of mankind to the prejudice of the commonwealth."[21] It was not until the passing of mercantilism that the ideas of either high wages or increased domestic consumption took root.

Mercantilist population doctrine was closely related to its low-wage policy. A large laboring population was considered the foundation of national wealth. The existence of low wages relied on a surplus of labor, because a scarcity of labor would place workers in an advantageous bargaining position. If, as already noted, the main source of economic value was the contribution of labor to production, then the larger the laboring population, the greater the potential wealth. At the very beginning of the mercantilist period greater emphasis was probably given to the military rather than to the economic advantages of a large population, but the latter soon took precedence.

The mercantilist emphasis was essentially on the quantity and industriousness of the population. Although the mercantilist state tried to attract skilled foreign labor and was anxious to preserve its own supply, all labor was generally regarded as equal, and the emphasis was on increasing their numbers and maintaining their industriousness rather than on the development of a more highly skilled group.[22] Size of population was considered of such vital significance that a direct relationship was frequently drawn between the wealth of a country and the numbers of its laboring population.

The doctrine of a large laboring population was not attended by any consideration for the provision of employment. The balance between population and employment was rarely achieved. Mercantilist thinkers were constantly concerned about surpluses or scarcities although they had little rational evidence for either. The only approved remedy for a surplus population was colonization because that would benefit no competing nations and would, if properly directed, be a source of wealth to the mother country. That was to be a source of conflict with the American colonies. The negotiations between the colonies and the mother country provided many examples of artful attempts by the colonists to use mercantilist population doctrine for their own ends. For example, Benjamin Franklin pointed out:

Thus there are suppos'd to be now upwards of One Million English souls in North America . . . and yet perhaps there is not one the fewer in Britain, but rather many more, on Account of the Employment the Colonies afford to Manufacturers at Home. This Million doubling, suppose but once in 25 Years, will, in another Century, be more than the People of England, and the greatest Number of English men will be on this Side of the Water. What an Accession of Power to the British Empire by Sea as well as land! What Increase of Trade and Navigation! What Numbers of Ships and Seamen![23]

Stability and Property

Social stability and the advancement of property were two major though not always harmonious poles of mercantilist economic policy. The conflict between them was finally resolved in the nineteenth century when property values became the primary focus of national policy. Mercantilism bridged the gap between the medieval and the modern world, and during its era there occurred marked and rapid changes in all aspects of life—social, economic, religious, and political. The emphasis on social stability, however, made possible a relatively smooth transition to the laissez-faire society to follow. For a century in England between 1550 and 1650, the conservative and stabilizing forces of the mercantilist state were in control, and even afterwards its influence was felt as a balancing force against the disruptive trends of the merging society.[24]

Like Hobbes, the leaders of the mercantilist state assumed that man's original condition was antisocial and conflict-ridden and that an irrevocable contract with unlimited sovereign power was necessary to save society from its own destruction. Mercantilist society was threatened by the uncertainties of the commercial market, unemployment and idleness, religious differences, and social discontent leading to violence and rebellion. The sovereignty of the monarch was not yet firmly established, and discontent was feared as kindling insurrection. Mobility of population greatly increased, and that alone acted as a source of much disorganization. No effective system of public safety had been established, and mobility increased the opportunities for thievery, disease, and political conflict.

The adverse effects of mobility and the desire for stability are illustrated by the plans for utopias of sixteenth- and seventeenth-century writers. In More's Utopia permission for travel must be obtained from the magistrates. However, if the travelers "stay in the place longer than a day, each of them follows his own occupation." But "if any man goes outside his district without leave and is caught without a passport from the prince, he is treated scornfully, brought back as a fugitive, and severely punished. If he does it again, he is made a bondsman."[25] In Francis Bacon's *New Atlantis* (1629) the king, "to give perpetuity to that which was in his time so happily established, therefore among his other fundamental laws . . . he did ordain the interdicts and prohibitions which we have touching the entrance of strangers . . . doubting novelty and commixture of manners."[26] In Harrington's *Oceana* (1656), "Lacedaemon, being governed by a King and a small Senate, could maintain itself a long time in that condition, because the inhabitants, being few, having put a bar upon the reception of strangers, and living in a strict observation of the laws of Lycurgus . . . might well continue living in tranquility. For . . . not receiving strangers into their commonwealth, they did not corrupt it."[27]

In its first century the mercantilist state met the dangers of instability by attempting to solidify already established social patterns. Mobility of the lower classes was rigidly limited, and their attachment to local employment enforced. "Masterless men" were searched out, punished, and returned to their place of employment. Agriculture was encouraged at the advantage of industry. The guild system was protected against the influx of industry and surplus labor. Large-scale agriculture through enclosures was discouraged, and landholding requiring a large labor force was stimulated. Agriculture was viewed as the most secure source of national wealth, stable employment, and military personnel.

Local responsibility was stressed, and lengthy attachment to local employment was the ideal of mercantilist labor policy. Control of wages hindered the development of a free and mobile labor market and at the same time guaranteed some minimum subsistence to the laboring classes. With the trend toward the emphasis of commercial interests after the middle of the seventeenth century, many of the policies limiting the activities of the merchant and manufacturing classes fell into disuse; but controls for the stability of labor remained in effect up into the next era.

As the stabilizing and paternalistic domestic policies waned, the rights of property interests were more strongly asserted. Even by the sixteenth century concerns of ownership outweighed obligations of responsibility. The Tudors and early Stuarts attempted to limit the freedom of owners and speculators. A legislative act of 1593 complained of "divers evil disposed persons commonly called Choppers or Jobbers of woolen yarn wanting fear of God, and caring only for their private gain, without having any regard of the maintenance of a common wealth." Some forty years later in a Star Chamber judgment against the increasing of the price of corn by withholding from the market, Archbishop Laud succinctly stated, "This last year's famine was made by man not by God."[28] Throughout this period the state tried to rectify the balance between the interests of property and the needs of society.

The development of the concept of private property in England since the medieval period had not been free of friction and opposition. The Pilgrimage of Grace in 1536 and the Norfolk Revolt of 1549 were responses by the rural population to the passing of land into modern private ownership. The uprising of 1549 was a large-scale insurrection involving a great proportion of the peasantry. Those who sympathized with the poor in the latter part of the sixteenth century merely wished that the medieval sense of responsibility would prevail. Thus Robert Crowley, a clergyman of the period, stated that he did not agitate "to make all thynges com-

mune. . . . If the possessioners woulde consyder them selves be but
stuardes, and not lordes over theyr possessions, thys oppression woulde
sone be redressed."[29]

The next major agitation against private property occurred during
Cromwell's period, when the Diggers under Winstanley took possession
of some untilled land near London. The movement was short-lived and
was brought to an end by government troops. Winstanley opposed private
property whether based on divine right or royal prerogative and pleaded
for general equality of wealth. The democratic ferment of the Levellers
and the Diggers as well as the Quakers had little effect on the entrenched
elements in Puritan society. The idea of private property had become well
established, and Locke's concept of social contract provided it with a philosophical justification.

By the first part of the eighteenth century Francis Hutcheson, Adam
Smith's teacher and predecessor at the University of Glasgow, summed up
the prevailing attitude:

Now nothing can so effectually excite men to constant patience and diligence
in all sorts of useful industry, as the hopes of future wealth, ease, and pleasure
to themselves, their offspring, and all who are dear to them, and some honour
too to themselves on account of their ingenuity, and activity, and liberality.
All these hopes are presented to men by securing to everyone the fruits of his
own labours, that he may enjoy them, or dispose of them as he pleases. If they
are not thus secured, one has no other motive to labour than the general affection to his kind, which is commonly much weaker than the narrower affections to our friends and relations. . . .

Nay the most extensive affections could scarce engage a wise man to industry,
if no property ensued upon it. He must see that universal diligence is necessary. Diligence will never be universal, unless men's own necessities, and the
love of families and friends, excite them. Such as are capable of labour, and
yet decline it, should find no support in the labour of others. If the goods procured, or improved by the industrious lye in common for the use of all, the
worst of men have the generous and industrious for their slaves. The most
benevolent temper must decline supporting the slothful in idleness, that their
own necessities may force them to contribute their part for the publick good.
Thus both the immediate feelings of our hearts, and the consideration of the
general interest, suggest that law of nature, "that each one should have the
free use and disposal of what he has acquired by his own labour;" and this
is property, which may be defined, when it is unlimited, "a right to the fullest
use of any goods, and to dispose of them as one pleases."[30]

By the beginning of the eighteenth century the paternalism and social obligations of mercantilism had given way to the ethic of individualism. Labor and industry, formerly the agents of national power and wealth, were now wedded to private ownership and gain. These alone would incite to maximum effort since social interdependence and the common good "could scarce engage a wise man to industry, if no property ensued." However, the foundation of private property rested on the social and economic measures of mercantilism. Without the stability and the encouragement of commercial activities by the mercantilist state, the road toward a laissez-faire society would have been exceedingly difficult.

2

Economic Assistance Programs of the Sixteenth and Seventeenth Centuries

Background

THE changing social conditions and ideologies of the sixteenth century were reflected in a new, or at least radically remodeled, series of proposals for solving the problems of economic security. The English and Western European programs were remarkably similar and indicated common problems and common modes of thinking. The salient issue was the growing numbers of poor, for which the established institutions of society provided neither sufficient nor satisfactory solutions. The actual extent of deprivation during this period is difficult to estimate. Modern historians have differed about the dearth of opportunity for earning a living. Some have maintained that there was ample employment available in the domestic system of industry and in agriculture or in a combination of both. Others have found the same sources of livelihood to be inadequate and considered the supplementation of industry by agriculture unrealistic in view of the separation of the artisan from the land.

A survey conducted in Sheffield at the beginning of the seventeenth century may throw some light on the extent of poverty as well as on the agricultural and other resources available to the town dweller.

By a survaie of the towne of Sheffielde made the seconde daye of Januarie 1615 by twenty foure of the most sufficient inhabitants there, it appearethe that there are in the towne of Sheffelde 2207 people; of which there are 725 which are not able to live without the charity of their neighbours. These are all begging poore. 100 householders which relieve others. These (though the best sorte) are but poore artificers; among them is not one which can keepe a teame on his own land, and not above tenn who have grounds of their own that will keepe a cow. 160 householders are not able to relieve others. These are such (though they beg not) as are not able to abide the storme of one fort-nights sickness but would be thereby given to beggary. 1222 children and servants of the said householders; the greatest part of which are such as live of small wages, and are constrained to work sore to provide them necessaries.[1]

The early development of large-scale industry and trade with a fluctuating market for British goods, the intermittent supply of raw materials for domestic manufacture, and the seasonal demands for some products affected employment in the sixteenth century.[2] Enclosures and commercial farming also added to the growing insecurity of the laboring population. These factors were exacerbated by rising prices, the falling value of money, and the failure of wages to keep up with these trends.[3]

Since little distinction between vagrancy and mobility was drawn in sixteenth- and seventeenth-century England, it is difficult to account for the amount of movement due to involuntary unemployment. Movement seems to have been an increasing phenomenon of Tudor England. There was much restlessness of labor. The migrant craftsman or worker dissatisfied with regular service at the usual wage was suspect as a source of crime and disorder. For many workers, however, mobility must have been a necessity, and the harshness of official policy toward migrancy indicated the breadth of the problem and the degree of governmental concern.[4]

The new approaches to poverty in the mercantilist period had their roots in a series of reforms in England and on the continent at the beginning of the sixteenth century. In the two decades between 1520 and 1540 a number of plans were developed for remedying the condition of the poor and preventing the disorganization resulting from poverty. As Vives, the most influential of the early reformers, pointed out, the disease, thievery, immorality, and other behavior of the poor threatened the welfare of all the members of the community. Vives proposed his plan for Bruges in 1526. In the previous year a scheme for Ypres had already been formulated, and Luther had promulgated his ordinance for Leisneck in 1523. Zwingli's program for Zurich was established in 1525, and the French city of Rouen organized its program in 1534. The reform of the English poor laws was enacted in 1536. The principles and practices of all these programs had much in common.[5]

Early Mercantilist Policies

During this period occurred the earliest efforts to develop a system of classification of the poor. At least two categories were specified in all the plans noted above although a third group was formally recognized in several and tacitly accepted in the others. The two largest types were the poor "not able to work," the "impotent, sick and diseased," and the poor "such as be lusty, having their limbs strong enough to labour," in the words of an English act of 1536. The third kind of poor, specifically mentioned by Vives, Luther, and Zwingli, were those who had fallen into "misfortune" through no fault of their own. These were to be called the "worthy poor" some three centuries later. According to Zwingli, these were "the pious, respectable poor citizens . . . who have worked all their days and taken trouble to maintain themselves honourably, who have not consumed their substance with riotous living but happen to be, through God's providence, unable to work any more to maintain themselves by reason of war, famine, accident, excess of children, old age or other infirmity."[6]

Classification of the poor was logically followed by differentiation of treatment. The major innovation of the early sixteenth century schemes was some provision for setting the able-bodied to work. While such provisions were not always carried out, they marked a transition from the punitive policies of previous eras, on the one hand, and from indiscriminate alms-giving, on the other. In the 1536 act no actual plan for setting the able-bodied to work was established, but the local authorities were directed upon punishment by fine "to cause and to compel all and every the said sturdy vagabonds and valiant beggars to be set and kept to continual labour, in such ways as by their said labours they and every of them may get their own livings with the continual labour of their own hands."[7]

In general, most plans had no provision beyond the admonition of setting the able-bodied to work. Vives, although recognizing "no scarcity of normal employment," suggested that "a certain number, however, may be allotted in the name of the public to individual manufacturers from those who are unable of themselves to obtain employment."[8] He also directed that public contracts be given those hiring the unemployed. In Rouen public works such as road-building were established, but there was little distinction between punitive and constructive work.[9] While emphasis on labor was present in all these programs, it is doubtful that any really constructive employment was introduced.

For the worthy poor Luther suggested that "a reasonable advance" be made "from the common chest" so that they might continue to "fulfill their labour honestly." These loans were to be "repaid" at some future time, but for those who could not repay through honest labor and industry, the loans would be "remitted for God's sake because of their necessity."[10] In Zwingli's ordinance for Zurich the overseers could "exempt from the duty of wearing the badge [of beggar] those who, though now in need of relief, were formerly people of position and who would be quite willing to work if they were able to."[11] These distinctions were made in English policy, and the worthy poor were generally the object of voluntary benevolence or mutual aid, such as friendly societies or fraternal associations where they existed. English poor law officials attempted to segregate the poor in jails, houses of correction, and workhouses according to their respectability or willingness to labor.

The tradition of community responsibility as defined in earlier medieval society was evident in these sixteenth-century plans. Although recognition of social responsibility continued to some extent, it was several centuries before the doctrine of responsibility was again as clearly defined as in the beginning of mercantilism. At the crossroads between the medieval and the modern, the schemes of the 1520s and 1530s emphasized the responsibilities of the well-to-do to their poorer neighbors and at the same time pressed for each man to contribute through labor to the community's welfare.

The Ypres scheme required "handy works" of "these stronge and lustye beggers also which haue no luste to work for their lyuinges . . . lest to the hurte bothe of them selves and also of the comen welth they synfully nourisshe their pernicyouse idlenesse of good mennes almose and so take profyte of other mennes laboure."[12] However, this demand for work was balanced by acceptance of responsibility by the community for the needs of the poor.

Poore men no doute are membres of the cyte as wel as ryche and they shulde be looked vpon a great dele the more for that they haue more nede than other and for that the poore mennes profyt may the better be furthered without contencyon and all things be done by the wyse aduyse and auctoritye of many men.[13]

Vives similarly remarked:

And just as in a wealthy house it were a disgrace for the father of the family to allow any to hunger, or go naked, or be disgraced by rags, so it is not seemly that in a city by no means needy the magistrates should permit any citizens to be harassed by hunger and poverty.[14]

In both of Vives' proposals and in the plan designed for Ypres the obligation of the rich to the poor was strongly supported. The advocates of the Ypres plan resorted to the medieval rationale of the relationship of the classes, "For no other cause dyd nature mengle poore and ryche togyther but that poore men shulde receyue benefytes of ryche men."[15] Vives, in the spirit of More and others who were critical of the materialism of the new age, spoke of the rich as "proudly and insolently abusing the riches which they have snatched from the poor and their like."[16]

Responsibility, however, was limited to members of the local community. The community was the center of economic assistance, and its benefits were to go only to those recognized as local dependents. Although local responsibility was of medieval origin, local exclusiveness conflicted with the universal nature of the medieval brotherhood of man. When the sacred authorities of the Sorbonne reviewed the Ypres scheme, they insisted on its coverage being extended to "the poor of neighboring villages" who "on no account" were "to be excluded by this scheme from the relief that is due to them."[17]

One of the major breaches with medieval tradition was the restriction of voluntary charity. If these plans were to be successful, the public authorities believed, they must centralize the distribution of aid so that it would be impossible for the poor to avoid public control. Otherwise the sturdy vagabond might continue to rely on alms and avoid labor. In addition, since the plans relied on voluntary donations to the public fund, they could not permit too great a diversion of resources. The English act of 1536 forbade alms-giving outside the common fund and provided for a fine of ten times the value of the money given privately. The Sorbonne authorities objected to a similar provision in the Ypres scheme and protected the traditional right of the charitable giver. The English provision was probably too radical a departure from previous practices and was not included in the later codification of the poor laws under Elizabeth I. By that time, however, the strengthening of the public program and the employment of taxes for relief may have indirectly discouraged the distribution of private charity.

The English and continental programs of the early sixteenth century marked the turning point in economic assistance policy for the able-bodied poor. The new programs demonstrated a beginning recognition that the normal channels of employment, even when supported by repressive governmental action against idleness, were insufficient to solve the problems of poverty in the rising commercial society. Deterrent policies, however, by no means slackened; they continued to play an important if not a primary role, along with the widening sphere of more positive measures.

The second phase of economic security policy in England encompassed the period from the second half of the sixteenth century, with the elaboration of Tudor mercantilist policy, through the close of the seventeenth century and the dissolution of internal mercantilist controls. For some students this phase of economic policy came to an abrupt end with the Puritan Commonwealth, and a new era emerged with the Restoration in 1660.[18] There was a distinct weakening of economic security policy and administration with the defeat of Charles I, but, on the whole, social responsibility remained the dominant philosophy, if not the practice, until the close of the century. The period 1590–1640 represented the high point of a national system of economic security.

To understand the total impact of mercantilist policy it is necessary to go beyond the narrow definition of poor laws to examine the broad area of economic measures. The theme of stability or conservatism predominated during the most active period of mercantilism. At the beginning stability was defined in the interests of the old, landed aristocracy, but power gradually shifted to the new commercial interests in the seventeenth century. The welfare of the lower classes was greatly affected by this change.

In general, the measures for the economic well-being of the able-bodied were undertaken with several purposes in mind, including the maintenance of the attachment of the working classes to employment, the provision of employment or the means of making a living, the guarantee of some minimal standard of living, and the provision of substitute means of support when employment was not available. These goals were closely related in the eyes of mercantilist statesmen, and there was an evident desire to correct all the abuses of the past and establish a total pattern for the future. During the most active period of governmental intervention centralized coordination was achieved by the Privy Council's control of the local justices of the peace, who were responsible for administration of all the important phases of labor policy. It should be recalled that there was state intervention in every aspect of social and economic life and that regulation of labor was only one feature of larger state policy.

The attachment of the worker to his employment was enforced by a series of measures that discouraged mobility and encouraged continuity or permanence of employment. The most drastic, though not necessarily the most effective, measures against mobility were the long series of statutes prescribing heavy punishments—at times death—for the increasingly large numbers of unattached laborers. An act of 1597, whose provisions were essentially incorporated in the famous Elizabethan Poor Law Act of 1601, included a fulsome catalog of rogues, vagabonds, and sturdy beggars from wandering scholars to "portending" Egyptians. The category "all wandering persons and common labourers, able in body, and refusing to work for the wages commonly given" was the most inclusive and the most pertinent. The punishments were whipping and return to place of residence, but commitment to a house of correction or jail and, in extreme cases, banishment and even death were prescribed. The suppression of vagrancy continued to be the last resort instead of a more constructive policy. The Commonwealth government, which for the fifteen years between 1645 and 1660 could not agree on a measure for the relief and employment of the poor, was, however, able to formulate a statute against vagrancy in 1657.[19]

The punitive aspects of poor law policy colored its more positive features. Thus the houses of correction, which originally provided opportunities for both correction and employment, finally became identified solely with correction. By 1609 an act requiring the construction of such houses in every county referred only to the punishment of vagrants by work. The local poor law officials, pressed by responsibilities beyond their competence, failed to discriminate among the various types of poor and were overwhelmed by the urgency of dealing with the most extreme problems requiring control. Whatever the original intention, the poor law administration gradually developed into a deterrent mechanism for the punishment rather than the relief of those in need of employment.

While the statutes against vagrants and vagabonds required attachment to employment, the Statute of Artificers of 1563 established in detail the conditions of employment. The pious "hope" was expressed that its execution would "bannyshe idlenes, avaunce husbandrie, and yelde into the hyred persone both in the tyme of scarcitie and in the tyme of plentie a convenyent proporcion of Wages."[20] By fixing the period of employment, the conditions for leaving employment, the requirements for admission to apprenticeship, the length of apprenticeship, and the methods of determining wages, the Statute of Artificers attempted to guarantee a stable labor market and stable labor conditions.

All hiring in crafts or trades was to be for a minimum of one year. As a contemporary commented, men hired for lesser periods "do not live in such obedience and good order, as beinge hiered by the yeare." They did not work regularly, engaged in vice and crime, "and so by sundry meanes undo themselfes and others also, whereof great misery and increase of roges and vagabounds growethe."[21] Workers could not leave their employment before the end of their term without the approval of the Justices of the Peace, and a quarter's advance notice was to be given by either party to the contract. Even at the expiration of his term of employment a worker could not leave the locality of his employer without a certificate of lawful departure.

The length of apprenticeship was fixed at seven years, but the minimum age for completion was twenty-one, and twenty-four in corporate towns. This provision had many values for stability. It made possible an apprenticeship long enough for the young to learn their trade fully; it permitted the employer to make a profit from the work of a skilled apprentice by the end of his period of training; it prevented young men from setting themselves up in business and in marriage too early; it limited the early start of independent artisans and thus protected the older craftsmen from the competition of the young; and it provided a longer period of control over the young and a foundation of support for their elders.[22]

Apprenticeship was not open to unskilled farmers or laborers unless they were wealthy, for entry into trades or crafts was limited to children of those already artificers. Thus the mobility of the poor was severely limited and the occupations of the skilled protected. The goal of occupational stability was paralleled by the desire to maintain a large agricultural population. Agriculture was considered the key to social and economic stability by early mercantilist statesmen. All able-bodied men between the ages of twelve and sixty not employed in other occupations were required to accept employment in agriculture. Only the wealthy were free from the demands of occupation, and in times of harvest all, no matter what their occupation, could be called upon to work in the fields.[23]

Finally, wages were to be fixed by the local Justices of the Peace, and both the payment and receipt of wages beyond the approved rate were to be punished. Encouraging mobility of employment through a free wage market was to be avoided by standardizing all the terms of employment. The wage assessment policy, however, had a relatively short history and fell into disuse well before the end of the seventeenth century.

Attachment to employment was also effected by the residence laws of the poor relief system. Even prior to the rigid formulation of settlement in the 1662 Settlement Act, parish relief and the poor law employment programs had been limited to the "settled" or locally resident poor. Previously, too, the laborer could have been penalized for leaving his place of abode, but strict enforcement of the act would have made it almost impossible to change community of residence. The act was frequently broken, and to a large extent it compounded rather than solved the problem for which it was designed. But it represented a further attempt to restrict workers to the local market and prevent their mobility, particularly with respect to rural employment.

Rationally there seemed little justification for the passage of the Settlement Act of 1662. Its goals were already established in earlier policy and practice, and its makers probably despaired of finding a solution to poverty and vagrancy in the second half of the seventeenth century. It also reflected the hardening attitude toward the poor that had grown during the Commonwealth period. When a century later those parts of the act preventing movement were officially abandoned, the continuance of local responsibility operated as a hindrance to mobility.

Local ties, however, were fundamental to a society trying to maintain social stability. Permanence of residence and enforced attachment to employment not only established clear economic relationships but also created social relationships that cemented duties and obligations. The poor law supported these responsibilities by establishing the boundaries of mutual liability. The Elizabethan Act of 1601 extended to grandparents liability for the support of their grandchildren. In general, the act attempted to fix responsibility for support within the family and upon those members who could be expected to be employed. Although the welfare function of local government was clearly promulgated, this function was delimited by the enforcement of family obligations. The latter, it was assumed, would both strengthen family ties and influence those responsible for support to remain at work.

The acceptance of public responsibility, as already noted, led to the lessening of the role of private relief. Charity had been looked upon as a strong influence toward idleness and thriftlessness. It was believed that the local authorities would be more discriminating and more efficient in their use of relief. The private charities turned to other functions such as education and hospitals. Even those, however, came under the surveillance of the public officials who were responsible for seeing that there was no misuse of private funds. In effect, the mercantilist state recognized the significance of philanthropy, and, like other important functions, it was not to be left entirely to the vagaries of private control.

More direct intervention in private enterprise occurred in the policies affecting employment. The state attempted to prevent the curtailment of jobs by private employers and to encourage the expansion of employment opportunities. During its period of greatest power, the first part of the seventeenth century, the Privy Council brought pressure on individual employers to maintain their workers in times of crisis. Pressure was exerted on merchants to buy and on manufacturers to produce even when there was no market. In 1622, when difficulties with Spain caused English merchants and manufacturers to dismiss workers because of poor trade, the Privy Council informed the justices of the counties:

We hereby require you to call before you such cloathiers . . . and to deale effectually with them for the employment of such weavers, spinners and other persons as are now out of worke. Where wee maye not omitt to let you know that as wee have employed our best endeavors in favor of the cloathiers. . . . Soe, may wee not indure that the cloathiers . . . should att their pleasure . . . dismisse their workefoelkes, who being many in nomber and most of them of the poorer sort are in such cases likely by their clamores to disturbe the quiet and governement of those parts wherein they live.

The Council concluded its admonition:

This being the rule by wch both the woolgrower, the cloathier and merchant must be governed. That whosoever had a part of the gaine in profitable times since his Maty happie raigne must now in the decay of Trade . . . beare a part of the publicke losses as may best conduce to the good of the publicke and the maintenance of the generall trade.[24]

With the disintegration of the Privy Council's control and the increasing opposition to direct intervention in domestic business following the Civil War, the policy of forcing responsibility on employers came to an end. The yearly hirings under the Statute of Artificers tended to maintain some stability in the labor market not only for the employer but also for the worker, who was protected from capricious dismissal. As one contemporary observer commented:

Some that have hiered servauntes for a whole yeare, when the thincke their tourne served, the will, longe before thende of the yeare or withoute any warninge, put their servauntes awaye . . . Some will not take the paynes to correct their servauntes for their offences, but will putt theim awaye. . . . Some will kiepe servauntes in their health and putt them awaye in their sicknes.[25]

However, neither statutes nor administrative action were sufficient to withstand the tendency of employers to look upon labor as merely one of the elements in the total process of manufacture and trade. Toward the end of the seventeenth century new relief schemes were developed that were intended to exploit the labor of the unemployed and at the same time be profitable.

There had always existed, as an alternative to private employment, the possibility of work provided by the public authorities. The early sixteenth-century poor law programs had emphasized employment of the able-bodied, but English poor law authorities were slow to move in this direction. In 1576, Parliament required of cities and towns a stock of raw materials so that

Yowthe may be accustomed and brought to Laboure and Worcke, and then not lyke to growe to bee ydle Roges and to the Entent also that suche as bee alredye growen up in ydlenes and so Roges at this present may not have any juste excuse in sayeing that they cannot get any Service or Worcke . . . and that other poore and needye persons being willinge to worcke maye bee set on worcke.[26]

By the acts of 1597 and 1601 all local authorities were to establish stocks for employing the able-bodied unemployed. As with the enforcement of employer responsibility, the period of greatest local authority activity corresponded to the greatest exercise of central government surveillance under the Privy Council. For example, the order affecting clothing merchants and manufacturers stated:

And if there shalbe found greater numbers of poore people then the clothiers can revieu and imploy, Wee thinke it fitt and accordingly require you to take order for putting the statute in execution, whereby there is provisione made in that behalfe by raising of publicke stockes for the imployment of such in that trade as want worke.[27]

The organization of work by the parishes did not differ essentially from the domestic system of production generally practiced during this period. Frequently the administration was placed in the hands of a local entrepreneur, such as a clothier, who gave out work to those applying and paid fixed rates for the work. Thus, apart from the local authority supplying the capital and establishing the wage, the arrangement conformed to typical employment.

There was much unemployment during the period of the Commonwealth, and Parliament deliberated lengthily on plans for the poor; but the system of employment by the parishes had almost vanished. A competent contemporary observer remarked in 1659, "It is rare to see any provision of a stock in any parish for the relief of the poor."[28] After the Restoration the earlier emphasis on parish employment was not revived.

The establishment of houses where the poor would be set to work was another major aspect of the mercantilist employment program. Those houses were the forerunners of the later factory system. Such institutions as London's Bridewell started in the middle of the sixteenth century. The example of Amsterdam's combined poorhouse, workhouse, and penal institution, where labor was conserved and used for the benefit of the whole society, influenced all of Europe. It was assumed that training and the development of habits of industry would make effective workers of those returning to the community.

The development of houses of correction was widespread in England by the early seventeenth century, but the penal rather than the work aspects of these institutions was dominant. In the years before the Civil War, there was a great increase in workhouses with the ostensible purpose of employment. Their growth may have been encouraged by the embezzlement of materials occurring when work was given the poor in their own homes and by the desire for a convenient place to train workers.[29] Many workhouses attempted constructive work programs, and some were under the expert supervision of skilled master artisans. In one such house in Yorkshire those employed were even paid the statutory wage for their kind of work.[30]

The second half of the seventeenth century was marked by more ambitious workhouse projects. They were motivated by the belief that the poor could be made a source of profit to the nation, and papers were written and schemes devised that purported to demonstrate that beneficial effect. The proponents of such schemes did not think that the labor of the poor would merely compensate for their own maintenance but expected a considerable profit. Such efforts rested on the mercantilist assumption that labor was the primary source of value and on the expansionist faith of the period that any enterprise harnessing labor power must necessarily be successful. John Locke, the philosopher and a member of the Board of Trade at the close of the seventeenth century, strongly supported such ventures, although his own proposals for employing the poor were of a much harsher variety. In keeping with the times, Locke found the causes of poverty in the low morality of the poor, and his measures included contracting out the able-bodied poor to private masters and the provision of partial employment of the less able, women, and children.

Some of the plans for the profitable employment of the poor, such as Sir Matthew Hale's in *A Discourse Touching Provision for the Poor,* were not inconsiderate of the needs of the poor. In advocating his plan for workhouses Sir Matthew pointed out:

No person will have need to beg or steal, because he may gain his living better by working; and no man will be so vain, and indeed hurtful to the public, as to give to such as beg, and thereby to encourage them, when he is sure they may gain their living by working. And all the laws against vagrants, beggars, and wanderers, will be then effectually put in execution, when we shall be sure they may be employed if they will; but till that, the interdicting and punishing of beggars and givers seems a most unreasonable piece of impudence as well as uncharitableness.

He maintained that as a result of his plan "the wealth of the nation will be increased, manufactures advanced, and everybody put into a capacity of eating his own bread."[31]

The idea of special corporations for employing the poor received much encouragement from the glowing reports of Bristol's experiment, which was begun in 1696. Similar workhouses that both employed and administered to the needs of the poor were set up in thirteen towns within fifteen years of the founding of the Bristol house. They were regarded as a substitute for the whole previous poor relief system. They were to educate the young, provide for the able-bodied, and care for the impotent. Attempts to have Parliament approve a national system of workhouses failed, though only after much deliberation. Daniel Defoe opposed such plans with the telling argument that the competition of such houses would destroy manufacturers and throw their employees out of work. If opportunities for enterprise were available, said Defoe, there was no need for special corporations; the normal channels would expand to employ the surplus labor.

Emigration to the colonies was also a popular remedy for unemployment. It was during this period that the principal American colonies were founded, and a great proportion of their population was made up of transported indentured servants and vagrants or pauper children whose passages were arranged by the poor relief authorities.

In addition to its efforts at maintaining employment, the mercantilist state supported the standard of living of the lower classes through the control of wages, the control of prices, the prevention of artificial shortages in the major staples, and the protection of workers from the unrestricted competition of a free labor market. The foundation of Tudor wage policy was laid in the Statute of Artificers of 1563, which differed from earlier legislation in not establishing a maximum wage. Instead the local justices of the peace annually set wages by "calling unto them suche discreate and grave persons of the said Countie or of the said Citie or Towne Corporate as they shall thinke mete, and conferrynge togither respectynge the plentie or scarcity of the tyme and other circumstaunces necessaryly to be considered."[32]

This policy permitted a flexible scale of wages that could be arranged according to the different costs of living in various parts of the country. The administration of the statute, however, was the measure of its adequacy, particularly with regard to the fixing of the basic rate since employers and workers could be penalized if wages above that rate were paid. The preamble of the statute proposed that there be provided "unto the hyred persone bothe in the tyme of scarcitie and in the tyme of plentie a convenyent proporcion of wages," and the Privy Council urged that workers not be "uncharitably dealth with."

In the clothing industry particularly there appears to have been efforts to protect the workmen; an act of 1608 established penalties for payments by clothiers below the wages fixed and further disqualified any clothiers from being "raters" of wages for those employed in their industry. In this statute the general complaint was made that "the rates of wages for poor artificers, labourers and other persons whose wages were meant to be rated . . . have not been rated and proportioned according to the plenty, scarcity, necessity, and respect of the time."[33] This act would appear to have established a policy of minimum rather than maximum wages for textile workers, who, on the whole, received more support than most workers in their struggle against the rising entrepreneurs of the new industry.

In accord with its ideological assumptions, the wage policy of the mercantilist period favored low wage standards. A commission at Sudbury appointed by the Privy Council in the early seventeenth century "found by experience that the raising of wages cannot advance the relief of the poor, but will prove inconvenient, for that they will not be set on so much work as if the wages were at the usual rate."[34] The administration of this time probably safeguarded the laborers against excessive exploitation while it prevented the pressure of the workers for increased wages. After all, the administration of the law was in the hands of men of property, and it was unlikely that they would go against their own best interests. In the case of the clothiers, the workers gained from the antagonism of the conservative landed aristocracy for the new commercial classes.

The established rates may often have acted as minimum rather than maximum wages despite the purposes of the law. Failure to lower wages during periods of reduced cost of living indirectly resulted in higher wage scales.[35] Effective wage regulation, however, like other controls over the internal economy, was undermined during the Commonwealth, and by the end of the seventeenth century, administration of wage assessments had markedly declined. With the reversion to local autonomy at the time of the Civil War, whatever bias previously existed in favor of the worker also rapidly disappeared. By 1675, Roger Coke criticized the Elizabethan poor law structure because it "encourages wilful and evil-disposed persons to impose what wages they please upon their labours."[36]

From the second quarter of the sixteenth century the government attempted to see that the poor could obtain corn and at reasonable prices. In periods of distress throughout the century the state attempted to prevent corn from being withheld from the market, to encourage the wealthy and the local communities to set aside stores of corn for the poor, and to have corn sold to the poorer members of the community at lower than the prevailing market prices. At times the prices of major foods, such as corn, butter, and poultry, were fixed by proclamation. Some of the larger cities, particularly London and Bristol, even imported grain in times of scarcity.

With the increased activity of the Privy Council during the years prior to the Commonwealth, regulations for the adequate provision of corn became more systematically administered. The export of corn and other staples was forbidden. Distribution of adequate supplies to all areas of the country was attempted. In times of scarcity the use of barley for malt and the sales of alehouses generally were restricted. In addition to food, some of the larger towns supplied fuel to the poor during the winter. These policies affected the laboring class generally, not only those classified as paupers.[37]

The distinction between programs for the economically dependent and the general paternalistic policies of the state for the welfare of the laboring classes was not sharply drawn prior to the end of the seventeenth century. The government's broad intervention in the economic life of the nation tended to make normal procedure of what was later interpreted as strictly assistance measures. The clear line between public and private matters that marked the later, laissez-faire, era had not yet been sharply drawn. The right of the poorer members to benefit from the general wealth was still recognized, although the rumblings about private rights were not far off. Even at the end of the sixteenth century one man who was fined and imprisoned for refusing to help the poor exclaimed, "They are knaves . . . my goodes are my nowne, they nor the queene nor the Councelle have to doe with my goodes, I will doe what I liste with them."[38] During the eighteenth century the rigorous push toward a commercial and industrial society made abnormal or unnatural the dependency on anything other than wages from private employment.

The state's programs for securing employment for the poor, whether in private enterprise or in public workhouses and parish stocks, bridged the gap between the institutionalized ways of gaining subsistence and later relief. In the early provision of work the poor were paid for their labor, and in some instances the rate of pay was specified as that "for such lyke work within the said parishe."[39] The later seventeenth-century plans for employing the poor were conceived of as strictly commercial enterprises that would provide profit as well as employment. In the eighteenth century work became merely instrumental to a deterrent relief system rather than a program in its own right.

Although work was prescribed for the able-bodied poor and correctional measures were employed when they were unwilling to work, it may be assumed that the able-bodied poor shared in the public and private provision for the impotent poor. While the local authorities were urged and ordered to provide work for the able-bodied, they were frequently incapable of or lax in the development of work programs. In view of the primitive administrative mechanisms at their disposal, their limited resources, and the complexity of organizing suitable employment, many of the smaller local authorities must have mixed a great deal of temporary aid to the able-bodied with their more permanent programs for the impotent poor. Apart from small monetary grants or doles, the dominant form of parish aid was the provision of shelter. The poor were permitted to build on the wastelands of the community. In some cases the parish provided rent-free cottages; in others, the parish might arrange for the payment of rent in private households.

Private charity continued to play an important role. Where there was no conflict with public policy, such as encouraging dependency, the national and local authorities supported the development and use of private resources, which lessened the burden on public taxes. In many of the communities private and public action tended to be blurred, and private funds were used for public policy. As in other aspects of life, the separation and specialization of institutions had not yet fully evolved.

3

The American Colonies During
the Mercantilist Period

Background

THE history of American economic security policy has been
affected throughout by trends in British social and economic policy, but
never more significantly than during the colonial period, when British
influence was direct and official. The prescription of colonial policy by the
central government, the important colonial offices held by citizens of the
mother country, and the loyalty of leading colonials to England and its
practices resulted in a fundamental unity of policy between England and
America. However, the informal factors of common culture and personal
relationships were more important in maintaining similarity of approach
to social and economic problems. Differences were present, of course, because of variations between the two countries, but even they did not make
for major deviations from the English pattern.

The New England colonies, most influential in determining American
assistance policies, were strongly identified with the economic and religious doctrines of the Puritan party in England. The emigrants in America were even more theocratically inclined than their counterparts at home.
While the New England and particularly the Massachusetts leaderships
were especially firm in discouraging economic assistance, the colonies as a
whole followed a policy of extremely limited responsibility for economic

welfare. Even New Amsterdam, which passed from Dutch to English rule during the colonial period, required no real change in economic assistance policy. The Dutch represented an even more thorough version of mercantilism then, and their assistance programs were the envy of the British. Whether Cavalier or Puritan, Dutch or English, William Penn or Roger Williams, mercantilist ideology created a unified approach to economic security.

The colonies differed from the mother country in one major aspect; they did not directly experience the feudal paternalism that colored England's sense of social responsibility. England's long and gradual evolution from a feudal society to a burgeoning commercial nation had not been part of colonial history. In fact, many of the early colonial leaders were identified with the groups in England who wanted to sweep away the remnants of earlier systems of interdependence and replace them with the ethic of individualism. While the central government and the Privy Council restrained these centrifugal forces, no such balance was achieved in the colonies. The mother country had no interest in developing a spirit of social responsibility in the colonies. The colonies were looked upon as a source of economic advantage, and the companies who helped finance the colonies were interested only in quick profit. When royal favorites were granted large personal holdings, exploitation for their own and England's benefit was the primary motive. As for the colonists themselves, the economy of the colony was identified with the interests of the permanent body of well-to-do settlers who had no traditional concern for the more needy with no established roots.

The colonies consisted of geographically separated settlements with little intercommunication. Surviving the rigorous physical environment and the Indian and foreign menaces required strict adherence to a code of local self-sufficiency and protection. Compared to England, where local interests continued to thwart national policy, the colonies were still in a primitive stage of local separateness. It is not surprising, therefore, that a sense of isolation and localism had an overwhelming influence on colonial assistance policy, which reflected a combination of parochial thinking and the views of productivity, labor, and profit prevalent in England at the end of the seventeenth century.

The idler or vagrant was a particular threat to colonial self-sufficiency. Economically, these communities could not afford to contribute to nonproductive members, and socially, they could not tolerate deviations from the norms of community life. The settlements were tight little communities that feared the corrupting effects of any foreign influence. In England gains from the introduction of foreign capital and skill outweighed concern about strange customs and behavior. Besides, the nation was large and sufficiently integrated to absorb differences. The colonies, however, looked with suspicion on all newcomers. Those who brought in strangers, whether from overseas or merely from outside the community, were held responsible, and the "warning out" system to prevent the establishment of residence was practiced almost indiscriminately in some of the colonies. Even prior to the passage of the Settlement Act of 1662 in England the New England colonies rigidly excluded migrants. Colonial attitudes were heightened by England's practice of exporting vagrants and petty criminals to the colonies. Long Island, for example, served as a natural refuge for criminals, and the local people, in addition to strict settlement laws, organized military assistance to prevent the entrance of undesirable newcomers.

All these factors resulted in the local community exerting much more control over the lives of its citizens than was the case in England. This control was for the protection of the community, not for the preservation of the individual. In Plymouth, for example, where there was rigorous intervention in all aspects of life, a statute of 1670 required that all persons live as part of some family. This act explained its purpose:

Whereas great inconuenience hath arisen by single psons in this collonie being for themselves and not betaking themselves in wel gourned families It is enacted by the Court that henceforth noe single pson be suffered to live of himselfe or in any family but such as the Celectmen of the Towne shall approue of.[1]

As in England, the stability of society was believed to rest on the members of the community recognizing and fulfilling their appropriate social roles. The enforcement of that belief, however, created greater problems for the colonies. Migration itself led to the loosening of social ties and class lines. In many instances the total social hierarchy was no longer present, and the differences among free men narrowed to the lower and upper middle classes. Slavery and indenture provided definite positions in the social structure, but the existence of free labor threatened the traditional pattern.

Because of the great need for labor, much higher wages were offered in the colonies than in England. High wages, however, conflicted with the mercantilist tenet of low wages and with strict adherence to class position. William Penn complained in 1698, "Were the 'generality' content with less luxurious expenditures, according to their rank, the price of labor would fall, manufacture would be cheaper, and a greater market provided." He concluded, "The temperance I plead for is not only religiously, but politically good."[2]

While Penn spoke moderately, the Massachusetts leaders reacted with great fervor to the luxurious living of the "lower orders." A bill for the regulation of wages and hours introduced in 1670 included the statement that in addition to acts of God affecting crops and the poor market for farm produce,

Difficultie and discouragmt is yet heaped and increasing vpon them and others by reason of the excessive deerenes of labour by artifficers, Labourers, and Servants, contrary to reason and equitie, to the great prejudice of many householders and their Familyes, and tending to their vtter ruein and vndoeing, and the produce thereof is by many Spent to mayntayne Such bravery in Apparell which is altogether vnbecomeing thier place and ranck, and in Idleness of life, and a great part spent viciously in Tavernes and alehouses and other Sinful practices much to the dishonour of God, Scandall of Religion and great offence and grief to Sober and Godly people amongst vs.[3]

Mercantilist doctrine was thus accentuated by Puritan asceticism, which had such a fanatical hold in New England. The number of free laborers or wage earners was relatively small in the seventeenth century. Free artisans and craftsmen were largely independent producers. Slavery and indenture were the basic sources of labor, but the indentured servant generally became a farmer rather than a wage earner at the end of his period of service.[4]

Despite the low status given to labor by the practice of indenture and particularly slavery, the free laborer achieved a higher position than his contemporaries in England and on the continent. The need for skilled craftsmen, their greater independence, and their higher wages raised them above similar labor in other places. It has been estimated that the colonial workman had a real wage 30 to 100 percent higher than his English counterpart.[5] In some of the northern colonies the working class even participated in town government. There were altogether greater opportunities for social advancement in the more fluid and labor-hungry society of America.

In the seventeenth century the colonies attempted to copy England's mercantilist controls on wages and working conditions. Massachusetts was most active in regulating wages and prices. In the spirit of the Privy Council, in 1633 Massachusetts fixed prices so that "honest and conscionable workemen should [not] be wronged or discouraged by excessive prices of those commodityes wch are necessary for their Life and comfort."[6] The efforts to control wages in the colonies were clearly unsuccessful. The shortage of labor and the opportunities available prevented any strict adherence to a labor code. In fact, labor was persuaded to come to the colonies by the promise of high wages. The natural advantages of the colonial labor market protected the interests of labor, and some of the regulations against arbitrary dismissals in the Statute of Artificers were introduced in the colonies.

As in England, industriousness was encouraged by punishment for vagrancy and forced employment or commitment to the workhouse. Some of the colonial statutes were borrowed directly from England, and the courts and local authorities rigidly required the worker to be employed at his vocation. All inhabitants might be expected to give some time to such necessary public works as highways, bridges, fortifications, and prisons. In the southern colonies this obligation tended to be limited to the lower classes and slaves, and even in some of the northern communities the upper classes were exempted. Labor might also be expected on private undertakings, and for projects desired by the local authorities, guarantees of a quantity of manpower would be made to the entrepreneur in charge.[7]

The attitude in the colonies toward wealth, property, and poverty reflected the great emphasis on individual enterprise. The influence of the Puritan ideology was widespread. Poverty, like wealth, demonstrated God's hand, and while riches were proof of goodness and selection, insufficiency was evidence of evil and rejection. The Reverend Thomas Hooker even rejected the idea that the poor should be aided from the same fund that supported the ministry, for the ministry, in his opinion, was honest labor and should be justly compensated from the wealth of the community. However, "neither rule nor reason leads us or allows us to relieve the poor by all our good things."[8] Cotton Mather maintained that "for those who Indulge themselves in Idleness [and poverty and idleness were synonymous in this context], the Express Command of God unto us, is, That we should let them Starve." For Mather, only the impotent or unemployable were worthy of charity, and for the remainder, "the best liberality to them" is to make them work.[9] Charity would only encourage idleness. The combination of Puritan morality and mercantilist labor doctrine resulted in an extremely repressive colonial poor law policy.

Colonial Assistance Programs

Economic assistance in seventeenth-century America was so little provided, as distinguished from England, as to be a negligible part of colonial administration. The colonies had sparse populations, and under the prevailing conditions informal, neighborly aid played a greater role in the closely knit frontier communities than did publicly organized programs. The administration of a vigorous settlement policy avoided responsibility for impoverished migrants; individuals were held accountable for those whom they brought in should need arise. Slavery and indenture also emphasized individual as against community responsibility for the economic well-being of dependent persons. The family responsibility of the English poor law was extended to other groups in the colonies to limit the sphere of community obligation.

Economic assistance would probably have been so negligible in early colonial times as to warrant no official attention had it not been for the sensitivity to idleness that made of even the most minor occasions of need gross examples of sin and delinquency. It is interesting to note that although there was much complaint against the idle and the poor by the colonists, the colonial governors generally reported to England that there was insufficient need to establish formal assistance programs. Some of those reports may have been prepared as defenses of the colonial administration with the object of warding off central government interference and so may have been overly optimistic. Allowing for understandable exaggeration, however, those reports painted a consistent picture. In 1678, Andros, who was to be governor of the ill-fated Dominion of New England and who was regarded as a harsh administrator, reported to the Lords of Trade that the New York province had no beggars and that the poor were being given proper care. The governor of Connecticut wrote in 1690, "For the poore, it is ordered that they be relieved by the townes where they live, every towne providing for theire owne poor; and so for impotent persons. There is seldom any want of releif; because labor is deare, viz., 2s, and sometimes 2s. 6d a day for a day labourer, and provision cheap."[10]

A few years later another governor of New York, Dongan, informed the Lords of Trade, "Every Town & County are obliged to maintain their own poor, which makes them bee soe careful that noe Vagabonds, Beggars, nor Idle Persons are suffered to live here."[11] In 1699, Governor Bellamont ridiculed a suggestion for a workhouse in New York City by stating, "There is no such as a beggar in this town or country."[12] In another connection an entrepreneur proposing a "bank of credit" to the Massachusetts Council in 1686 remarked that it would be unnecessary to include small loans to the poor as there were so few, and employment at comfortable wages was available to all.[13] In general, conditions in the colonies did not seem to require the elaborate plans of the mother country for dealing with poverty.

The administration of poor relief followed the English pattern. In New England the town was the chief unit for providing aid. In the southern colonies the parishes were the principal agents, and they were accountable in turn to the county courts. During New York's history under the Dutch, assistance was a church function, but secular administration was substituted after New York was ceded to the British.

The New England communities soon established detailed provisions for supervising the poor. Their main goal was to prevent the possibility of anyone requiring relief from the public treasury. A Plymouth law of 1654 required all persons of "small means" and "suspected" of living "idley" and "loosely" to give an account of themselves to the authorities.[14] The details of administration were made more explicit in 1658:

for the preventing of Idlenes and other euills occationed thereby It is enacted . . . that the Grandjurymen . . . take a speciall view and Notice of all manor of psons married or single dwelling within theire seuerall townshipes that haue smale meanes to maintaine themselues and are suspected to liue Idlely and loosly and to require an account of them how they liue and such as they find delinquent and cannot giue a good account with them that they cause the cunstable to bring them before the majistrate in theire towne if there bee any if there bee none before the Celect Men appointed for such purpose that such course may be taken with them as in theire wisdomes shalbee judged just and equal.[15]

Informal control of the lower classes by their superiors had a long history, but the establishment of town officers with formal powers and responsibilities went back to the censors of the poor provided for in most of the early sixteenth-century mercantilist statutes.

Soon after their founding colonial communities followed the policy of restricting entry and deporting undesirables. The definition of undesirable covered a variety of factors, although potential economic dependency was the primary concern. Strangers were carefully scrutinized as to their likelihood of becoming local "charges," and measures were taken to establish the responsibility of their hosts or employers or of the masters of the vessels on which they arrived. In the New England colonies probationary periods of three months to a year were required before the status of resident was acquired, but an extensive "warning out" system further limited the acquisition of such status. As in England, guarantees of support were expected from the community of prior residence when the immigrant moved from another settlement.

The middle colonies had especially rigid residence restrictions because of the heavy flow of immigrants into these areas. When New York was under Dutch rule, it was a favorite refuge of bonded servants fleeing from the English colonies. In 1642 the Dutch Director-General forbade the entertaining of strangers or the providing of more than one meal or one night's lodging without his knowledge.[16] In response to New Amsterdam's complaint that it was burdened with the poor of other villages, Peter Stuyvesant ordered:

That from this time forward, no assistance shall be given by the Deacons of this City New Amsterdam, to any persons residing outside the jurisdiction of this City, unless they bring with from the Deacons or Overseers of the Poor at the place of their residence a certificate of their character and poverty.[17]

The city, however, followed the practice of assisting only its own poor.

Under the English a settlement act for New York was passed in 1683, "for the prevention and discourageing of Vagabonds and Idle persons to come into this province from other parts, and also from one part of the Province to another."[18] This act followed the New England colonies in distinguishing between those without estate or skill and those having a "manuall craft or occupacon." The latter could "at all times come and inhabitt in any part within the Province and bee always admitted."[19] As in

England, settlement policy did not prevent the entry of desirable laborers so much as limit the mobility of the less adequate and potentially more burdensome.

The rudimentary nature of colonial programs for the poor was reflected in the makeshift plans for their care. The most common method was the boarding of the poor in private homes. The local authority would pay the total cost or supplement the contribution made by the recipient from employment or other resources. The poor might also receive aid in their own homes, and relief was given to cover such exigencies as medical expenses. Poorhouses, whether workhouses, houses of correction, or almshouses, were not practicable in most communities. The population was insufficient to support the need for such enterprises. In Virginia plans for a poorhouse to be sponsored by three parishes were drawn up but were not carried out.[20] Some of the larger towns, such as Plymouth, Boston, and New York, established houses in the seventeenth century. In New York the Dutch Reformed Church provided houses for aged or ill who could not be cared for otherwise. The houses in New England were of a general type and served all purposes. In Massachusetts, after the first almshouse built in 1660 was burned down, a recommendation that a workhouse be provided was not acted upon, and a second general almshouse was erected.[21] The next century, however, was to see the widespread development of workhouses, but they were probably reserved for the more recalcitrant poor who were given punitive labor much as in the houses of correction.

Although the local authorities themselves provided little work directly, extensive efforts were made to see that the able-bodied were employed. The practice of binding out poor widows into service was followed in the New England towns.[22] The Dutch organized local work-relief programs in some of their settlements during critical periods. The poor were employed at public expense in the building of barns and fences, enlarging churches, constructing public granaries, and in other projects necessary for the welfare of the community that would ordinarily have been done through regular employment.[23]

The reduction of taxes and the provision of food and clothing at low prices were other measures favoring the poor. In New England towns grain was supplied the poor below the market price, and town cows were maintained for milk for the poor. On the whole, the colonial situation in the seventeenth century made few demands on those responsible for the poor, but where help was required, it tended to be negative in spirit and practice. As one writer has well summarized the period:

The duty of the state to assist directly in the creation of individual well-being was never clearly accepted. Although regulation of the economic activity of the individual was highly paternalistic, it was essentially repressive rather than assisting. Laws were designed to restrain excessive expenditures, excessive prices or excessive wages. But the seventeenth century offered little in the direction of true constructive intervention. Mercantilists tend to look upon labourers as enemies, and the colonial labour laws in general have a distinct mercantilist flavour. Maximum wage laws were far more frequently enacted than minimum wage laws; the less fortunate members of society were more often legislated against than legislated for. This is illustrated in the matter of poor relief. It is true that the relief of the poor was not a serious problem during the seventeenth century. State action was therefore infrequent, but that which did emerge was ill devised.[24]

4

Significance of the
Mercantilist Period

DURING the mercantilist era the foundation of modern economic security policies was established. Not until the twentieth century were there comparable efforts in England and the United States to develop a national program for economic welfare. During the intervening centuries new ideologies and the changing social and economic scene caused important changes in the concept of economic security, but the legacy of mercantilism continued to influence welfare planning. The status relationships mercantilism inherited and built upon have never been wholly absent as an important source of social policy. Such fundamental questions were raised during this period as the role of the state in the economy, the function of economic security programs in a commercial and industrial society, the balance between local and national interest in economic security measures, the relationship of special legislation for the poor to general measures concerned with the social and economic welfare of the nation, the social and psychological implications of the use of the community's wealth for individual and family security, and the influence of economic security programs on the economic, social, and political structure of the nation.

While these questions were not entirely new, having been recognized to some extent in earlier periods, it was during the mercantilist era that the first serious and considered efforts were made toward their solution. Mercantilism, in effect, represented a staging and rehearsal of the principal elements in much of future welfare policy. It was a period of experimentation in welfare strategy supported by a climate of social responsibility combined with state interest. Both the principles and practices explored during this time have been significant for the whole of later welfare planning.

During the mercantilist period the principle was established that economic security involved more than the mere provision of assistance to those who, for whatever reason, had insufficient means for their own subsistence. The focus of economic security became the relationship between social provision and employment. "The question," as Alfred Marshall later stated, "was, in fact, one of unemployment rather than poor relief, [and] to both 17th and 18th century writers the crux of the problem was the position of the able Poor."[1] The mercantilist experiments in work programs for the unemployed able-bodied poor were far from successful, and their faith that the able-bodied could be absorbed into industry was not borne out. By the end of the seventeenth century work as a constructive or positive form of public planning for the unemployed ceased to be a paramount issue, and work was relegated to the repressive and institutionalized system of relief. However, this represented more the frustration of failure than the denial of the principle that the crux of the problem of poverty was employment. Later programs attempted to approach the problem indirectly or obliquely, but even the most harsh and destructive policies of later years were rationalized as leading to this goal.

The acceptance of the link between employment and economic security was closely related to a second fundamental principle of mercantilist policy: the stability of society required direct and active intervention in overcoming the threat of poverty. The informal customary methods of assistance had acted as a stabilizing force prior to the sixteenth century, when society was made up of small and isolated units, and stability could be achieved on a relatively intimate level. In the increasingly complex world of the mercantilist statesmen, economic security was no longer the casual by-product of other relationships but required the attention of specialized institutions.

A third principle growing out of the other two was the necessity of the state's playing a major role in welfare planning. The amount and enthusiasm of public effort have varied over the centuries since mercantilism, and other institutions have either by necessity or by choice filled the vacuum left by limited public action, but the principle of public responsibility has never been entirely denied. Even during the decades of greatest opposition to public action the continued presence of public programs has belied the strength of their critics.

Despite the recognition of national interest in a stable economy during the mercantilist period, the emphasis on local administration of welfare programs led to much confusion. This resulted from the conflicts between the immediate concerns of the local areas and the broader policies of the national government as well as from the administrative ineptitude of most local units. The traditional responsibility of local areas for the poor meant one thing when poor law policy was primarily a matter of providing for the local needy impotent, but it was entirely different when the prosperity of the nation and the employment of the able-bodied were involved. Although the restrictive approach of the local communities was harmful to all groups, it was especially detrimental to the wage-earning population. Apart from the brief period when the Privy Council enforced national policy in England, the local authorities made little serious effort to meet the problem of economic security. Fundamentally concerned with lowering the cost of public aid and protecting the interests of local employers, the localities frequently followed the paradoxical policy of restricting the mobility of surplus labor and limiting their financial responsibility for the poor. The Settlement Act of 1662, new in neither principle nor practice, formalized the restrictive nature of local responsibility. The Act itself may have been an immediate response to the demands of the large municipalities being flooded with migrant labor during a difficult period or may have represented more thorough rejection of national controls following the Restoration. In any case, it symbolized the disintegration of earlier, more constructive policies for economic security. By the end of the century the Act was liberalized by giving local authorities the power to guarantee the security of their residents in other communities and thus made possible greater movement of workers. The issue of local responsibility, however, remained a continuing obstacle to rational welfare planning and later became tied to economic liberalism in the struggle against the expansion of social provision. It was ironical that the feudal notion of

CARNEGIE LIBRARY
LIVINGSTONE COLLEGE
SALISBURY, N. C. 28144

local responsibility should have become the handmaiden of the ideologies of the rising commercial and industrial classes.

It became apparent, however, that the goal of local responsibility was not the establishment but the abandonment of responsibility. The local authorities discouraged marriage and families among the laboring population to reduce the potential numbers of dependents. Available living quarters were destroyed to prevent families from residing in them. Thus, Lord North said at the end of the seventeenth century:

It is another very great Destruction of People, as well as an Impediment to the Recruit of them, that Gentlemen of late years, have taken up an Humour of Destroying their Tenements and Cottages, whereby they make it impossible that Mankind should inhabit upon their Estates. This is done sometimes bare faced, because they harbour the Poor that are a charge to the Parish.[2]

The parishes also used other approaches that conflicted with national policy. Although the Statute of Artificers had been established for the purpose of stabilizing the labor market through long hirings, the parishes fostered short periods so that there would not be sufficient time for the worker to settle. Immorality and family irresponsibility were fostered if they would free the parish of the charge of its settled poor. Marriage was a greater offense than an illicit relation, in the eyes of parish officials, for the former resulted in the parish being saddled with legitimate children to support. Poverty became a criminal offense, and, in turn, the poor were often obliged to turn to crime to provide for themselves.[3]

Perhaps the redeeming feature of local controls was its inefficiency. Local officials were unpaid amateurs to whom office was a temporary burden. In view of their other interests, they could give little time or energy to administering the welfare programs of their communities. The 1572 act establishing the office of overseer of the poor recognized the reluctance of those chosen by providing a fine for refusal to serve. In England, even at the height of central government control, the Privy Council had to maintain constant surveillance over the local authorities and rarely received more than minimal cooperation.

The failure of the local authorities to establish work programs for their able-bodied poor was one of the most significant defeats of mercantilist economic policy. The administrative complexities were too great, and the expenses were prohibitive, from the local authority's point of view, whatever the resultant national dividend. Small pensions were easier and less costly than the provision of work. With the breakdown of Privy Council authority, the natural inclination of the localities was to abandon efforts to set the poor to work or at most to establish workhouses. It was hoped that the workhouses would provide care, discipline, and financial support, if not profit.

Apart from immediate administrative problems, the seventeenth-century experiments in the employment of the poor were beset by many difficulties. The parishes soon turned over the management of both their domestic and their workhouse programs to private entrepreneurs. It was felt that there was a need for experienced businessmen with knowledge of production and market conditions. Employment programs, whether in workhouses or on parish stocks, had inherent limitations. The parish was not able to market its products profitably if the cost of production was similar to that of private enterprise because it was the lack of market for such goods at regular prices that frequently caused the unemployment the parish hoped to correct. On the other hand, if the parish sold below competitive market prices, it forced out of employment workers engaged by private employers. Generally the parishes could not find a field of profitable business that would not compete with private enterprise.

The work programs of the parishes were hampered by the labor force at their disposal. Unable to be selective, the parish officers were saddled with workers whom private employers rejected or workers who themselves avoided employment. It is not surprising that the parish programs were not successful and often reflected the discipline of a house of correction. The reformers of the latter half of the seventeenth century who substituted efficient commercialism for inefficient poor relief appear to have been no more successful than their predecessors in making the work of the parish poor profitable.

The experiments with work programs as ventures in productive employment were largely abandoned by the end of the seventeenth century. The pressure on private employers to maintain employment even in periods of poor markets had disappeared even earlier. The state, through the poor relief system or other measures, had gradually receded from positive action with respect to the economy. Work for the poor remained but was transformed into one of the more noxious aspects of the deterrent assistance policies of the local authorities.

Part II

FROM MERCANTILISM TO LAISSEZ-FAIRE

5

The Transition to Laissez-Faire

BETWEEN the end of the seventeenth century and the first part of the nineteenth century, laissez-faire succeeded mercantilism as the dominant ideology in England. The contract society whose seeds were laid in the mercantilist period reached its fruition in the policies of the famous Poor Law Commission of the 1830s. The Poor Law Reform Act of 1834 was the first major poor law legislation since the Elizabethan Act of 1601 and marked, as did the earlier act, the culmination of a new era. It is noteworthy that the sponsors of the 1834 Reform Act considered it less a revision of than a return to the basic principles of the Elizabethan Act. According to the critics, the original purposes of the Elizabethan Act had been confused by policies founded on the out-worn status principles the act hoped to reform.

The new legislation sought to correct this situation, and its goal was complete assumption of responsibility by the able-bodied for their own economic security. A poor law providing for the employable worker conflicted with the most fundamental ideals of the new society, and its continuance represented a compromise with anachronistic mercantilist principles. The new poor law expanded the contract aspects of earlier law and sloughed off the remaining status commitments. When such questionable policies as local settlement were retained, it was for the purpose of limiting social responsibility even though these policies were antagonistic to the nature of a contract society. The replacement of local responsibility with national responsibility would have meant broadening the base of social support, and this was more objectionable to the proponents of laissez-faire than a continuation of the inefficient and outmoded practices of previous eras.

While the roots of modern economic assistance policy may be traced to the Elizabethan poor laws and the preceding period, it was the accommodation of those early programs to the new social and economic demands of the eighteenth and nineteenth century that provided the most direct antecedents of modern policy. Contemporary policy can be traced to the redefinition of Elizabethan policy and the discarding of the last status remnants at the beginning of the nineteenth century.

Social and Economic Trends

During the eighteenth century occurred the development of large-scale production in agriculture and industry with the expansion of enclosures and the introduction of the factory system. While neither of these phenomena was unknown prior to the eighteenth century, it was their intensification at this time that revolutionized the social and economic basis of society. By the beginning of the nineteenth century agriculture in England ceased to provide support for a sizable number of small landowners or to provide supplementary income for those engaged in other pursuits.

These shifts in the economy made the great mass of the working population more dependent than ever on the flux of the commercial market. Wage earning was for most the primary, if not the only, form of subsistence. Correspondingly, the success of business enterprise required the presence of a large and regular labor supply. The introduction of machinery meant that industry was centralized, and the factory system depended on the presence of a large and disciplined supply of workers.

The advent of machinery and the factory system corresponded with the growth of large urban centers. By itself the latter would have caused great dislocations of population, but with the changes in the means of livelihood there was widespread instability for the lower classes. Long periods of war and vast increases in population aggravated these conditions from the latter part of the eighteenth century. Throughout the eighteenth century England had more years of war than peace, but the war with France between 1793 and 1815 was especially costly. Goods and food were scarce; prices increased at a much greater rate than wages; markets and employment were unstable; and the demand for labor fluctuated greatly.

Despite these unfavorable conditions population increased at a greater rate during the second half of the eighteenth century and the first decades of the nineteenth century than during any prior period. Before 1750 the estimated diennial increase was 3 percent. From 1751 the diennial increase rose steadily from 6 to 18 percent in the first two decades of the nineteenth century. The bulk of this increase was in the industrial population; the absolute numbers and the relative proportions of the agricultural population steadily declined.[1]

The economic hardships of the period were not mitigated by the system of social supports. The dwindling sense of social responsibility of the merchant aristocracy, already present at the end of the seventeenth century, was heightened with the transition to an industrial society. Whatever social ties remained were replaced by the cash nexus of the business culture that permeated farming and created a gulf between farmer and agricultural laborer.[2]

The disintegration of the relationship between employer and employee was not replaced by any effective cohesion within the working class. The rapidity of change had created a large working population with neither organization, power, nor clearly defined goals for their own well-being. Organizations of workers had existed throughout the eighteenth century, but they were mainly small, local, and limited to the skilled trades. In many cases these early worker's societies laid greater emphasis on "friendly" or "mutual benefit" functions than on obtaining employment advantages. Some of the early reactions of workers to the hardships of the new industrial system took the form of riots rather than systematic opposition. The displacement of workers by machines led to sporadic outbursts of machine-breaking, the most famous of which was the Luddite movement of 1811. Burnings and rioting occurred in rural districts during acute periods of distress, and in 1830 there was widespread revolt in the southern counties against the growth of harsher poor law policies. The government and the upper classes strongly repressed any demonstrations of the lower classes. Alarmed by the revolutionary doctrines of the French Revolution and the violence across the Channel, the government saw every spark of opposition as kindling the fire of revolution. All efforts of the lower classes to redress their grievances were viewed as conspiracies. The Combination Acts of 1799 and 1800 suppressed trade unions, and the government restrained all forms of organized labor activity, political or industrial. These acts remained in force until 1824, when the fear of revolution subsided and when more liberal leadership prevailed in Parliament.

The period from 1760, and particularly after 1790, was marked by severe hardship for the laboring population. The number and variety of proposals for reducing the extent of poverty were indicative of the severity of the problem as well as the degree of contemporary concern. It has been estimated that real wages of labor decreased by one third between 1760 and 1820. Some of the general causes have already been suggested: costly wars, economic dislocation following upon rapid industrial change, and poor agricultural years. Workers were burdened with high food prices resulting from bad harvests. During the war years inefficient governments placed heavy taxes on the laboring population. Systematic procedures for employment and payment of wages had not yet become part of the industrial pattern. Arrangements were frequently made in taverns, and this encouraged irregular labor practices and dissolute working habits. Wages were often paid in worthless currency or in overpriced goods. In the case of the agricultural worker, cottage rents were rising, and farmers were destroying cottages previously permitted on waste lands. Supplementation of wages by rights on land and pasturage had been cut off, and agricultural wages were kept at a low level.[3] The general insecurity of the times did little to encourage industriousness and providence.[4]

Despite these hardships—the increasing separation of classes and the inability of the lower classes to improve their own condition—the position of workers had changed markedly since the seventeenth century. The standard of living had risen during the first half of the eighteenth century. Some of the increase in population itself, particularly at the end of the century, may have been due to the better health and sanitary conditions, which produced a sharp decline in the death rate. The plague, which had afflicted previous periods, had all but disappeared, diet had improved, and advances had been made in medicine.

The laborer at the end of the eighteenth century could not be lumped indiscriminately with paupers and vagabonds as in previous periods. The manners and morality of the lower classes had improved, and their expectations had increased. A visitor who had been living in the United States for twenty years noted the following changes in the life of the English working class:

There is an ambition in parents to give a better education to their children than they have received themselves, more apparent here than perhaps anywhere else, the desire and the hope of ameliorating their situation are general; and such is the proper sense every individual entertains of his rank as a man, that there is not one so low as to suffer the treatment he would have borne in former times. The usual language of masters to servants, and of superiors to inferiors, is infinitely more guarded and considerate than it used to be, blows and abusive epithets are known in old novels and on the stage—the pictures of obsolete manners. The poor are becoming less ignorant and less abject.[5]

Contemporary Ideologies and Social Policy

The solutions proposed at the beginning of the nineteenth century for the problem of economic security fell into three categories: those offered by the supporters of economic liberalism or laissez-faire, those that appealed to the Tory leaders who emphasized the traditional pattern of mutual obligation of classes and particularly the responsibility of the powerful and wealthy for the welfare of the weaker and poorer, and those favored by reformers trying to readjust the balance of social, economic, and political forces so that the disadvantaged might achieve a more equitable distribution of the benefits of society. In terms of the concepts of status and contract, they may be designated respectively as solutions of a contract society, solutions of a paternalistic status society, and solutions of an equalitarian or democratic status society. Although the differences among the three approaches were great enough to distinguish clearly each from the others, actual proposals often overlapped. The proponents of economic liberalism frequently accepted governmental intervention. The solutions of the status oriented were frequently weighted with contract assumptions and could be designated status policies in a contract society. The issues were usually of balance and goal.

Mercantilist society had represented the bridge between the static order of the medieval world and the triumph of individualism in the modern. The dissolution of definite obligations had occurred over several centuries, but the sharpest awareness of change took place at the beginning and end of mercantilism. In the earlier period, as noted in such works as More's, there was a marked dissatisfaction with the destruction of established values. In the later period these values were no longer mourned, but the problem remained of substituting some rationale for the void created by the absence of any organized pattern of social responsibility.

The dominant philosophy of the nineteenth century was founded on the axiom of individual liberty, which manifested itself in politics, industry, religion, and all other significant aspects of society. The major question for advocates of the new liberalism who were concerned with social or ethical problems was the kind of society that could be built on the exclusive contribution of individual interest and action. What centripetal forces were there to maintain the notion of social good and social welfare present in earlier societies? That issue had never been so forcibly present before because the overriding nature of social institutions had created a coalescence of individual and social interests. The new liberalism was faced with the task of finding the cement for a cohesive foundation among the separate and uniquely shaped stones of the liberal society. Was individual self-interest enough, or was it only sufficient for the primitive behavior of economic exchange? If there was more to society than individual self-interest, how were these goals to be achieved?

In the seventeenth century, during the Puritan revolt from the mercantilist controls of the monarchy, there was clear dissent from the notion of social obligation. Concern with more than the individual was looked upon as unnatural. Each was his own master and responsible for his own well-being. In fact, the emphasis on achievement made each individual view himself, as well as others, as an object in his drive for almost impersonal success. While he would exploit himself and others for gain, the gain itself was not to be used for his own or others' satisfaction.

In the eighteenth century this type of crude individualism no longer entirely prevailed. Although the philosophers and political economists of the eighteenth century denied the organic concept of earlier societies, they were still concerned with the existence of social goals. The eighteenth century was marked by a resurgence of humanitarianism, which made more salient the dilemma between individual action and social welfare.

The Nature of Society

The belief that society was composed of isolated individuals, each of whom was the best judge of his own interests, dominated thinking from the beginning of the eighteenth century. Organized institutions, such as the state, were looked upon as fluid conveniences that could be dissolved if they conflicted with the interests of those who, according to Locke, entrusted them with certain limited powers. Later, Benthamism's concentration on man's secular goals and Evangelicism's concern with religious life reinforced the principle of individualism by abandoning traditional structures and appealing to the personal and individual interests of man.

The scientific justification of the contract conception of society was to a great extent abandoned by the end of the eighteenth century, and had little practical impact. The welfare of the whole was seen as the function of the activities of the members rather than the welfare of the members being determined by the desires of the whole. Any interference with the freedom of the individual's behavior in his own interests was a blow at both the individual and the social good, which were synonymous. This belief was based on natural law, which effected the natural harmony of the free play of discrete forces.

Whatever the rationale, unfettered self-interest was the goal. Institutions of control, such as government, were essentially evil because they were restricting and represented a cultural lag. Differences occurred about the necessity of tolerating the evil according to one's estimate of man's social capacity. Paine, with faith in man's social instincts, minimized the need for government under ideal conditions. Bentham, less idealistic, was not as optimistic in his assessment of man's impulses. Hobbes, one of the earlier social contract theorists, assumed that the hostile, aggressive, and competitive nature of man could achieve no harmony without a strong external control. In effect, the state was society's defense against man's own antisocial nature. In his famous parable Mandeville denied the existence of altruistic sentiments and satirically suggested that the well-being of society was dependent on the immoral interests of man. Theorists, more theologically oriented, turned to the supernatural and referred to the "invisible hand" guiding harmonious relationships. The problem of social good arising from individual action troubled even Adam Smith, who accepted an ultimate theological explanation. Since direct divine intervention or traditional religious explanations were not acceptable to eighteenth century man, what was the force or motivation establishing harmony among self-interested individuals? Could a moral society be created by men starting with essentially asocial standards?

The supporters of natural order avoided the dilemma of individual interest and the social good by using an analogy from the model of the physical universe. Social bodies, like physical bodies following their own paths, were obeying the laws of a predetermined harmony much in the style of Newton's findings. Smith, for example, was skeptical of the substitution of conscious altruistic behavior for self-interest. That would have been comparable to one of the planets unilaterally seeking to improve the harmony of the whole. The duty of individuals and planets was to follow their natural paths.

While the perfection of the system was recognized, there were still attempts such as Newton's, to understand the forces responsible. Both Hume and Smith, anticipated to a large extent by George Berkeley, postulated as one of the instinctive or natural elements of man a "sympathetic" sense in behalf of his fellows. Berkeley, alluding to the attraction of physical bodies stated:

After the same manner, in the parallel case of society, private passions and notions of the soul do often obstruct the operation of that benevolent uniting instinct implanted in human nature; which, notwithstanding, doth still exert, and will not fail to show itself when these obstructions are taken away. . . .

And as the attractive powers in bodies is the most universal principle which produceth innumerable effects, and is a key to explain the various phenomena of nature; so the corresponding social appetite in human souls is the great spring and source of moral actions. Thus it is that inclines each individual to an intercourse with his species, and models everyone to that behavior which best suits the common well-being. Hence that sympathy in our nature whereby we feel the pains and joys of our fellow creatures. . . . In a word, hence arises that diffusive sense of Humanity so unaccountable to the selfish man who is untouched with it, and is, indeed, a sort of monster and anomalous production.[6]

Hume similarly distinguished between "self-love" or private actions and benevolent or public actions. He was especially critical of those who saw private gain as the motive for all public action. "We have found," he wrote, "instances, in which private interest was separate from public; in which it was even contrary. And yet we observed the moral sentiment to continue, notwithstanding this disfunction of interests." Therefore, he contended, "We must renounce the theory, which accounts for every moral sentiment by the principle of self-love. We must adopt a more public affection, and allow, that the interests of society are not, even on their own account indifferent to us."

Hume conceded that the motivation toward "private good" was much stronger than concern for the "general interests of the community."

Sympathy, we shall allow, is much fainter than our concern for ourselves, and sympathy with persons remote from us much fainter than that with persons near and contiguous; but for this very reason it is necessary for us, in our calm judgments and discourse concerning the characters of men, to neglect all these differences, and render our sentiments more public and social.

However, he concluded that:

A tendency to public good, and to the promoting of peace, harmony, and order in society, does always, by affecting the benevolent principles of our frame, engage us on the side of the social virtues. And it appears, as an additional confirmation, that those principles of humanity and sympathy enter so deeply into our sentiments, and have so powerful an influence, as may enable them to excite the strongest censure and applause.[7]

The complexity of the liberal position was mirrored in Adam Smith's two great volumes, *The Theory of Moral Sentiments* and *An Inquiry into the Nature and Causes of the Wealth of Nations*. There has been much speculation about the extent of philosophical unity represented by those volumes.[8] The moral or social emphasis of the *Moral Sentiments* was not reflected in the *Wealth of Nations,* and the separation may well have symbolized the contemporary conflict between the social and bartering aspects of society. The greater fame and influence of the *Wealth of Nations* showed which of the two volumes appealed most to the dominant groups of the period.

In *The Theory of Moral Sentiments* Adam Smith, like Hume, proposed sympathy as the force drawing men together:

However selfish soever man may be supposed, there are evidently some principles in his nature which interest him in the fortune of others and render their happiness necessary to him, though he derives nothing from it except the pleasure of seeing it. Of this kind is pity or compassion, the emotion which we feel for the misery of others when we see it or are made to conceive it in a very lively manner.[9]

Smith described the function of sympathy:

As we have no immediate experience of what other men feel, we can form no idea of the manner in which they are affected, but by conceiving what we ourselves should feel in the like situation.[10] . . . By changing places in fancy with the sufferer . . . we come either to conceive or to be affected by what he feels.[11]

Like Hume, Smith is careful to point out that sympathy is not self-serving and is not founded on "self-love" but indicates the recognition of others with whom "I change persons and characters."[12]

Although Smith did not believe that "the welfare of society" was "the sole virtuous motive of action," he thought that "in any competition it ought to cast the balance against all other motives."[13] The impression is given, however, he wrote in the *Moral Sentiments,* that benevolence or concern for the welfare of others is primarily an attribute of the Deity, and that "so imperfect a creature as man . . . must often act from many other motives. The condition of human nature were peculiarly hard if those affections which, by the very nature of our being, ought frequently to influence our conduct, could upon no occasion appear virtuous or deserve esteem and commendation from anybody."[14]

While he had high regard for "beneficient virtues," Smith did not see them as necessary for society. "The mere want of the beneficient virtues, though it may disappoint us of the good which might reasonably be expected," he maintained, "neither does, nor attempts to do, any mischief from which we have occasion to defend ourselves."[15] Society must rely on more mundane motives for its stability. "Society may subsist among different men, as among different merchants, from a sense of utility, without any mutual love or affection; and though no man in it should owe any obligation or be bound in gratitude to any other, it may be upheld by a mercenary exchange of good offices according to an agreed valuation." In the final analysis, it is the formal institution of justice that, according to Smith, guarantees us our rights.[16]

In his *Wealth of Nations,* the bible of the new order, Smith analyzed the functions of benevolence and self-interest with the merchant society as his model:

Man has almost constant occasion for the help of his brethren, and it is in vain for him to expect it from their benevolence only. He will be more likely to prevail if he can interest their self-love in his favour, and shew them that is for their own advantage to do for him what he requires of them. Whosoever offers to another a bargain of any kind, proposes to do this. Give me that which I want, and you shall have this which you want, is the meaning of every such offer; and it is in this manner that we obtain from one another the far greater part of those good offices which we stand in need of. It is not from the benevolence of the butcher, the brewer, or the baker, that we expect our dinner, but from their regard to their own interest. We address ourselves, not to their humanity but to their self-love, and never talk to them of their own necessities but of their advantages.[17]

The conflict between the status-oriented, sympathetic, benevolent impulses and the contract-oriented, self-interest motivations was assumed by Smith. While admiring the former, he depended on the latter to supply the foundation of social responsibility:

Men, though naturally sympathetic, feel so little for another with whom they have no particular connection, in comparison of what they feel for themselves; the misery of one, who is merely their fellow creature is of so little importance to them in comparison even of a small convenience of their own; they have it so much in their power to hurt him, and may have so many temptations to do so, that if this principle did not stand up with them in his defense and over-awe them into a respect for his innocence, they would, like wild beasts, be at all times ready to fly upon him; and a man would enter an assembly of men as he enters a den of lions.[18]

Hume, too, as already noted, though giving more scope to the influence of sympathy on behavior, recognized its limited effect. Where Smith relied on justice to counterbalance the weakness of sympathy as a socializing force, Hume turned to the rational forces of man.[19] Self-interest, for Smith, must be conditioned by justice, but justice was not to be left to the "freedom of our own wills" but "may be extorted by force."[20] The natural harmony of interests was insufficient to provide justice, one of the few areas in which Smith saw a function for the state.

The tortuous path that led Smith, though aware of the virtues of benevolence and interest in others, to concentrate on self-interest as the basis of society reflected the victory of the commercial society. Malthus and Ricardo justified the inevitablity of the laissez-faire system in terms of practical considerations. The nature of society had already been settled, and the contributions of Malthus and Ricardo merely confirmed that it could not be otherwise. The interests of society could be attained only through unfettered self-interest. Direct concern for the welfare of others was self-defeating and bound to result in frustration and failure.

The reaction against laissez-faire arose from other ideologies. Classical economics itself, however, provided significant sources for change. Its assumption that a contract society was dependent on free interchange of equals suggested necessary reforms in the direction of social and economic democracy. The assumption that the purpose of society was the happiness of all provided a measure against which society might be evaluated. The doctrines of equality and happiness were forcefully promoted by the most influential of the early nineteenth century schools of laissez-faire, the Utilitarians, of whom Bentham and James Mill were the most prominent.

Although the concept of natural law had emerged as the dominant philosophy during the eighteenth century, two other ideologies persisted and became increasingly important during the nineteenth century in spurring the reaction against laissez-faire. The paternalistic concept of society drew its roots from traditional societies of earlier eras and was supported by wealthy and powerful groups; and the equalitarian or democratic concept of a status society had its background in such earlier movements as the Levellers during the Puritan era but did not come to the fore until the latter half of the nineteenth century, when the labor movement and socialist ideologies arose.

The supporters of a paternalistic society attempted to maintain the established social and economic distinctions of society, which were rapidly being destroyed by the dominant commercial and industrial interests. Their ideal was a society of duties and obligations carefully balanced by rights and privileges. Prominent among its leaders were the poets Coleridge, Southey, and Wordsworth, forerunners of the later nineteenth-century romantics, and the Tory politicians Sadler and Oastler, who were active in the Evangelical movement. The Evangelical movement of the late eighteenth and early nineteenth centuries combined in its religious appeal an emphasis on individual responsibility with an acceptance of a social order of regulated distinctions and functions. This position was represented by the Reverend Thomas Chalmers, who worked to replace the public system of poor relief by self-reliance supplemented by voluntary communal help. Public assistance, in his opinion, bred an unhealthy reliance on social support and discouraged the informal loyalty of neighbors and the charitable efforts of the wealthy. The goal was to reestablish a sense of interdependence within classes and between classes as a means of educating the lower classes toward morality and self-support.

The clearest exponent of a paternalistic society at the end of the eighteenth century was Edmund Burke. Reacting to the French Revolution and the doctrine of natural rights, Burke stressed the binding nature of man's obligations rather than the inherent nature of his liberties. Burke's social harmony rested on the existence of an aristocracy that accommodated the interests of classes. Thus he saw as destructive to the social good any effort to incite antagonism between classes or to incite the poor against their guardians and protectors.[21]

The paternalistic attitude of the upper classes had been undermined by the trend toward individualism and a society of contract relations. Yet much of the earlier thinking remained. Even among the rising commercial leadership there still remained the belief that the more well-to-do should take some responsibility for those less well off, and, in turn, workers relied on the good will of their "betters." The Evangelical movement effected a bond between the old paternalism and the new individualism.[22] While inculcating the lower classes with the morality of self-reliance, the Evangelical preachers emphasized the duty of Christian charity and the unity of the Christian community. Unlike some of the Tory reformers and the utopian socialists, the Evangelical leaders opposed state intervention as the means of social change. The Evangelical leadership was indifferent to the influence of the social environment and turned to individual character as the basis of social reform. Individual moral behavior assumed the acceptance of their mutual responsibilities by the rich and the poor, by the employer and the worker.[23]

The Evangelical social philosophy was well illustrated by Hannah More, the founder of charity schools for the lower classes. In 1801, a year of bitter poverty, she addressed the workers:

You will guess I allude to the continuation of the scarcity. Yet let me remind you that probably that very scarcity has been permitted by an all-wise and gracious providence to *unite* all ranks of people *together* to show the poor how immediately they are dependent upon the *rich,* and show both *rich* and *poor* that they are all dependent on *Himself.* It has also enabled you to see more clearly the advantages you derive from the government and constitution of this country—to observe that benefits flowing from the distinction of rank and fortune, which has enabled the *high* so liberally to assist the *low:* for I leave you to judge what would have been the state of the poor of this country in this long, distressing scarcity had it not been for your superiors. I wish you to understand that *you* are not the *only* sufferers. You have indeed borne your share, and a very heavy one it has been, in the late difficulties; but it has fallen in some degree on all ranks, nor would the gentry have been able to afford such large supplies to the distresses of the poor had they not denied themselves for your sakes many indulgences to which their fortune at other times entitles them. We trust the poor in general, especially those that are well instructed, have received what has been done for them as a matter of *favour*, not of *right*—if so, the same kindness will, I doubt not, always be extended to them, whenever it shall please God so to afflict the land.[24]

The Evangelical group did much to lessen the isolation of the poor. At a time when the liberal economists were denying the responsibility of the upper classes for the poor and maintaining that the display of such responsibility could only have disastrous economic effects, the Evangelical preachers found a place for the working class within the total social fabric.[25] At its inception, under Wesley's guidance, the new movement recalled many of the virtues of the medieval status society. Wesley favored just wages and fair prices based on ethical standards rather than on the free market. The use of wealth was for Wesley not a matter of personal and independent choice but, apart from the satisfaction of individual needs, a community responsibility. "To feed the hungry and cover the naked with a garment" were the philanthropic prescriptions of Wesley as opposed to the storing up of surplus for personal advantage. Masters were to look upon their workers as "secondary children," and workers were expected to exercise moral suasion over their employers. Early Methodism did not exhibit the rigid demarcations of social inequality and subordination of the poor that developed in the nineteenth century.[26]

While Methodism held out other-worldly rewards to the poor, the extension of middle-class morality to workers and the emphasis on education, albeit limited, made possible tangible gains in this world. Many Methodists following the precepts of the church were able to improve their social and economic status. Methodism provided a channel for social and economic mobility.

The third of the major conceptions of society, the equalitarian or democratic status society, had the least support at the beginning of the nineteenth century. The labor movement had only begun to take root, and much of the working-class opposition to the inequities of the Industrial

Revolution was an immediate reaction to hardships rather than a long-term point of view. The Combination Laws prevented the development of any overt, organized defense of the workers. The leadership of the working class was divided. Francis Place, most responsible for the later repeal of the Combination Laws, was an economic liberal who believed that once the inequities were taken care of, workers would follow the middle class in adhering to the dominant laissez-faire principles of the period. A great deal of working-class energies were absorbed in the struggle for the Electoral Reform Act of 1832, which extended the suffrage to the middle class. While the lower classes themselves obtained no benefits from the reform, their agitation consolidated their desire for political rights and laid the groundwork for the Chartist movement of the next decade.

By the time of the Poor Law Reform Act of 1834 trade unionism had spread, and there were even abortive attempts to establish national trade unions. Linked to the trade union movement and largely under the influence of Robert Owen was the growth of cooperative societies. Owen did not consider the industrial era the source of all difficulty, as did Cobbett and others. The new cooperative movement hoped to harness industrial progress in the interests of society by substituting a cooperative for a competitive environment. The cooperative leaders, on the one hand, and Godwin with his anarchistic leanings, on the other, agreed that reforming the competitive economy would provide the foundation for a better society. Disregarding the pessimistic views of Malthus and Ricardo about the nature of man and society, the early trade union and cooperative leadership foresaw a society of friendly rather than selfish and competitive enterprise.

Those beginning attempts to reform the core of society were doomed to failure because of their impracticality and the weakness of their supporting forces.[27] But they were not without influence, and they added new dimensions to economic policy. The new democratic, cooperative, and trade union movement furthered the belief that society should provide economic security to its members, not as an outgrowth of the competitive employment market or in response to the paternalism of the upper classes, but as a right of equal membership in society. In addition, and this conflicted even more radically with the dominant ideologies, it was proposed that a cooperative system sharing wealth among its members would not only increase their material well-being but would also improve moral character and social relations among all members of society.

Though there were fundamental differences at the start of the nineteenth century about the kind of society desired, there was general agreement about the ultimate purpose of society. The primacy of social ends present in previous eras gave way to the satisfaction of individual interests.[28] The idea that individual happiness is the goal of life, to which the interests of society are subordinate and instrumental, originated as far back as the Renaissance and the rise of secularism. In the eighteenth century the goal of individual satisfaction was not so frankly recognized as in later centuries, and increases in material enjoyment were rationalized as instrumental to social gain. Thus a contemporary writer stated, "The word luxury hath usually annexed to it a kind of opprobrious idea, but so far as it encourages the arts, whets the inventions of men, and finds employments for many of our own people; its influence is benign and influential to the whole society."[29] Hume asserted this view more explicitly:

The encrease and consumption of all the commodities which serve to the ornament and pleasure of life, are advantageous to society; because, at the same time that they multiply these innocent gratifications to individuals, they are a kind of *storehouse* of labour, which, in the exigencies of state, may be turned to public service. In a nation, where there is no demand for such superfluities, men sink into indolence, lose all employment of life, and are useless to the public, which cannot maintain or support its fleets and armies, from the industry of such slothful members.[30]

Hume thus found a rationale for private gratification in its public function. However, he had progressed far from the Puritan obsession with the sinfulness of gratification.[31] Adam Smith, on the other hand, had divorced himself entirely from both Puritan and mercantilist ideologies. Hume still shared the mercantilist concern for increased labor and productivity as an end in itself, but Smith recognized consumption as the only true end of the economy. This he stated unequivocally:

Consumption is the sole end and purpose of all production; and the interest of the producer ought to be attended to, only so far as it may be necessary for promoting that of the consumer. The maxim is so perfectly self-evident, that it would be absurd to attempt to prove it.[32]

Human happiness as the purpose of life and the goal of society was crystallized in the Utilitarian doctrine of "the greatest happiness of the

greatest number," and a measuring rod of its accomplishment was provided in the "felicific calculus." Wealth was recognized as a primary
source of happiness in the calculus. As Bentham wrote, "To every particle of wealth corresponds a particle of the matter of happiness. . . . So
far as depends on wealth,—of two persons having unequal fortunes, he
who has most wealth must by a legislator be regarded as having most
happiness."[33]

The Utilitarian emphasis on happiness and its relationship to income or
wealth was of critical importance to the development of welfare policy.
The Utilitarians defended themselves against a charge of hedonism, but
wealth, which was a source of happiness for many Utilitarians, made it
possible for each man to select his own happiness or satisfactions through
his mode of consumption. The connection between wealth, choice, and
satisfaction may have been oversimplified by the Utilitarians and their
successors, but the Utilitarian model at least provided a guide for examining economic policy in social terms.

In addition, the Utilitarians made a radical departure from earlier systems by their equalitarian assumptions. No distinctions were made among
the members of society. Each member, each unit of society, was equal to
every other unit without reference to social position and had an equal
right and potential to fulfill his expectations of happiness. The greatest
happiness of the greatest number was an aggregate of individual states of
happiness, and the goal of national policy was to increase this sum for all.

The Utilitarian approach to social justice had been anticipated by earlier philosophers and political economists. Hume and Smith had questioned the morality of a society in which too great a disparity of wealth
existed. Hume maintained:

A too great disproportion among the citizens weakens any state. Every person, if possible, ought to enjoy the fruits of his labour, in a full possession of
all the necessaries, and many of the conveniences of life. No one can doubt that
such an equality is most suitable to human nature, and diminishes much less
from the *happiness* of the rich than it adds to the poor. It also augments the
power of the state, and makes any extraordinary taxes or impositions be paid
with more chearfulness. Where the riches are engrossed by a few, these must
contribute very largely to the supplying of the public necessities. But when the
riches are dispersed among the multitudes, the burthen feels light on every
shoulder, and the taxes make not a very sensible difference in any one's way
of living.

Add to this, that, where the riches are in few hands, these must enjoy all the power, and will readily conspire to lay the whole burthen on the poor, and oppress them still farther, to the discouragement of all industry.[34]

Hume concluded that "where so considerable a number of the labouring poor as the peasants and farmers are in very low circumstances, all the rest must partake of their poverty."[35]

This represented a sharp break with earlier mercantilist thinking, which viewed the poverty of the lower classes as an advantage to the national welfare. Adam Smith, following Defoe's earlier attack, questioned the mercantilist belief in low wages as an incentive to industry.

The wages of labour are the encouragement of industry, which, like every other human quality, improves in proportion to the encouragement it receives. A plentiful subsistence increases the bodily strength of the labourer, and the comfortable hope of bettering his condition, and of ending his strength to the utmost. Where wages are high, accordingly, we shall find the workmen more active, diligent, and expeditious, than where they are low.[36]

Smith also pointed out that since labor constituted "the greater part" of society, its welfare closely influenced the welfare of all.

What improves the circumstances of the greater part can never be regarded as an inconveniency to the whole. No society can surely be flourishing and happy, of which the far greater part of the numbers are poor and miserable. It is but equity, besides, that they who feed, cloath and lodge the whole body of the people, should have such a share of the produce of their own labour as to be themselves tolerably well fed, cloathed and lodged.[37]

While Utilitarians accepted happiness as the end of life, not all agreed on the relationship between the distribution of wealth and happiness. Some rejected outright the connection between wealth and happiness, and others rejected the possibility of effecting the distribution of wealth at all or for any constructive purpose. Paley, one of the leading theologians of the latter part of the eighteenth century, firmly rested Utilitarian doctrine on God's will.

The method of coming at the will of God, concerning any action, by the light of nature, is to inquire into "the tendency of the action to promote or diminish the general happiness." This rule proceeds upon the presumption that God Almighty wills and wishes the happiness of his creatures; and, consequently, that those actions, which promote that will and wish must be agreeable to him; and the contrary.[38]

But Paley, though cognizant and critical of the abuses of inequality of property, concluded that wealth was a necessary "evil" because it stimulated industry.[39] He did not consider income a source of happiness and concluded that "happiness is pretty equally distributed among the different orders of civil society."[40] In fact, Paley endeavored to prove that the poor might actually be better off than the wealthy.[41]

The most rigorous attack on the principle of more equitable distribution of wealth came from two of the foremost figures of the "dismal science" of economics, Malthus and Ricardo. Avoiding sentimentality, they concerned themselves with the practical possibilities of introducing such a policy. For different but related reasons they concluded from their analyses that equalization of wealth conflicted with the basic laws of society and economics as they defined the workings of these systems. Malthus, selecting Godwin as his antagonist, argued that given man's nature, any equal distribution of wealth would soon be upset. The precarious balance between population and subsistence would be disturbed as each man followed his own passions and selfish interests, and poverty and misery would inevitably be reestablished at the cost of even greater suffering. Only, as Malthus suggested as an afterthought, through the lower classes exercising prudence and postponing marriage and childbearing could the law of nature enforcing inequality of income be thwarted.[42]

Ricardo similarly had little faith that the natural harmony of classical economics would provide a better life for the lower classes. Like Malthus, he believed that wages would tend toward a susbsistence level. This belief was based on the popular wage-fund theory, which assumed a fixed fund out of which wages were paid; increases in population would always keep wages at the "natural price of labour," i.e., that necessary for the subsistence and perpetuation of the laboring population. Malthus and Ricardo modified mercantilist subsistence theory by recognizing the possible influence of changing standards within the laboring population that would modify population increase and "natural price."[43] Despite these qualifications, however, Ricardo's name became identified with the "iron law of wages," one of the most accepted axioms of economic liberalism. Nassau Senior, a most influential member of the Poor Law Commission and an orthodox laissez-faire economist, contended that even a shortening of the work day would be disastrous because the first part of the day provided the compensation for labor and the last hours the profits. Reduction of hours would thus destroy the incentive of the entrepreneur.[44]

Bentham, the chief exponent of British Utilitarianism, took still another position on the practical consequences of greater equalization of wealth. There was no question of the importance of happiness and its relation to wealth. The issue for Bentham was whether pressure toward equalization would threaten the whole wealth-producing system and thus so severely limit whatever was available for distribution as to make any such scheme impractical. Bentham concluded that the protection of property was more essential to the welfare of the community than the creation of equality. Bentham explained his reasoning in giving priority to the "security providing principle" over "equality-maximizing" or "inequality-minimizing":

Thus it is, that if the effects of the first order were alone taken into account, the consequence would be, that, on the supposition of a new constitution coming to be established, with the greatest happiness of the greatest number for its end in view, sufficient reason would have place for taking the matter of wealth from the richest and transferring it to the less rich, till the fortunes of all were reduced to an equality, or a system of inequality so little different from perfect equality, that the difference would not be worth calculating.

But call in now the effects of the second and those of the third order, and the effect is reversed: to maximization of happiness would be substituted universal annihilation in the first place of happiness—in the next place of existence. Evil of the second order,—annihilation of happiness by the universality of the alarm, and the swelling of danger into certainty:—Evil of the third order,—annihilation of existence by the certainty of the non-enjoyment of the fruit of labour, and thence the extinction of all inducement to labour.

Independently of the destruction which would thus be produced by carrying, or even by the known intention of carrying to its utmost possible length the equalization, or say levelling system, as above, diminution would thus be effected in the aggregate of happiness, by the extinction of the fund afforded by the matter of abundance for keeping undiminished the stock of the matter of wealth necessary for subsistence.[45]

In keeping with this approach, Bentham did not advocate government interference to redress economic inequality. He and his followers, the Philosophical Radicals, supported extension of suffrage so that the interests of all the governed might be fully represented in the determination of governmental policy.[46] In the long run the Utilitarians assumed that the happiness of the greatest number would best be served by each individual having the freedom to pursue his own interests rather than through any directed policy of government.

Wesleyanism approached the problem of material wealth and inequality from an entirely different set of premises and reached much the same conclusion the Benthamites did. Wesley exhorted his flock to take advantage of the opportunities available and "live thou today." Methodist preachings in the early years emphasized success and satisfaction in this world in the spirit of the Utilitarians. While he was not an apologist for the inequities of the period, Wesley felt that security from interference with property was essential for the exercise of personal freedom. Without the certainty of his material possessions, man could not exercise his talents to the fullest. Neither Wesley nor Bentham were unaware of or depreciated the problems of economic maldistribution, but both believed that any disturbance of the right to property would cause more harm than good. The reform of social injustice, however, was not entirely dependent on the logical precision of liberal economists, Utilitarians, or religious reformers. A new humanitarian spirit was becoming evident, and its influence balanced, and in some instances defeated, the reasonableness of self-interest with the warm breath of sympathy.

The New Humanitarianism

The changing ideas on the nature and purpose of society were paralleled by changes in the definition of the membership or constitution of society. The humanitarianism of the eighteenth and early nineteenth centuries was reflected in a variety of reforms correcting the gross abuses of the period. Legislation and philanthropic action broadened the base of social responsibility by recognizing more of the population as being within the boundaries of social concern. To list but a few of the "causes" indicates the breadth of reform interest at the time: abolition of badging relief recipients, prohibition of slave trade, limitation of the use of the pillory, abolition of the whipping of women, protection of animals from cruelty, and correction of factory abuses.

Naturally not all parts of the population were accorded full and equal membership. Class differences were carefully maintained. The type of education provided for the poor, the social gospel of Wesleyanism, and the restricted suffrage of the Electoral Reform Act all supported the notion of a highly structured class society. However, the humanitarian reforms of the period, no matter how limited, reduced the gap between the poor and the rest of society. The poor were conceded human qualities comparable to those of the more privileged and rights as human beings to a more adequate share of the social resources.

The roots of eighteenth-century humanitarianism were complex, and its spirit was by no means universal. Some of the background of humanitarianism lay in traditional patterns of paternalism. The Civil War and the rise of the merchant and industrial classes had disrupted the earlier static feudal society. More stable conditions were evolving, and the wealthy entrepreneur classes were assuming some of the status and responsibility formerly held by the landed aristocracy. On the other hand, since their struggle for power was not over, they catered to the interests of the lower classes in order to bind the working population to them as allies. The movement for Parliamentary reform illustrated such a combination of the middle and lower classes.

From another point of view the humanitarianism of the period was an integral part of the spread of democratic thinking in the western world. Subordination of the working class and inhumane treatment of even the most humble conflicted with new doctrines of freedom and equality. Although in response to the French Revolution the upper classes in England barricaded themselves against any change for a brief period, democratic concessions were inevitable. In addition to social and political advances, humanitarianism found support in the growing rational and scientific spirit of the age. Outworn and outmoded solutions to problems were questioned and abandoned, and efforts were made to find demonstrably effective approaches. Experimentation was in the air, and it affected social as well as physical problems.

Poverty for the lower classes, as already noted, was no longer considered an unmixed blessing. The low-wage policy of mercantilism was questioned on both economic and ethical grounds. Even those who continued to accept the traditional assumption that only through necessity could the lower classes be made productive, modified or refined their concept of necessity. For example, Colquhoun distinguished between poverty and indigence. Poverty was a constant pressure exerted on all "who must labour for subsistence."

It is the lot of man—it is the source of *wealth*, since without poverty there would be *no* labour, and without *labour* there would be *no* riches, no *refinement*, no *comfort*, and no *benefit* to those who might be possessed of wealth—inasmuch as without a large proportion of poverty surplus labour could never be rendered productive in procuring either the conveniences or luxuries of life.[47]

The degree of necessity associated with indigence, in Colquhoun's opinion, had only destructive effects. This necessity "is known to be one of the chief incitements to vice and depravity. From a state of indigence, wretchedness, and despair, the transition is easy to criminal offenses."[48]

Apart from the distinction between poverty and indigence, Colquhoun indicated a recognition of the effects of indigence that had not previously been present. Poverty was no longer wholly the result of the vices of the poor, and dire poverty itself was accountable for some of the difficulties of the "inferior ranks." By the end of the eighteenth century causes other than the poor themselves were being discovered to explain the presence of poverty and misery. The Society for Bettering the Condition of the Poor, founded in 1796, proposed:

Let us . . . make the inquiry into all that concerns the poor and the promotion of their happiness a science. Let us investigate *practically,* and upon *system,* the nature and consequences, and let us unite in the extension and improvement, of those things which experience hath ascertained to be beneficial to the poor.[49]

Malthus, too, remarked on the concentration in the past on the affairs of the upper classes and on the need for much attention to the lower classes.[50]

Abstract study of the poor and poverty, however, engaged much less contemporary effort than did attempts at practical social reform. Humanitarianism was not so much a planned approach as an intense emotional reaction to the cruelty and degradation of the past. There was an extension of the social conscience to those who had been viewed as uncivilized and almost animal-like and who were now recognized as humanly sensitive to oppression and suffering.

Some, like Adam Smith and Sir Frederick Eden, the great student of the poor law and conditions of the poor, even wondered whether the only lot of the lower classes was "unremitting labour." In his painstaking and authoritative work, Eden remarked:

Though labour is indispensable, it is by no means consonant to the physical or moral nature of man that he should, like an ass in a mill, apply solely to bodily exertion from week's end to week's end. Nor has the state any reason to complain, if he, who can earn enough in four days to maintain him for seven, chooses to spend the remaining three in idleness and relaxation.[51]

This point of view was by no means common in Eden's time, but it would have been heresy less than a century before.

Smith noted that the complaints of the idleness of labor were frequently unjustified. "Excessive application during four days of the week is frequently the real cause of the idleness of the other three," he said. "Great labour, either of mind or body, continued for several days together, is in most men naturally followed by a great desire for relaxation."[52] These statements sounded a new note in an era when the only reason for the existence of the lower classes was work, and recreation by laborers was considered a vice.

The major impetus for humanitarian action, however, did not come from the enlightened followers of laissez-faire who developed, as Schumpeter so aptly termed it, a "meta-economic" doctrine to support their sympathy for the underdog.[53] The strongest pressure for reform came from those who continued to emphasize the traditional responsibilities of the "better" classes to their "inferiors" or those who, like the Evangelical preachers, attempted to establish a sense of mutual obligation in an industrial society. While these groups assumed the subserviency of the poor, they at least attacked the isolation of the lower classes, which had grown since the Puritan Revolution and which continued under the leadership of the nineteenth-century liberals. It was well into the nineteenth century before the liberals became identified with reform, and by then the laboring classes were organized in their own interests.

Humanitarian efforts and proposals for reform were strongly influenced by contemporary beliefs about the nature of man, and specifically lower-class man. If man was fixed and unchangeable in his nature and governed by irrational and immoral passions, the most well-meaning reforms were doomed to failure. If man was mutable and responsive to rational influences, the outlook for improvement of the lower classes was optimistic. The forces for change might come from either of two directions: improvement of the circumstances of the poor or reform of the character of the poor. Broadly speaking, there were those who thought the lives of the lower classes could be bettered by improving the social and economic conditions surrounding them, and there were those who thought that the sources of change lay within the poor themselves and that all change must start inwardly and work outward. But even those who recognized that circumstances might cause the differences among men were not always ready to tolerate any tinkering with the environment of the poor. For although man's limitations might be the result of external circumstances, those circumstances were not considered subject to man's control. The natural order was represented by the contemporary system, i.e. the status quo, and any interference would conflict with the immutable laws of nature. Thus the burden of reform fell heavily on the potentialities of man himself as his own prime mover.

Man was viewed by one school of thought as so controlled by his passions that there was little possibility for reform. This conception of man was held by a large number of eighteenth-century thinkers who emphasized that reason was subservient to passion in the determination of man's behavior. Hume, the exponent of the experimental method in the study of morals, concluded that while reason was useful in understanding behavior, it was not a determinant of behavior. Behavior was a response to the passions and was, therefore, controlled by emotion. This was essentially Malthus' argument when he maintained that any scheme for social improvement must take into account the "deeper-seated causes of evil which result from the laws of nature and the passions of mankind."[54] The imbalance between population and the resources for survival was caused by the domination of man's sexual urge and the failure of reason and prudence to curb instinctive behavior. In a sense, poverty and starvation were God's punishment for man's giving vent to his evil nature or more generally to his emotions, since the passions could produce no moral behavior. Intervention, said Malthus in refuting Godwin, was not only foolhardy and doomed to failure because of the immutability of human nature but was also immoral because it interfered with God's just retribution and His design for the universe.

Although Malthus started from the assumption that men's, or at least the lower classes', emotions were alone sufficient to explain their condition, he was not entirely consistent in his analysis. Influenced perhaps by criticisms of the fatalism of his doctrine and of its implicit defense of the negative recourses of vice, misery, war, and disease in maintaining the natural order, Malthus examined the possibility of reform in man's basic nature. He did not revise his view that man was the cause of his own predicament, but by posing the notion of a "preventive check," Malthus

found a way for man to correct his own situation. Poverty and its se-
quence of moral ills were not inevitable if man learned to use reason to
control his passions.

The bettering of man's condition rested with man himself. Only by increasing his moral qualities could man ward off misery for large segments
of the population. Since Malthus held the lower classes responsible, it was
they who must change if society were to be saved from recurrent disaster.
Middle-class behavior was Malthus' model, and the "preventive check"
meant emulation by the lower classes of middle-class responsibility and
prudence. Malthus expected the class balance in the population to shift
heavily in the direction of the middle class. "It seems probable," he said,
"that our best-grounded expectations of an increase in the happiness of the
mass of human society are founded in the prospect of an increase in the
relative proportions of the middle parts."[55] So encouraged was Malthus by
the vision of the lower classes achieving the position of the middle class
that he even allowed them the possibility of romantic love, a concept heretofore reserved for their "betters."

Malthus saw education as the means of lower-class improvement.
Through education the poor would aspire to a higher standard of living,
and their understanding would be enhanced. They would be less influenced by radical and ill-founded schemes. Their morality would be improved as a result of all these changes. Malthus had opened the way for
an escape from the inevitability of contemporary conditions, but it was not
an easy way, and as a result of Malthus' analysis there remained the impression that there was little chance for reform in the reasonable future.
The task was Herculean; the weight of Malthus' own historical analysis
and his sharp indictment of the character of the lower classes served as a
strong counterweight to any optimism about improving the conditions of
the poor.

While Malthus contemplated the possibility, albeit reluctantly, of the
lower classes altering their character through self-improvement, some of
his contemporaries were dealing directly with the problem. Like Malthus,
they looked to education as the savior, but their goals were limited to preparing the lower classes for their already determined station in life. They
gave no indication of high expectations of the potential of the lower
classes, and their concern with maintaining social stability conflicted with
any notion of education raising the position of the lower classes or eras-

ing class differences altogether. Education for the poor was looked upon with suspicion, if not antagonism, by those who feared that it would only lead to dissatisfaction and to disruption of the existing order. Even the charity schools were seen as radical ventures. Hannah More defended herself by stating:

My plan for instructing the poor is very limited and strict. They learn of week-days such coarse works as may fit them for servants. I allow no writing. My object has not been to teach dogmas and opinions, but to form the lower classes to habits of industry and virtue. I know no way of teaching morals but by infusing principles of Christianity, nor of teaching Christianity without a thorough knowledge of Scripture. . . . To make good members of society (and this can only be done by making good Christians) has been my aim. . . . Principles not opinions are what I labour to give them.[56]

Colquhoun, the author of many practical plans for reforming poor law policy at the beginning of the nineteenth century and an ardent advocate of education, remarked similarly:

Let it not be conceived for a moment, that it is the object of the author to recommend a system for the poor that shall pass the bounds of their condition in society. Nothing is aimed at beyond what is necessary to constitute a channel to *religious* and *moral instruction*. To exceed that point would be utopian, impolitic, and dangerous, since it would confound the ranks of society, upon which the general happiness of the lower orders, no less than that of those in more elevated stations, depends.[57]

Colquhoun thought that in many cases circumstances were often the cause of lower-class immorality and recommended "religious and moral habits" as the "best security against indigence, vagrancy, and criminal offenses."[58] However, "deficient education," "temptations," and "want of religious and moral instruction" were not sufficient to account for the state of the poor. In his opinion, it would be impossible wholly to banish criminal offenses and indigence "since in the tumultuous and ill-regulated passions incident to human nature, these evils must continue, to a certain extent, to afflict the community."[59]

By the beginning of the nineteenth century there was growing acceptance of the potential use of education in inculcating the approved virtues through appeal to the rational side of human nature. In addition to formal education, there was a trend toward informal and individualized service for the lower classes by the more well-to-do as a technique of initiating the poor to proper habits and values. This approach was strongly advocated by the Scottish minister Chalmers and has been recognized as a forerunner of modern social casework. Chalmers was among those who placed responsibility for the condition of the lower classes on themselves and believed that the only significant change in their condition could come about through changes within themselves. The necessary force for change would be the development of the individual's interest in his own welfare. The Society for Bettering the Condition of the Poor referred to Adam Smith's belief in "the desire implanted in the human breast for bettering its conditions" as the "master-spring of action" and concluded that any program for dealing effectively with the poor must be founded on the "idea of choice and free will,"[60] an idea fundamental to later social work.

Wesleyanism, the first major Protestant movement in England to be concerned about the lower classes, did not share earlier pessimistic views about man's nature. For the Wesleyans, man was essentially good, but he had become corrupt, and the task was the restoration of man to his original state—the state God had intended for him. Man had the potential for original perfection and could recapture it. The way back was through the moral improvement of man himself rather than through a rearrangement of the environment, as the utopians suggested. It was not outward circumstances that accounted for man's debasement but his own internal corruption. Social institutions represented divine will; and man's failure, his own defective will. The Wesleyan position thus differed from that of Malthus and other reformers who, while emphasizing the individual as the fulcrum of change, only grudgingly accepted his potential for change. The Wesleyan movement introduced a confidence that man, particularly lower-class man, could overcome his moral weakness. Immorality was not his innate nature and could be discarded if he struggled toward reform with God's help.

Least influenced by the notion of innate passions guiding behavior were the classical economists and the Utilitarians under the leadership of Jeremy Bentham and James Mill. Behavioristic in outlook, they found the explanation of behavior in the outward circumstances conditioning man's life. Smith, following Hume, was impressed by the basic similarity in the capacities of men:

The difference of natural talents in different men is, in reality, much less than *we* are aware of; and the very different genius which appears to distinguish men of different positions, when grown up to maturity, is not upon many occasions so much the cause, as the effect of division of labour. The difference between the most dissimilar characters, between a philosopher and a common street porter, for example, seem to arise not so much from nature, as from habit, custom, and education. When they came into the world, and for the first six or eight years of their existence, they were, perhaps, very much alike, and neither their parents nor playfellows could perceive any remarkable difference. About that age, or soon after, they come to be employed in very different occupations. The difference of talents comes then to be taken notice of, and widens by degrees, till at last the vanity of the philosopher is willing to acknowledge scarce any resemblance.[61]

The Utilitarians assumed the fundamental similarity and equality of men. Their faith in representative government relied on the belief that through education the lower classes could effectively care for their own interests. While Adam Smith's education of the "inferior ranks" was limited to preparation for their own occupations and lives and the maintenance of the stability of society, the Utilitarians stressed the "unlimited possibilities of moulding human beings to fit them for a new order."[62] They were little concerned about the inner man, and their system operated with an average man responding rationally to external forces. The psychology of the Utilitarians differed radically from those who emphasized the fixed nature of passion divorced from rational controls. Motivation, the core of the school of passion and morality, was abandoned by Bentham, and the consequences of behavior, their external effect, were all that required appraisal. The pleasure-pain or felicific calculus exploited egoistic hedonism for social ends and was the product of a psychology concerned with making individual rational choices conform to ethical purposes. Given a rational universe and rational individuals, the consequences of self-interested action could be made to harmonize with the best interests of the greatest number.[63]

The beginning of the era of laissez-faire coincided with the disappearance of the vestiges of medievalism inherited by way of mercantilism. With the abandonment of earlier controls there flowered a belief in the immense potential for progress, primarily material, but also social and cultural. Faith in the possibility of social betterment depended ultimately on contemporary views of man himself. To those for whom man was passion-ridden and beyond the influence of rational experience, there was little hope for improvement. At the other extreme were those who looked upon man as a *tabula rasa* to be educated toward making the proper choices for himself and his fellows. Between these positions were those less optimistic about man's potential for change but still sufficiently sanguine to embark on humanitarian efforts in behalf of the less fortunate.

The Scientific Approach to Social Problems

Whatever their convictions about society and man, students of the late eighteenth and early nineteenth centuries diligently resorted to science as the foundation for their arguments. The optimism of a Godwin and the pessimism of a Malthus were equally dependent on scientific support. The rationalism of the period rejected both authority and sentimentalism in understanding society and proposing reforms. There was also an impatience with abstract thinking and an urgent desire to get at the facts. Whether establishing grand theories, like Smith, Malthus, Bentham, and Ricardo, or attempting less ambitious studies, like Eden, Chalmers, and Colquhoun, empiricism was the order of the day.

Analyses of the poor and their problems were part of this trend, and humanitarianism turned to science for direction. Writers and reformers were critical of vague generalization and assumed that the poor must be known if anything was to be done about them. The Report of the Society for Bettering the Conditions of the Poor referred to two centuries of "speculation," not "fact," and urged that knowledge of the poor rather than the assumptions of the writer be the starting point for reform.[64] Chalmers, too, introduced his proposals for the poor by emphasizing the need for case studies of the poor instead of general assumptions about the poor as a class.[65]

The enquiries leading to the recommendations of the Poor Law Commission of 1834 demonstrated the full force of contemporary scientific spirit. The Commissioners were not wholly open minded, and their methodology would hardly satisfy the modern social scientist; but the enquiry was an impressive effort at obtaining a picture of current relief practices and the factors influencing dependency. A survey schedule of some sixty pages was administered over a wide variety of poor law areas, and the data collected supplied the foundation for the recommendations of the Commission.

The revolt against impulsive projects for the poor, although influenced by the general move toward science in human affairs, was particularly stimulated by the continued failure of poor law policies. To Malthus, Ricardo, Chalmers, and Bentham the previous haphazard treatment of the poor was not only undirected, but it was also misdirected so that it aggravated the very evils it attempted to correct. Whether or not poverty was accepted as a necessary and universal condition of society, its evil effects had to be mitigated. Science was to be put to the wheel of social reform. The Utilitarians stood ready to translate their scientific knowledge into the art of practical affairs. Bentham, in distinguishing his own approach from Adam Smith's, stated:

He has not taken for the sole or for the principal, or even for any part of the professed object of his enquiry, the question how, with regard to all these matters, the law ought to be; he has considered principally the science: what he has said of the art has come in rather incidentally than professedly. . . .

The great object, the great *desideratum,* is to know what ought and what ought not to be done by government. It is in this view, and in this view only, that the knowledge of what is done and takes place without the interference of government can be of any practical use. Otherwise than in this view the knowledge of what spontaneously takes place is a matter of curiosity rather than use. The only use of the science is the serving as a foundation to the art. For what purpose does it concern us to know how things are? Only in order that we may know how to deal with them, and to dispose of ourselves in respect of them.[66]

During the nineteenth century the tools for organized change were being sharpened through the improvement of government structure and personnel, reforms with which the Utilitarians were closely connected. As the Poor Law Commissioners noted, the failure of poor law policy was not only a failure in principles of action but also a failure in organization and administration. In the first part of the nineteenth century governmental reform made possible the practical translation of policy in ways that had theretofore not been true. The beginnings of modern government departments in England have been traced to the last two decades of the eighteenth century, but the transition to a competent administrative organization was slow, although the Parliamentary and municipal reforms of the 1830s provided a healthy impetus.[67]

Poverty and the Lower Classes

Mercantilist society had emphasized the value of poverty for increasing the national wealth. Poverty provided the incentive to work and restricted domestic consumption, thus encouraging production for foreign trade, and gave domestic industry a competitive advantage in foreign trade through low labor costs. These principles remained popular well into the laissez-faire period. The poor laws themselves were favored by some because they maintain a low-wage policy without discouraging population growth and reducing the livelihood of the poor below the level of subsistence. Supplementation of wages according to the price of goods, as in the Speenhamland policy, by the public assistance authorities was preferred to any substantial increase of wages. However, during the eighteenth century some of the basic mercantilist tenets supporting a low wage or poverty standard were beginning to be attacked.

The belief that poverty or necessity were the only definite incentives to the productivity of the laboring class was seriously questioned. This reliance on the effectiveness of poverty closely reflected contemporary views about the laboring class. If workers were not constantly goaded by need, they would be slothful and lazy. Any excess over subsistence would be wasted in dissipation and would discourage serious effort. This doctrine of the value of lower-class insecurity was challenged on several counts. The effects of poverty were reexamined. Along with others, Malthus, while not denying the significance of poverty as a "great spur to industry," pointed out that beyond "certain limits" poverty "ceases to operate" in a positive fashion. He distinguished, as did Colquhoun, between poverty and indigence:

The indigence which is hopeless destroys all vigorous exertion, and confines the efforts to what is sufficient to bare existence. It is the hope of bettering our condition, and the fear of want, rather than want itself, that is the best stimulus to industry; and its most constant and best directed efforts will almost invariably be found among a class of people above the wretchedly poor.[68]

Although Malthus attacked the dogma of dire poverty, his own population theory supported the tolerance of poverty, not because of its incentive value but rather because of its function in the population-subsistence balance. Malthus' tolerance of poverty was not due to a cold or unsympathetic attitude toward the poor, as is frequently assumed, for he recognized its destructive psychological effects and was distressed by them. Poverty could not be tampered with because it was an integral and inevitable concomitant of natural law.

The relationship between poverty, idleness, and immoral behavior was a deeply ingrained belief. Chadwick, an ardent Utilitarian, referred to this relationship as "one of the most powerful arguments" for promoting popular education. His Utilitarian philosophy favored equality of income, but his adherence to the belief that affluence in the laboring class encouraged dissipation made him question the value of high wages without raising the workers' "intellectual and social condition." He was of the opinion that "an increase of wage to any considerable extent" would be "equivalent to a proportionate increase in drink."[69]

As during earlier periods, the relationship of poverty to industriousness rested on the assumption that labor was intrinsically unpleasant, and therefore extremely distasteful consequences must follow idleness in order to enforce any degree of effort. The classical economists assumed that leisure was man's natural state and that labor was a sacrifice of this utopian condition. Wages were the compensation for this sacrifice and induced men to give up their leisure. Wages must then provide men with significantly greater satisfactions than they might have without working. High wages, which might directly compensate for the renouncing of leisure, were not popular with those in power. Chadwick's opinion that the working class, not motivated like their superiors toward self-betterment, would use high wages to avoid employment and to squander their surplus in immoral ways was widely held. In addition, there still remained the belief that low wages gave a country a competitive advantage in foreign trade.

Although these assumptions were challenged, they were commonly enough held to remain effective. Hume attacked the heart of mercantilist and classical labor policy by suggesting that work might be a satisfaction, not a sacrifice. He added a new element, "action," to the accepted elements of happiness, "pleasure" and "indolence." In contrast to the popular belief that indolence or the desire for leisure was the primary motivation and that action or labor was a painful sacrifice, Hume reversed the order. Action was the fundamental satisfaction, and indolence was dependent on action for its value.

Indolence or repose, indeed, seems not of itself to contribute much to our enjoyment; but, like sleep, is requisite as an indulgence to the weakness of human nature, which cannot support an uninterrupted course of business or pleasure. The quick march of the spirits which takes a man from himself, and chiefly gives satisfaction, does in the end exhaust the mind, and requires some interval of repose which, though agreeable for a moment, yet, if prolonged, beget a languor and lethargy that destroys all enjoyment. . . . In times when industry and the arts flourish, men are kept in perpetual occupation, and enjoy, as their reward, the occupation itself, as well as those pleasures which are the fruit of their labour. The mind acquires new vigour; enlarges its powers and faculties, and by an assiduity in honest industry, both satisfies its natural appetites, and prevents the growth of unnatural ones, which commonly spring up, when nourished by ease and idleness. Banish those arts from society, you deprive men both of action and of pleasure; and leaving nothing but indolence in their place, you even destroy the relish of indolence, which never is agreeable, but when it succeeds to labour, and recruits the spirits, exhausted by too much application and fatigue.[70]

The distinction, already referred to, between the positive effects of necessity and the negative consequences of indigence or extreme poverty, though apparently a refinement, was of more than passing significance. This distinction provided an important defense against those who denied the responsibility of society for any level of subsistence. While it might be maintained from a purely laissez-faire point of view that each must rely on his own resources, society could not be blind to the problems resulting from indigence. Though the predominant motif was the pressure of necessity toward industry, it was also clear that necessity beyond a certain point was a threat to the welfare of even the most individualistic society. Thus, despite abstract protests against the continuance of any system of economic support, complete abandonment was never attempted. But the fine line between appropriate minimum and overly generous subsistence remained a vital issue in assistance policy.

In general, the low-wage policy reflected the employers' low opinion of the lower classes, the disregard of the welfare of the working population, and the inability of the workers to defend their own rights. Some of the doubts about the validity of a low-wage policy were paralleled by changes within the lower classes. Workers no longer automatically accepted their inferior position and began to demand respect and consideration. Working-class leaders themselves expressed dissatisfaction with the pauperizing effect of the poor laws. A resolution at a Manchester workers' meeting in 1818 declared:

That any Employer offering to recommend a Labourer to an Overseer for Parochial relief as a part of the reward for his Labour, is an insult, and such Employer should be held up to public indignation.[71]

The upper classes became aware of differences within the lower classes. All could not be considered the same ruffian rabble. Efforts were made to appeal to the respectable workers to obtain their support for upper-class reforms. Thus one journalist seeking working-class support for the deterrent poor law reform of 1834 wrote:

A great deal of lackadaisical sympathy has been exhibited by the poor-law agitators, for the pauper class, whilst you, my hardworking, honest friends, who live by the sweat of your brow, who toil from morning to night, exposed to the heats of summer and the winter frosts; you, who thus labour for a scanty pittance, barely sufficient to keep body and soul together, and to obtain clothing for yourselves, and wives, and little ones, and to keep a roof over your heads; you, I say, are left almost, if not altogether, out of the question, without a single tear of pity. Pauper woes and pauper wrongs have drained their fountains dry. This whimpering over the workhouse tenant, who is better fed, better clothed, and better housed by far than the independent labourer, is to me truly sickening.[72]

While the sincerity of such approaches might well be questioned, they indicated that working-class influence was worth courting and that there was a section of the working class who, it was believed, could be induced to identify with upper-class policy.

In addition to the reasons already considered, the low-wage or poverty doctrine for the working class was challenged in the interests of national prosperity. Adam Smith and other critics pointed out that not only would higher wages result in greater productivity and an increased laboring population, but the prosperity of the country would be heightened by the increased money for consumption in the hands of the working population. Defoe had recognized this oversight in mercantilist policy at the beginning of the eighteenth century when he called the high cost of labor in England "the vast hinge on which the wealth of the nation turns." He noted that the "expense of the poor . . . causes a prodigious consumption both of the provisions and of the manufactures . . . of our country at home and this creates what we call inland trade."[73]

This point of view differed from the emphasis of mercantilist policy on foreign trade. High wages and high internal consumption were not the goal and conflicted with mercantilist efforts to attain a favorable balance of trade. A well-paid laboring population not only increased the cost of production but also consumed expensive finished products at home when it was preferable for these products to draw foreign purchasers. Some mercantilists showed interest in the national market when there was a surplus of goods, but on the whole, the internal market as a source of wealth was not appreciated, and its recognition was an important factor in supporting a high wage or high standard of living for the poor. Adam Smith suggested an additional value of high wages. High wages and high labor cost encouraged the producer to improve the efficiency of production in order to reduce his labor cost. This provided incentive toward further division of labor and the invention of machinery so that a "smaller quantity of labour" might "produce a greater quantity of work."[74]

The major reasons for a low-wage and, broadly speaking, a low-income policy for the lower classes were now open to question. A subsistence standard of living was no longer categorically accepted. The term "poor" had signified a class of people who could never anticipate more than a minimal share of the country's economic resources, but to the eighteenth- and nineteenth-century mind, the inevitability of poverty was not self-evident. The weight of evidence still fell on those who denied the "dismal" conclusions of Malthus and Ricardo; but the subject was approached with less finality, and the position of such men as Hume, Smith, and Eden was becoming more common. In the words of Eden:

The greatest praise that can be given to any government is a statement that there is employment for all, that their cottages are comfortable, their food wholesome, and their children well fed. The prosperity of the country depends on the welfare of its labouring Poor, and no estimate can be formed of its population, industry, strength, virtue, and happiness without considering their condition.[75]

Even those who were pessimistic about the chances of the lower classes did not deny their right to a better way of life. The question for them was not "should," but rather "could" the poor be better cared for. Most liberal economists saw little hope for change since the shares of the various factors in production could not be tampered with. Both Malthus and Ricardo, however, permitted themselves the luxury of extenuating circumstances permitting an improvement in the standard of living of the poor. Changes in the way of life of the lower classes, in their opinion, could in turn result in a share beyond the inevitable subsistence level.[76]

6

The Reform of the Poor Law

The Ideological Background

THE theoretical and practical reasons supporting a more adequate level of living for the lower classes were not reflected in poor law policy. In general, defending or opposing the notion of better economic conditions for the poor made little difference with respect to governmental intervention. Whatever the position, there was agreement that government's role could at best be ineffectual and at worst disastrous. Classical economics, with its faith in laissez-faire, dominated the political and economic thinking of the time.

The growing objection to the Elizabethan poor laws, particularly as they were administered from the closing years of the eighteenth century, was that they implied an obligation of society for the economic security of its able-bodied members. Some critics maintained that the original act was at fault in providing at all for the able-bodied; others denied that the act had ever been intended to relieve the able-bodied and maintained that the act had been perverted by later administrative practices.

The Poor Law Commission of 1834, responsible for the reform of the poor law, made clear its position when it concluded that "the most pressing of the evils [of poor law administration] . . . are those connected with the relief of the Able-bodied." The "relief of indigence; not the relief of poverty" was the business of government. Indigence, for the Commission, was "the state of a person unable to labour or unable to obtain in return for his labour, the means of subsistence." Poverty was defined as the "state of one, who in order to obtain a mere subsistence, is forced to have recourse to labour."[1] It was assumed by the Commission that all who were capable of working would find work and would earn enough for their needs. Only the totally or the partially handicapped who could not demand a full wage were eligible for social support.

Poverty, the natural state of the working class in a low-wage market, did not involve social intervention, in the Commission's opinion. The economic level of the poor was determined by the employment market, which was not within the purview of social reform or government action. Opposition to any acceptance of social responsibility was widespread because of its alleged pauperizing effects. The independence of the working man, it was believed, would be undermined by any system of public responsibility. It was the task of the Poor Law Commissioners to demonstrate that even their proposals involving a minimum of public aid would avoid the menace of pauperism.

Malthus probably represented the most generally held opinion when he stated:

But there is one right which man has generally been thought to possess, which I am confident he neither does nor can possess—a right to subsistence when his labour will not fairly purchase it. Our laws indeed say that he has this right, and bind the society to furnish employment and food to those who cannot get them in the regular market; but in so doing they attempt to reverse the laws of nature; and it is in consequence to be expected, not only that they should fail in their object, but that the poor, who were intended to be benefited, should suffer most cruelly from the inhuman deceit thus practiced upon them.[2]

Even Sir Frederick Eden, whose interests and investigations showed his sympathy for the poor, stated:

It may, however, be doubted whether any right, the gratification of which seems to be impracticable, can be said to exist. A legal provision for the poor, on the contrary, seems to check that emulative spirit of exertion, which the want of the necessities, or the no less powerful demand for the superfluities, of life gives birth to; for it assures a man that, whether he may have been indolent improvident, prodigal, or vicious, he shall never suffer want.

Eden "confessed that many able writers, who have investigated this subject, are of a very different opinion."[3] He was not, however, impressed by their arguments. Ricardo had no patience with the whole poor law system. He criticized Malthus, who suggested a gradual abolition of the poor laws, as having an "immediate and temporary" view. Ricardo stated bluntly for himself, "No scheme for the amendment of the poor laws merits the least attention which has not their abolition for its ultimate object."[4]

Government's responsibility for programs dealing with poverty was considered by most observers to be the major issue because the public authorities had administered the poor laws for over two centuries and were the recognized mechanism for economic aid. But men such as the Reverend Chalmers and the Reverend Townsend and a great host of other ministers and "pious laymen" (as the Webbs described them) advocated the expansion of private or voluntary charity. They viewed governmental intervention as artificial and advocated voluntary help as the appropriate or natural way of meeting economic need. The kindness of the wealthy for their neighbors was to be substituted for any publicly organized attempt to correct the inroads of poverty on the working population. This point of view appealed to the Wesleyans and others who had little faith that external conditions could affect the lives of the poor. Dependence on public relief was synonymous, in their eyes, with improvidence, laziness, and vice, and abject poverty was the symptom rather than the cause of dependency. Dependency could not be cured by any large, organized program. In fact, the reverse was held to be the most common result. The Wesleyans were proud of the numbers whom they had influenced to eschew public aid. Through religious teaching and, where necessary, individual philanthropic effort, the capacity for independence and self-support was reawakened.

Whatever the justification for a voluntary system of charity in earlier eras, reliance solely on voluntary activity for economic aid represented at this time a reversal of the principle of social responsibility. By the beginning of the nineteenth century economic security had become so closely related to governmental action that removal of governmental aid was virtually a rejection of social responsibility. It is noteworthy that the Poor Law Commissioners, who would certainly have been sympathetic to any reasonable alternative to governmental responsibility, did not give much consideration to the function of voluntary charity. The Commissioners spoke of the charitable foundations as being wasteful and "mischievous" in encouraging poverty and feared that the charities might "interfere with the efficacy of the measures recommended."[5]

Of course, there were those who criticized any system of social provision, whether public or private. Benjamin Franklin, visiting England in 1766, objected to all aid, for any help, in his opinion, made the poor "idle, dissolute, drunken and insolent." He advised the English:

The day you passed that Act [of 43 Elizabeth] you took away from before their eyes the greatest of all inducements to industry, frugality and sobriety, by giving them a dependence on somewhat else than a careful accumulation during youth and health for support in age and sickness. . . . I think the best way of doing good to the poor is not making them easy in poverty, but leading or driving them out of poverty. . . . There is no country in the world where so many provisions are established for them, so many hospitals to receive them when they are sick or lame founded on voluntary charities; so many alms-houses for the aged of both sexes, together with a solemn general law made by the rich to subject their estates to a heavy tax for the support of the poor. In short, you offered a premium for the encouragement of idleness, and you should not now wonder that it has had its effect in the increase of poverty.[6]

The differences, the contradictions, the variations, and the doubts of the leaders of classical economic and Utilitarian thinking about poverty and social responsibility were lost in the general impression that any demonstration of public responsibility was not only ineffectual but would also conflict with the progress of society. This conclusion rested on Adam Smith's free and unfettered society, where the whole was served by the enlightened self-interest of the members; the belief that the welfare of workers could be entrusted to the enlightened self-interest of the employer; the population theory of Malthus that poverty was inevitable as long as the natural increase in population went unchecked; the wage-fund concept in all classical economic writings from Smith onwards, which predicated the existence of a fixed amount of capital or wealth available for the wage-earning class that could not be altered; the combination of the wage-fund and population theories in the Iron Law of wages, i.e. wages gravitate toward the subsistence level;[7] and the general belief that the social system had an inexorable logic that could not be altered through intervention.

Together these doctrines supplied the rationale for avoiding any real responsibility for economic security. The solution of the Poor Law Reform Act of 1834 was a negative one: relief was not to be abolished, but it should be made so unpleasant as to be undesirable. The principle of social responsibility for poverty was not totally abandoned. Even the classical economists, despite their loyalty to laissez-faire, found room for assigning a variety of welfare functions to government. At one time or another they espoused such causes as public education, restriction of child labor, medical care, emigration of the poor, housing and health regulation, public works, employers' liability, prison reform, social insurance, and poor relief. These proposals for reform served as a foundation for later, more active intervention of government in social and economic welfare.

Nassau Senior, a leading economist of the early nineteenth century who participated influentially in the Poor Law Commission of 1834, illustrated the classical position. Senior accepted the idea of government intervention when "accident or error" prevented the laborer from obtaining his subsistence. Private philanthropy was not, in his opinion, equal to the task of relieving the poor, and government could meet the demand as well as distribute the burden more equitably.[8] Senior was particularly sympathetic to the claims on society of the sick and the orphan. Society, however, must guard itself against taking responsibility belonging to the individual. Care of children and provision for old age were contingencies within the foresight of every man and should be reckoned to his individual account. Senior advised:

Every man knows that in old age his personal wants will be greater than they are in his youth and middle age, and his earnings less. Assure him that the differences will be made up by the public and you diminish in him the motives both of providence and of industry. You weaken still more the benevolent feelings of those around him.[9]

Senior was strongly opposed to any measure that would interfere with the relationship of the able-bodied to the employment market.

We deplore the misconception of the poor in thinking that wages are not a matter of contract but of right; that any diminution of their comforts occasioned by an increase of their numbers without an equal increase of the fund for their subsistence is an evil to be remedied not by themselves, but by the magistrate—not an error, or even a misfortune, but an injustice.[10]

If government could be of aid "without materially diminishing industry, forethought, and charity," then it is the "imperious duty" of government to provide relief. Senior had little faith in government's achieving this aim, however. "The power of human laws directly to punish the want of these qualities is very slight; their power directly to create them still slighter; their power to destroy them, almost irresistable."[11] Individual responsibility was the primary goal of Senior, and anything that would modify self-reliance was a threat to the good of society.

Senior's writings occurred more than fifty years after Adam Smith's great classic, when the ghost of mercantilist policy had already been laid to rest. The laissez-faire society had triumphed, but the polemical writings of the leading figures indicated that opposing figures were constantly in the wings. The contract basis of society, never fully accepted by its faithful exponents, was threatened by paternalistic humanitarianism as well as by the resentment of the lower classes. While the dominant commercial and industrial interests adhered to laissez-faire and employed it to their own advantage, the lower classes, on the whole, never recognized or acceded to the virtues of a contract society. Constant war had to be waged against the medieval status mentality of the lower classes. Their willingness to depend on social support had to eradicated. For the laboring class, government was still considered an instrument for restoring "the just balance of society."[12] One of the primary functions of the Poor Law Commission of 1834 was to rectify this state of mind so that the laboring population would recognize that economic security was an individual obligation in the natural order of the economic market.

The Issues at Stake

In the beginning of the nineteenth century the pressure for reform of the poor law became increasingly great. The immediate cause was the inefficient and in many instances corrupt system of relief identified with the Speenhamland policy of subsidizing wages, particularly in agricultural districts. That reform had not been hastened was probably due to the unsettled state of affairs following the French Revolution and during the Napoleonic period. The reform of the poor law was not an isolated issue. It was an integral part of the growing body of changes necessary for England's transition to an industrial and commercial society. Speenhamland and the poor law policy founded upon it represented one of the last reminders of the status ancestry of the evolving society.

The poor law policy prevalent prior to the Reform Act of 1834 was the subsidy of wages from the public poor-relief funds. The Speenhamland justices had introduced the policy of making up the difference between agricultural laborers' cost of living and the wages paid by their employers. The result was that the cost of labor was shared by the local taxpayers. Under such a system it was generally believed that the large farmers gained most because they were the major employers of labor and were, in effect, being subsidized by their poorer neighbors. In addition, since the support of the poor was a local responsibility, poor rural parishes were thought to be taxed far beyond their resources, and wealthy industrial parishes, where few of the poor had settlement, were relatively free of the burden of support. Wages were also thought to be kept low by the expected supplementation from the taxes.[13]

The combination of wages and poor relief did not, however, provide a secure or adequate income to the laborer. Prices had greatly outdistanced wages during the later eighteenth and the early nineteenth centuries. The allowance system, on the other hand, had been greatly curtailed, and enclosures and large-scale farming had almost eliminated any opportunity for supplementary income in kind from small holdings.[14]

The allowance system represented the final stage in the conflict between the paternalistic mercantilist philosophy and the new laissez-faire economics. Among the major criticisms of the system was that it had caused a great increase in population by taking responsibility for family support. The common belief was that it had permitted early marriages and large families as well as a great amount of illegitimacy.[15] However, these were primarily problems from the point of view of the new political economists. For mercantilists overpopulation was of no real concern because increases in the laboring population automatically increased the national wealth. This position continued to be espoused by such writers as Weyland, who disagreed with the growing belief that England was overpopulated. Weyland argued that a large working population was in the interests of the national state and its defense. The rigors of war and the need to maintain even in peace an adequate army and navy were, in his opinion, a continuous drain on the population.

Differences in attitudes on overpopulation, however, did not alone distinguish the neomercantilist or Tory position from that of the advocates of laissez-faire. The neomercantilist pointed to social causes for the increased dependency of the lower classes and was willing to accept responsibility for the welfare of the poor. The poor laws provided for a large

population and had the effect, according to Weyland, "of training a surplus population as much to their improvement in morals and utility, as to
their relief."[16] Finally, Weyland maintained that the benefits of the poor
laws outweighed their disadvantages. "If the poor laws keep wages low,
and nevertheless encourage early marriages, and promote population, by
holding out a prospect of support in old age, these benefits should not be
thrown away if a few men have taken advantage."[17]

The social and economic readjustments following the end of the Napoleonic wars and the impact of the sharply increasing poor rates and
numbers receiving assistance greatly strengthened the opposition to the
prevalent allowance system. The almost universal theme in the contemporary criticism of the poor law was its effect on productivity. Productivity was seen as the basis of national wealth, and the poor law was considered a deterrent to increased industry and national wealth. The poor
law undermined the efforts of the normal economic market to stimulate
economic growth. The specific effects attributed to the poor law indicated
the changing attitudes toward labor and the poor at the time of the Industrial Revolution as well as the current social and economic trends.

Relief as a Claim on the Social Resources

The allowance system particularly, but the poor law generally, was
considered by contemporaries to imply the right of the poor to some claim
on the nation's wealth. Apart from other consequences, the idea of society's responsibility for the standard of living of those with low incomes
was totally abhorrent to the leaders of the new economy. They did not
view the function of society as guaranteeing a living wage for the exchange of its least skilled labor.

The policy of the old poor law administration, which the reformers attacked, was more fundamental than maintaining the relationship between work and subsistence. The underlying issue was the responsibility
for subsistence alone. Early poor law policy had required the provision of
work for the unemployed able-bodied by the overseers of the poor. The
system of parish employment, however, had never really been effective
except for a brief period at the beginning of the seventeenth century. The
failure of the parish to find employment resulted in the able-bodied poor
being given relief both in and outside workhouses without having to
labor for their subsistence. In time, the duty of the poor to labor became

overshadowed by the duty of the parish to provide relief. Since it was the responsibility of the parish to provide employment, it became its responsibility to see that the poor had some livelihood even when employment was not provided.

This transition in policy occurred during the middle of the eighteenth century and may be noted by the differences between the Workhouse Test Act of 1723 and Gilbert's Act of 1782. During this period the growing sense of moral responsibility and humanitarianism as well as changing beliefs about the value of poverty were paralleled by increasing disillusionment with the workhouses because of their inefficiency and expense. The local authorities were quietly abandoning more and more the application of the rigid system of workhouse relief.[18]

The new approach was incorporated in an act of 1782 for "the better Relief and Employment of the Poor," popularly known as Gilbert's Act. The most controversial feature of this act, at least for its later critics, was its provision for the able-bodied.

Any poor person, or persons, who shall be able and willing to work, but who cannot get employment, the guardian of the poor of such parish . . . is required to agree for the labour of such person or persons at any work or employment suited to his or her strength and capacity, in any parish or place near the place of his or her residence, and to maintain, or cause such persons to be properly maintained, lodged, or provided for, until such employment shall be procured.[19]

In addition, under the act the parish was expected to make up any deficiency between wages and "maintenance."

Under the Speenhamland approach, this policy of guaranteeing employment and wages was carried over into private employment. The criticisms of the Gilbert and Speenhamland policies centered around the implied guarantee of employment and provision of subsistence whatever the source of income. Sir George Nicholls, a poor law commissioner and secretary to the Poor Law Board, attacked the assumption of Gilbert's Act "that there can never be a lack of employment, that is of profitable employment, and it makes the guardian of the parish answerable." Nicholls contrasted the "uncertainty" of other "callings" with that of labor and wondered why the laborer led "a charmed life in this respect."[20]

The growth of industrialization at the close of the eighteenth century, the widespread unemployment at the beginning of the nineteenth century, and the changed nature of the labor market made the guarantee of employment or subsistence a much more complex issue than it had been previously. The critics of the poor law were not only specifically attacking the Speenhamland policy of subsidizing wages but were also questioning the transformation of the earlier duty of labor into the modern right to labor.[21] They were not merely concerned that the poor law was providing maintenance regardless of labor; they would not have been willing to accept a system in which relief would be given only in return for employment. They wished to break away from any practice that implied the right to employment and the parish's responsibility for employment.[22]

As distinguished from other periods, the early nineteenth century was faced with a great surplus of labor, and there was little concern about the value of each productive unit of labor. The popularity of Malthus' writings is symptomatic of an era plagued by the problem of excess labor. Thus the factors that had formerly made for parish responsibility for employment were no longer present, and the goal was to narrow the responsibilities of the poor law administration. After 1834 provision of employment was no longer a poor law policy. The pattern of emphasizing employment or combining relief and employment had been replaced by a purely relief policy, with work merely a form of administering relief.

The Threat to Property and Wealth

One of the most serious objections to the poor law was its threat to an economy founded on private property. When faced with the principles of security and equality, Bentham, as already noted, made security of property the governing principle. If security of property were undermined by an emphasis on equality, he maintained, wealth would diminish, and all would be the poorer. The critics of the poor law stated that "a compulsory system of relief must ultimately annihilate all property unless it were abolished."[23] Ricardo contended that the poor laws not only failed "to amend the condition of the poor" but actually worsened "the condition of both the poor and rich."

Instead of making the poor rich, they are calculated to make the rich poor, and whilst the present laws are in force, it is quite in the natural order of things that the fund for the maintenance of the poor should progressively increase, till it has absorbed all the net revenue of the country, or at least so much of it as the state shall leave to us, after satisfying its own never failing demands for the public expenditure.[24]

In addition to the pernicious effects of giving wealth to the idle, the diversion of economic resources from productive to unproductive channels was thought to reduce the nation's potentiality for growth and to limit the general well-being. Thus Ricardo concluded, "The principle of gravitation is not more certain than the tendency of such laws to change wealth and power into misery and weakness."[25] Nassau Senior's criticism of the introduction of a labor rate in agriculture involved the assumption that there was an essential contradiction between a system of inviolate private property and economic assistance. He said that a labor rate would admit "the most dangerous of all principles, the principle that the poor are in fact the owners of the land, and that to the extent of their wants."[26] The riots of the agricultural laborers in the 1830s certainly heightened the fear that regard for private property was seriously threatened by the poor's expectations of support.

As a result of their investigations the Poor Law Commissioners maintained that the assessments for the poor rates had absorbed the profits of property and led to the "neglect and ruin of the land."[27] The Commissioners cited instances of loss of rent, decrease in value, and total abandonment of property.[28] The contemporary impression was that the value of property, particularly in agriculture, was being destroyed by the rising poor rates and that the nation could not survive this channeling of wealth from productive enterprise.[29]

Industriousness Penalized and Idleness Encouraged

As a corollary to their effects on property and productivity, the poor laws were condemned for penalizing the industrious laborer. This was believed to occur in several ways. The discouragement of enterprise limited the opportunities for employment. Where employment was available, the industrious were often discriminated against because the employer preferred to hire workers on assistance, some of whose wages would be paid by the parish. Further, it was to the interest of the parish to find employment for those on assistance so that they would be occupied and some of their maintenance taken care of. Workers with any independent property or savings were handicapped because it disqualified them from assistance when they were unemployed. It was to the worker's interest never to be provident enough to possess assets that would result in his being treated less favorably than his neighbors. The wages of independent laborers in competition with workers on the allowance were forced down to assistance standards, and according to the contemporary wage-fund theory the wages available to the independent workers were reduced by the amount distributed in assistance to the idle.

Because of the confused pattern of wages and allowance, no distinction was made between the worker entirely dependent on wages and the worker receiving an assistance allowance. The Poor Law Commission lamented:

The pauper is not distinguished from other labourers under circumstances to familiarize them with pauper feelings and habits. Out-door labour without the workhouse has also the great and generally inseparable disadvantage, that it is a form of relief which is peculiarly liable to be made subservient to plans for pauperizing the independent labourer, inasmuch as it is a form of relief presenting in some degree the aspect of his regular employment.[30]

There was little incentive to industriousness, according to critics of the poor law, since the idle were cared for as well as the industrious. The employer of a worker on assistance tended to be less demanding because part of the wage was from the parish rate, and the worker was correspondingly less attentive to the demands of the employer because the parish guaranteed subsistence.

The alleged differences in the habits and character of the independent worker and the worker receiving aid were emphasized by critics of the assistance administration. Not only were the assistance recipients said to be lazy and improvident, but it was also believed that they were generally less honest and virtuous. The Poor Law Commissioners did not find poverty to be the cause of crime, but, rather, they associated pauperism, the willful neglect of responsibility, with the increase of vice and crime. The Poor Law Commission concluded that the poor law administration repealed "the ordinary laws of nature."

To enact that the children shall not suffer for the misconduct of their parents, the wife for that of the husband . . . that no one shall lose the means of comfortable subsistence whatever be his indolence, prodigality or vice. . . . Can we wonder if the uneducated are seduced into approving a system which aims its allurements at all the weakest parts of our nature; which offers marriage to the young, security to the anxious, ease to the lazy, and impunity to the profligate?

Restriction on Mobility

The poor law was not only believed to encourage the increase of population because it removed the responsibility for support from parents, but it was also accused of artificially restricting the distribution of population by its settlement provisions. Modern scholars have tended to balance Adam Smith's assumption that "there is scarce a poor man in England, of forty years of age" who was not affected by the Law of Settlement, with Eden's belief that settlement was more of a nuisance than an absolute limitation of mobility. The testimony before the Poor Law Commission indicated that contemporary observers in the early nineteenth century believed that settlement had widespread influence.[32] The effect of settlement, in their eyes, was to stifle the urge toward seeking jobs outside the area where poor law relief was provided and as a consequence to saddle areas with the least resources with the greatest number of dependents.

By the end of the eighteenth century it was not so much removal from the new parish of residence that restricted mobility as the fear of loss of maintenance from the old. An act of 1795 had limited removal to those who had actually become chargeable, thus preventing the practice of removing persons suspected of potential dependency. Industrial areas and large cities were eager to attract labor, but workers often preferred the certainty of maintenance to the uncertainty of work. This situation became increasingly critical during the twenty years preceding the reform of the poor law in 1834, when agricultural employment was decreasing and the agricultural population was growing.

Maintenance of Class Relationships

The function of the poor law system in maintaining social stability during a critical period of social and economic change has already been remarked upon. The examples of political uprisings on the continent and the dissatisfactions of the lower classes in England made it politic to provide at least some minimum of economic security, a minimum described by the Hammonds as "not the minimum on which the labourer could live, but the minimum below which rebellion was certain."[33] To the critics of the poor law it symbolized a society of paternalistic benevolence in conflict with the emerging business society. The administration of local relief had previously been supported on the grounds that it permitted a close knowledge and supervision of the recipient. The reformers, however, questioned the desirability of such personal relationships in a society of formal agreements. Relationships in local areas tended to emphasize personal dependency and to confuse public and private action. Sir Thomas Bernard, secretary of the voluntary Society for the Improvement of the Poor, was criticized for using his office as magistrate to order relief without parish vestry approval. It was maintained that he had confused private "benevolent action" with his responsibilities as a public official. The traditional system of local relief supported the old relationships between the gentry and the lower classes.[34]

The local administration of relief was also charged with using personal management for the corruption of assistance administration. Some of the illustrations brought to the attention of the Poor Law Commission were clearly of a fraudulent nature. By the end of the eighteenth century efforts were made to substitute a paid and organized bureaucracy for officials dependent on personal influence for their appointments.[35] In its first report the newly appointed Poor Law Commission examined the problem and concluded:

Where the districts are small, the dispensers of relief act more closely within the sphere of their own connexions; proprietors are more frequently called upon to decide upon applications from their smaller tenants or dependents, or from the connexions of their dependents; occupiers who serve parochial offices are exposed by solicitations from their own labourers.[36]

The critics of the poor law administration saw the task as rooting out a system that had emphasized the traditional responsibility of the well-to-do for the local poor. In their opinion, by encouraging the expectation of support from the upper classes, the poor law not only increased the dependency of the lower classes but was also a continuing source of class friction in a mobile society. The lower classes must be weaned from relying on assistance, and the upper classes must be prevented from using assistance for their personal and private ends. The usefulness of the assistance system as a social stabilizer was over, and all classes must face the hard realities of the commercial and industrial world that was growing swiftly about them.

Solutions to the Problem of Economic Insecurity

From the latter half of the eighteenth century on, there were an increasing number of proposals for solving the poverty of the able-bodied worker.

The reforms finally adopted were extremely narrow and were by no means representative of the breadth of the alternatives suggested. The solutions under consideration in the first part of the nineteenth century were of four general types: measures to reduce the general extent of economic insecurity, measures to guarantee income to the employed, measures to encourage individuals to provide for their own security, and measures to provide alternative income.

Reduction of the General Extent of Economic Insecurity

Measures affecting the general economic security were least popular during this period. The decline of mercantilist policy and the rise of laissez-faire policies caused the economic welfare of the nation to become a matter of natural or free growth rather than of determined policy. The Tudor and Stuart monarchs had shown sensitive interest in the economic stability of the nation. Economic stability was no longer the primary national concern and was certainly no longer a concern of government. The free interaction of the variety of separate interests had supplanted the concentration on an organic and orderly society. Imbalances and frictions were a normal part of the system, and a continuous state of unhampered readjustments was the ideal. Theoretically, the existence of any coercive force was inimical to the nineteenth-century liberals, and the most inexcusable interference would be that of government.

Education. Education was the most popular measure suggested for the reduction of economic insecurity. The most enthusiastic advocates of laissez-faire recommended education as the panacea for the ills of the lower classes. Malthus and the population theorists thought education would give greater play to reason and intellect and would eventually check the increase of population. To others, less concerned with population statistics, education would imbue the lower classes with the habits of morality and industry necessary for making a living. During the poor law inquiry evidence was cited on the value of education, and it was recommended that some plan for education be included if the prevention of pauperism was considered part of the responsibility of public relief. The Commission, however, made no recommendation for the spread of education to the low-income population.

Employment Service. A measure that found favor with the Commissioners was the organization of what might be termed a national employment service. Impressed as the Commissioners were by the heavy burden of some parishes, particularly in the rural South, they tried to arrange employment for surplus agricultural labor in industrial districts. In their first report, the Commissioners stated:

So far as any proceedings for influencing the direction of circulation of labour come within our province, which we conceive they do under the very peculiar circumstances of the change of system we are charged to conduct, we feel it is our duty to the pauperized labourers themselves to direct them to the sources of the highest wages; and we believe that this course of proceeding will be conducive to the most enlarged public interests.[37]

No formal service was established, but the Commissioners used their own and their staff's knowledge and influence to route workers from areas of low to areas of high employment.

Emigration of Labor. While the Commission took steps to locate employment, it hoped that there would be "spontaneous" migration without official intervention. At the same time, it also encouraged a policy of emigration of labor to the colonies. Emigration had always been popular with those who were convinced that England suffered from a surplus of population. The Reform Act of 1834 provided for loans from the national treasury to aid the emigration of poor persons. The Commissioners complained that insufficient advantage had been taken of this provision.[38]

Employment. Provision of employment had been the major method for reducing economic security prior to the poor law reform. The object of the 1834 reform was to correct a situation that, in effect, committed the parishes to a full-employment policy. The three most common programs through which the local authorities became involved in employment were the roundsmen system, the labor rate, and the allowance system. In the first, unemployed men were sent "round" the parish for employment, part of the wages being paid by the employer and the rest by the local authorities. In the labor rate, each ratepayer had either to employ at a set wage his quota of labor or had to pay the rate to the parish in lieu of providing employment. Finally, in the allowance system, the parish subsidized those who were already employed but whose wages were insufficient for subsistence. While these schemes differed in form, their common effect was to make the parish a partner in the provision of employment and wages.

The Poor Law Commission objected to all three schemes because they benefited employers at the cost of other ratepayers, gave the recipient of assistance an advantage over other labor, and failed to distinguish the independent worker from the relief recipient. These schemes conflicted with the very nature of employment as conceived by the Commission. In its criticism of the labor rate the Commission made clear its opposition to all schemes involving public responsibility for employment.

> The labourer is employed, not because he is a good workman, but because he is a parishioner. He receives a certain sum, not because it is the fair value of his labour, but because it is what the vestry has ordered to be paid. Good conduct, diligence, skill, all become valueless. Can it be supposed that they will be preserved? We deplore the misconception of the labourers in thinking that wages are not a matter of contract, but of right; that any diminution of their comforts occasioned by an increase of their numbers, without an equal increase of the fund for their subsistence, is an evil to be remedied, not by themselves, but by the magistrates; not an error, or even a misfortune, but an injustice. But can we more effectually maintain this state of feeling than by proclaiming that, at the expense of the landlord, the tithe-owner, the small farmer and the shopkeeper, all the labourers of the parish are to be kept at the ordinary wages or nearly the ordinary wages of the district, in a state free from anxiety, restriction or degradation, however great their numbers, however little their diligence, or however reckless their profligacy or their improvidence?[39]

By the nineteenth century any belief that constructive employment could be provided by the parish ceased to exist. The experiences of the local authorities over two centuries in developing schemes for profitable employment had left no illusions, although Gilbert in 1775 and Pitt some twenty years later still suggested workhouses as places of productive employment. Parish workhouses had come to be recognized as instruments for discipline and deterrence rather than schemes for employment. As such, they became an essential part of the Poor Law Commission's recommendations for the able-bodied unemployed. Relegation to the workhouse was important in distinguishing between the recipient of assistance and the employed worker with the right to normal conditions of life.

Guarantees of Adequate Income

The parish employment programs discussed above might be classified as measures for guaranteeing adequate income to the employed. While in theory, for example, the allowance system provided for the making up of wages to meet subsistence living standards, in reality it was an employment scheme in which the parish and the employer shared the wage bill.

Minimum Wage. By the middle of the eighteenth century, if not earlier, the mercantilist practice of wage regulation had fallen into disrepute. In 1757 the last major controversy over wage regulation was settled in favor of the employers in the clothing industry. In the previous year the weavers had obtained Parliamentary support for a reenactment of the assessment provisions of the Elizabethan period. However, the justices empowered to make assessments were impressed by the arguments of the employers and refused to issue an order fixing the wages of weavers. In 1757 Parliament repealed the act of 1756; that action symbolized the formal discarding of wage regulation and the sanctioning of laissez-faire in the country's major industry.

The abandonment of wage policy, however, did not signify that there was no need for some standard of wages. With some few exceptions mercantilist wage policy had functioned to control the demands of labor and to provide a stable, low wage market for the employer. With the changing economic situation the employer preferred to rely on the free competitive market to determine the price of labor. It was now labor that required some protection if it was to receive an adequate wage. The practice of parish rates subsidizing wages pointed to the inadequacy of wages. The allowance system seemed to be preferred by those in power to the establishment of adequate wage standards. In 1795, Whitbread introduced a minimum-wage bill almost at the same time as the Speenhamland policy took shape. Despite influential support, the House of Commons under the leadership of Pitt rejected Whitbread's proposal. Whitbread introduced similar measures in subsequent Parliaments but they received practically no consideration. There was continuing agitation, however, and in 1827 the idea of a legal minimum wage was revived again before a Parliamentary committee but was rejected as "absurd" and "extravagant."[40]

Pitt's opposition to the original Whitbread bill remained the classic answer to all suggestions for establishing a legal minimum wage. Pitt referred to earlier wage regulation as a protection against combinations of labor rather than a measure to keep wages in line with the cost of living. He argued, "Trade, industry, and barter would always find their own level, and be impeded by regulations which violated their natural, and deranged their proper effect."[41] Even Lord Grey, who had backed Whitbread in 1795, rejected the idea of a minimum wage when as Prime Minister he was faced with the agricultural laborers' riots in 1830. He commented:

Raising wages would no doubt have a good effect. But any resolution of this sort published by the magistrates would evidently appear to be dictated by fear and would operate as a premium to violence, in quarters which this spirit has not yet reached. Besides, what authority have the Magistrates or can they have to direct any measure for this purpose? They cannot prescribe to me what wages I am to pay my labourers, or what rents I am to receive from my tenants.[42]

Grey's position is particularly significant because he did not represent so much the rising commercial and industrial class as he did the former paternalistic landed aristocracy, which had become identified with the principles of economic liberalism.

Minimum-wage legislation received no consideration in the Poor Law Reform of 1834. Wages for the able-bodied were a matter for determination by the free market. The allowance system that had acted as a haphazard substitute was the enemy of the Commission, which would sanction no other interference in the natural relationship of workers and employers.

Loans. In his omnibus bill of 1796 for reforming the poor law, Pitt proposed, among other schemes, the provision of loans for purchasing livestock or for setting up the needy in business where there was a prospect of self-support. This was in line with Pitt's general policy of preventing, not merely relieving, destitution. As he stated:

The law which prohibits giving relief where any visible property remains should be withdrawn; no temporary occurrence should force a British subject to part with the last shilling of his little capital, and compel him to descend to a state of wretchedness from which he could never recover, merely that he might be entitled to a casual supply.[43]

Pitt's bill, however, was not supported by the government. Like employment, loans were tied to the relief system rather than seen as a positive preventive program for economic security. The Select Vestry Act of 1817 gave the parishes the power to advance relief as a loan when it appeared that the applicant because of "extravagance, neglect, or willful misconduct" was unable to maintain himself. This was a punitive rather than constructive use of loans. The Poor Law Commission of 1834 recommended the continuation of this policy, and the Act itself included a provision for the attachment of wages. Relief in the form of loans, however, was rarely given; it was probably considered a poor practice since borrowing was not thought to encourage the habits of thrift considered so important for the working class.[44]

Cottage Allotments. Enclosure and large-scale farming had led to the loss of lands formerly available for small cultivation by cottage owners. The decrease in holdings of the cottager and his loss of rights to the common were roughly paralleled by the increasing dependency of agricultural workers at the end of the eighteenth century. The cottage allotment, formerly a basic source of income for rural families, was becoming more important as a supplement to income from other sources or as an alternative source of income during periods of hardship. Limited attempts at providing small allotments to the poor had been made by philanthropists and progressive landholders. Although successful, this approach did not receive widespread acceptance.

A series of acts in the early nineteenth century, starting with the Select Vestry Act of 1819, permitted parishes to let "small portions" of land "to any poor and industrious inhabitant of the parish." The parishes might also acquire land for employing the poor on parish farms and this latter use, rather than individual cultivation, became the common practice. A system of small allotments had been recommended to the Poor Law Commission by one of its own staff. On the basis of his observations, he concluded, "It calls into action industry, the source of all capital, under the influence of the best feelings of our nature."[45] The Commission, however, did not include allotments in its recommendations. It noted that small allotments to laborers had been effective as a supplement to irregular income from employment, but it viewed this as a matter for private arrangement between landholders and laborers, not for official action.

There was some strong opposition to allotments. Employers opposed allotments because they freed the worker from total dependence on the wages offered. Nicholls, both as a local poor law official and later as a poor law commissioner, objected to the parish farm and allotments, and as he later summed up his position:

No person now doubts the pernicious effects of forced or artificial employment, or is blind to the consequences of tampering with the market for labour, whether by the parish or in any other way; but the conviction in this respect was not then so strong in general, and a middle course was resorted to, in the hope probably of averting the consequences of such interference, by letting portions of land to the persons whom the parish would otherwise have to relieve, or set to work on its account. The objection, however, applies with about equal force in either case. Both modes of employment are artificial, and calculated to raise up and retain a larger number of labourers in a district than there is legitimate employment for; and consequently by such excess of supply over demand, to lower the price of labour to an amount incompatible with social or physical well-being.[46]

Finally, Chadwick, the most earnest and possibly the most influential of the poor law reformers, swept away all consideration of allotments by declaring that laborers with allotments were worse off than those without. "It was demonstrated," he maintained, "that the labouring man never works for so bad a master as when he works for himself; that the poor man must make a poor master, and that it is better for himself that he should serve a rich one."[47]

Diet Reform. The alternative to an adequate level of wages was to lower the cost of living of the lower classes. If the consumption habits of the lower classes could be changed so that they would be satisfied by cheaper dietary staples, then dissatisfaction would be reduced without an increase in income. Supplying the staples essential to the laborer's diet at lower cost would also compensate for low money wages. Reforming the diet of the poor received enthusiastic attention.[48] Consumption of expensive foods such as the "finest" bread and teas were attributed to the thriftlessness and immorality of the poor. The selection by the laborer of anything but the cheapest and coarsest food was looked upon as an inexcusable indulgence.

The Poor Law Commission of 1834 was mystified by the stubborn adherence of laborers to their habitual diet. The reformers found little gratitude among the poor for their endeavors to substitute economical foods for those consumed by the poor. When Chadwick, as part of the Poor Law Commission's investigations, inquired about the standard of living of independent agricultural laborers, he was regarded with suspicion and was advised that this was to be expected "as the independent labourers really believed that mischief commonly followed even well-intentioned interference with their affairs by the gentry."[49]

In addition to the usual desires of people to satisfy their own tastes and the resentment of laborers at the interference of their superiors, there were reasons for the resistance to change of diet. The monotony of diet, the limitations of choice, the lack of foods that provided balance in the diet of the upper classes, and the scarcity of fuel for cooking all made the laboring class dependent on such staples as bread and tea and unwilling to accept less palatable alternatives.

The luxuriousness of the laborer's diet was, no doubt, exaggerated by contemporary critics. The purpose of Chadwick's inquiry had been to discover whether inmates of workhouses and prisons had a superior diet to the independent laborer. He found the weekly diet of able-bodied paupers and prisoners considerably better than the diet of agricultural laborers. He concluded that the diet of the former was far too generous, but his evidence may have more validly indicated that the diet of the independent laborers was exceedingly modest when the food allowance of a transported thief was two and a half times the independent worker's budget for solid food.[50]

The efforts to change their consumption habits, as noted, received little encouragement from the lower classes. A few philanthropists initiated projects to supply the poor with desired foods at low prices. These were, however, limited, and the government took no part in regulating the prices of necessities, as it had during the mercantilist period. The corn laws passed during the latter half of the eighteenth century affected the price of wheat, but after 1791 they were primarily intended to keep agricultural prices up in the interests of farmers and thus were opposed to the interests of wage earners. The philosophy of free trade, except where it conflicted with the interests of the dominant groups, was everywhere in the ascendency. In 1722, for example, during a period of scarcity Parliament repealed statutes against monopolistic practices in the marketing of food products with the ostensible purpose of benefiting the poor. Nicholls later remarked that the act required "political courage . . . for the measure was not only opposed to popular prejudices, but was calculated, as the people then for the most part believed, to raise prices and increase their privations."[51]

For Malthus, proposals to supply cottagers with the means of their own subsistence, such as land and cows, and proposals to introduce a cheaper diet for the poor were equally untenable. Both would result in encouraging population growth beyond the demands of capital and employment. The eventual effect would be "more dreadful" than when the price of labor was regulated by the price of more expensive foods. There always remained the possibility of resorting to cheaper foods in times of scarcity. The temporary expansion of resources for the poor, in Malthus' opinion, would not check but would rather support the growth of a surplus population.[52]

Encouragement of Individual Provision for Security

Friendly Societies. During the second half of the eighteenth century there was a great development of friendly societies insuring their members for a variety of contingencies. Friendly societies were not new to the working class. The guilds had in many respects operated as friendly societies by contributing to their members when in need and at times of illness or death. Many of the early friendly societies, however, could not perform effective economic security functions for their members.[53] A great number were financially unsound and did little more than provide occasions for drinking and contribute to expensive and elaborate funerals for their members.

Later in the century the friendly societies appealed to many reformers as the remedy for the dependence of the labor population on the poor laws. By insuring himself and his family with a friendly society the poor laborer would be cared for in times of need without resorting to parish relief. A variety of proposals were made, and some were even introduced in Parliament, to establish insurance programs under the management of the parish authorities. Some involved compulsory membership, some were voluntary; others were compulsory for low-income groups but voluntary for wealthier persons. Some schemes provided for subsidies by the employer or by the parish, while others were to be financed wholly by contributions and the income from investment. Actuarial tables were drawn up relating risks, contributions, and benefits.

These insurances, it was hoped, would not only reduce dependency on the poor rates but would also educate the lower classes to habits of saving and self-provision. Colquhoun, an advocate of a national system of friendly societies, stated that his plan would improve the working class by rewarding the virtue of saving, increase the self-respect of the lower classes, promote "virtue, morality, and industry," ensure the "loyalty and subordination" of the poor by giving them "an interest, a stake in preserving, manufacturing and defending the laws and constitution of the country," and divert capital "into useful purposes, calculated to invigourate labour and to increase the national income."[54]

The risks to be provided for varied, but many plans included a large assortment. Colquhoun's, for example, provided for sickness and accident, childbirth, death, and losses due to accident and fire. Allowances were to be made to widows according to size of family, for apprenticeship of children, and for the aged and infirm.[55] Other plans were more modest in scope and were concerned primarily with retirement. It is interesting to observe, in comparison with modern plans for retirement, that the bill introduced by Baron Maseres in 1772, which passed in the Commons but failed in the Lords, set the age of annuities for men at fifty and for women at thirty-five.[56] Acland's proposal in 1786 included medical care among its benefits.[57]

Insurance through friendly societies was primarily conceived of for the low-income classes. The Parliamentary committee appointed in 1817 "to consider the Poor Laws, and to report their observations thereon" recommended the establishment of parochial benefit societies throughout England. Recognizing the heavy financial burden on large families receiving assistance, the committee suggested that the parishes contribute toward their membership in the benefit societies, although the total payment should gradually be assumed by the families themselves.[58] Among the variety of proposals incorporated in Pitt's ill-fated bill of 1796 was the provision by the parishes for sickness, infirmity, and old age through insurances to be financed by both private donations and the poor rate.[59]

None of the recommendations for the establishment of publicly administered benefit societies, whether national or local, received Parliamentary approval. Malthus and others opposed compulsory programs and preferred to leave these early efforts at social insurance in voluntary hands. Malthus' objections were fourfold: universal compulsory schemes would add to the cost of labor and would be borne eventually by the consumer; the funds would be unsound if the idle and dissolute were included, so there could be no guarantee of right of benefit; the cost of membership would increase indefinitely with the inclusion of bad risks who would seek unlimited benefits; and the benefits might reflect need rather than equity based on contributions.[60] Malthus concluded that a universal compulsory system would be "merely a different mode of collecting parish rates." Since most proposals provided for some subsidy by the parish, there would be great pressure for liberalizing benefits to be paid out of parish funds. Malthus had little faith that the contributions to the insurance schemes would keep up with the demands of a constantly increasing population.[61]

Rather than supporting the development of publicly sponsored insurances, the central government encouraged voluntary benefit societies. An act of 1793, "For the Encouragement and Relief of Friendly Societies," was introduced with the statement that voluntary "separate funds for the mutual relief and maintenance of the said members in sickness, old age, and infirmity, is likely to be attended with very beneficial effects, by promoting the happiness of individuals, and at the same time diminishing the public burthens."[62] The act made lawful the organization of societies of "good fellowship" for such purposes and empowered the justices of the peace to examine and approve their rules and regulations. In addition, the act exempted members of friendly societies from removal under the settlement laws until they actually became chargeable. Two years later, in 1795, this privilege was extended to the whole of the population. The sole exclusion of members of friendly societies in the earlier act gave them a distinct advantage over their neighbors, as one organizer of a local friendly society noted in regretting the passing of the act of 1795:

The locomotive faculty also derived from the certificates of friendly societies is a very obvious advantage; and I was sorry to be obliged to give way to the authority of the legislature, in adoption of a general principle of this nature with respect of the poor, by the passing of an act for preventing vexatious removals; which has taken away, or at least diminished much, this inducement for entering into friendly societies.[63]

Although proposals for government-sponsored societies, forerunners of modern social-insurance programs, were not accepted, there was a vast growth of voluntary friendly societies by the end of the eighteenth century. That some of these were sound ventures, rather than the haphazard clubs of the previous era, is attested by the numbers still functioning in the twentieth century. Of societies founded before 1800, 191 were still in existence in 1905, and despite the vicissitudes of wars and national health schemes, 52 survived into the middle of this century.[64]

Savings Banks. The skepticism of Malthus and others about friendly societies, and particularly state-administered insurance, was balanced by their enthusiasm for savings banks. Malthus wrote:

Of all the plans which have yet been proposed for the assistance of the labouring classes, the savings banks, as far as they go, appear to me much the best, and the most likely, if they should become general, to effect a permanent improvement in the condition of the lower classes of society.[65]

Savings banks, according to Malthus, encouraged the habits of "prudence and foresight" and offered a means of individual planning for responsibilities rather than a scheme smacking of shared responsibility for individual contingencies. While Malthus recognized that savings banks could not be an immediate substitute for poor relief, he thought they would play an important part in the gradual abolition of the poor laws.[66]

The Parliamentary committee in 1817 "to consider the Poor Laws" recommended the newly established institutions of saving banks as promising "very beneficial results, not only in affording to the industrious poor a secure deposit for their savings, but in familiarising them with a practice of which the advantage will be daily more apparent."[67] Two acts were passed in the years 1817–18 regulating bodies for receiving small savings. The banks were to be nonprofit organizations and were to provide compound interest on deposits. The size of the deposits was limited, and the money was to be invested by the National Debt Office. Careful accounting of the sums deposited was provided for as well. The popularity of savings banks was shown by their rapid growth. By the end of 1833, 408 savings banks held almost £14,500,000 for some 425,000 depositors.[68]

Apart from other considerations, the emphasis on friendly societies and savings banks indicated a new view of the poor. The expectation that either of these plans would be successful depended on the assumption that the poor were capable of appreciating and cooperating with these organizations. Both the savings banks and the friendly societies required of the lower classes some sophistication in the culture of a commercial society and motivation toward thrift and planning. The successful expansion of the banks and societies suggested that the lower classes were in the process of accommodating themselves to the new society and deserved better opinions than the descriptions of some contemporary poor law commentators.

Provision of Alternative Income

The Workhouse. The Poor Law Commissioners explored most of the contemporary proposals for administering assistance. Their final recommendations, however, for the able-bodied needy centered on one approach —the workhouse. The workhouse was for the Commissioners the single simplest solution for meeting society's obligation to the able-bodied individual and his family. This was by no means a novel solution. Workhouses had existed for centuries prior to the Commissioners' inquiry and had always been an important component of poor law policy. Even the use of the workhouse to deter the able-bodied poor from applying for assistance was not an innovation in itself. The "offer of the house" as a deterrent to accepting assistance was sanctioned in 1723, and its value for this purpose had been determined by earlier experiments. What was new was the single-mindedness of policy that the workhouse symbolized in the 1834 reform of the poor law.

While the workhouse for the able-bodied had had deterrent aspects, it had also been considered, prior to 1834, a place of potentially profitable employment and a place for training in vocational skills. "Schools of Industry" was a popular euphemism in the eighteenth century, and the workhouses mentioned in Pitt's bill were so named. In the century preceding the 1834 reform the function of the workhouse had frequently changed, and often several purposes were served by the same institution. The role of the workhouse had also been influenced by the fact that the workhouse was usually only one of several ways of providing assistance to the able-bodied. In 1834 the workhouse became the sole means of assisting the able-bodied, and its goal was the discouragement of dependence on assistance.

Poor law policy from the Tudors until 1834 had ranged over a broad area of economic programs and the poor law authorities and the state generally had dabbled, at times, in almost every aspect of society affecting the economic security of its members. The reforms of the Poor Law Commission of 1834, however, clearly indicated not only that public assistance was no longer a right but that need and the expectation of help itself were tantamount to antisocial behavior.

As conceived by the Poor Law Commission, the workhouse served as a place for segregating the able-bodied needy from the respectable employed. With the workhouses becoming merely institutions for the able-bodied on assistance, the parishes stopped supplementing private employment and engaging in the direct provision of employment. Through the practice of less eligibility, the able-bodied person receiving assistance was to be treated as less eligible than "the situation of the independent labourer of the lowest class." The distinction between private employment and assistance was to be made so clear that it would be obvious to all that private employment was the only acceptable way of earning a livelihood.

Outdoor Relief. With their emphasis on the workhouse as the source of relief for the able-bodied and their families, the Poor Law Commissioners deliberately rejected outdoor relief or assistance to the able-bodied in their own homes.[69] Among other reasons, the Commissioners found outdoor relief antipathetic because it was so closely identified with the previous practice of parish employment, which they so strenuously opposed. The Commissioners stated unequivocally that all the weaknesses of earlier policy might be corrected, but if the principle of less eligibility, which in practice meant the workhouse, was not introduced, the whole would fail.

The Commissioners' recommendations, although interpreted by them in the "spirit and intention" of the original Elizabethan Act, were definitely a departure from previous policy. Outdoor relief had been an integral part of all poor law administration from its beginnings. The Commission was also rejecting the reforms incorporated in Gilbert's Act of 1782, which had specifically provided for the maintenance of the able-bodied unemployed within the community. In supporting his act, Gilbert stated:

It deserves therefore very serious consideration, whether the inclinations of the poor, in this particular, may not in some degree be in union with the true policy that should be observed in their concerns; and whether it is not as unwise, as it is cruel, to break through all the connections of life, and shut up part of a family in a workhouse, without first trying whether they may not be equally useful to themselves, and society, at their own homes. . . . The interest of the parish and the comfort of the individual, should be consulted according to the occasion; it being always to be remembered, that, with all our plans for good management, the effectual relief, maintenance, and employment of the poor is never to be cramped by ill-placed economy; which would be sacrificing the *end* to the *means,* and disappoint the whole scheme of beneficial regulation.

Gilbert concluded with the "hope . . . that all endeavors will be made to employ people out of the workhouse, not only as contributing to the health of the poor, but because this scheme will be attended with less danger of misapplication and mismanagement."[70]

Gilbert's objections to the inhumane aspects of the workhouse were not shared by the Commissioners in 1834. In fact, it was the very unpleasantness of the workhouse that made it the core of the new policy. The Commission considered one of Gilbert's alternatives, a mixture of outdoor and indoor relief but rejected it for the able-bodied because it would have required handling cases on a more individualized basis, and the Commissioners preferred the security of general rules for all. They feared that individualizing would erode the deterrent principles on which the whole system was founded. They believed that the general benefits of their approach compensated for any individual hardship and were convinced that, on the whole, the workhouse was the most just treatment for all able-bodied applicants. In their opinion, the principle of less eligibility must govern, and where a workhouse for any reason could not be established, then relief in kind, i.e. food and other necessities, should be provided rather than money. Relief in kind was clearly recognizable as relief and left no freedom for "indulgence" of personal tastes or inclinations.[71] It thus bore the closest resemblance to the workhouse itself.

Administrative Problems

The effectiveness of the reformed policies and practices for the treatment of the poor were greatly influenced by the administrative structure established for their implementation. The failure of previous poor law practices, according to critics, had been due as much to their administration as to the policies they reflected. In the minds of the reformers, policies and practices were so intertwined with administrative structure that it was difficult to distinguish the weaknesses of one from the other. The administrative problems considered were of two major types: the governmental level to be responsible for administration, and the type of personnel to be in charge. These problems were interconnected since the domination of poor law administration by unpaid or voluntary officials had been an outgrowth of local administration.

National or Local Control. Traditionally, poor law administration had been a parish function, and its philosophy and practice had been dominated by local interests except for the brief period prior to the Puritan Revolution when the Privy Council exercised some central control. Despite the principle of local responsibility, several measures had been introduced to increase the jurisdiction of the local poor law unit beyond the parish. The Elizabethan Act of 1601 had extended the levying of funds for poor relief beyond the parish if "the inhabitants of any parish are not able to levy among themselves sufficient funds." An act of 1722 permitted smaller parishes to unite for the maintenance of workhouses or to arrange for the use of workhouses in larger parishes. Gilbert's Act of 1782, while attempting to remedy some of the abuses of contracting out the poor under the act of 1722, further encouraged the combining of parishes. Gilbert's Act required that parishes incorporating be no more than ten miles from the workhouse, but this policy was only loosely observed. In addition to these unions of parishes, the combining of parishes under special acts of incorporation had been taking place since the end of the seventeenth century. It has been estimated that by the nineteenth century the proportion of united parishes was an eighth of the total.[72]

Thus, by the time the Poor Law Commission conducted its investigations and made its recommendations, there had already been a sizable trend toward the organization of parishes into larger units for poor law administration. However, the traditional pattern still conformed to local financing and control. Even in unions of parishes the poor in workhouses were charged to their parish of settlement. For some, the reform of the poor law meant an opportunity to abandon the whole system of local poor relief. Colquhoun, for example, wrote of the nation as "one family," and though no advocate of a liberal policy toward the poor, he favored a national approach to relief. As he explained:

His majesty is entitled to the allegiance of all his subjects, as members of the state; and are they, on account of the calamity of indigence, to be imprisoned within a particular parish? Their country should be their settlement, and the legislature their guardians.[73]

Within the Poor Law Commission there were supporters of a national system of administration, and in their report the Commissioners weighed the possibility of such a plan. The Commissioners recognized its advantages. It would do away with settlement and all its inconveniences, including the osbtruction to the mobility of labor. It would result in more efficient and uniform administration. While the Commissioners believed that at first a national program would significantly improve the poor relief system, they tended to be pessimistic about its long-term effects. Eventually the administration, not spurred on by "private interest," would become lax; the workhouses would "cease to be objects of terror" and would become filled, and the overflow would be cared for through outdoor relief; politicians would exploit poor relief for their own ends; and the collection of taxes for a national program would be too complicated.[74]

Although the stated objections of the Poor Law Commissioners to a national system of poor relief were considerable, they do not seem convincing when the evidence of the Commission's investigations of local administration are balanced against them. Perhaps more significant was the fact that the country was not ready for such a large-scale change, as was indicated by the reaction even to the more modest central control established by the Reform Act of 1834. In addition, a national system, in the Commissioners' opinion, would have given approval and stability to a program several of the Commissioners hoped would eventually be greatly reduced, if not abandoned. National responsibility must in many ways have recalled the more active policy of the mercantilist monarchs. "To promise, on the part of the government, subsistence to all, to make the government the general insurer against misfortune, idleness, improvidence and vice," the Commission found to be "objectionable in principle."[75]

The support for local control should not be taken as concern on the Commission's part for more personalized relationships in the administration of assistance. It was only later that the issue of personal and moral controls for improving the poor became an argument for localizing the administration of relief. Chalmers, who stressed the value of personal relationships in assistance, was opposed to any system of public assistance, local or national, and supported voluntary aid. On the other hand, the Poor Law Commissioners sought uniformity and impersonality of administration even under a system of local relief. They wished to avoid any situation that would permit individual discretion. Their recommendation and the Act constituted a compromise between national and local responsibility. In principle, local parish control was left intact, but a body of three national commissioners or a Control Board appointed by the Crown was to supervise and direct the administration of relief. The commissioners were empowered to make and issue all rules, orders, and regulations necessary, although they could not "interfere in any individual case for the purpose of ordering relief."[76]

The Control Board was given almost *carte blanche* in determining policy and practice and in changing the administrative structure. The Board could on its own initiative and without the agreement of other bodies unite parishes for the administration of relief. This power in the hands of a body desirous of reorganizing the inefficient system of local control might well result, as it did, in a total restructuring of the poor law administration from a multitude of small, varied, and independent units to a relatively limited number of uniformly organized jurisdictions.

Local responsibility, however, was maintained by keeping each parish within the union liable for the expenses of its own poor. Settlement, which determined the financial responsibility of the parish, was simplified but by no means abandoned. Abolition of settlement had been in the minds of the Poor Law Commissioners. Theoretically and practically settlement limited the free movement of labor, and the Commissioners could find little rationale for its existence. It resulted in preferential employment for some, such as the settled laborer with a large family, who might become a heavy burden on the parish. But the Commissioners were not willing to abolish settlement by recommending relief as a national charge, and apart from attempting to reduce some of the sources of greatest conflict within settlement law, they left its abandonment to future generations.

The Reform Act of 1834, though a conciliation of the national and local interests, made a significant advance toward national control. Despite the objections to pushing ahead with a national system, the beginnings were evident in the power given the national Central Board. National control would have meant a more rational administrative structure, more clearly defined policy, and less obstruction of the needs of the economic market. Although for these reasons the Commissioners opposed local control, the continuance of local administration conserved the traditionally deterrent and parsimonious nature of local relief under the oligarchy-dominated local government.[77]

Salaried or Voluntary Officials. The reforms resulting in the establishment of a Central Board on the national level were paralleled on the local level by the introduction of paid local officials. Efficient administration relied on the presence in the local areas of a bureaucracy capable of implementing the policies of the Board.

Permanent officers, salaried assistant overseers, were gradually being appointed in the period immediately prior to 1834. This practice, however, had affected only about one seventh of the localities, generally the larger ones.[78] The Reform Act provided for the widespread development of a salaried local officialdom and made this new bureaucracy directly responsible to the national Board. The commissioners were empowered to direct the local authorities to appoint paid officers, set the qualifications for these officials, regulate their duties, establish their salaries and terms of office, and remove them from office. Although the introduction of a national system had been avoided, paid local officials directly responsible to the national commissioners who had broad controls over local affairs could have much the same result. No immediate attack was made on the existing local officials, although the evidence and recommendations of the Poor Law Commission had been severely critical of the influence of magistrates on local relief policy. The Reform Act gave the commissioners some control over these officials, too, since they could determine the qualifications of persons elected to the position of Guardians of the Poor in the projected unions of parishes.

The regularizing of administration and the development of a responsible paid staff, as already noted, were not for the purpose of permitting greater discretion within the framework of established policy. The system the reformers hoped to displace had been faulty, in their opinion, because of the inconsistencies and variations attributed to local and personal control. In its report the Commission stated:

The bane of all pauper legislation has been the legislating for extreme cases. Every exception, every violation of the general rule to meet a real case of unusual hardship, lets in a whole class of fraudulent cases, by which the rule must in time be destroyed.[79]

The idea that individualized relief was not within the functions of government received formal approval from the Commission when it concluded, "Where real cases of hardship occur, the remedy must be applied by individual charity, a virtue for which no system of compulsory relief can be or ought to be a substitute."[80] Such was to be the division of public and private action. The public program would be governed by general regulations applied indiscriminately; private programs would adapt themselves to individual differences. The Commission identified uniformity with efficiency. For the later critics of public relief, this was to be an important element in their attack on government's administration of assistance. The rigidity of the Commission's policy was considered an admission of the State's inability to cope with the problem of providing aid in the most effective fashion.

Conclusions

The policies acceptable to the leadership of the reform of the poor law in 1834 were among the narrowest in the broad spectrum of available solutions. The triumph of laissez-faire in the Reform Act of 1834 was marked by the radical decline of public responsibility for economic welfare. The offer of the workhouse was arranged to evoke refusal rather than acceptance of social aid. The goal was the abolition of support for those who could not provide sufficient income for themselves from employment. The able-bodied poor were subject to the most deterrent policy, but the principle applied to all. Carried to its logical conclusion, and many in the reform party did carry it that far, poverty due to old age, sickness, or other contingencies was a normal risk to be accepted and planned for during the most active periods of life and employment. There was hardly an economic difficulty that could not, therefore, be charged to the account of the individual involved.

The poor law administration had, in effect, given up responsibility for poverty. Poverty, it was insisted, was the normal condition of those dependent on labor. To interfere with poverty was to interfere with the natural course of events, a law of nature as right and sacred as Newton's promulgation on gravity. The task of the poor law was to deter those without income from sinking into dependency or pauperism and to limit the spread of dependency where it had already occurred. To guarantee adequate income to the employed, to reduce the general extent of economic insecurity, or even to encourage positive measures for self-provision, all were viewed by the adherents of laissez-faire as wholly outside the sphere of governmental action.

Limiting the scope of poor law policy signified that in the future the solutions for the broad problems of economic security would have to be looked for outside the realm of the poor law. During the height of the mercantilist period the poor law administration had been viewed as the organ of the state with broad powers for meeting economic need. For a brief time between the end of the eighteenth century and the first decades of the nineteenth century the poor law structure had again attempted, but unsuccessfully, to guarantee some minimum of economic security. After 1834 the poor law administration was clearly designed to perform a negative role—to increase the fear of insecurity rather than to check its causes or alleviate its problems. The movements for both individual and social reform lay outside its province.

While the disavowal of responsibility for economic security by the poor law authorities resulted in the development of new institutions for economic welfare, similar changes were taking place in other areas of need as well. The poor law structure had been the catch-all for all types of maladjusted people—the criminal, the handicapped, the sick, the aged. Gradually these groups became separated from the poor law system. By the nineteenth century the lumping together of the criminal and dependent populations had greatly lessened. The Vagrant Act of 1824 separated from the poor law administration, as criminals, several classes of persons who had previously come within the authority of the poor law officials. The punishment of vagrancy had become a police function distinguished from the relief of destitution. The use of the poor law administration for preventing mobility was rejected by the Poor Law Commissioners. Mobility and vagrancy had been synonymous in the past, and the settlement provisions of the poor law had been used punitively against transient labor. The Commissioners wanted to encourage a fluid labor market. The term "casual labor" used by the Poor Law Commissioners and their insistence that relief should "precede inquiry into settlement" were indicative of the new approach. Needless to say, this policy was strongly opposed by many local officials who continued to view mobility as vagrancy and mendicancy.[81]

The general effort to limit social responsibility and government intervention was part of the background of the new industrial era. The reformers considered it necessary to root out the last vestiges of the old status system if the new economy was to have a healthy development. Ironically, because of international and national conditions, in Speenhamland the new era was faced with the greatest recrudescence of paternalistic poor law policy since the seventeenth century. For the reformers, an abrupt break with the past was the only way to guarantee a favorable social and economic climate for the expansion of commercial and industrial life.

Although the ideology of economic liberalism had triumphed, within its wake there remained the currents of continued social responsibility for economic welfare. To achieve their goal of individual responsibility, the reformers of 1834 laid the foundation for the most effective administrative structure for dealing with economic security since the Privy Council of the early Stuarts. Central control, larger and more uniform administrative areas, and salaried personnel, all in the service of checking the growth of dependency, might equally be applied in time to the expansion of social responsibility. Benthamite administrative reforms might easily provide for more rather than less governmental intervention. The mere existence of so elaborate and specialized an administrative structure would itself have important consequences.

The followers of Bentham, notably John Stuart Mill, in their quest for "the greatest good for the greatest number" gradually shifted from the earlier Utilitarian adherence to laissez-faire and classical economics. When it became clear that self-interest and justice were far from compatible, humanitarian or social concern began to take precedence over the previous faith in salvation through self-interest. The Benthamite recognition of the potential of government and the important administrative reforms encouraged and introduced by Utilitarians like Chadwick were a valuable contribution to later social reformers. The humanitarian interest of the early period of laissez-faire, blocked either by faith in natural harmony or by despair at influencing the mysterious pattern of natural law, was now released for more positive ends.

Several other trends were also noticeable that indicated that the reforms of 1834 were the climax as well as the triumph of individualism. While individualism continued to be the dominant philosophy for the remainder of the century, there was a slow but constant erosion of the pinnacle achieved in the first part of the nineteenth century. Just as the shift from mercantilism to laissez-faire was earliest evident on the domestic scene, so, too, the influence of laissez-faire waned in internal policy before the change affected foreign trade. The spirit of paternalistic benevolence, briefly submerged, continued to act as a force for social responsibility. Governmental action was viewed as an extension of private concern, just as the dominant landholding class in the past had mingled public and private functions.

Finally, the roots of social responsibility were laid down in still another direction, in the working-class movement and among the idealists and reformers who were the forerunners of the socialists. Their goal was economic security for the lower classes and the extension of democracy into all spheres of life. Inequality, of whatever sort, was not to be tolerated. There were differences among the more radical reformers about how much their goals could be achieved within the framework of a society established in the laissez-faire era and how fundamental a reorganization of society would be required to achieve the social, economic, and political ends desired.

7

The American Scene

Trends in American Society

THE growth of a complex commercial and industrial society revolutionized the British scene during the eighteenth and nineteenth centuries. During the eighteenth century the bonds that had unified British society during the major part of the mercantilist era were loosened, and the new social, political, and economic ideologies replaced earlier systems of thought and provided the rationale for a contract society. The poor law reform of 1834 symbolized the triumph of the new era. In America, too, assistance policy showed striking parallels with the formula of the English Poor Law Commission. The series of state reports in the 1820s in New York, Massachusetts, New Hampshire, and Pennsylvania, as well as policies in other states closely resembled the dominant British trends. There were, however, some essential differences between the British and American programs, and they grew during the following periods.

One of the major differences, mentioned earlier, affecting British and American assistance policy was the absence in America of a well-established system of status relationships. Superficial similarities appear between the large landed estates in America founded on royal charters and the feudal proprietaries in England. The American landed aristocrat, however, was primarily a land merchant, not a landlord. The American landholder, whether in the period prior to the Revolution or after, was fundamentally an exploiter of the resources of land. He was a promoter of schemes for the sale and increase of land values and was primarily concerned with the profits to be made from speculation, tenancies, and production.[1] While his British counterparts had also moved energetically in this direction, the American landholder was not burdened with a system of traditional rights and relationships requiring consideration of, and conciliation with, prior status privileges. The American landed gentry had not inherited the system of responsibility to dependents his British contemporaries were seeking to dislodge. The American landowner could practice the principles of enclosure with complete freedom, but for the British lord enclosure signified a lengthy struggle toward commercialized agriculture.

The American land proprietor and the growing merchant class were not affected by the last intensive outburst of responsibility that infused the internal mercantilist policies of the Tudors and early Stuarts. The American colonist represented the external or foreign aspects of mercantilism, and his function was the creation of profits for the mother country rather than the establishment of a cohesive internal social structure. America was a society in flux seeking balance and stability rather than a society in balance trying either to avoid flux or to incorporate flux within an already established system of relationships.

The motivation and attitudes of the upper classes, apart from the slave plantations, were paralleled by other forces that militated against the development of a closely knit status society. The diverse backgrounds of the mass of American settlers provided little basis for a system of fixed relationships. The early immigrants came from many areas and did not have a foundation of cultural homogeneity to compensate for the absence of established relationships. A mixture of small tradesmen, farmers, criminals, paupers, and adventurers, they would not adapt easily to a society of predetermined and mutual responsibilities. They were, on the whole, a mobile group.

Thus, at both ends the social structure of America differed from England's. From the start American society conformed to the commercial ideal of the Protestant ethic. Contract was the foundation of the social system, and no people had so literally absorbed the notion of the social contract as the early Americans. From the contractual agreements founding the New

England settlements to the Declaration of Independence, the Articles of Confederation, and the Constitution, the idea of contract was imbedded in the contemporary reality of America. The major problem was the terms of the contract among the great variety of interests in America. That their solution to some extent resembled that of England was not fortuitous. The dominant groups in America were of British origin, but there were sufficient deviations to create uniquely American solutions.

By the end of the eighteenth century in America there was a widening of differences between the wealthy and the lower middle classes, between the agricultural and manufacturing interests, between the rich and the poor, between the property holders and the nonpropertied, and between the creditors and debtors. While British society recognized the unequal position of the lower orders in the social and economic system, American society had little rationale to justify class relationships. On the contrary, one of its pervasive ideologies was the equality of man, and there was constant friction where the reality did not conform to the ideal.

The sparseness of population, the presence of only a handful of thickly settled areas, and the continuous mobility of people contrasted with the relatively static condition of British society. By 1770 there were some two and a quarter million white settlers, but only five communities had a population of 8000.[2] Fifty years later the population had increased almost fourfold, and about one quarter were settled beyond the Allegheny Mountains.[3] While the West may not have been the resource for the lower classes that has sometimes been assumed, it did provide an outlet that prevented the flooding of the labor market and the consequent lowering of wages. In addition, it furnished a way of life for those who did not desire to rely directly on others for their employment and economic subsistence.

Similarly, the industrial system did not hasten the growth of sharp distinctions between employer and employee. Because of the scarcity of labor and the degree of opportunity, labor was free to shift about. Large-scale manufacturing had been hindered by British mercantilist policy, and the Industrial Revolution, which had been so influential in transforming British society by the beginning of the nineteenth century, did not gain momentum until the end of the first quarter of the nineteenth century in America. For the greater part of the eighteenth century and even in the nineteenth century, there was only a relatively small number of people dependent on wages from employment. The lower classes were primarily artisans, small landowners, tenants, traders, and urban mechanics. Manufacturing was frequently done in the household or according to the putting-out or domestic system. Income from manufacturing was supplemented by small subsistence farming. There was much identity of interest between the master craftsman and his workers. While there were a few strikes and some sporadic organization of labor prior to the second quarter of the nineteenth century, there was no real consciousness of a working class with workers' interests. Even in New England, where large cloth mills were introduced by the beginning of the nineteenth century, factories were not seen as permanent places of employment, as they were in England. They were manned to a considerable degree by young women trying to put aside small savings before marriage or by men planning to enter independent occupations.[4]

By the 1820s, however, a noticeable change had begun to occur in the system of manufacturing. The stifling effect of British colonial policy had worn off, and manufacturing appealed to those with capital as an important source of income. The merchant-capitalist rather than the employer-manufacturer became the dominant figure. The similarity of interest between the master craftsmen and his workers dissolved. Employers became merely labor contractors, and the increased profit of the employer was viewed as dependent on the reduced cost of labor. As a result, there were increasing numbers of strikes and the growth of stable and active labor organizations in a great variety of trades.[5]

Despite his growing opposition to the wage system, the American worker did not see himself as rooted in the role of wage earner. While agitating for higher wages and better working conditions, he was really espousing the perennial cause of the poor against the rich, the underprivileged against the privileged. He had not ceased to view himself as the small producer of the pre-Revolutionary era. The *Mechanic Free Press* in 1830 complained:

We are fast approaching those extremes of wealth and extravagance on the one hand, and ignorance, poverty and wretchedness on the other, which will eventually terminate in those unnatural and oppressive distinctions which exist in the corrupt governments of the old world.[6]

The reforms labor organizations pressed on the political front were little related to the problems of a wage-earning class but rather largely to lower-middle-class goals. In education, for example, labor opposed any system oriented to preparation for a worker's role, the predominant pattern of British lower-class education. Thus American labor leaders attacked Robert Dale Owen's plan of free boarding schools where mechanical and industrial subjects would be emphasized. A large body of labor leaders preferred the traditional education received by upper-class youth in preparation for professional careers.[7]

Despite the sparseness of population, the optimism of labor, and the general expansiveness of the American economy, there were problems of poverty. The continuous accommodation of new settlers to the demands of a strange economy was a constant source of difficulty. Some of the new immigrants had been paupers and petty criminals in their homelands, and many had no fixed trades and arrived penniless. Whatever small savings they had, had been used to pay for the journey to America. In contrast to their expectations and the blandishments of ships' agents and others interested in encouraging the influx of labor, many immigrants suffered extreme privation and illness from the voyage and required extensive aid before they could find their own way in the new country.

Although the major waves of immigration into New York City occurred after 1815, by 1796 the commissioners of the almshouse and bridewell of the city complained of the "enormous and growing expense . . . not so much from the increase of our own poor, as from the prodigious influx of indigent foreigners in this city."

For many of them have paid their last shilling to the captain, are landed destitute and emaciated, and we are sadly sensible of the effect of such numbers of these poor people huddling together in cellars and sheds, in and about the Ship-Yards the last summer and fall.[8]

Some twenty years later the Society for the Prevention of Pauperism in New York City listed "emigrants to this city from foreign countries" as the most important source of pauperism. Its annual report stated:

This inlet of pauperism threatens us with the most overwhelming consequences. From various causes, the City of New York is doomed to be the landing-place of a great portion of the European population, who are daily flocking to our country for a place of permanent abode. . . . Many of them arrive here destitute of everything. When they do arrive, instead of seeking the interior, they cluster in our cities. . . depending on the incidents of time, charity, or depredation, for subsistence. . . . They are frequently found destitute in our streets; they seek employment at our doors; they are found in our almshouse, and in our hospitals. . . . For years and generations will Europe continue to send forth her surplus population. The winds and the waves will still bring needy thousands to our sea-ports, and this city continue the general point of arrival. Over this subject can we longer slumber?

New York is the resting place and is liable to be devoured by swarms of people. . . . Where is this evil to stop, and who can compass its magnitude?[9]

The majority of those in almshouses were foreign-born, and many had required assistance since the time of their arrival. The port cities were particularly burdened. In the 1830s the governor and legislature of Massachusetts became greatly concerned over the arrival of foreign paupers encouraged by European states, particularly England.[10] Although the amount of officially inspired pauper-dumping may have been exaggerated by the American authorities, great numbers of immigrants required considerable aid.[11] During the years of the Irish famine, 1846 to 1848, there was an endless stream of immigrants, who, though possibly the more active and enterprising, had little resources or capacity to establish themselves in entirely strange surroundings. In addition, few of their compatriots were, as in later years, in a position to give any substantial help.[12] While many of the new immigrants required aid, many of the older residents, too, shifted about with greater rapidity than in the more static societies of Europe. Seeking opportunity, moving from urban to rural communities, from settled to new areas, all entailed difficulties of adjustment often involving the provision of aid.

Apart from the special problems of individual adjustment in a new land, eighteenth- and nineteenth-century America was not spared the common crises arising from epidemics, wars, and the uncertainties of foreign trade. Under British rule, America's economy was affected by England's wars and the varying nature of colonial policy. The more restrictive mercantilist measures after the French wars of 1763, for example, resulted in economic depression and stimulated lower-class opposition to British rule. Small tradesmen were forced to close their shops, farmers suffered from loss of markets and currency contraction, the fur trade was decimated, and there was widespread unemployment. Following the Revolution conditions were even more unstable, with America's loss of its place in the British colonial system and with the necessity for adjustment after a long and costly war. Shays' Rebellion was indicative of the critical state of New England small farmers whose property was being foreclosed by creditors in the 1780s. The *New York Daily Advertiser* reported as late as 1791 that "many of our small tradesmen, cartmen, day labourers and others, dwell upon the borders of poverty and live from hand to mouth."[13] A few years later a widespread epidemic of yellow fever in New York City resulted in the closing of many businesses and a general disruption of the life of the city. Unemployment spread, and several thousand of the city's population were forced to rely on public and private charity.

America's relations with Europe were especially complex during the period of the Napoleonic Wars. Jefferson's embargo policy (1807–1809) caused a tremendous decline in American foreign trade and depressed the total economy of a country heavily engaged in foreign commerce. The most drastic recession followed the conclusion of the Napoleonic Wars, when an overexpanded American economy was confronted with a resumption of European competition as well as a general period of decline in European commerce. At the height of the depression it was estimated that some 500,000 were unemployed.[14] In Philadelphia alone, of 9,700 employed in thirty establishments, 7,500 were discharged in 1819.[15] Properties of farmers and small businessmen were taken over by creditors. Again in 1829 a decline in business conditions resulted in many workers applying for assistance. The *New York Times* reported:

Thousands of industrious mechanics who never before solicited alms, were brought to the humiliating condition of applying for assistance, and with tears on their manly cheeks, confessed their inability to provide food or clothing for their families.[16]

During the latter part of the eighteenth century and the early nineteenth century there was in America a large population living on the edge of poverty—some heavily in debt, others totally dependent on their immediate earnings. Any crisis affecting the economic stability of the country had serious repercussions for their economic welfare.

American Social and Economic Thought

American social and economic thought, while reflecting familiarity with contemporary English and continental trends, was impatient with the theoretical refinements of the European political economists. To some extent differences between European and American thinking were due to the pace of diffusion of ideas. Many of the leading intellectual and political figures in American society at the time of the Revolution were under the influence of seventeenth- and early eighteenth-century writers, such as Harrington, Hobbes, Locke, Hume, and Montesquieu. Differences with their English contemporaries, particularly the liberal economists and Utilitarians, such as Smith, Malthus, and Ricardo, were also in part the result of differences in the economic and social conditions prevailing in America. On the whole, Americans were not so much interested in grand theories as in practical guides for the immediate problems of the new nation.

While there were major conflicts in theoretical orientation between the Jeffersonian Democrats and the Federalists, they were often resolved by agreement on practical issues because both parties supported the growth of the commercial interests of the nation. Rigid orthodoxy of principle was not the way of the American leaders, who combined to varying degrees the roles of politician-statesman, propagandist, philosopher, and businessman, as is evidenced by so many of their careers. The British political economists alienated Americans not only by the complexity of their theories but also by what Americans considered their skepticism and their pessimism. Having an unquestioning faith in national growth and an unlimited future, American scholars and policymakers were antagonized by British doubts about the rightness of the current economic structure. Smith's concern about labor receiving its rightful share, Malthus' about the value of population, and Ricardo's about the appropriate function of rent were not welcomed by those who preferred to think that each of these issues was satisfactorily resolved on the American scene.[17]

Laissez-faire doctrine dominated the American political and economic arena. The writings of Smith and McCullough or popular revisions of their work were standard college texts when economics in America became sufficiently divorced from earlier theological influences. While classical economics was accepted in principle and no major American writing proposed an alternative system, there was, in fact, much deviation from the classical economists in American thought and policy. A great deal of American thought was mercantilist because the leadership sought justification for policies to strengthen the internal and external position of the new nation. In encouraging self-sufficiency or a balanced economy, in maintaining a favorable balance of trade, in developing a large and low-paid supply of labor, many American statesmen fitted the mercantilist mold in viewing the economy as a whole rather than as the sum of varied and discrete parts.

Even beyond economic policies that might be considered strategically advantageous to a new nation in the eighteenth century, there were social and political ideologies in America closer to mercantilist than to liberal thinking. The Federalist view of society and government that dominated the constitutional convention of 1787 resembled more the Hobbesian conception of society in conflict than Locke's assumption of a cooperative society with the freedom to abrogate unsatisfactory political arrangements. Conscious of the self-interested or "economic man" of the classical economists, the Federalists did not have faith in the socially benevolent nature of man. They assumed neither that reason would act as a corrective nor that the interests of the individual were harmonious with the interests of the whole. Madison's discussion of the threat of "factions" to a well-organized state makes clear the Federalist view of society.

The latent causes of faction are thus sown in the nature of man; and we see them everywhere brought into different degrees of activity, according to the different circumstances of civil society. A zeal for different opinions concerning religion, concerning government, and many other points, as well of speculation as of practice; an attachment to different leaders ambitiously contending for pre-eminence and power; or to persons of other descriptions whose fortunes have been interesting to the human passions, have, in turn, divided mankind into parties, inflamed them with mutual animosity, and rendered them much more disposed to vex and oppress each other than to co-operate for their common good. So strong is this propensity of mankind to fall into mutual animosities, that where no substantial occasion presents itself, the most frivolous and fanciful distinctions have been sufficient to kindle their unfriendly passions and excite their most violent conflicts. But the most common and durable source of factions has been the various and unequal distribution of property. Those who hold and those who are without property have ever formed distinct interests in society.[18]

The Federalist position was also made clear on the issue of checks and balances in government.

It may be a reflection on human nature, that such devices should be necessary to control the abuses of government. But what is government itself, but the greatest of all reflections on human nature? If men were angels, no government would be necessary. If angels were to govern men, neither external nor internal controls on government would be necessary. In framing a government which is to be administered by men over men, the great difficulty lies in this:

you must first enable the government to control the governed; and in the next place oblige it to control itself. A dependence on the people is, no doubt, the primary control on the government; but experience has taught mankind the necessity of auxiliary precautions.[19]

Society was viewed as a conflict of interests motivated by selfish passions, the most dangerous of which were founded on differences of property. The function of government was to conciliate the discordant interests. Under those circumstances the contract of society could not be a mutable instrument, and the Federalists proposed rigid obstacles to any change in the basic structure of government. That the terms of the contract proposed by the Federalists favored the interests of property was not surprising in view of their own diagnosis of human behavior.[20]

Opposing the Federalists were those who have been broadly termed Jeffersonian Democrats, of whom Tom Paine was one of the most influential spokesmen. Less organized and less unified in their thinking, this group included a range as wide apart as Benjamin Franklin and Joel Barlow. For their philosophical substance they drew upon French radicalism as the Federalists had upon English conservatism. They emphasized the basically benevolent nature of man. Accepting the dominant belief of the Age of Enlightenment that man was a rational being, they rejected what Jefferson described as the view that "men in numerous associations cannot be restrained within the limits of order and justice but by forces physical and moral, wielded over them by authorities independent of their will."[21] Rather than a strong centralized government to restrict the passions of individuals, the Democrats advocated the elimination of formal institutions that hindered the achievement of social justice through the free interplay of the members of society. As Paine stated in *The Rights of Man:*

The more perfect civilization is, the less occasion has it for government, because the more does it regulate its own affairs, and govern itself. . . . All the great laws of society are laws of nature.[22]

The Democrats, who had faith in the natural order of man, were more positive than the British liberal economists and Utilitarians, who emphasized the egoistic and selfish nature of man. The ideal of the Democrats was a collection of agricultural freeholders. It was a closely knit society with democratic principles, a society of yeomen governed by informal relationships rather than an urban industrial world of contract agreements. On principle, the Democrats opposed the national bank, the power of the Supreme Court, and the growth of powerful economic institutions—the symbols of a contract society. In practice, the Democrats no less than their Federalist opponents favored the expansion of the country's resources and economic interests.

Fundamental to the differences between the British liberal economists and the French political philosophers was the British emphasis on a society of identity of interests as contrasted to the French concern for equality of rights. The liberal faith in identity of interests was largely limited to the economic sphere and involved no strong commitment to political democracy. While the economic well-being of the whole might be best assured by each of the members following his own interests, it did not follow that the happiness of society would be accomplished by the free and equal functioning of its members on the political scene. Even Joseph Priestly, an intimate of Jefferson and an English political liberal much in advance of his colleagues, believed that political liberty could function only in a small state.[23]

The belief in equality of rights, the ideology of the French Revolution, was supported in America primarily by Tom Paine. However, the majority opinion defined the issues in terms of interests rather than rights, a trend critically remarked on by Condorcet soon after the Declaration of Independence.[24] The notion of a society of rational individuals, as conceived by Paine and Godwin, endowed with natural rights and reaching a state of natural harmony or fusion of interests without political coercion was not acceptable. As Jefferson wrote to John Adams:

One of the questions . . . on which our parties took different sides, was the improvability of the human mind in science, in ethics, in government, etc. Those who advocated a reformation of institutions *pari passu* with the progress of science, maintained that no definite limits could be assigned to progress. The enemies of reform on the other hand denied improvement and advocated a steady adherence to the principles, practices, and institutions of our fathers which they represented as the consummation of wisdom and the acme of excellence beyond which the human mind could never advance.[25]

The "enemies of reform" dominated the constitutional convention and the early years of the new Republic. The protection of the propertied interests from the uncontrolled passions of the poor and unpropertied was one of their major concerns. There were few advocates of the franchise for the unpropertied, but Jefferson conceived of a society with no extreme contrasts of wealth, in which all might be small property holders and the poor would be improved both intellectually and morally under the influence of education and progress.

The conservatives, on the other hand, had little faith in the lower classes and saw in them a constant threat to the well-being of society. In contrast to Jefferson, Hamilton viewed society as composed essentially of two groups, the rich and the poor, with the disparities between them increasing rather than decreasing with time. Whether or not Locke's emphasis on society's responsibility for the preservation of property was too literally interpreted, the rights of property heavily permeated the thinking of the most influential Americans.[26] The Federalist position dominated the leading educational institutions, and Chancellor Kent of New York state and professor of law at Columbia College summed up the Federalist philosophy when he defined society as "an association for the protection of property as well as life," and added that "the individual who contributes only one cent to the common stock, ought not to have the same power and influence in directing the property concerns of the partnership, as he who contributes his thousands."[27]

The concern of the propertied with maintaining control was not entirely an abstract issue, as was illustrated by the famous letter of General Knox to Washington at the time of Shays' Rebellion.

Their creed is, that the property of the United States has been protected from the confiscation of Britain by the joint exertions of all, and therefore ought to be the common property of all. . . . This dreadful situation, for which our government had made no adequate provision, has alarmed every man of principle and property in New England. They start as from a dream, and ask what can have been the cause of our delusion? What is to give us security against the violence of lawless men? Our government must be braced, changed, or altered to secure our lives and property. We imagined that the mildness of our government and the wishes of the people were so correspondent that we were not as other nations, requiring brutal force to support the laws. But we find we are men—actual men, possessing all the turbulent passions belonging to that animal, and that we must have a government proper and adequate for him.[28]

This attitude toward the lower classes was similar to the fears of British conservatives but was not mitigated by the paternalism of the British aristocracy. The interests of the commercial classes were the primary concern of national policy. It was assumed that what was good for the wealthy must be in the interests of the poor because the poor were totally dependent on the rich for their welfare. In the controversy over the national bank Daniel Webster supported the national bank by pointing out that even if the banks were primarily of value to the rich, "the rich will take care of the poor." The care to which he referred was not the benevolent concern of the rich for the poor but the identity of interests that gave the poor a stake in the profitable ventures of the wealthy. As Noah Webster remarked somewhat later:

What would become of the poor without the rich? How would they subsist without employment, and how could they be employed, without the capital of the rich? Who but the wealthy can pay the public expenses? Who can furnish the capital for canals, and railroads, and all other public improvements?[29]

While this general point of view was acceptable in England, too, there were important differences between American and British social and economic philosophy. Americans adhered to the mercantilist high-population and low-wage policy as a positive good, but such British economists as Smith, Malthus, and Ricardo deprecated the effects of increasing populations and subsistence wages even while accepting their inevitability. The achievement of national wealth at the expense of the lower classes, a fundamental tenet of mercantilism, was seriously questioned by British liberal economists and Utilitarians from both a practical and an ethical point of view. In their emphasis on national progress Americans gave little attention to this issue. It is true that the question of overpopulation was not pressing and that the Americans did not have before them the ravages of the Agrarian and Industrial Revolutions in England. However, even when they hypothesized such possibilities, they were willing to tolerate much social dissatisfaction in the name of economic growth.

For the influential groups seeking America's competitive advantage in international trade, a large and low-paid working class appeared of primary importance. American writers and theorists of the early nineteenth century, such as Tucker, Cooper, and Everett, were more concerned with the value of population density as a stimulus to trade and industry than with its consequences for the welfare of the laboring population. Even when they agreed with Malthus' analysis, they preferred to leave the problem of the working population to the natural checks of population pressure. Tucker in 1827 even saw the panacea for slavery in Ricardo's subsistence wage. For "when the wages of free labor are nearly reduced to bare subsistence," he said, "then it will be more expensive to keep slaves than hire free labor."[30]

No one spoke for the employed poor in American society. The Jeffersonian Democrats, while identified with the small man, saw the small man as an independent farmer, not as an urban worker or a wage earner. The Federalists were conscious only of the affairs of merchants and were identified with capital growth, production, and trade. With the subordination of agrarian democracy to the rising merchant and industrial interests even this obstacle to the rigors of a contract society passed away. Unobstructed economic individualism became the dominant political and social philosophy.

Causes of Poverty

American explanations of poverty closely resembled those popular in England. If anything, American opinion tended, as might be expected, to place greater weight on individual shortcomings than did the British. Unwilling to view poverty as a fortuitous or capricious event, the Puritan mentality compulsively searched for the causes in personal behavior. After all, in the land of expanding opportunity it was almost paradoxical for poverty to exist unless it was a sign of individual weakness.[31]

Mathew Carey, a Philadelphia businessman interested in the conditions of the working class and a warm advocate of reform, summed up the prevailing viewpoint about the poor:

1. That every man, woman, and grown child, able and willing to work, may find employment.
2. That the poor, by industry, prudence, and economy, may at all times support themselves comfortably, without depending on aid—and as a corollary from these positions.
3. That their sufferings and distresses chiefly, if not wholly, arise from their idleness, their dissipation, and their extravagance.
4. That taxes for the support of the poor, and aid afforded them by charitable individuals, or benevolent societies, are pernicious, as by encouraging the poor to depend on them, they foster their idleness and improvidence, and thus produce, or at least increase, the poverty and distress they are intended to relieve.[32]

The "idleness," "dissipation," and "extravagance" of the poor was emphasized in all investigations of the causes of poverty. During the first two decades of the nineteenth century the increasing demands on public and private aid stimulated investigations by public and philanthropic bodies. The Report of the Humane Society of New York City in 1809 was typical of these examinations of poverty. It began:

Associated for the purpose of relieving the indigent, our attention has been naturally drawn to the causes which produce the extreme poverty and misery, which have so much increased among our labouring poor. . . . To obtain more perfect information in relation to these subjects we lately appointed a committee to investigate them; and their report . . . we now lay before you, hoping that when your attention shall be awakened to a consideration of the evils which it details you will concur in endeavoring to effect a radical reform.[33]

Thereupon the Report found the causes of indigence to be vice and particularly intemperance. Similar reports by other committees found similar causes; differences were largely restricted to the more detailed delineation of individual shortcomings. Thus, the 1818 Report of the Society for the Prevention of Pauperism in New York City listed "ignorance," "idleness," "want of economy," "imprudent and hasty marriages," as well as "intemperance," which was referred to as "the cause of causes."[34] In 1817 it was estimated that of the 15,000, one seventh of the total population, on charity in New York City, seven eighths were pauperized by liquor.[35] The Yates Report suggested that intemperance was the cause of two thirds of permanent dependency; and that was a conservative estimate when compared with those of other public officials, who regarded intemperance as the sole cause.[36] Reports on poverty were also critical of the presence in the community of pawnbrokers, lotteries, houses of ill-fame, gambling houses, and even of courts and prisons which, it was maintained, encouraged the increase of vice and pauperism. The numerous immigrants requiring help in the port cities were reflected in the attention given to immigration as a cause of dependency.

Wars and their aftermath were given special consideration among the few social factors considered responsible for poverty. "Want of employment" was mentioned in the 1821 Report of the Society for the Prevention of Pauperism at a time of general depression. Mathew Carey vigorously challenged the belief that employment was universally available. There was also some recognition of the effects of inadequate wages, unequal distribution of property, and industrialization on the growth of poverty.[37]

Alongside vice, ignorance, and other symptoms of personal inadequacy, the most popularly cited cause of increasing dependency was the encouragement given idleness by the presence of many public and private relief agencies. Malthus' criticism of relief as stimulating rather than alleviating dependency was generally accepted. Contemporary criticisms of the English public assistance system only further confirmed already deep-rooted suspicions of the corrupting influence of relief. Franklin, as already noted, had on the basis of his own observations advised that the major obstacle to an industrious laboring population in England was the widespread system of public relief. By the end of the century, influential Americans were convinced of his judgment in view of the ever-increasing assistance and the continued difficulties of the English local authorities. Governor DeWitt Clinton of New York expressed the general opinion when he said, "Our statutes relating to the poor are borrowed from the English system. And the experiences of that country as well as our own, show that pauperism increases with the augmentation of the funds applied to its relief."[38]

The poor laws were seen as the source of other evils beyond encouraging dependency alone. Although in-door relief was strictly adhered to, the almshouse was criticized for demoralizing the poor, and was blamed for the hostility, impudence, and ingratitude of the poor. The opinion was held that provision of relief from tax funds weakened normal ties with family and friends, and that industry and thrift were threatened by the transfer of wealth from its rightful owners to the undeserving.[39]

The extent of responsibility for pauperism put on public or private charity appears to have varied with the observer. Legislative committees emphasized the indiscriminate nature of public relief and recommended private charity as a corrective. On the other hand, private charitable organizations referred in their reports to the availability of relief from so many private sources as a primary cause of dependency. However, voluntary societies were credited with one advantage over public assistance; they offered "no certain support of the poor."[40] Thus, their unreliability was seen as a virtue. Private charity was also thought to avoid the stigma of pauperism and to establish a bond between the rich and the poor.

Social responsibility for poverty received little or no recognition. Tom Paine was an effective political propagandist, but his schemes for old-age pensions and work for the unemployed did not draw support. In Louisi-

ana, Edward Livingston, a Jeffersonian Democrat, advised the state legislature that unemployment was the result of the workings of the economic market and that workers who had been productive in times of
prosperity should not be left to starve or become objects of charity in
times of crisis. In making his plea for a public relief system Livingston
did not refer to the responsibilities of the community to its members but
rather to the morality of a "just" commercial society. "Can it be supposed," he said, "that any just contract could stipulate that one of the
contracting parties should die of hunger, in order that others might enjoy, without deduction, the whole of their property?" Livingston, however, failed to convince his colleagues.[41]

Programs of Assistance

Writing on America during the Revolutionary era, Anthony Trollope
commented, "This new people, when they had it in their power to change
all their laws, to throw themselves upon any Utopian theory that the
folly of a wild philanthropy could devise . . . did not do so."[42] Trollope's
observations were more than justified in the field of assistance policy. The
programs of economic assistance after the Revolution were fundamentally the same as those of the colonial period. The changes in political and
social philosophy marked by the Revolution were not reflected in the programs for the indigent. The poor laws of the new states were borrowed
from those of the mother country, and during the early years of the Republic England's lead continued to be followed. Colonial assistance policy
had been rudimentary prior to the Revolution and remained so in the
period after it. Although the colonies and the new states had not experimented, as England had, with a variety of forms of relief for the able-
bodied, they anticipated England in turning to the workhouse as the sole
form of assistance.

Without having had a liberal policy of relief, there was much less reason for the states to settle on a primitive approach to assistance, and the
absence of a prior era of responsibility meant there was nothing to leaven
the effects of even more restrictive measures. While from the latter part
of the eighteenth century England was establishing larger administrative
areas of responsibility for assistance, the Americans were doing the opposite. Existing state and county systems gradually gave way to entirely

local control and more rigid settlement restrictions. These trends were particularly significant in view of the efforts of the Federalist leadership to plan for the economy on a national rather than a local basis in such matters as banking, tariffs, and public works.

In general, the able-bodied needing assistance, except for periods of dire emergency such as epidemics or severe business depressions, were treated as petty criminals, and destitution itself was viewed as a crime. Not that the aged or sick received more favorable treatment, for all were cared for in much the same manner. There was, however, even less acceptance of the able-bodied as a public responsibility. The Yates Report of 1824 in New York State recommended that no able-bodied person between the ages of eighteen and fifty be supported at public expense. This was even more drastic than the policy of the 1834 English Poor Law Commission, which, though equally unfavorable to assistance for the able-bodied, provided for their care in workhouses. To the Yates Committee all able-bodied needy were beggars and vagrants, and the workhouse became a penitentiary. The workhouse test of the English system relied on discipline and deprivation for its deterrent effects; the American states, on the other hand, introduced punitive measures usually reserved for criminals.

The movement toward public indoor or institutional relief gathered momentum during the 1820s, although in many states actual provision followed slowly upon legislative action. The pressure for assistance in institutions was accentuated by restrictions on the provision of assistance to the poor in their own homes. In New York and Michigan, for example, no more than ten dollars could be given a person or a family without special approval of the superintendent of the poor of the county. In Kentucky legislative authorization was required. Approval was usually limited to the aged or feeble or those "who cannot be conveniently removed to the poorhouse."

There had been some early outdoor relief in the colonies and the states, but it had been a minor element in the total provision and had occurred either in exceptional circumstances or where sparseness of population had discouraged any more complex program. The chief forms of assistance were "contracting out" and "auctioning off" of the poor to private persons who gave minimal care to the poor at a low cost to the public authority and exploited the labor of those relieved. It was as a reaction to this system that measures to set up public almshouses were instituted. The latter were considered to be cheaper, more deterrent, and more efficient than other forms of care. In his report to the New York state legislature Yates favorably compared the low incidence of dependency in Rhode Island, Delaware, and Virginia, states having public poorhouses, with New York, Massachusetts, Connecticut, and Pennsylvania, which had no poorhouse system.

The goal of the reforms in the states during the first part of the nineteenth century was the substitution of directly administered public programs for the previously subsidized private programs. Steps to restrict private contracting had been taken in England as early as 1782 and 1805. However, Gilbert's Act of 1782 established outdoor relief and employment of the able-bodied as the alternative rather than the more rigid institutional system recommended in the states. Some of the state committees emphasized opportunities for work in the projected institutions, but they frequently did not materialize. In Massachusetts a committee of the state legislature commented, "It is in affording the poor the means of labor instead of a support independent of labor, that your Committee thinks a judicious change can be made in the system of State Charity."[43] Yet county houses of correction rather than houses for work were established. In New York City the Society for the Prevention of Pauperism was influential in having a treadmill installed in the local penitentiary in 1823 as a punishment for vagrants (including the able-bodied unemployed), but it proved so physically damaging to the inmates and so ineffective that it was abandoned after a short time. The few attempts to develop meaningful and profitable employment in institutions failed. In Boston a group of private citizens established a spinning school for the employment of the poor, but it became insolvent within five years. The products of most institutions and farms for the poor were mostly consumed within their boundaries.

The shortcomings of the local assistance programs were most sharply revealed during periods of emergency arising from economic reversals, war, or disease. At such times the communities and states, public and private efforts, strained themselves to the utmost. Such crises, however, only succeeded in demonstrating the administrative and financial limitations of the assistance programs. It was evident that the relief system was not designed to deal with the needs of the normal unemployed but was geared to the punishment of vagrants and beggars.

The conflict between the expectations of the unemployed and community attitudes toward assistance was portrayed in the clash of the Mayor of New York City with the unemployed during the period of the Embargo Act of 1807–1809. The unemployed seamen petitioned the city for assistance. The Mayor disapproved of their "mode of application." The Corporation, he said, would "provide for the wants of every person without distinction who may be considered proper objects of relief." The seamen pointed to the embargo as the source of their distress and replied to the Mayor:

You tried to dissuade us from our purpose, mentioning that provision was made for objects of pity. We are not objects of pity yet, but shall soon be, if there is not some method taken for our support. We are for the most part hale, robust, hearty men, and would choose some kind of employment rather than the poorhouse for a livelihood. We humbly beg therefore, you will provide some means for our subsistence or the consequences may not only prove fatal to ourselves, but ruinous to the flourishing Commerce of America, as we shall be necessitated to go abroad on foreign vessels.[44]

The terms of the demands of the seamen and their rejection of the Mayor's position indicated differences between the belief of the seamen in the right to assistance and the city's attitude of charity to its "objects of pity." The seamen sought recognition as equal and contributing members of the community while the Mayor and the Corporation viewed them as dependent and inferior. The conflict was resolved by the city arranging with the navy yard for their employment. The cost of maintenance would be paid by the city, and the unemployed seamen would be under the heavy discipline of the navy.[45]

During these emergency periods the public and private benevolence of the local communities was supplemented by state and federal resources. Outdoor relief, largely in kind, was expanded. Haphazard attempts at work relief were made through public works. In the larger cities voluntary societies attempted to control and supervise the giving of assistance through district committees and visitors. Generally, the total resources of the communities were overtaxed, and while the failure to cope with emergency situations led to much dissatisfaction, it did not result in more effective programs of assistance. The experiences during these periods seemed to confirm the prejudice against all forms of economic aid and to support the position of those who believed personal limitations and the moral degradation of the poor to be the cause of their dependency.

The few proposals to apply broader policies to economic insecurity gained little backing. Tom Paine's scheme for old-age pensions and David Stirrat's program of public works for keeping the economy in balance and preventing the fall of wages and prices were much in advance of their times. Measures that might have had support earlier were no longer acceptable in the era of laissez-faire. Thus, although the system of land tenancy resulting in the loss of farms for the poor farmers was complained of in the Yates Report, the granting to poor persons of land from the village commons, which occurred a century earlier, was no longer considered a possible alternative. Even up to the middle of the eighteenth century petitions for establishing monopolies were approved on the grounds of their employment of the poor.[46] On the whole, although there was recognition in some quarters of the need to provide opportunity through employment or land, few such opportunities were arranged in the first half of the nineteenth century.

Since the major cause of dependency was believed to be the moral state of the poor, most solutions were designed to combat immorality. There was a general impression at the beginning of the nineteenth century that dependency and crime had increased at a much greater rate than the rate of population growth. This heightened the concern with immorality generally. Temperance societies were founded in the decade between 1810 and 1820, and following the hard times of 1816, a great number of voluntary bodies were formed to inquire into and deal with the sources of pauperism and crime.[47] These organizations were critical of public and private efforts for their failure to discriminate between the deserving and the unworthy poor and for their inattention to other than the material needs of the poor. In their opinion, catering to the physical wants of the poor merely increased dependency. The task was essentially the development of sobriety and industry.

The great panacea recommended on all sides was education. There was, however, much difference of opinion about the function of education. Some, like Hamilton and the conservative Southern journalist and economist Jacob Cardozo, saw education as the means of indoctrinating the lower classes with respect for the status quo. Hamilton favored the establishment of charity schools for workers to counteract the influence of radicalism in the cities. Cardozo thought that when the lower classes

were educated to the workings of society, they would be "brought to submit to temporary deprivations of employment, as the law of our social
condition."[48] For a second group, education for the masses would be restricted to its most elementary aspects, and its major contribution would
be the improvement of the moral habits of the poor. This point of view
closely paralleled the Evangelical Sunday School movement in England.
With the spread of education for the lower classes Sunday schools in
America became identified with strictly religious training.[49]

The most acceptable function of education to liberal reformers as well
as to labor spokesmen was preparing the lower classes to improve their
social and economic position. A broad system of public education for rich
and poor alike would dispel the ignorance at the root of immorality
and idleness. Through education the lower classes would be stimulated
to ambition, would learn the skills necessary for their betterment, and
would become the equals of their superiors.

Next to education the encouragement of saving was the most popular
of the constructive reforms and had much in common with the purposes
of education. By saving, the lower classes would learn the habit of thrift,
would gain a conservative interest in the welfare of society, and would
improve their own positions. The establishment of savings banks and insurance benefit societies was supported by all groups. The Pennsylvania
Society for the Promotion of Public Economy approached the problem of
thrift by emphasizing the necessity of reducing the expenditures of the
poor for shelter, food, and clothing. In most instances, however, savings
were not openly equated with a reduced standard of living.

Savings, like education, appealed to both the laboring groups and the
social reformers. Many mutual benefit societies existed for artisans and
mechanics. Typical journeymen societies had funds for protection against
illness, accident, death, and other misfortunes. An important motivation
for such funds was the desire to avoid the invidious state of receiving
public or private charity. Membership in a workers' benevolent society
gave members the right to assistance which membership in the general
community did not.[50] Another popular form of mutual aid was the
nationality benefit societies, which acted as benevolent societies for their
members and aided newcomers. By the beginning of the nineteenth
century national societies had been organized among the English, Scots,
Germans, French, and Irish in America.

By the nineteenth century several important trends were discernible on the American scene. Although a system of public assistance was present, it took little or no responsibility for the able-bodied needy. Measures for the economic security of the able-bodied poor were limited by the belief that dependency was the result of individual failings, not of social and economic conditions. Programs for the able-bodied, apart from education, were largely under the aegis of private organizations and combined paternalistic benevolence and moral reform. The limited role of the public authorities and the provision of aid by workers' and other benevolent societies indicated that private bodies would independently attempt to meet the challenge by assuming major responsibility for economic security.

Part III

THE ERA OF LAISSEZ-FAIRE

8

The Foundations of British Policy

Social and Economic Trends

DURING the period after 1834 the new industrial society in England became firmly established. Modern economic security policies can be directly traced to their foundations at this time. The Poor Law Commission of 1834 had attempted to wipe the slate clean and begin anew with policies suited to an established industrial society. The reforms of the Commission removed some of the last vestiges of mercantilism. The old poor law had survived by only a few years the great reform of Parliament that symbolized the power of the new business interests. The revision of mercantilist labor and wage policies had been completed, and modern factory legislation had its start in the second decade of the nineteenth century.

As much as any organization could disinherit its past, the new Poor Law Commission and its heir, the Poor Law Board, vigorously attacked the remains of previous administrations. Armed with the principles of the new era, they attempted thoroughly and rigorously to root out the practices of the former system, and they were sensitive to any backsliding on the part of the local authorities. Any delay by the local authorities in carrying out the new policies, however, was not necessarily a reflection of conservatism. The new principles did not fully meet contemporary demands. For example, the attack on outdoor relief for the able-bodied, while defensible in view of earlier experiences with the allowance system in agricultural communities, was not appropriate for the same reasons in the growing industrial and commercial centers. The continued resistance to outdoor relief by the central administration represented an almost fanatical concentration on anachronistic issues. The policies of 1834 were better suited to reforming past conditions than to meeting present and future problems. During the nineteenth century Utilitarian and laissez-faire philosophies were tested against the demands of an increasingly complex industrial society, and by the end of the century there arose a new formulation of social responsibility comparable to the Elizabethan advances following the feudal era.

"By the middle of the nineteenth century," as a Royal Commission succinctly stated, "Great Britain had become the workshop of the world."[1] Throughout the century there was a growing concentration in mining, factory production, and shipbuilding and at the same time a relative diminution of agriculture. This growth in trade and industry was paralleled by the rapid development of great cities and a persistent trend toward the concentration of population in urban and industrial areas. While in 1801, 49 percent of the population of Great Britain resided in urban and industrial areas, by 1861, 60 percent of the population was found in these areas, and by 1901, 69 percent.

At the same time, there was a vast increase in the total population. In 1801 the population of Great Britain was 10.5 million; by 1861 it had increased to 23.1 million; and in 1901 it was 37 million.[2] The concentration of population in the major commercial and industrial centers was followed by even somewhat larger concentrations of the gainfully employed in these areas. In 1801, 45 percent of the gainfully employed was distributed among the major regions of commerce and manufacture. By 1861 the proportion had increased to 62 percent, and in 1901 to 70 percent.[3] The decreasing significance of agricultural occupations and the vast expansion of large-scale industrial and commercial employment resulted in considerable changes in the social and economic life of the nation and in the types of plans necessary for economic security.

The growth of complex urban centers, the expansion of communication and transportation, and the flow of population to the centers of employment led to a set of circumstances markedly different from the society to which the principles of 1834 had been applied. It is noteworthy that the Poor Law Commission's analysis of the critical conditions underlying the need for reform in 1834 gave relatively little attention to urban areas. The goal of maintaining a stable working population with traditional ideologies in agricultural regions was not relevant to the social and economic life of the industrial centers. The availability of a surplus population who could perform the relatively unskilled tasks required made unnecessary the organization of a static labor force by the industrial entrepreneur. These were the issues with which the Poor Law Commission dealt, and the principles formulated by the Commission led to the fitting of a rural model to an industrial economy.

Old-fashioned individualism, although kept alive by some political economists and social philosophers, was no longer a practical issue in the latter part of the nineteenth century in England. Inroads on individualism had been increasing throughout the century. The state had moved far from being a casual enterprise of squires and large landholders. The extension of the franchise in 1832 gave political representation to the already established middle-class interests. Labor, too, recognized the importance of government as the means to social and economic reform. The Chartist movement had turned into political channels energies which earlier, under radicals like Owen, had been directed at immediate social and economic change.

The state, particularly the central government, was now able to take effective administrative action. While the theoretical rationale for laissez-faire in earlier periods may have been open to question, the practical weakness of government lent much support to the classical economists. To some extent, laissez-faire may be considered a reaction to the political realities of the time.[4] No one could be totally unaware of the inefficiency and corruption of English government in the eighteenth century.

The situation changed radically in the second half of the nineteenth century. As Clapham concluded:

The state, purged and trained fine, better informed and better equipped, could supervise the carrying out of its decisions with a certainty which would have been unthinkable two generations earlier. Whatever the conscious or subconscious doctrines about the proper sphere of its action by which legislators were influenced, it was probable, perhaps inevitable, that the organism of state, more sinewy and efficient, would also become more active.[5]

A whole series of reforms laid the groundwork for the state's effectiveness as an instrument of social policy. Major political institutions—Parliament, the municipalities, and the guardians of the poor—had been reorganized. The philosophical radicals, followers of Bentham and James Mill, had emphasized the application of scientific knowledge to governmental matters. Officials, like Chadwick, approached their positions and instilled their subordinates with a respect for disciplined work and familiarity with the daily tasks of government. The differences between Chadwick and the Commissioners on the Poor Law Board may be partly traced to the conflict between the new type of bureaucrat and the old casual, albeit well-intentioned, gentleman administrator.[6] For the former, the honors of office were not a sign of political favoritism but an opportunity for effective intervention in the social and economic affairs of the nation.

Like the middle class, the working class during the nineteenth century turned to exploiting the conventional channels of power in its own interests. At the beginning of the nineteenth century the working class looked toward utopian experiments and syndicalist action. During the second half of the century trade unions overcame their earlier organizational difficulties, and by 1870 their membership increased to approximately 250,000 and within twenty years to one million.[7] The franchise was extended to the working class in 1867 and 1887, and the legislation of the 1870s removed the remaining legal restrictions to union activity. At the same time, the trade union movement was growing more conservative in its goals and policies and represented primarily the interests of the more skilled, better paid, and better organized workers. By the close of the nineteenth century, however, the trade unions, some of the more radical labor leadership, and social reformist groups decided that government was a major, if not the major, route to their social and economic goals; they founded the Labour Party. Alongside and closely related to trade unionism there also grew a large cooperative movement that extended beyond the borders of the working class.

During the period after 1850 the general conditions of workers improved significantly. The standard of living rose, and social legislation began to correct some of the evils of the Industrial Revolution. Yet despite the favorable economic position and the wealth of the country as a whole, poverty had by no means been eliminated, and during the last quarter of the century there were serious economic crises and unemployment. In contrast to earlier periods, the problem of poverty now occurred in a relatively affluent society—in a society capable of producing enough for the needs of all its members.

The reform of the franchise, compulsory education, and the growth of trade unions and cooperatives were all indicative of important social changes in British society. While nineteenth-century England might not be considered an equalitarian society, the strongholds of privilege had been greatly reduced. The important extension of the franchise in 1867 occurred calmly in comparison to the bitter struggle over the Reform Act of 1832. The initial fears of democratic change, influenced by the revolutions on the continent in the first half of the century, gave way to a relatively calm acceptance of democratic evolution. During the Victorian era the stability of the country, its internal prosperity, and its strong international position provided the background for social change without the threat of upheaval.

Attitudes Toward Work, the Working Class, and Poverty

In this period, as in the preceding one, attitudes toward work, the working class, and poverty were closely interrelated and influenced the nature of economic security policy. The victory of laissez-faire, with its strong emphasis on work and its rejection of poverty as a social responsibility, was followed by a reaction to its harsh and inhumane policies. Although the poor law reformers of 1834 had defeated what they considered an anachronistic reliance on social support, they had abolished neither poverty nor the need for help for those unable to gain an adequate living. The principle of work as the only approved source of income reinforced by the policy of less eligibility had not made work more available or more remunerative.

The issue of work and wages remained the core of economic security policy throughout the remainder of the century, but there were significant shifts in emphasis. The monolithic concern about work and productivity of the early years slowly gave way to a concern about the distribution of the wealth arising from work and productivity. In addition, the nature of work itself was examined more closely—the conditions under which it took place, its possible satisfactions, and its effect on the lives and character of those dependent on it for support. A number of factors were influential in this more thorough attention to the phenomenon of work. Some were humanitarian, some practical, some political, but all resulted in a reconsideration and, in some instances, a reformulation of the work-wage formula and its relationship to the well-being, economic and spiritual, of men.

The shifting attention from production to distribution indicated the division between classical and neoclassical economics, between the early nineteenth-century economists under the influence of Adam Smith and those after John Stuart Mill. The conservative economist Sidgwick, writing in the last part of the century, remarked that the "desirable result" of political economy had changed from merely increasing national productivity to making "a given amount of wealth as useful as possible." The purpose became "to apportion the produce among the members of the community so that the greatest amount of utility or satisfaction may be derived from it."[8] Alfred Marshall, the most renowned economist at the end of the century, commented on the previous lack of concentration on the problem of distribution of wealth. "In earlier generations," he stated, "many statesmen, even some economists, neglected to make allowance for considerations of this class [distribution] . . . and their words or deeds seemed to imply a want of sympathy with the sufferings of the poor; though more often they were due simply to want of thought."[9]

The shift in theoretical emphasis was frequently greater than the changes in actual policy. Smith and, to an even greater extent, Bentham were aware of the limitations of distribution under laissez-faire. But their belief that productivity, of prime importance to the welfare of society, depended on the free flow of the market resulted in a reluctance to tamper with the distribution of wealth. The pessimistic school of Malthus and Ricardo, while entertaining the possibility of interference, could foresee only the direst consequences. The neoclassical economists' measurement of the wealth of the nation in terms of utility or satisfaction rather than of absolute productivity provided a new measure of value but did not of necessity result in changes in policy. Satisfaction, too, might be augmented by noninterference with the market economy, just as earlier theorists had argued in the case of productivity. Nor should it be assumed that the concentration on distribution resulted in the neglect of production. For most economists and statesmen optimum distribution required "making the proportion of produce to population a maximum." Proper distribution might in itself be seen as a means of increasing production, as Marshall clearly indicated when he criticized "the older economists" for taking "too little account of the fact that human faculties are as important a means of production as any other kind of capital."[10]

Whatever the rationale, the emphasis on distribution, with its utilitarian assumption that individual satisfactions were a primary goal and that increased satisfactions were inversely proportional to the amount of previous satisfaction, was influential in modifying earlier notions about the appropriate division of wealth. Of significance also was the growing belief that interference with the market distribution could not only take place but could actually have beneficial results for the total economy. The simple relationship of work and earnings no longer held, and reasons were found for providing income to individuals, even if only indirectly, outside the normal mechanisms of the market.

While the doctrine of work as the only basis for income was being modified, the view of work itself was also undergoing change. To the early classical economists and Utilitarians work was an unpleasant exercise that interfered with man's natural state of intertia or leisure. Wages were paid to offset man's reluctance to part with his freedom. The Utilitarians reinforced the compensations of work by increasing the pains of leisure through the workhouse test, indoor relief, and the principle of less eligibility.

The discommodity of work remained a tenet of the neoclassical school. It fulfilled the theoretical need of explaining the rate at which the wage earner was willing to accept employment where the exchange of satisfactions was the fundamental market unit. Despite this theoretical construct, the economists of the latter part of the century recognized that work was not wholly a source of dissatisfaction. Marshall, for example, skirted the problem of the unpleasantness of work by defining labor "as any exertion of mind or body undergone partly or wholly with a view to some good other than the pleasure derived directly from work."[11] In fact, Marshall recognized that "pleasure predominates over pain in a great part even of the work that is done for hire."[12] He also indicated that it was not so much work itself that was unsatisfying as the conditions under which it took place.[13] His belief that a man "out of work for some time" would be willing to work for nothing merely to enjoy the sense of work sharply contradicted the assumptions of mercantilist and classical economic thought.

While Marshall's more positive ideas about work may have reflected the changing times, they also revealed a new awareness of the psychological and social meaning of work. When Marshall questioned the very emphasis on work as the purpose of life, particularly for the lower classes, he removed himself even further from earlier political economists and social philosophers. While concentration on work may be valuable for the exceptional, he stated, "for ordinary people, for those who have no strong ambitions, whether of a lower or a higher kind, moderate income earned by moderate and fairly steady work offers the best opportunity for the growth of those habits of body, mind, and spirit in which alone there is true happiness."[14] This conflicted with much previous thinking, which accepted leisure for the elite but considered work the only proper function of "ordinary people." For Marshall and others of his generation the function of work became more complex than it was in societies that had been almost totally dependent on work for mere subsistence. Now, in addition to its other functions, work was seen as character-building exercise endowed with intrinsic ethical values.[15]

At the same time the orthodox economists were revising their views on work and distribution, more radical positions were being taken by dissident thinkers. Men such as Carlyle, Ruskin, Morris, and the Christian Socialists were shocked by the ravages of the industrial system. For them, work should provide a creative experience, and they suggested ways by which society might turn or return to a life founded on the satisfactions of artistry and skill. The trade union leadership and the Fabians, on the other hand, accepted the contemporary view of work, but tried to change its conditions and organization. They assumed the unpleasantness of work in an industrial system and hoped to mitigate its evils through more humanitarian conditions and through a more efficient and less exploitative system of management or ownership. John Stuart Mill, the Christian Socialists, and others, too, believed that cooperative forms of ownership would result in greater satisfactions for workers and less industrial conflict.

The efforts to reform the nature and conditions of work partially reflected changes within the working class itself. The rising standard of living, increasing education, the growing strength of the trade unions, and labor's political activity all distinguished the laboring population of the late Victorian era from the poor of Malthus' time. At the end of the century labor was no longer a surplus commodity, and it became more prized as the birth rate dropped off enough to cause concern about a decreasing labor supply. Then, too, the kind of working population that seemed adequate in the early years of the Industrial Revolution was no longer appropriate in the later years. By the second half of the century there was a growing realization that skilled workers rather than merely a large undifferentiated supply of labor was needed.

The possibility of developing a skilled working class conflicted with the labor and wage theories popular since Malthus and Ricardo. It was believed that a skilled laboring population based on a higher standard of living and higher wages would be constantly frustrated by the unrestricted growth of population and the limitations of the available wage fund. While classical economists from Adam Smith to John Stuart Mill were often critical of the smallness of labor's share, their pessimism about any change under the laws of the system, as they defined the system, generally left them in the position of rationalizers of the status quo. J. S. Mill, for example, though favoring the rights of workers to combine into unions and strike as a measure of freedom, saw little long-run gains from such action because the result would be merely the benefit of some workers to the disadvantage of others. Mill also considered ineffectual all efforts to influence workers' incomes through minimum wages, wage subsidies, guaranteed employment, and agricultural allotments because they would only be undermined by eventual increases in population.[16]

On the other hand, Alfred Marshall in the next generation of economists clearly favored a high-wage policy. He maintained that "any change in the distribution of wealth which gives more to the wage receivers and less to the capitalists is likely, other things being equal, to hasten the increase of material production, and . . . it will not perceptibly retard the storing-up of natural wealth."[17] Improving the ability of labor and increasing its incentives would raise the share of all. Investment in this generation would pay future dividends in the greater competence of its children. Marshall's marginal utility theory was criticized as merely another version of the iron law or subsistence theory of wages.[18] Marshall denied that interpretation, and his proposals indicated his support for more adequate wages. Despite his reluctance to interfere with the free market, he approved of a legal minimum wage.[19]

The doctrine of investment in people, which Marshall espoused, was an important contribution to modern economic security policy. Marshall's position was founded on the Utilitarian conception of satisfaction as the ultimate measure of wealth, the marginal utility postulate of the diminishing returns in satisfaction of additional units of consumption, the assumption that a redistribution of wealth in favor of the less fortunate would be neither self-defeating nor destructive to the economy, the belief that investment in people "might do more in the long-run to promote the growth of even material wealth than great additions to our stock of factories and steam-engines,"[20] and the acceptance of government's role of increasing income indirectly through such services as education, recreation, and public health and through more direct intervention in income distribution as well.

Marshall's approach was significant not only because he was the leading British economist of his period but also because his position was essentially conservative and rooted in the prevalent value system.[21] He was identified with the progress made under a laissez-faire society and rested his faith for the continued advance of society on the business acumen and personal character of the middle class. His support of programs for the working class was based on neither paternalism nor socialist concern about labor's appropriate share. He assumed the continuance of a fluid capitalist society in which working men would have the opportunity for increased contribution for the benefit of all. As he pointed out:

About three-fourths of the whole population of England belong to the wage-earning classes; and at all events when they are well fed, properly housed and educated, they have their fair share of that nervous strength which is the raw material of business ability.[22]

"There is no extravagance," he maintained, "more prejudicial to the growth of national wealth than that wasteful negligence which allows genius that happens to be born of lowly parentage to expend itself in lowly work."[23]

As might be expected, Marshall did not recognize poverty as the inevitable condition of the great mass of wage earners. His optimism was buoyed by the "steady progress of the working classes during the nineteenth century."[24] John Stuart Mill had not been nearly so sanguine. He belonged to the generation disillusioned by the effects of the Industrial Revolution but unable to see a way out. In his later years Mill himself questioned the fundamental soundness of the free-market economy and gave some consideration to socialism as a possible alternative.

Marshall, however, could see no reason why the problems of his period could not be solved under the present system. His more benign attitude as compared to Mill's was indicated by his treatment of poverty. By the middle of the nineteenth century there had already been some progress toward viewing poverty as a socially caused phenomenon. That this progress was slow is indicated by Schumpeter's comment that the Poor Law Report of 1909 "taught many an economist who stood in need of such a lesson that unemployment was at times very little influenced by factors under the workmen's control."[25] For Mill, the size of the laboring population was the key to their poverty, and he believed that at least part of the responsibility must be shared by those who sought gain from a large laboring population. Marshall, on the other hand, was more concerned about the effects of poverty than its causes. He did not feel that a low-wage system was essential to the economy of society or that it was necessary to reform the foundations of society to reduce poverty. He saw poverty as the cause rather than the result of "physical, mental and moral ill-health," and believed that the low-wage system and the consequent lack of financial reserve of workers that were identified with poverty could be corrected in an expanding free-enterprise society.[26] The liberal economists and politicians of Marshall's era, no longer obsessed with a rigid adherence to laissez-faire, saw no limit to the possibility of integrating social and economic justice into the contemporary competitive system.

The Nature of Society

After the 1830s there was a growing dissatisfaction with laissez-faire, and even its most faithful exponents rejected many of its tenets. It was less and less assumed that man was a consciously rational being whose acts of intelligent self-interest resulted in a society of natural harmony. The idea of rationality was not toally discarded, but the faith in a rational universe as the sum or totality of rationally motivated individuals no longer held sway.

There were those who preferred to rely on the rationality of individuals as the foundation of society even though they were skeptical of the ultimate rationality of society. For them, such a society was more acceptable than a possibly more rational society that dispensed with the freedom of individual action. Others, less impressed with man's rationality and less concerned with maintaining man's economic freedom, were willing to substitute a rationally organized society for what they conceived to be an irrational arrangement of presumably rational beings. The difference between the two positions suggests the dilemma of the Benthamites. To what extent should society rely for its harmony on mutual self-interest and to what extent should it rely on the artificial creation of mutuality? While Bentham and his followers certainly favored the harmony arising from self-interest, they also provided for the possibility of an externally determined harmony if individual self-interest did not conform to the good of society.

Although rationality, whether individual or social, remained the keystone for most, there were those who rejected it as the basis of individual and social action. Individual experience was considered primarily emotional, and the important elements of society were seen as emotional and spiritual rather than as logical and intellectual.

The stimulus for these new schools of socially oriented thought in the second part of the nineteenth century arose from the failure of laissez-faire to provide a sound basis for social organization. As already noted, the great problem of earlier rationalist and individualist philosophers was to discover the catalytic agent for social cohesion. Even when individual gain or satisfaction was supplemented or expanded to include ethical behavior, such as Adam Smith's "sympathy" or John Stuart Mill's interpretation of Utilitarianism, the orientation still remained individual rather than social. The social instinct appeared like an artificial grafting on self-interest.

During the latter half of the century the emphasis shifted noticeably toward approaching society as a social entity rather than as an aggregate of individuals. This development of interest in the social aspects of society may be traced to a number of sources. Disquiet with the sterility of earlier doctrines and the kinds of societies associated with them has already been mentioned. Theoretical contributions to the understanding and classifying of society had been made by Comte, who influenced John Stuart Mill, and others who saw the nature of society as an entity in its own right. The concept of social evolution, developed and popularized by Spencer, also drew attention to the social structure. In addition, Spencer had made sufficient references to biological organisms to encourage a simple organismic conception of society. Socialist thinking, both early utopian and later Marxist, had stressed the complex cooperative unity of society. Stemming from Ricardo's theory of rent, there was a growing recognition that the shares in the economic market could not be simply divided. Ricardo had interpreted value as a function of complex social and economic factors, and much later Henry George and others supported a tax on land as the return on the social contribution to the value of property. The Fabians extended George's notion of land to all types of property. All value arising from agriculture and industry was viewed as socially rather than privately created and should be treated as social rather than individual wealth.

Finally, the notion of an organic, integrated society was paralleled by the sense of national unity associated historically with nationalism. The spirit of nationalism was more sharply evidenced on the continent during the latter part of the century in the struggles of such nations as Germany and Italy for unification. Even in England, however, the long period of Tory control and empire building during the Victorian era marked the growth of national consciousness.

All these developments were in contrast to the ideologies of the preceding period. In demolishing mercantilist society, the ideal of the eighteenth and early nineteenth centuries was the free-moving relationship of the parts of society. If society was seen as a social machine, it was a social machine in which the individual units had a logic of their own that geared them to the smooth working of the whole. At most, society through government might provide the lubrication for the whole to run more smoothly, but there was no need to guide or plan the operation. Like the heavenly bodies of Newton's finite and contained universe, men, too, moved independently and freely in the course of their callings. In the latter part of the nineteenth century stress was laid upon the interdependence and interaction of social groups in an organically structured society.

The New Psychology

The new conceptions about the nature of society were paralleled by new ideas about the nature of man. Earlier pessimistic pictures of society drawn by such writers as Malthus reflected their view of man. Malthus' doubts, if not his convictions, about the continuing course of social events were based on his belief that lower-class man was ruled by passion and sinful desire. Even though he introduced the idea of "preventive check" into his later editions, there is little reason to believe that he placed great faith in rational and moral restraints overcoming the baser nature of the poor.

During the first part of the nineteenth century, under the influence of the Benthamites and their associationist psychology, the pendulum swung toward an environmentalist position. Man was plastic, easily molded through the appropriate association of his experiences with his fundamental drive to increase pleasure and avoid pain. Man's educability was the foundation of progress. Faith in education included broadly the influence of all constructive environmental changes. In abandoning earlier notions of man as inherently depraved, the associationists also abandoned any emphasis on the innate nature of man or the possibility of innate differences among men. Given the proper environment, all men had similar potential.

In the second half of the nineteenth century both theoretical speculation and empirical study focused on the innate elements of human behavior. John Stuart Mill criticized his father's failure to allow for differences in intellectual abilities due to "natural aptitude."[27] But Mill himself was still sufficiently under the influence of associationist psychology to consider the "greater part" of differences among "individuals, races, or sexes" as stemming from "differences in circumstances." The acceptance of "innate" and "indelible" factors in human nature was for him "one of the chief hindrances to the rational treatment of great social questions, and one of the greatest stumbling blocks to human improvement." He decried the tendency to emphasize innate behavior as "agreeable" to "conservative interests generally."[28]

Conflicts about the nature of mind had been based largely on logical and philosophical grounds. During the second half of the nineteenth century the experimental method began to invade psychology, and a series of empirical studies were undertaken that supported the notion of innate and hereditary differences. Galton and Pearson found major variations among the populations studied and hypothesized that such variations were essentially determined by heredity. Differences in innate ability, it was assumed, were reflected in the social class structure with the upper classes populated by the most able.

The doctrine of inherited characteristics received strong theoretical stimulus from the popular evolutionary beliefs of the period. The evolutionary point of view stressed variations founded upon hereditary differences. These variations reflected the differential adaptive capacities of individuals or groups to their environment. The struggle over nature versus nurture became a matter for scientific proof. Because of the complexity of the problem and its obvious social significance, as Mill had noted, the issue continued to be strongly connected with ideological positions. Views about the causes and consequences of intellectual and moral differences provided important rationales for positions on social and economic matters.

Psychological research on inherited characteristics had its greatest impact on the field of education. Research on intelligence and learning capacity was of immediate importance to the formulators of educational policy. The findings of Galton and others were used to confirm the established belief that the spread of education to the lower classes was impractical since it could not overcome their "evident" inferiority. As one contemporary authority stated in 1682:

There is little or nothing in the profession of an elementary schoolmaster, in this country to tempt a man having a respectable acquaintance with the elements of even humble learning to exchange the certainty of a respectable livelihood in a subordinate condition in trade or commerce, for the mean drudgery of instructing the rude children of the poor in an elementary school.[29]

Publicly sponsored secondary education made exceedingly slow progress during the Victorian era. The Royal Commission of 1894, considering the "best methods of establishing a well-organized system of secondary education," oriented its deliberations along class lines. "Secondary education," it concluded, "may be described as education conducted in view of the special life that has to be lived with the express purpose of forming a person to live in it."[30]

Ability and intelligence were viewed as exclusively innate characteristics well into the twentieth century in educational circles.[31] However, it was not the assumption of heredity alone but its association with particular classes in society that gave the doctrine of heredity its influence on social policy. As one supporter of the heredity school, who was a critic of its class implications, remarked:

The evidence presented by Galton is taken to imply that membership by birth in a distinctive group—intellectual, artistic, or noble—is *ipso facto* a warrant of inherited power, and conversely that membership in a class of lower social grade or in an inferior race can be assumed to mark a low calibre. The educational inference from such judgments readily follows: these families or classes, it is argued, merit special attention both in education and in other forms of nurture, so that they may render back to the community a measure of service proportionate to the high qualities with which they are endowed. Briefly it must be replied that there is no scientific evidence, in the records of any homogeneous community such as Great Britain presents, to warrant this social prejudice.[32]

Not until the act of 1902 did secondary education receive any real stimulus, and it was several decades before secondary education affected any large number of youngsters in Britain.[33]

Interest in heredity and the improvement of the race in England was stimulated by the founding of the Eugenics Society in 1907. The *Eugenics Review,* the journal of the Society, and the Eugenics Library in London have been influential in spreading knowledge about the field of human heredity. Galton was followed by such eminent scholars as Karl Pearson, R. A. Fisher, and L. S. Penrose.[34] Generally speaking, adherents of the doctrine of the innate inferiority of the lower classes deprecated any move aimed at improving their capacity or the spread of democracy.[35]

For others, however, the existence of a large group of the population in a state of poverty and misery could not be easily reconciled with their vision of social progress. The issue became even more salient as the trend toward democracy resulted in greater equality for the "inferior" elements of society. Earlier generations had kept nature and status in balance by reserving the dominant positions in society for the superior classes. But attempts in the later nineteenth century to emphasize social class differences, even when presumably supported by scientific findings on heredity, conflicted sharply with the trend toward social and economic equality.

Those who disregarded or disagreed with the inferences of class differences drawn from the evidence of psychological research received support from several sources. Studies of the poor at the end of the century by Booth and Rowntree emphasized the inadequate living conditions of the poor. Social critics like Shaw and the Webbs pointed up the gross injustice of the Victorian era. The limitations of the environment of the British lower classes made academic any question of grading opportunity to ability. For the reformers, the imbalance would have to be corrected before there could be any realistic concern about the basic distinction in the population. Whatever these latter differences were, they were far outweighed by the existing differences in standards of living.

The attack on rational self-interest as the single or most influential factor in human behavior also tended to make less significant the findings of a psychology that measured differences in rational capacities. On the social side, the effects of laissez-faire and the Industrial Revolution led to disillusionment with a society based on the rationally self-interested actions of its members. From the individual point of view, there had already been recognition that all individuals were not equally capable of making judgments in their own behalf, but there was also a growing belief that there was more to human behavior than the rational faculties. The Romantics with their antirationalistic bent were emphasizing the emotional content of behavior as its most important element. Even John Stuart Mill was critical of the underestimation of "feeling" in Utilitarian psychology. Mill commented on the later shift from overemphasis on rationality:

What we principally thought of, was to alter people's opinions; to make them believe according to evidence, and know what was their real interest, which when they once knew, they would, we thought, by the instrument of opinion, enforce a regard to it upon one another. . . . I do not believe that any one of the survivors of the Benthamites or Utilitarians of that day, now relies mainly upon it for the general amendment of human conduct.[36]

Finally, the new ideologies of the nineteenth century, Romanticism and socialism, were advocating the responsibility of society for the individual, and concern with the contribution of the individual became much less important, for the moment, than the social context that surrounded him and made possible an individually and socially satisfying contribution.

9

The Major Ideologies

Liberalism: The Society of Individual Rationality

DURING the Victorian period continued support for laissez-faire came from the inheritors of the old liberal creed of the classical economists and Utilitarians and from the followers of the new social evolutionary theories of Herbert Spencer. Spencer's social Darwinism supported the decaying faith in enlightened self-interest and natural harmony. After the middle of the nineteenth century the conflict between individual and social interest became apparent to even the most obdurate of the liberal school. In Spencer's theories, however, the frictions and disharmonies were made to serve a positive function; they were indigenous to the process of social evolution. Through the free play of the interacting forces in society, the most adapted, the most fit of individuals and institutions survived and the least capable were abandoned. Interference with this process of natural evolution was even more dangerous to the interests of society than interference with the natural law of the earlier advocates of laissez-faire. According to Herbert Spencer and Sir Henry Maine, the present competitive society represented an evolutionary advance over more primitive cooperative societies.

Despite the strong ideological support given laissez-faire by Spencer, he appears to have had little influence on practical social and economic policy. It may be that the dominant forces in British society found too little acceptable in the kind of world preferred by Spencer or that, as Mill advised Comte, the English were no longer willing to accept any full-blown social theories and were amenable only to an empirical or practical approach to social phenomena. The strongly individualistic doctrine of Spencer no longer fitted into the body of British liberal thinking, which, ever since John Stuart Mill, had turned away from a dogmatic adherence to the ideal of a contract society. Thus, W. Stanley Jevons, one of the pioneers of the marginal utility theory, objected to the social evolutionists' absolute "principle of freedom." "The principle of equal freedom," said Jevons, "is ... put forth as an all-extensive and sure guide in social matters," but for Jevons there was no "sure guiding light."[1] "We must consent to advance cautiously, step by step, feeling our way, adopting no foregone conclusions, trusting no single science, expecting no infallible guide."[2]

The abandonment of a strict liberal policy incensed Spencer. As he rightly noted, the chasm between the differing schools of social and economic thought had greatly narrowed in his generation, and the advocates of "compulsory cooperation" were to be found in all camps. Thus the liberals at the close of the nineteenth century differed only relatively from their opponents.[3] Perhaps the major contribution of social Darwinism to Victorian liberalism was its faith in progress through the perpetual compromise of change with continuity.[4]

The followers of the liberal tradition, like their socialist critics, were concerned with the problem of distribution of wealth. Gross inequalities leading to extreme poverty for some and luxury for others were inexcusable.[5] The liberal political economist abhorred the waste caused by the failure to make maximum use of the nation's resources, human and material. Increased efficiency resulting in greater national wealth would result in more income for all. The belief of Malthus and Ricardo that growth of productivity would eventually be balanced by growth of population and result in no ultimate gain for the lower classes had been almost completely dropped. J. S. Mill, brought up on Malthusian and Ricardian economics, relinquished the wage-fund theory toward the end of his life. Even Fawcett, Marshall's predecessor at Cambridge and a staunch advocate of Malthusian moral and economic principles, assumed that increased national wealth would be reflected in an improved standard of living for the working classes.[6] Marshall and Jevons, a generation after

Fawcett, had faith that the "natural forces of evolution" were working to bring about that change, which Fawcett had been disappointed not to observe.

In favoring both a more equitable distribution of wealth and an increasing national product, liberal and socialist thinkers were in agreement. They agreed, too, on the virtues of a cooperative society. From J. S. Mill on, the classical economists had been impressed with the idea of a society in which social cooperation would replace individual competitiveness. In the eyes of liberals, however, the achievement of such a goal seemed utopian. Whether it could ever be accomplished depended on man's capacity to shift from selfish to social behavior. Mill and Fawcett considered the possibility of combining enlightened self-interest with mutual interest in cooperative schemes between capital and labor. The general opinion, however, was that "energetic cooperation in unselfish work for the public good" would require vast changes in human nature. In this the liberal economists went along with Spencer, who stated that the goal of cooperation would be achieved only when through the lengthy process of evolution there would arise "the ultimate man . . . whose private requirements coincide with public ones." For even Spencer viewed the final goal as one of "greater mutual dependence" without, of course, trespassing on the rights of individuality.[7]

For the liberal, cooperation, though earnestly desired, was still ephemeral, while the reality of competition was by no means wholly to be decried. After all, in the opinion of liberals, competition was responsibile for the tremendous advances during the nineteenth century. If there was any fault, it was not with the principle of competition so much as with the ways in which it had taken place. In fact, it was only through the harnessing of the competitive system that the gains of the past would be maintained, progress assured, and the possibility of future cooperation realized.

The improvement of society, in liberal opinion, was dependent on the improvement of its individual members. Evolutionary thinking provided great faith in the improvement of man. Even the conservative Fawcett wrote:

It would be presumptuous to place any definite limits to the possible development of man as a moral and responsible being. . . . The time may come when no one will show any anxiety to escape his due share of labour, and when all will recognize the grave responsibility incurred in not making adequate provision for those who are dependent upon them. If man should ever obtain this ideal social state, poverty will be exterminated, many of the most perplexing economic problems will have solved themselves, and many questions which are now of the greatest practical importance will cease to possess any but speculative interest.[8]

The contemporary competitive society was the best environment to assure the development of the characteristics essential for the progress of man and society.

The liberal point of view continued to emphasize the essentially rational nature of man. As Marshall stated, "The human will, guided by careful thought, can so modify circumstances as largely to modify character."[9] Through the growth and application of man's rational faculties in a competitive society would come the better society. Sidgwick well summarized this position:

If our orthodox economists have not gone the length of maintaining that distribution by free competition is perfectly *just,* as proportioning reward to service, they have still generally maintained it to be practically the best mode of dividing the produce of the organized labour of human beings; they have held that through the stimulus it gives to exertion, the self-reliance and forethought that it fosters, the free play of intellect that it allows, it must produce more happiness on the whole than any other system, in spite of the waste of the material means of happiness caused by the luxurious expenditure of the rich.[10]

The main difference between the earlier and later orthodox economists in the nineteenth century was the latter's willingness to tolerate state intervention for the purpose of increasing the total wealth and making more "just" the distribution of wealth. This intervention was not to substitute for, or even to complement, the free economy, but rather to make more effective the workings of the competitive system. The fundamental element of the system remained the "exertion, the self-reliance and forethought" of the participants, and the reforms supported by the liberals would permit the greatest flowering of the individual potential. There would be no direct redistribution of wealth, but opportunity would be made more equal so that the underprivileged could compete more adequately. Through improving the capacity of the poor, they would be able to increase their share of the wealth as well as increase the total social wealth.

The reforms of the later nineteenth-century liberals were not bound by doctrinaire notions of private property, individual rights, and state intervention, as were their predecessors. Although they were governed by no absolute laws, they were inclined to be conservative for fear of upsetting an essentially sound system. As Marshall explained:

It may be well therefore to note that the tendency of careful economic study is to base the rights of private property not on any abstract principle, but on the observation that in the past they have been inseparable from solid progress; and that therefore it is the part of responsible men to proceed cautiously and tentatively in abrogating or modifying even such rights as may seem to be inappropriate to the ideal conditions of social life.

By the 1880s, Jevons, more rash than Marshall, pointed out "the difficulty of defining what is . . . own property" and commented favorably on the extent to which "this absolute right has been invaded in every conceivable way."[12] The issues of "special urgency" posed by Marshall illustrated that flexibility of late nineteenth-century liberal thinking. Such traditional tenets as "economic freedom," the "institutions of property," "increasing national wealth," "justice," "the energies of the leaders of progress," and "the existing forms of division of labour" were balanced against "more equal distribution of wealth," "work of a more elevating character," "cooperative management of business," "collective ownership," and "government intervention."[13] "The question simply is," Jevons stated, "by what least sacrifice to approximate to a sounder state of things."[14]

The "least sacrifice" was continued faith in the fundamental principles of the liberal society—economic freedom, individual initiative, and private property modified to guarantee some degree of social justice. Without interfering with private ownership and control, the wealth arising from private enterprise should be so distributed that many members of society would receive larger benefits than would normally be their share if they depended entirely on their compensation in the economic market. Standards for conditions and wages of work and trade union bargaining were acceptable, and even state or collective provision of such strategic services as health, education, and recreation could be tolerated.

On the issue of social interference with individual liberty, liberal thought at the end of the nineteenth century deviated widely from Herbert Spencer's position. The "first principle" of Spencer's philosophy was freedom of individual action, and the only limit to freedom was the possibility of all exercising similar liberties. Spencer thought the problem of his society was guarding the individual against intervention by the state. He reminded liberalism that its function in the past was opposing the power of kings and concluded that "the function of true liberalism in the future will be that of putting a limit to the powers of Parliament."

In principle there was much agreement with Spencer's point of view, but principle was of limited importance to a generation oriented to meeting their problems empirically. For example, Sidgwick, following Mill's dictum, said:

The sole end for which mankind are warranted, individually or collectively in interfering with the liberty of action of any of their number, is self-protection. . . . The only purpose for which power can be rightfully exercised over any member of a civilized community, against his will, is to prevent harm to others. His own good, either physical or moral, is not a sufficient warrant.[15]

However, Sidgwick qualified this position:

I do not mean to imply that all governmental interference which is individually "paternal" ought therefore to be rejected without further inquiry. I consider that so uncompromising an adhesion to the principle "that men are the best guardians of their own welfare" is not rationally justified by the evidence on which the principle rests. I regard this principle as a rough induction from our ordinary experience of human life; as supported on an empirical basis sufficiently strong and wide to throw the *onus probandi* heavily on those who advocate any deviation from it, but in no way proved to be an even approximately universal truth. Hence, if strong empirical grounds are brought forward for admitting a particular exception to this principle . . . it would, I think, be unreasonable to allow these practices to go on without interference, merely on account of the established general presumption in favor of *laissez faire*.[16]

In weighing the possible circumstances for interference, Sidgwick did not limit himself to the positive promotion of the interests of any particular body of the citizenry but found reasons to support "socialistic" measures involving the redistribution of wealth. The "justification" for such action, in his opinion, occurred only when it was a "supplementary and subordinate element in a system mainly individualistic."[17] Sidgwick decided that it was the interest of the "community at large—as distinct from that of the individuals primarily concerned" that justified intervention for the purpose of redistribution. As a result of his analysis, Sidgwick concluded that he favored "at least a removal of the extreme unequalities, found in the present distribution of wealth and leisure . . . if it could be brought about without any material repression of the free development of individual energy and enterprise, which the individualistic system aims at securing."[18]

Sidgwick's argument was typical of the nineteenth-century liberal. While devoted to individualism in the abstract, he found so many exceptions in practice that it was often difficult to distinguish the true nature of liberalism. Recognition of the organic nature of society led to the conclusion that interference which at first glance might seem to be for the benefit of some might really be for the benefit of all. Furthermore, interference, whatever its form, might actually strengthen the individualist system by remedying those weaknesses that threatened the continuance of the liberal society.

T. H. Green, the most influential liberal philosopher of the late nineteenth century, provided a bridge between the atomism of earlier laissez-faire thinking and the later liberal support of state intervention. Green's solution was in the identification of individual and social morality. Freedom became not the ability to do as one pleases, but the capacity to choose the good identified with the common good. Individual and social good were indistinguishable, but true morality and the good society existed only in an atmosphere of moral freedom for the individual. Authority as a restrictive force destroyed individuality, but authority as a liberating force permitted the full realization of morally autonomous individuals.

Like Bernard Bosanquet and F. H. Bradley, Green conceived of citizenship as incorporating the rational, the moral, and the social and symbolizing the fulfillment of the highest level of individual conduct. Morality was self-realization through commitment to society, and rational behavior was the consequence of recognizing the underlying social or harmonious core of all human activity. The concept of the inseparability of man and society, while not always clearly expounded, integrated the rational and the romantic, the individual and the social into an organic view of the state.[19]

Green's approach gave much support to the idea of social reform. "Every injury to the health of the individual is so far as it goes," he stated, "a public injury. It is an impediment to the general freedom; so much deduction from our power as members of society, to make the best of ourselves."[20] That position led Green to favor a broad range of measures to strengthen the independence of the lower classes. Where intervention had been seen as threatening, it could now be viewed as releasing the individuality and independence of the lower classes. Even Spencerian doctrine was revised by the popular Benjamin Kidd at the end of the nineteenth century to favor social legislation. In order to thwart socialism and encourage the most effective private enterprise, the masses must be strengthened by social legislation to engage in the competitive struggle. Social legislation would be the bulwark of the competitive system.[21]

However far liberalism might go in embracing the idea of social intervention, there always remained a basic skepticism about the ability of government as the instrument of intervention to carry out its responsibilities effectively. All liberals would not agree with Spencer that progress could come only through the natural process of evolution and that the history of social intervention was bungling failure. Society, in Spencer's opinion, was not sufficiently knowledgeable about the laws of social change to participate effectively in its own reform. Although others shared his general concern for the sensitively balanced mechanism that might be thrown abruptly off the track if amateurs started tinkering with the works, they did not have Spencer's fanaticism about individual liberty when they preached caution in interfering with the system they felt was still the best available.

Differences among liberals and between liberals and other groups often narrowed to the amount of social intervention acceptable. Liberal doctrine tolerated intervention only as a means to the ultimate end of a society of rationally motivated individuals participating in a laissez-faire economy. In the opinion of some liberals, any compromise with the principle of unfettered individual action must have dire consequences. Fawcett was convinced that those who were aided by government would be lulled into apathy, and those who were not would see little advantage in being self-sustaining if society contributed to the welfare of others. The provident would be penalized for the benefit of the improvident, and the latter would not be helped thereby to independence. It was rare that those who opposed intervention did not refer to the alleged pauperizing effects of the early nineteenth-century Speenhamland policy.

On the other hand, for many liberals the possibility of the success of the liberal society depended on the underprivileged attaining the qualities necessary for functioning effectively in such a society. All must be given the opportunity to make the best use of their talents. Social and economic reforms would produce a generation of independent and thrifty workers, some of whom might even attain the position of the superior classes. Where the desire for independence was lacking, it could be developed, and the best way was to make possible a successful experience of self-reliant employment.

Liberalism in the Victorian era was strongly identified with the spirit of humanitarianism. There was a sympathy for the weak and even an antagonism for the strong who took advantage of the underprivileged. But again there were difficulties in the implementation of the feeling. Fawcett maintained that publicly supported education and foster care for children might seem commendable at first glance, but they were inherently dangerous. Relieving the parent of his responsibility was more threatening than whatever ills might befall the child through lack of education. Marshall, on the other hand, clearly supported measures for redistribution on the Utilitarian grounds that "a pound's worth of satisfaction to an ordinary poor man is a much greater thing than a pound's worth of satisfaction to an ordinary rich man."[22]

Diversity among its followers and its internal contradictions were indigenous to liberalism in the Victorian era. It was a fluid compromise sensitive to many influences but with the goal of enhancing the possibilities of individual and independent action. It had moved, however, a long way from its predecessors, as the conditions included by Bagehot in describing the Victorian ideal so clearly indicated:

That when no blinding passions prevent individuals from discerning what is their greatest pecuniary interest; when their pecuniary interest coincides with that of the nation at large; and when also the pecuniary interest of the nation is coincident with the highest interests and highest duties—the welfare of the nation will be better promoted by leaving every man to the exercise of his own unfettered discretion, than by laying down a general rule for the observance of all.[23]

Earlier thinkers had no doubts about the "natural" relationship of the individual and the society and saw no need for provisional statements about their congruence.

Socialism: The Society of Collective Rationality

In the late nineteenth century the distinction between the followers of the liberal tradition and the advocates of a planned society was neither sharp nor absolute. In practical policies and even in theoretical heritage there was often more agreement than difference. The absence of orthodoxy and the wide range of views among British socialists often resulted in closer ties with liberals than with their socialist colleagues.

The program of the Liberal Radicals of the 1880s closely resembled the platform of the socialist groups, and important segments of the socialist movement in the trade unions and the Independent Labour Party were more strongly identified with liberal reformism than socialist change. Joseph Chamberlain's program for the Liberal Party incorporated the ideas of Henry George and the socialists and differed little, if at all, from the reforms supported by most labor and socialist leaders. The recognition of most socialists of the difference between the practicable and the ideal made for much similarity in the immediate proposals of the less orthodox liberals and the evolutionary socialists. In such matters as the payment of high taxes by the wealthy, free education, improved housing, social services, and Parliamentary reform, there was general agreement.[24] The failure of Joseph Chamberlain to win over the Liberal Party to his reform program sharpened the line between liberal and socialist policies toward the end of the century. Throughout the last decades of the nineteenth century, however, Liberal-Labour cooperation on the local level was extensive, particularly in London, where Fabian leadership permeated the combined Progressive Party.[25]

After the debacle of Chartism in the 1840s the trade union movement turned to more conservative goals. The trade unions representing the more skilled and better-compensated trades accommodated themselves to the dominant liberal philosophy. They attempted to improve the standards of their own trades through agreement with employers rather than by reliance on any thoroughgoing reforms affecting the working class as a whole. As each new wave of workers was organized, they, in turn, concentrated on consolidating their own gains in the employment market. The more successful of the working class accepted the tenets of liberalism strongly buttressed by Methodism. Self-reliance, reward for virtue, and fear of the pauperizing effects of relief were widely held values. The working class was emulating middle-class standards. The Majority Report of the Poor Law Commission of 1909 noted with approval that the "improved position" of the working class was related to efforts "to further strengthen their independence by a variety of forms of thrift." Between 1854 and 1906 savings depositors increased from 1,300,000 to 12,100,000. Membership in friendly and benefit societies was 14,600,000 in 1905. Trade union membership, which frequently also provided for insurance benefits, rose to 2,100,000 by 1906.[26] In general, the principle of self-provision spread to large segments of the population.

The unsettled economic conditions of the last decades of the nineteenth century and the failure of the Liberals to support the reforms desired by labor resulted in a disillusionment with liberalism and a revival of labor's enthusiasm for socialism. The form of socialism popular with British workers was not Marxist or revolutionary but reformist. It was an emotional and ethical reaction to the suffering and injustice of capitalist society. Political power was sought to rectify those conditions of society that caused human suffering and prevented full achievement of a decent standard of living and happiness. While the slogans of the new socialism did not differ markedly from those of the radical Liberals, there was a much stronger emphasis on collective action. The better society was not to be achieved through a more socially oriented system of individual enterprise but through a socially planned and organized system of collective bodies.

The emotional conviction of those identified with ethical, cooperative collectivism was paralleled by the rationalism of the rising Fabian socialists. Though concerned with social justice, the Fabians were primarily reacting against the waste, inefficiency, and irrationality of contemporary society. The significance of the Fabians for welfare policy was great not only because of the personal involvement of the leaders but because welfare reform was an essential part of the Fabian concept of a rational society. The Fabians drew much from the neoclassical economists and liberal reformers. They were not Marxists but, like other reformers of the period, were empiricists rather than doctrinaire followers of any school of thought. They incorporated much of the spirit of the earlier Philosophical Radicals as well as John Stuart Mill's refinements of classical economics and Utilitarianism. Most congenial to the Fabians were the Utilitarian impatience with tradition and their emphasis on research, administrative planning, expertise and efficiency, social equality, and social wealth. The Utilitarian emphasis on individualism and laissez-faire were not found, however, in Fabianism.

No figure bore so close a resemblance to the Webbs, as Professor Tawney has remarked, as the early nineteenth-century Benthamite reformer Edwin Chadwick.[27] Chadwick's interest in social planning and the extension of the public services and his intolerance of waste were similar to the Fabians'. The Webbs, like Chadwick, planned for social wholes rather than individual differences. They concentrated on creating a rationally organized society rather than on dealing with the subtle and unique elements of individuality; and, as Margaret Cole has observed, the Webbs were insufficiently aware of and "underrated the powers of irrational emotion."[28] Like the Utilitarians, they concentrated on the larger view, and Finer's sketch of Chadwick might be applied equally to many of the Fabian leadership, particularly the Webbs:

Chadwick was instantly fired by any and every feature that caused unnecessary suffering, disease, and economic waste, and equally enthusiastic for all suggestions that promised to increase efficiency, wealth, and well-being. If it is true that he thought in wholesale and not of individual, it is none the less true that it was of others that he thought. One must picture him not as a humorless drudge but as an ardent crusader in other people's causes, moving ruthlessly and fanatically to his own preconception of what he thought was good for them.[29]

The socialism of the Fabians stemmed from their view of society as a social organism rather than from any doctrine of the right of labor to enjoy the products of its own effort, so fundamental to Marxist socialism. The Fabians were shocked by the injustice as well as by the irrationality of an economic system that caused some members of society to live constantly at marginal or submarginal levels while others enjoyed wealth toward which they had made little contribution. The Fabian position involved not so much the restoration to the underprivileged or the "exploited" of their due, as the command of the general wealth for the common good. This would naturally result in some redistribution of wealth as a "national minimum standard of civilized life" was established and as the unearned social surplus was withdrawn from the idle classes and placed at the disposal of society.

The national minimum was connected more with the Fabian desire for rational social planning and efficiency than with any guarantee of individual rights.[30] The Webbs rigorously condemned parasitic industries that impoverished their own labor supply and were consequently subsidized by the resources of society as a whole. The object of the national minimum emphasized by the Webbs was "to secure the community against the evils of industrial parasitism."[31] No industry was to be "carried on under conditions detrimental to the public welfare."[32] The national minimum would keep workers "in a state of efficiency as producers and citizens."[33] It would be a standard "determined by practical inquiry as to the cost of the food, clothing, and shelter physiologically necessary, according to national habit and custom, to prevent bodily deterioration."[34] The establishment of the national minimum was a practical goal related to effective social contribution, not to individual satisfaction.

For the Fabians, collective ownership was neither a fundamental principle nor an end in itself. Collective ownership was the means by which society as a whole received its rightful share and controlled the use of economic and social resources in its own interests. Ricardo's concept of unearned increment in rent was expanded to all types of ownership, and the role of government was to collect society's rent from agricultural and industrial enterprise for the good of the whole.

The view of society as an organic whole was among the earliest and most strongly held positions of the Fabians. The "social organism" was more than a mere collection of the parts of which it was composed. It was independent of and more important than its units, which were the product of the organized social system. Sidney Webb formulated the Fabian concept of social organism in 1889.

A society is something more than an aggregate of so many individual units . . . it possesses existence distinguishable from those of its components. A perfect city became recognized as something more than any number of good citizens—something to be tried by other tests, and weighed in other balances than the individual man. The community must necessarily aim, consciously or not, at its continuance as a community: its life transcends that of any of its members; and the interests of the individual unit must often clash with those of the whole. Though the social organism has itself evolved from the union of individual men, the individual is now created by the social organism of which he forms a part: his life is born of the larger life; his attributes are moulded by the social pressure; his activities, inextricably interwoven with others, belong to the activity of the whole. Without the continuance and sound health of the social organism, no man can now live or thrive; and its persistence is accordingly his paramount end. . . . We know now that in natural selection at the stage of development where the existence of civilized mankind is at stake, the units selected from are not individuals, but societies. . . .

If we desire to hand onto the afterworld our direct influence, and not merely the memory of our excellence, we must take even more care to improve the social organism of which we form part, than to perfect our own individual developments. Or rather, the perfect and fitting development of each individual is not necessarily the utmost and highest cultivation of his own personality, but the filling, in the best possible way, of his humble function in the great social machine. We must abandon the self-conceit of imagining that we are independent units, and bend our jealous minds, absorbed in their own cultivation, to this subjection to the higher end, the Common Weal. . . .

This new scientific conception of the Social Organism has put completely out of countenance the cherished principles of the Political Economist and the Philosophic Radical. We left them sailing gaily into Anarchy on the stream of *laissez-faire*. Since then the tide has turned. The publication of John Stuart Mill's *Political Economy* in 1848 marks conveniently the boundary of the old individualist Economics.[35]

In later years both Bernard Shaw and Sidney Webb suggested that perhaps too little attention had been given to "human volition" as a force in social development.[36] The Fabians were not entirely indifferent to the question of individual rationality and morality, but, in contrast to most other contemporary groups, they viewed individual behavior as a function of the social system. A cooperative social system combined with education would identify the individual with social purpose and morality. The competitive society, in the opinion of the Fabians, stunted both individual and social growth. The Fabians were sensitive to their "alleged indifference to character"[37] and frequently referred to the ultimate goal of the improvement of individual intellect and character. Since they emphasized the determining role of social conditions, however, the main task for them was the social reforms that would make possible the flowering of individual capacities. As the Webbs maintained:

Anyone conversant with the life-histories of families below the "Poverty Line" learns to recognize a sort of moral malaria which undermines the spiritual vitality of those subjected to its baleful influence and . . . gradually submerges the mass of each generation, as it grows up, in coarseness and bestiality, apathy and cynical skepticism of every kind.[38]

Thus, the Fabians in general concentrated on social rather than individual change. They viewed social problems and social reform as dependent on a great number of factors and were critical of those who accepted single causes and advocated single solutions. The orientation of the Fabians toward scientific study and their impersonal attitude on social issues made them more ready to agree with the findings of Galton and Pearson on innate differences. They disagreed with the social Darwinists, however, about the practical consequences. While the social Darwinists concluded that the less interference the better the chance for an improved society, the Fabians showed no faith in the process of natural selection and advocated maximum intervention. It was not out of sentimentality that the Fabians objected to the workings of natural evolution, for, as one Fabian wrote, "The real danger of Collectivism, indeed, is not that it would take the form of charity that fosters a degraded class, but that it would be as ruthless as Plato in the direction of 'social surgery.' "[39]

Although the Fabians identified the efficiency of society with the encouragement of its productive elements and the elimination of the unfit, they denied that the struggle for existence in a competitive society resulted in this end. The individual was not affected by his biological inheritance alone. He was conditioned as well by his social inheritance, which, although transmitted differently, was equally effective in determining the individual's potential. According to the Fabians, the social environment limited modes of adaptation and represented, for practical purposes, the inheritance of acquired characteristics.

In addition to their objection to the social Darwinist conception of the "natural," an objection shared by others, the Fabians had their own views about the improvement of the race. For them, the laissez-faire of the social Darwinists would lower rather than raise standards. Like the social Darwinists, they were critical of the encouragement given by private philanthropy to the least effective members of society, but they accepted as inevitable this counterselective process. Private charity would always choose the weakest as the object of its aid. The poor law, too, encouraged the unfit to have children by providing special benefits such as maternity care. The more wealthy responded to their higher standard of living by limiting the size of their families. For all these reasons, the Fabians thought that social intervention was necessary. They advocated a policy of reducing the burden of children on the lower-middle and artisan classes and of segregating the clearly unfit to prevent their having children.[40]

Despite their awareness of the threat of the unfit to the rational, efficient society, the major attention of the Fabians was given to the reform of social institutions. Social problems must be viewed primarily in a social, not an individual, context. In considering proposals for alleviating unemployment, for example, the Minority Report of the Poor Law Commission, which represented the Webbs' point of view, stated:

We have deliberately subordinated the question of personal character, because in our view . . . it does not seem to us to be of significance with regard to the existence or the amount of Unemployment. . . . But speaking broadly, employers take on the labour they have occasion for, and no more; and the aggregate amount of their wages bill from week to week does not depend on the habits of the workmen.[41]

At another point, the Report concluded:

In short, it is just because the bulk of the Unemployed are, like other men, full of faults and shortcomings, that is of such vital importance to the community to put an end to the incalculable waste, misery and deterioration that Unemployment at present causes.[42]

The Fabians shared their era's general faith in progress. Progress, for them, was not a natural function of the free interchange of the individual members of society. Progress was rather a social venture in which cooperative action provided the opportunity for individual fulfillment. The goals of the planners became synonymous with progress. While the classical economists were studying the existing system as a model of progress, the socialist planners were busy defining progress and the mechanisms for its achievement. The goals of the planners were gradually absorbed into the general societal notion of progress and became important measures of advance, whether society was dominated by individualist or collectivist ideologies. The Fabian assumption that "important organic changes" in society could only be "democratic," "gradual . . . causing no dislocation," "constitutional and peaceful," and viewed as moral actions by the citizenry set the pace for social reform.[43]

Even in the famous poor law dispute of the first decade of the twentieth century, the recommendations of the Webbs and their Minority colleagues were not so strikingly radical or sharply contradictory of the Majority Report as the Webbs and their followers maintained.[44] In such specific measures as their opposition to the social insurances, they were even more conservative than the Majority Commissioners. Beveridge has commented that the differences between the Charity Organisation Society (COS) and the Socialists were more nominal than real. "At about the time of this report [Poor Law Report of 1909], I used to say that C.O.S. and SOC (ialist) were only different ways of spelling the same thing."[45]

There was, however, one major and fundamental difference between the Webbs and their socialist colleagues and the supporters of the Majority plan. The Webbs did not see the poor law reform entirely in terms of the immediate situation. They concentrated on laying the foundation for a general system of social services that would provide healthful living for all members of the community, whether or not economically dependent. In this respect Fabian influence immeasurably broadened the welfare responsibilities of the state beyond what was at that time recognized. Thus, principles of governmental social responsibility and the state's role were established that have been continuous guidelines for the development of British welfare policy.

The Minority proposals also reflected the Fabian desire for a planned and rationally efficient society. Despite their criticisms of the compulsory aspects of the Majority plan, the Webbs' recommendations provided for a much more considerable intervention in what were ordinarily defined as the private aspects of individual and family life. Because of their emphasis on the social contribution of the citizenry, there is little that society should not concern itself with, in their opinion. All aspects of human behavior come under the guidance of the state. While the end was a cooperative society of responsible individuals, the means was a society of highly regulated action for social purposes.

Any form of socialism would be immoral if it denied the necessity of individual responsibility. It may also be urged that the compulsory elevation by municipal and state activity of the most degraded classes is a necessary preliminary to their further elevation by individual effort and voluntary association.[46]

Although as middle-class reformers the Fabians were particularly distrustful of the morality and habits of the lower classes, they were not inspired with a general confidence in human nature, and their proposals indicate society's need to enforce its demands on primarily self-interested individuals.[47]

Romanticism: The Society of Collective Stability

The Romantic ideology, sometimes allied with liberalism, sometimes with socialism, had a significant role in British social reform during the second part of the nineteenth century. To a greater or lesser degree all movements toward social change came under the Romantic influence. The liberalism of Lord Shaftesbury, the conservatism of Disraeli, and the socialism of William Morris all bear witness to the influence of Romantic thought. More specifically, two major social welfare developments—the growth of charity organization and the settlements—owed much of their philosophy to Romantic ideologies. As the forerunners of modern social work practice, they reflected the social philosophies of an important segment of Victorian reformers. The principal issues of Romantic thought as represented in these organizations are thus significant for the growth of welfare policy.

The breadth of the Romantic influence on social policy may be illustrated by the names of a few of the prominent figures and movements most closely connected with the development of the Romantic ideology. Among poets, Coleridge and Southey were forerunners. Among writers and reformers, Carlyle and Ruskin were particularly outspoken and influential. Leaders of organized movements were Maurice, Ludlow, and Kingsley in Christian socialism; Cardinal Newman in the Oxford movement; Disraeli in Young England; Arnold Toynbee in the university settlements; and William Morris in the Socialist League. However, the Romantic movement was so much a part of the spirit of the nineteenth century that few writers or reformers were not to some extent within its ranks. Dickens, Wordsworth, Byron, Scott, Shelley, Tennyson, to name but a few, were among the host of Romantic figures of the century. Even John Stuart Mill, heir to the leadership of rationalism and utilitarianism so opposed by the Romantics, was swayed by his contacts with English and continental Romantics.

Romanticism was a reaction against the emphasis on materialism, rationalism, and self-interest that had become increasingly dominant in British life since the end of the eighteenth century. More specifically, the attack on these values was linked, by the middle of the nineteenth century, with the reaction against the social and economic order associated with the triumph of the Industrial Revolution. The Victorian era was marked in the eyes of its critics by the corruption of significant human values. The individual and society had been perverted by concern with selfish economic gain. Individual satisfactions and social good had not proved to be congruent, as the laissez-faire political economists had maintained. Instead there were gross disparities between the sensual luxury of the rich and the degrading poverty of the poor. The gulf between them was continually widening, and the increasing wealth of the country was reflected neither in the standard of living of the majority nor in the cultural level of the wealthy. Antagonism between the classes had grown, and there was much concern that the increasing political and economic power of the lower classes would be used to overthrow abruptly the whole contemporary order. If the stability of society was to continue, the lower classes must be educated to use their new powers wisely and safely, and the structure of society must be strengthened against the disintegration of individual and class relationships.

The Romantics sought to replace the emphasis on rational self-interest with recognition of social obligations and responsibilities. However, this goal was not to be accomplished by dissolving the individual into the group or by giving group interests priority over individual interests. Rather, a fundamental tenet was the expansion or increase of the individual's own sense of self. Through concentration on the whole man, rather than merely the economic or rational man, the individual's own limits would be expanded to social fulfillment. As William Temple, later Archbishop of Canterbury, stated, Wesley and the earlier evangelical revival had emphasized the "impulse to personal religion," and the Oxford movement of the nineteenth century had "supplemented" this by its "insistence on the essentially social or corporate nature of historic Christianity."[48] The very concern with the "historic," traditional, or developmental aspect of society was in itself a facet of Romantic thinking. Not only was man linked to his contemporaries, but society had roots in the cultural heritage of his past. This contrasted with Benthamite rationalism, which rejected the influence of the genesis of society and recognized as reality only the mechanical ordering of the present.

The wholeness of the individual, in the Romantic view, was a spiritual wholeness. In its fullest expression, it was individual integrity based on the emotional, the intuitive, and the spontaneous. Spitual, moral, and esthetic values and interests were to be substituted for the rational and materialistic. Society itself, as the eminent Victorian philosopher T. H. Green enunciated, was founded upon faith. The spiritual identification of the individual with the group was substituted for the atomistic contract of self-interest.

For many Romantics this conjunction of the individual and the social often led to the idealization of earlier status societies when the interpersonal strands of duties and obligations were closely intertwined. Thus the charge of conservatism, reaction, and paternalism has frequently been leveled at the Romantic reformers because of their direct or indirect patterning of goals on feudal society. Mill, for example, found the Romantic picture of society "seductive": "As the idea is essentially repulsive of a society only held together by the relations and feelings arising out of pecuniary interests, so there is something naturally attractive in a form of society abounding in strong personal attachments and disinterested self-devotion."[49] But Mill rejected the notion of a paternalistic society based on the dependency of the lower classes on their superiors. He pointed out that the power of superior groups had always been used for their own benefit and concluded:

This, at least, seems to me undeniable, that long before the superior classes could be sufficiently improved to govern in the tutelary manner supposed, the inferior classes would be too much improved to be so governed.[50]

Mill's objection to the Romantic ideal of interdependence was on two grounds that were not, on the whole, within the stream of Romantic thought. First, Mill's acceptance of individual liberty and democracy conflicted with any system in which freedom and equality were to be subjected to the domination, whether physical or moral, of superior classes. Second, Mill did not see the possibility of wiping out class interests and differences through the assertion of a nebulous ideal of social cohesion. "The working classes," he maintained, "have taken their interest into their own hands, and are perpetually showing that they think that the interests of their employers are not identical with their own, but opposite to them."[51]

On both counts the general trend of Romantic thought differed. Romantic allegiance to individual liberty and equality was strongly tempered by a belief in the rightful leadership of the more successful groups in society, whether the landed aristocracy of Disraeli's Tory socialism or the merchant and industrial classes represented by other Victorian social reformers. Further, in their rejection of the morality of individual self-interest the Romantic reformers behaved as if class interests would vanish in a society of benevolence and spiritual cohesion. In this they differed from Mill and the liberal reformers, on the one hand, and from the socialists or supporters of collective rationality, on the other. For while both of these schools of thought emphasized progress toward a more cooperative society, they both accepted rational self-interest as the major motivation. For the liberals, individualism and competition would be modified as the elements in production found it to their advantage to engage in cooperative practices. For the collective rationalists, the gains of rational and efficient social planning would be sufficient inducement for all to recognize the value of the cooperative endeavor.

The charity organization societies and the university settlements originating in the last third of the nineteenth century shared to a large extent a common Romantic leadership and philosophy. The London Charity Organisation Society was founded in 1869, and Toynbee Hall, the first of the university settlements, was opened in 1884. An association to support the creation of a university settlement had been formed in Oxford in 1867, and Edward Denison was a pioneer settler in London in the same year. It is interesting to note, too, that Ruskin, probably the leading Romantic figure of the period, was active in the establishment of both settlement and charity organization movements. The origin of the settlement idea has been attributed to a meeting in 1868 at Ruskin's house to consider ways of helping the poor.[52] Ruskin was a founder and vice president of the London COS and in its earliest days gave the society crucial financial support. As its name implies, the COS was originated for the purpose of organizing charitable relief for the poor into a more efficient service through the establishment of cooperative planning among those engaged in charitable effort and through the introduction of more effective techniques in dealing with the relief of the poor and in "repressing mendicity."[53]

Charles S. Loch, the influential leader of the London COS during its formative years, broadly described the philosophy of charity organization as "an enthusiasm, as of religion, for the common good." Loch said it aimed "to ennoble citizenship and to perfect it, and for the relief of distress . . . to realize the duties of individual to individual, and to promote the fulfillment of these duties by co-operation."[54] While the charity organization movement recognized other methods of preventing pauperism, it placed primary responsibility on the case or individual approach.

The settlements, on the other hand, approached the problems of pauperism primarily from the community context. The first object of the settlements was to make friends with the neighborhood and to become part of the common life of the community. At their origin the university settlements were literally missions to the slums of the great urban centers. Through direct contact with and knowledge of the poor and their conditions, the way would be found to save the inhabitants from material and cultural poverty. More specifically, the methods emphasized were the scientific study of neighborhood and community life, the broadening through education of the horizons of the inhabitants, and the provision of leadership.

The Good Individual

Although different in form and function, the charity organization and settlement movements were similar in their common Romantic base. The foremost sign of Romanticism was its emphasis on man's moral nature. It was the character of man, rather than any external or environmental trappings, that accounted for the weakness or strength of society. The goal of the Romantic was the improvement of man's inner nature. Only through man's free will morally directed could man and, consequently, society progress. Both Carlyle and Ruskin, the chief apostles of Romanticism, had stressed that social reform must begin with the individual. Any mere change of social conditions was artificial; real change was founded on personal moral reform. Ruskin stated his views:

All effective advancement towards the true felicity of the human race must be by individual, not public effort. Certain general measures may aid, certain laws guide, such advancement; but the measure and law which first have to be determined are those of each man's home.[55]

Both the charity organization and settlement movements recognized this fundamental tenet of individualism. For both, the "character" of the poor was a fragile flower that must be cultivated and nursed to its full bloom. There could be no compromise here. It might be necessary to be harsh, and even at times cruel, but those given the responsibility of leading or helping the poor must ever be on their guard against the smug satisfaction of sentimental charity.

For the founders of Toynbee Hall it was the spiritual poverty of East London rather than its material poverty that provided the call to action. The Christian Socialist forerunners of the settlement movement had early identified individual improvement as the source of social reform. In his "Parson Lot" letters Kingsley had admonished the Chartists of 1848 for their impatience:

God will only reform society on condition of our reforming every man his own self, while the devil is quite ready to help us to mind the laws and the Parliament, earth and heaven, without ever starting such an impertinent and "personal" request, as that a man should mend himself.[56]

Samuel A. Barnett, the illustrious first warden of Toynbee Hall, was equally convinced that change meant change in the inner man. Being poor, while associated with limitations in education and occupational skill, was primarily the effect of character. Like the leaders of the COS, Barnett was opposed to the practice of outdoor relief because it encouraged the weak and stimulated dependency. "The poor are weak," he wrote, "and a good scheme of relief must include means for strengthening them to choose the good and refuse the evil."[57] Moreover he considered want as "not so much a want of money . . . as want of the common virtues of ordinary life." The poor appeared to have no moral idea, and "spirituality" to them was "as little understood in idea as in word." He thought the lesson must be brought home to the poor that "poverty was but the material result of their sinful, self-indulgent lives."[58]

Mrs. Barnett points out that her husband was less concerned with social justice than with the shouldering of individual responsibility. While at times Canon Barnett might question the rightness of the distribution of wealth, he never wavered "in his conviction." According to his wife, "he saw, without a shade of reservation from pity, that a man's soul was more important than a man's suffering, and held that it was spiritual murder to act as to nullify for him the results of his own actions."[59] Though in his role as an Anglican minister Barnett tended toward religious modes of expression, it was not the immortal soul of man but the temporal strength of character required for independent living to which he referred. He was critical of the Webbs and their goal of "national efficiency." For him their scheme was "like the Catholic Church without the Pope, like the garden of flowers without the roots." What will "inspire and guide the conduct of each?" he asked.[60]

That the fundamental gospel of the settlements had a religious tone was not accidental, in view of the affiliations of its earliest organizers and of the prominent role of Canon Barnett as head of the first university settlement. Toynbee, whose personal example was so much an inspiration to the university settlement movement, was a deeply religious young man who believed that "the triumph of righteousness" is dependent upon "the efforts of individual will" identified with the "perfect holiness" of "God Eternal."[61] The combination of religious impulse and Romantic faith in "individualistic" morality rather than in social or environmental forces made the development of individual character the focus of the early settlements.

In general, the Victorian era was heavily influenced by a Puritan revival that affected all schools of religious thought. The emphasis on moral character, the conception of life as moral welfare, and the rigid distinction between good and evil were an integral part of the Romantic ideology of such men as Carlyle and Kingsley. Combined with the Romantic emphasis on moral regeneration, the Puritan spirit accounted for the earnest, almost fanatical zeal that pervaded the charity organization and settlement movements in their rooting out of all obstacles to the development of moral character in the lower classes.

To the charity organization movement individual character was the fundamental, if not the only, moving force. For the charity organization leader, as represented by Helen Bosanquet, to raise the question of circumstances or environment was merely to becloud the issue: "It is always the man in his selective activity," she stated, "who makes his circumstances, who chooses what his world shall be, even though he may let them afterwards mold his life by the habits they encourage."[62] In the eyes of the COS, the life of the poor was an eternal struggle between dependence and independence, between worthiness and unworthiness. To a great extent the charity organization emphasis on individual strength and character reflected a social Darwinist point of view. The environment must not be made easier, for it is the struggle against his environment that brings about man's natural adaptive power.

To deprive an individual human being, then, of the necessity—the stern necessity, if need be—of planning his life for himself, is to deprive him of his natural power of "progressive development" to close the door which Nature has left open.[63]

The Romantic emphasis on individual morality was thus flavored in the charity organization movement by a strong infusion of both social Darwinism and the Protestant ethic. Life was a struggle for existence in which the superior or fittest won out. The struggle was primarily in the economic sphere, and destitution or economic failure was the sign of moral failure. Bernard Bosanquet maintained that he was opposed to socialism if it meant the "total supression of the personal struggle for existence." Charles S. Loch cogently summed up the argument.

That the head of the family should provide against the ordinary conditions of life is the condition of self-preservation in a civilized community. In other words, care and foresight in the use of wages and property is to the family in civic life what quickness of sense and strength are to the brute in the competition of wild beasts. If this care and foresight be present, there is at least the foundation of a progressive family life; if it be not present, the very pressure of the ordinary needs of life will reduce the family to incompetence, weakness, and savagery. Thus, rightly considered, the economic basis is a moral basis.[64]

The charity organization movement thus veered toward the more individualistic and Calvinistic aspects of Romanticism as represented by Carlyle. The support of laissez-faire by the charity organization leadership was far more inflexible than the position of the leading liberal economists of the day. For the charity organization bodies, the fundamental principles of social responsibility had been established by the English Poor Law Commission of 1834. Any deviation from this high-water mark of laissez-faire was considered a flagrant encouragement of dependency. Loch himself made a scathing attack on Alfred Marshall, the most prominent neoclassical economist of the period, for Marshall's criticizing the 1834 policies as unnecessarily harsh.[65]

Thus, although they had much in common in their emphasis on moral character, the settlement and charity organization leadership differed in their definition of character and in their assessment of the extent to which circumstances influenced the development of character. For the COS, character was synonymous with material independence—the economic man of the Protestant ethic. Bernard Bosanquet rationalized the significance of private property as the singular social institution that provides man the opportunity to display the full powers of adulthood. Through freeing himself from the economic dependence of the child, the adult became a complete individual. It was the ability to deal with one's material resources that was the index of character. Loch was critical of the studies of poverty made by Booth and Rowntree because, he said, they were not truly studies of social facts and habits.

It is not the greater or lesser command of means that makes the material difference in the contentment and efficiency of social life, but the use of means relative to station in life and its possibilities.[66]

A clear portrayal of the charity organization view of the "ideal economic man" was given to contrast his qualities with those of the failures of society.

The ideal economic man, as we know, is remarkable for his foresight and self-control, in the residuum these qualities are entirely absent. In the place of foresight we find that happy faith which never fails, that "something will turn up," and instead of self-control the impulsive recklessness which may lead indifferently to a prodigal generosity, an almost inconceivable selfishness. The true type of this class lives in the present only . . . there is no development . . . all is aimless and drifting.[67]

Here lay the distinction between the worthy and the unworthy, between candidates for charitable help and for public relief. The "question" for the Society, as it stated in its Report for 1909–10, was the "start and initiation in self-support,"[68] because for the majority of people "the way to independence is opened up by the necessity of earning a living."[69]

The settlement's view of character was, however, broader. Although economic independence was stressed, the description of character in material terms was not merely insufficient but was considered inappropriate. Influenced by the Romantic revolt against the vulgarization of man by the industrial capitalism of the Victorian era, the settlement movement spoke of a spiritual awakening of the whole man. Ruskin, Arnold, Carlyle, and Morris had deprecated the barbarous materialism of the age and had sought the full play of man's creative faculties. It was a revolt in which the spiritual, the esthetic, the imaginative, and the humanistic aspects of life were arrayed against the narrow materialism of the contemporary society. Ruskin preached a redefinition of work—work as a way of life, as a good and satisfaction in itself, not merely as a man's means of bartering energy for subsistence or profit.

This was the view of man the settlement movement presented. Its Christian Socialist predecessors had founded the Working Men's College to bring education and culture to the lower classes. The settlements continued this mission of education in the widest sense for citizenship and human satisfaction, through art, music, philosophy, and political science. Even the emphasis of Ruskin and Morris on the direct enjoyment of labor was given attention by training in arts and crafts.

The conflict between the goals of the COS and those of the settlements was brought into the open by the Barnetts' criticism of and gradual alienation from the London COS. Mrs. Barnett differed with those who stressed improvement of material conditions and who used "getting on" as a "stimulus" for change. Rather than "getting on," she said, it may result in "going back" because it may sap "the one virtue which is strong and beautiful in the lives of these people, their communistic love."[70]

Barnett himself spoke out forcibly against the influence of "scientific charity" as making "the working man too thrifty to pet his children and too respectable to be happy." He summarized the situation:

Those who have tried hardest at planning relief and at bringing to a focus the forces of charity, those who have sacrificed themselves to stop the demoralizing out-relief and restore to the people the spirit of self-reliance, will be the first to confess dissatisfaction if they are told that the earthly paradise of the majority of the people must be to belong to a club, to pay for a doctor through a provident dispensary, and to keep themselves unspotted from charity and pauperism. There is not enough in such hope to call out efforts of sacrifice, and a steady look into such an earthly paradise discloses that the life of the thrifty is a sad life, limited both by the pressure of continous toil and by the fear lest this pressure should cease and starvation ensue.

The poor need more than food; they need also the knowledge, the character, the happiness which are the gifts of God to this age. The age has reserved His best gifts, but they have fallen mostly to the rich.[71]

Those who care for the poor see that the best things are missed, and they are not content with the hope offered by "scientific charity."[72]

The cleavage between the goals of the charity organization and the settlement view of the nature of character was further sharpened by differing conceptions of the factors responsible for the development of character. While both started from the same principle—the necessity for inner moral reform—they diverged on the way in which this inner moral reform was to come about. For the COS inner change depended largely, if not entirely, on the individual's own potentialities for growth as he faced the responsibilities of his life. While also stressing the need for independent growth, the settlements recognized to a much greater degree the limiting as well as the liberating influence of circumstances.

The Good Society

The charity organization movement thus heavily emphasized the importance of the contribution of the individual over environmental contributions. The "inner heart of the trouble" was the "want of goodwill, the central preservative force of the individual soul."[73] This contention was supported, according to Loch, by the studies of the Galton Laboratory, which "point to the outstanding importance of heredity as against environment."[74] Helen Bosanquet wrote:

It is futile to say that the social organisation is at fault, and must be reconstructed throughout to improve their circumstances. They are themselves part of the social organism which chiefly affects the circumstances in question; and it is their sheer incapacity which makes and keeps them poor.[75]

This acceptance of hereditary or intrinsic differences was fundamental to Romantic doctrine. In general, the Romantics assumed an ordered society integrating essentially superior and inferior members through a system of status relationships based on authority. Ruskin referred to the "unconquerable differences in the clay of human nature" and believed that occupational and social stratification reflected the real differences of inherited characteristics.[76] In rejecting laissez-faire the Romantics also rejected its underlying assumption that men were essentially equal, rational creatures who could freely interact in their own interests. They also rejected the doctrine of radical liberalism, which attempted to balance the competitive system by equalizing opportunity and improving the lot of those disadvantaged by circumstances.

For the charity organization movement the primary issue was the kind of environment that stimulated to the maximum the demands on the individual for self-action. While on the one hand self-maintenance was the goal, on the other hand self-maintenance became the means to the goal. The process was a continuing upward spiral: self-maintenance demanded "energy and endeavor," which in turn resulted in self-maintenance.[77] To obtain this effect, the environment must encourage the greatest degree of self-reliance. Such an environment was not, as the socialists proposed, created by a system of social intervention that at the same time tried to influence individual behavior through social controls; this attitude placed too much emphasis on man as a "social animal." Charity organization focused on man as an individual and depended primarily on individual initiative rather than on social forces as the stimulus to change.[78] There was no room for compromise here. Social reform must be carefully evaluated. According to Loch, the weight of evidence not only was against its effectiveness but actually pointed to its harmfulness.[79]

The emphasis on individual morality motivated by self-reliance and suspicion of the destructive effects of social intervention led the charity organization movement to a categorical acceptance of laissez-faire.[80] Thus, although sharing the Romantic ideal of personal morality, the charity organization movement did not accept the general Romantic criticism of the excess of the industrial society as the major cause of spiritual decadence. The charity organization leadership reversed the situation by maintaining that it was the decline from pure principles of economic liberalism rather than their overemphasis that accounted for moral deterioration.

The settlement movement incorporated not only the Romantic concern with individual reformation but also the dissatisfaction of the Romantics with the contemporary state of British society. On the whole, the Romantics were not radicals and, except for Morris and possibly Ruskin, envisioned no radical change in the contemporary order. The Romantic ideal was not a more democratic society, socially or economically, but a reweaving of the texture of society into a more cohesive whole. The failure of the natural harmony of individual self-interest and social good was to be replaced by the harmony of individual morality and social duties and responsibilities.

The Romantic point of view, as evidenced in the settlement movement, always carefully balanced individual responsibility and social intervention. Canon Barnett succinctly summed up this position when he wrote, "But with our belief in human nature we believe also in the power of circumstances over character."[81]

Toynbee stated:

We have not abandoned our old belief in liberty, justice and self-help, but we say that under certain conditions the people cannot help themselves and that then they should be helped by the state representing directly the whole people. In giving this state help we make three conditions: first, the matter must be one of primary social importance; next, it must be proved to be practicable; thirdly, the state interference must not diminish self-reliance.

We differ from Tory Socialism insofar as we are in favour, not of paternal, but of fraternal government, and we differ from continental socialism because we accept the principle of private property, and repudiate confiscation and violence.

To a reluctant admission of the necessity for state action, we join a burning belief in duty, and a deep spiritual idea of life.[82]

Aside from a fervent spiritual note, there is little here to differ from the more advanced liberalism of the period, whether in the politics of Joseph Chamberlain or in the political economy of W. Stanley Jevons or Alfred Marshall.

The early settlement leaders were aware that their point of view on the influence of "circumstances" and their readiness to accept state interference went beyond the laissez-faire philosophy of the COS. Mrs. Barnett, in a full-scale attack on the Society, criticized its failure to be concerned with the reform of social conditions.[83] Her husband pointedly remarked that "the most earnest member of a Charity Organisation Society cannot hope that organised almsgiving will be powerful so as to alter conditions as to make the life of the poor a life worth living."[84]

For the early settlement leadership the ideal of the thrifty and temperate economic man of the COS was a delusion. Poverty could not be obliterated by moral virtue alone. Poverty was the reality of the poor, and it accounted for their condition. Social reform must erase the gulf between the rich and the poor. The poor must be provided with the cultural opportunities of the rich, and the vulgar and conspicuous materialism of the rich must be uprooted. Continuous contact with the poor brought Barnett to conclude that "the conditions in which people live" must be the core of any program of reform.

Though at times the early settlement workers might have sounded socialistic, socialism as a formal system disposing of private property, establishing collective ownership, and equalizing wealth had little appeal for the Romantics generally. The Christian Socialists had experimented with various forms of cooperative enterprise, and that was as far as they conceived radical reform. Nationalization meant to the settlement leaders the provision of municipal services through tax funds. More idealistically expressed, it was the nationalization of "beauty, knowledge, and righteousness."[85] Housing, schools, libraries, parks, museums, baths, sanitation—these would provide the poor with the opportunities for the fuller life enjoyed heretofore only by the wealthy. In addition, the settlement movement identified with the collective efforts of the workers themselves to improve their own conditions. Trade unions, the abolition of casual work, and the improvement of skills were seen as means by which the lower classes could redress the uneven balance of wealth in society while at the same time increasing their own independence and initiative rather then depending on state benevolence.

Although the Romantics viewed the morality of the individual as the starting point and the change agent for the better society, they did not stop with the individual. In contrast to laissez-faire reliance on the natural harmony of rational individuals, the Romantics did not rely entirely on the emergence of the good society as a natural outgrowth of the free relationship of moral individuals. The Romantics had a vision, sometimes blurred but reasonably consistent, of what the good society was. They believed, too, that the achievement of individual morality must go hand in hand with the establishment of society as a moral organism. The reform of society itself along the lines of the Romantic ideology was necessary for the optimum accomplishment of individual reform.

The revolt of the Romantic movement, as discussed above, was founded on its disillusionment with the chaos of the contract society of rational liberalism. Social relationships had broken down, mutual responsibility had vanished, and the poor had been abandoned. Social classes were in conflict, and community life had disintegrated. A cohesive society must be reestablished on the foundation of individual and social morality. Friendship must be reestablished among the conflicting groups whose "enlightened self-interest" had acted as a centrifugal rather than centripetal force. Among most Romantics there was a yearning for the olden days when the bonds of man to man were strong and persistent. Some Romantics sought literally to reestablish the order where:

> Each knew his place—king, peasant, peer, or priest,
> The greatest owned connection with the least;
> From rank to rank the generous feeling ran,
> And linked society as man to man.[86]

Other Romantics, while accepting the industrial order, hoped to re-create the spirit of the earlier system of relationships. One such type is satirized by Dickens:

I do my duty as the Poor Man's Friend and Father, and I endeavor to educate his mind by inculcating on all occasions the one great moral lesson which that class requires. That is, entire dependence on Myself. They have no business with—with themselves.[87]

The Romantics visualized a society in which formal relationships would be largely replaced by the informal and the voluntary. However, this society was not an egalitarian society but a society whose cohesion would come about through acceptance of leadership by the upper classes and recognition of this leadership by the lower classes. "Benevolent industrialism" is descriptive of the ideal of many Romantics.[88] As Ruskin put it, there would be "no liberty, but instant obedience to lay and ap-pointed persons; no equality, but recognition of every betterness and reprobation of every worseness."[89] The Romantic society was a society of authority in which order, reverence, and leadership would be the norms of daily behavior.

The upper classes must be prepared for their role of leadership. In an industrial society, this meant that the "captains of industry" and the middle classes generally must recognize their responsibilities. To many the revival of the social gospel of the church acted as a lever for instill-ing this sense of responsibility and even dedication. There was guilt for the comforts of the wealthy in a society in which there was so much deg-radation among the poor. Thus Arnold Toynbee's apologia to the poor:

We—the middle classes, I mean, not merely the very rich—we have neglected you; instead of justice we have offered you charity, and instead of sympathy we have offered you hard and unreal advice; but I think we are changing. If you would only believe in us and trust us, I think that many of us would spend our lives in your service. You have—I say it clearly and advisedly—you have to forgive us, for we have wronged you; we have sinned against you grievously— not knowingly always, but still we have sinned, and let us confess it; but if you will forgive us—nay, whether you will forgive us or not—we will serve you, we will devote our lives to your service, and we cannot do more.[90]

The responsibility of the upper classes toward the lower was broadly conceived. First, society depended for its moral health on the interde-pendence of the leadership and the great masses. Second, the leadership must provide a model of individual morality for the lower classes. The example of the spiritual soundness of the upper classes would have a significant influence on the lower classes. Finally, the upper classes must feel a warm, human interest and sympathy for the lot of the lower classes. In the Romantic tradition this humanitarian feeling arose, on the one hand, out of a romanticizing of the virtues of simple labor and the common man and, on the other hand, out of sympathy with the injustice suffered by those who had not received a fair share of society's riches.

The charity organization movement was permeated to only a limited degree by the social doctrine of the Romantics. Charity organization followed what Loch called the "Christian theory of society," which "accepts the structure of social life as it finds it."[91] In effect, whereas the Romantics denied the intrinsic morality of the contemporary contract society, the charity organization movement started with society as an irrevocable reality. Thus, greater social cohesiveness would have to be adjusted to the norms of individual self-reliance and a society emphasizing freedom of contract as the foundation of its economic system. It is true that the charity organization leadership referred nostalgically, as did more orthodox Romantics, to the golden days of earlier eras. But the lesson was not a return to, or a revival of, earlier systems but the recognition that in each period the optimum society encouraged the type of dependency appropriate for its time. Thus almsgiving was acceptable in the early medieval church, but times had changed and the system appropriate for interdependency in the small community no longer fitted a growing urban, industrial society. The focus now was the self-sufficient individual. The previous units of natural dependency, instead of being broadened in an expanding society, had become narrowed. The only acceptable dependency in the nineteenth century was dependency on self or within the family unit, which was an extension of self. The goal of charity organizations was to keep the notion of social interdependence within the narrowest possible limits.

At most, when the line of defense was weakened, the individual might turn to those who in the past had recognized him as part of their group— "relations, former employers, and friends."[92] However, charity organization preached no doctrine of responsibility to friends and relatives or to the upper classes. To do so would have encouraged the dependency that the charity movement tried to stem. Turning to other groups beyond the family was merely accepting the least of all evils in view of the ever-present possibility of the poor law and its wider implications of social support. For COS leaders, to whom meals for poor children were seen as a threat to the independence of family life, there was little room for compromise. As Bernard Bosanquet put it, the woman volunteer helping the poor must appreciate "the bearing of her work, not only on the immediate sufferer . . . but also on progress or retrogression in the whole condition of the poor, and consequently in the welfare and good life of society as a whole."[93]

The role of the charity organization worker was complex. He had to effect change through personal contact, but he had to be wary of providing any basis for the assumption of the rightness of interdependency. The personal touch was important because it was through "personal influence" that dependency might be prevented or cured.

It will make all the difference in the world whether it comes to him from the poor-rate, unwillingly paid, unaccompanied by personal interest, unadapted to his particular difficulties or circumstances; or whether it is the wise gift of an understanding and sympathetic friend, planned to be the stepping-stone to future independence.[94]

The element of personal influence conformed with Romantic doctrine, but not the tenuousness of relationships which the charity leadership emphasized. The clearly voluntary nature of the charity movement helped to insure the slim hold of the recipient upon his benefactors. In fact, this aspect was clearly recognized by the charity organization movement, and its values were stressed in contrast to public aid. There was no "claim or right of membership" in charity.[95]

Gratitude in exchange for kindness was the only basis of communication. Gratitude was appreciation of the help given by acceptance of the approved road to independence. In a sense, the gratitude-kindness complex was a substitution of emotional coin for the more literal exchange of contract in the market place. As in the market place, those who would not or could not pay the price were excluded. This distinguished the worthy from the unworthy. The latter were not acceptable as candidates for help because they did not fulfill the expectations of the charity system.

In contrast to the Romantics, the charity organization movement had little sentimentalism for the poor as a class. For them the present system of society was right. They did not consider the poor the victims of injustice, nor did they feel any sense of personal guilt for the state of the lower classes. In fact, it was the charity movement and society that were righteous, and the poor were the malefactors. Sir Charles Trevelyan, one of the early influential participants in the London COS, had little patience with proposals for national education when the problem was how to deal with "this young proletaire rabble."[96]

Whatever its goals, the London COS during the nineteenth century never achieved any effective system of personal relationships between its workers and the recipients of help. Its concern with organizational problems and its extraordinary sensitivity to the possibilities of undermining independence led to an almost exclusive concentration on the administrative aspects of its function. Investigation of applicants for help, collection of funds or stimulation of aid, and surveillance of recipients took precedence over the development of friendly relations between the well-to-do and the destitute. Loch referred with admiration to the friendly visiting of the Boston Associated Charities, in which "cases are not, as in most charity organisation societies, decided, and then, unless there is some special reason for keeping touch of them, allowed to slip out of sight." In London, he remarked, "any general approach to any system" whereby a friendly visitor was available in case of need was "a far-off vision."[97] Despite the charity organization identification with the Romantic belief in personal relationships as the source of reform, it was here that least was accomplished. There was, said Loch, "amongst us a certain want of faith in the strength of individual effort" to promote the social good.[98]

For the settlement movement the establishment or reestablishment of friendly relations between the rich and the poor, between the classes of society, was so closely intertwined with the accomplishment of all other goals that it became the fulcrum of the settlement program. The bringing together of the rich and the poor as "neighbors" and the establishment of the "brotherhood of man," "class solidarity," the "sense of fellowship," or "friendship" were the most repeated goals of the settlement leader. "No social reform will be adequate," said Barnett, "which does not touch social relations, bind classes by friendship, and pass, through the medium of friendship, the spirit which inspires righteousness and devotion."[99]

The breakdown of "class distinctions, class prejudices and class antagonisms" and the "acknowledgment of a common responsibility for the common good" were stressed by the chairman of the council of Toynbee Hall as the most important criteria of its success.[100] This was "the spirit to be engendered" in society. Through the incorporation of the settlement in the community, a mechanism was provided for cementing relationships between the classes. In addition, the means of making the slum neighborhood into a healthy community was also present, for the urban community of the poor would be balanced by a public-spirited and educated citizenry who "elsewhere in England uphold the tone of Local Life and enforce the efficiency of Local Self-Government."[101]

It is difficult to say to what extent the early settlement workers felt that the interest of the rich in the poor and the leadership of the rich would be the answer to social problems. However, at least in theory, if to a lesser extent in practice, the settlement movement rose above the paternalistic benevolence and authority often present in the Romantic conception of society. The settlement leadership was sensitively conscious of the spread of mass democracy and of the need for an enlightened total citizenry if democratic government was to be successful. As the chairman of the council of Toynbee Hall stated, "apathy, isolation, ignorance, selfishness in the masses—these are the powers of resistance to be vanquished before, by any chance, a self-governed people can possibly come to a well-governed people."[102] There was also recognition that through informal organizations such as trade unions the lower classes would gain the knowledge and spirit that would enable them to take responsible social and political action.

Of course, strongly mixed with this belief in the need of the lower classes to shoulder their responsibilities was the heavy and patronizing tone of the mission of the upper classes to the poor and ignorant. The sense of mission was greatly stressed in recruiting and stimulating the university settlers. "Sacrifice of self" and "doing something for the poor" were obligations of the well-to-do and the better educated. Nor were these obligations that could be fulfilled by proxy or by donation. The demand for action, often couched in religious terms, required personal involvement. Speaking of the residents in university settlements, a prominent leader of Toynbee Hall stated:

The charity which consists in subscriptions, bazaars, and public meetings cannot satisfy their desires. They long to come into personal contact with human suffering, to bind up the wounds with their own hands, to pour in oil and wine from their own stores, to give up their own beast and go on foot themselves, and to welcome the afflicted to their own society and their own abode.[103]

The settlement movement, by its emphasis on broad human fellowship and its demands for personal sacrifice and action, reflected major elements of the Romantic spirit. The rich must "give of themselves and of their substance." Through sacrifice, personal service, and example the wealthy would bring their influence to bear. The example demanded by the settlement movement was religious and spiritual. The Christian Socialist appeal to social justice and humanitarianism gave the settlement movement a philosophy broader than that of the charity organization movement. The religious ethic of the settlement leaders did not tolerate the judicious and discriminating weighing of souls employed by the charity organization societies but rather required "the recognition of the image of God in the most fallen and debased of the human race."[104] The Barnetts themselves were strongly critical of the holier-than-thou attitude of the charity organization movement. They felt that charity organization had not resulted in sufficient contact between the rich and the poor, and that the kind of contact was not really sympathetic or human. The Barnetts found the charity organization movement to be more negative and rejecting than positive and supporting. In 1894 Canon Barnett wrote of the Society:

The thoroughness with which they inquire into causes has not always been undertaken in Christ's spirit of tenderness. Human beings are too often regarded as "cases," and memories are touched with so rough a hand that the relief fails to heal the wound.[105]

Perhaps it is in this respect that the major contrast between the influence of the Romantic ideology on the charity organization and settlement movements is summed up. The Romantic trend, aside from its other aspects, had been born of a concern with the fullness of life and the spiritual wholeness of man, which its supporters felt had been denied by the emphasis on materialism and rationality. The settlement movement incorporated this concern and reflected it in a faith in the "capacity of everyone to rise to the highest," as God and nature had designed. The charity organization movement, on the other hand, more influenced by earlier fundamentalist Protestant philosophy, was more pessimistic in its interpretation of God's design and less willing to include the poor and the sinful within God's kingdom on earth. The good society was not the society of all, but the society of the select and those who accepted the leadership of the select.

10

British Welfare Policy

ECONOMIC security programs in the second half of the nineteenth century focused around three basic issues: the right to support, the right to opportunity, and the right to work. Although there was some overlapping, each of these "rights" was predominantly the concern of one school of thought or faction. For example, the most avowed supporters of laissez-faire, the charity organization societies, the central poor law administration, and the Majority of the Poor Law Commission of 1909 concentrated on the right to support. Such liberal economists as Marshall, Sidgwick, and Jevons as well as Liberal politicians like Joseph Chamberlain emphasized equality of opportunity. The labor movement and the socialists considered the guarantee of work the most important problem for economic security.

The poor law reform of 1834 withdrew the right to support, the basis of policy in the several prior decades. In addition, the responsibility for the provision of work was abandoned. The Commission maintained that this responsibility involved the poor law in the universal problem of poverty, whereas its function was to care only for dire destitution. The Poor Law Reform Act of 1834 provided the narrowest base for social responsibility. The poor law officials struggled to maintain and even to limit the grudging amount of support provided. A writer sympathetic to their approach could validly state at the end of the century:

Since the year 1834, if we except, perhaps, the Union Chargeability Act of 1865, no Poor Law legislation of the first importance has been added to the statute book. The later history has been concerned rather with a controversy than with definite acts of legislation.[1]

At the opposite end of the scale from the issue of support stood the right to work or the guarantee of employment. In a society dominated by the ideology of liberalism, the only appropriate source of income was employment. The trade unions and the socialists attempted to insure employment and an adequate wage to all able-bodied persons. Between those who would at best provide minimal support to persons in absolute need and those who would make society responsible for a living wage for all stood the liberal reformers. Seeking the optimum of laissez-faire, they considered equality of opportunity the norm of social responsibility. Handicaps of education and health were recognized as limiting many of the participants in the economic market from using to the fullest their own potential and from contributing effectively to society. To a large extent, the greatest part of the nineteenth century was given over to removing these limitations and insuring some degree of opportunity for all to meet the expectations of the employment market.

The Right to Support

The controversy over the right to support fell into three categories: minimal or no right to support, right of support determined by merit, and a general right to support. At times these positions were blurred in practice, but on the whole they represented distinct social philosophies.

Minimal or No Right to Support

The advocates of no social responsibility for support were primarily the firm supporters of the poor law reform of 1834. At most, like the Commissioners of 1834, they would accept a minimal responsibility for absolute destitution. Neither the Commissioners nor their partisans could completely rescind the traditional recognition of responsibility, although some of the Commissioners and others continued to hope that through a stern policy both destitution and any recourse to the poor law would be eliminated. The major problem of the central government officials throughout the century was the maintenance of the principles of 1834 against the lenient practices of the local poor law guardians. There was a constant struggle reflecting the impossibility of enforcing a system that conflicted with the social and economic realities of the time.[2] Toward the end of the century the central administration, under the Local Government Board, made a valiant attempt to revive the spirit of 1834 when it was evident that radical changes were near at hand.

The central government policy after 1834 demonstrated a faith in laissez-faire as the corrective of all economic maladjustments and indicated a clear point of view about the causes of destitution. The primary assumption of the advocates of minimal support was that poverty resulted from the moral defects of the poor rather than from social and economic circumstances. In addition, the existence of the poor law itself encouraged the poor to acquiesce to their own weaknesses. The two major Poor Law Commissions after 1834, in 1893 and 1909, consistently pointed to individual responsibility for destitution. Although these later Commissions considered much evidence suggesting other factors, the majority of their Commissioners still held that the problem was essentially personal and moral.

Those who emphasized individual responsibility sought justification for their position in a variety of factors. It was believed that the poor had the highest incidence of moral defects—intemperance, thriftlessness, laziness, and so forth—and therefore personal characteristics were the most influential determinants of economic position. The poor were found living under the most unsatisfactory conditions with regard to housing and sanitation, and it was believed that they either selected or created that way of life because those were the circumstances most comfortable and agreeable to them. They could have lived otherwise if they had chosen, it was believed, and the proof of that, apart from the general faith in opportunity, was that some low-wage earners—those who did not suffer from want of character—managed to live "respectable" lives. Finally, there were those who maintained that although the standard of living and circumstances generally had improved, they noticed no commensurate change among the lower classes. Thus there was obviously something indigenous to the nature of the poor that made them impervious to better external conditions.

The Majority Report of the Poor Law Commission of 1909 still suggested the influence of the philosophy of 1834. More sensitive than earlier commissions to the many dimensions of pauperism, the Commissioners listed a wide variety of possible causes: the displacement of older men in the labor market, sickness, housing, casual labor, child labor, unsatisfactory working conditions, and low wages.[3] In most cases, however, the Commissioners found that the underlying factor was individual character defect. The problem of the older worker was associated with "low earning power, drink, or thriftlessness."[4] Drink was considered "the most potent and universal factor in bringing about pauperism."[5] As for housing, the Commission concluded that the "unsanitary conditions of a house are so frequently due to the character of the people living in it, that it is sometimes difficult to disentangle cause and effect."[6] The question was also raised whether the poverty associated with casual labor was the cause or effect. Even child labor was related to the imprudent habits of the lower classes in sending their children too early into industry and cutting off their opportunities for education and skill.

The Majority members were definitely disappointed by the results of social reform. During the latter part of the nineteenth century they maintained that there had been significant progress in education, wages, opportunities for thrift, and public health without any noticeable change in the amount of pauperism.

It is very unpleasant to record that, notwithstanding our assumed moral and material progress, and notwithstanding the enormous annual expenditure . . . upon poor relief, education, and public health, we still have a vast army of persons quartered upon us unable to support themselves, and an army which in numbers has recently shown signs of increase rather than decrease.[7]

The single most constant factor was thus considered to be the defective character of the destitute. With this view of causation, the method of relieving society of the burden of pauperism must be of a personal rather than of a social or economic nature. The most simple and acceptable solution was a continuation of deterrent policies based on the earlier pleasure-pain psychology. The function of the economic assistance program was to exercise a restraining and discouraging influence on the growth of pauperism.

The Majority Report found that given the dependent nature of the pauper class, the administration of the poor law itself was the greatest force affecting the amount of dependency.

It will be generally acknowledged that, in so far as people are induced or en-couraged to receive from the Poor Law, for themselves or their dependents, what they are capable of providing by their own exertions, to that extent a pauperism is being manufactured which would not otherwise exist.[8]

The Majority found that "careless" administration resulted in a large amount of poverty and distress and had "destroyed the qualities of independence and mutual helpfulness, and substituted the desire to make out a good case for the relieving officer."[9]

Although "some" individuals would be "physically or morally incapable" under any circumstances, "very many . . . simply follow the line of least resistance," the Majority concluded. They could support themselves but were "drawn into loafing and thriftlessness by the prospect of relief."[10] The Majority Report gave almost exclusive attention to this latter group. An examination, however, of the Commission's Report does not support this emphasis on the able-bodied or potentially employable. It was estimated in 1906, for example, that approximately 45,000 able-bodied men were relieved as compared to a total poor law population of between 1,500,000 and 2,000,000.[11] Even if it is assumed that each able-bodied man was responsible for four others on assistance, this would not account for more than a sixth of the total poor law recipients. The Report itself referred to one fifth of the adults on relief as able-bodied. Since adults were 70 percent of the total, then 14 percent of the total were able-bodied adults on the basis of the Report's estimate. However, the Report's definition of able-bodied adults included all temporarily disabled persons above the age of sixteen with no upper age limit and all able-bodied women, whether single, married, or mothers.[12] Thus, the Majority's figures would appear to have exaggerated the incidence of the employables on the relief rolls.

The alleged number of able-bodied on public assistance has in all periods been the focus of the attacks on assistance programs. As Barbara Wootten remarked in the middle of the twentieth century, "This little company of individuals so persistently resistant (whether by design or misfortune) to assimilation, seems however to exercise a real fascination over the authorities responsible for their welfare."[13] The Majority members of the Poor Law Commission sympathized with the thesis of the central government officials that the local authorities had been lax in providing outdoor relief and had been too generous even in the care of those in institutions. The failure to apply strictly the principles of the workhouse test and less eligibility was in large measure held accountable for the size of the population on assistance. However, even the Majority Report's statistics indicated a reduction in the total rate of dependency in the fifteen years prior to 1905.[14] There was no increase in the overall rate of dependency of the able-bodied in this period, but, commensurate with the growth of the urban population, a greater proportion of the able-bodied on relief came from urban areas.[15] The Majority members ignored that fact and chose to find the increase in the absolute number of able-bodied urban dependents peculiarly significant.

The consideration of these statistics leads to the conclusion that it is in regard to the able-bodied that least progress has been made. Indeed it would appear that there has recently been a considerable retrogression in this branch of the Poor Law. Either the urban population is becoming less fitted for maintaining their independence, or the facility with which relief may be obtained and the immunity from labour which it confers are enticing a larger number of persons to avail themselves of Poor Law relief.[16]

Like their predecessors in 1834, the Majority started from the assumption that any dependency, no matter how small, was a symptom of moral failure nourished by corrupt relief practices. Successful policy would have involved a continuous reduction of rates without regard to the social and economic problems in the surrounding environment. The Majority members, even though aware of the need for, and of the Minority members' emphasis on, preventive measures, eschewed any such recommendations because they were "reluctant to enlarge the scope of public assistance for the needy in such a way as to lead to a sapping of the spirit of self-maintenance."[17]

Under such circumstances the concern of the Majority with able-bodied dependents was to be expected. For as in 1834, it was the able-bodied who were the core of the assistance problem. If the able-bodied were forced to become fully responsible, they would carry the total burden of dependency. They would care for themselves and their dependents during all periods of crisis. The Majority felt certain that the increasing number of aged needy merely reflected the laxness of family support.

In our opinion, the increase of aged pauperism, and the decrease in filial duty, are both alike, effects of a common cause, viz., the general feeling that the State is able and willing to make provision, and even lavish provision for parents whose sons fail to support them. We believe that if the position is clearly defined and a consistent policy laid down both as to pensions and Poor Law relief, the natural feeling between parents and children will again assert itself.[18]

A contemporary writer, Thomas MacKay, clearly summed up the overall position:

In the more modern controversy this contention has been expanded, and may be summed up generally in the proposition that the able-bodied period of life is equal to maintaining the not able-bodied period. The responsibility of the able-bodied must not be narrowed down to cover the period of his own working life only, but must be extended to take in his times of sickness and old age, and the dependent period in the life of his family.[19]

For the Majority members of the 1909 Poor Law Commission the central issue of poor law administration was proof of need or the right to support. By keeping the social services in the hands of the public assistance system, the broadening of social responsibility could easily be limited. The social controls directly present within the poor law structure and supplemented by other services were not disregarded by the Majority. They concluded their evaluation of the existing administration:

More especially, it must extend its policy of making the giving of relief conditional upon the recipient accepting a way of life likely to restore him to independence. . . . It has proved, indeed, impossible to push a curative policy any further in its absence; sickness cannot be cured . . . unless the patient will accept conditions; economic evils cannot be combated unless those who suffer from them will conform to conditions; moral weakness cannot be strengthened unless the authorities have power to impose conditions.[20]

The support of voluntary assistance agencies by the Majority members was not entirely consistent with their desire to minimize the extent of dependency. In their opinion, the voluntary bodies were more discriminating in aid and more effective in restoring independence, but staunch advocates of limited social responsibility saw voluntary agencies, like outdoor relief, as a threat to the tight ship of public assistance. For them the solution to public assistance was a system "completely subject" to unified direction. MacKay, for example, opposed the Charity Organisation Society by questioning the efficacy of private charity as the savior of the public system. He maintained that private charity was itself unmanageable and that its success depended on an effective public program.[21] In general, however, those favoring limited public responsibility for support believed that the voluntary agencies had the cure for dependency. In this they were encouraged by the leadership of the voluntary charities, and the Majority Report gave the voluntary societies a primary role in the public system.

The advocates of limited support favored the continuance of local financing and administration of public assistance. The issue of national control had been in the forefront of the public assistance controversy since the reforms of 1834. For many of the same reasons for which national administration had been rejected in 1834, it was opposed by the Majority in 1909. Local control and local financing signified a policy of parsimonious and deterrent assistance despite the dissatisfaction of the central government's officials with the efficiency of the local authorities.

The Minority of the Commission, which envisioned a larger role for public responsibility, differed strongly from the Majority in their recommendations on administration. The Minority recommended the breaking up of the old poor law by distributing its functions among several local authority units with parallel central government bodies for the exercise of national responsibility. There would be five national offices to deal with education, health, mental defectives, old age pensions, and assistance for the handicapped, in place of the former single organization supervising assistance. The major innovation of the Minority Report was the removal of the able-bodied entirely from local control and placing. them under a new Ministry of Labour.

Right to Support According to Merit

The right to support according to merit provided the broadest base for agreement among the contending philosophies of public assistance at the end of the nineteenth century. The existing public assistance administration, the charity organization and voluntary societies generally, the trade unions, and the Fabians all believed that applicants for assistance should be distinguished according to personal merit. There were few who did not support the idea that those who were deserving should receive help from society when in need. The major points of difference involved who were the deserving and the kinds of treatment to differentiate them from the undeserving.

In practice, the public assistance system had always made rough distinctions among its clientele. Since 1834, although the central government boards had continuously pressed for indoor relief for all, their primary concern had been to see that the able-bodied did not escape the workhouse test. The destitution of the able-bodied was an obvious indication of poor character, but the handicapped might be tolerated because they could not be accused of avoiding work. The unemployable were generally permitted to receive outdoor relief, but there were constant pressures to maintain the able-bodied in workhouses. A minority maintained throughout that this was an inconsistent application of the principles of 1834 and that all should receive aid within poor law institutions.

The Fabians and some of their trade union colleagues were, if anything, less friendly toward the unemployed able-bodied and more generous to the handicapped. Those who could earn and did not were more reprehensible to the Fabians than to the more conservative poor law reformers. The Fabians had replaced the latter's distinction between citizens and paupers with one between "workers" and "drones."

The real line of demarcation is between those who do or have done service *to* the community which is an adequate return for what they receive *from* the community, and those wasteful, even criminal, classes, both at the top and at the bottom, which live idly at the expense of the rest.[22]

Those who would not work should "be dealt with under some form of the criminal law," for "to live without working is a crime."[23]

The "scientific" distinction of the Fabians between workers and drones was paralleled by similar attempts by others. The Majority of the Poor Law Commission used such traditional terms as industrious, frugal, and provident, but they covered much the same ground as the Fabians. Perhaps the economist Marshall's definition of the worthy poor came closest to hitting the mark in describing the employable or previously employable who should be eligible for assistance without stigma: "thrift combined with the absence of notorious ill-conduct."[24]

While there were disagreements about classifying the more and less deserving of public aid, major differences occurred over the policies to be applied once the distinctions were made. The Webbs and the Minority of the Poor Law Commission believed that removing the whole of the social services and economic assistance from the poor law system would revolutionize British welfare. By tying the needs of those requiring financial help to the type or cause of need, the Minority hoped to broaden the population served and to reduce their vulnerability to attack solely on the grounds of destitution. Since society would be responsible for providing services or employment, those who refused to work or neglected their families would be ineligible for support and passed on to the correctional system.

The Majority of the Poor Law Commission and the Charity Organisation Society leadership sought a system of support that would clearly reward virtue. Those destitute who demonstrated the moral qualities considered necessary for rehabilitation would become the clients of the voluntary societies. Those for whom there was little or no hope would be the recipients of the minimum subsistence of public aid. The voluntary societies, it was assumed, would be free to make extraordinary provision without the problems of a public bureaucracy. Reward of merit was essential to such a plan of treatment. If merit was not to be rewarded, Marshall suggested, the program should have been reversed with the more difficult cases going to the voluntary agencies, which were presumably equipped to supply more intensive services.[25]

George Bernard Shaw also criticized the voluntary societies and remarked on the paradox of charity that helped those who could help themselves and left the others to their own devices.[26] On the other hand, John Burns, the labor leader, attacked the charities for encouraging "the loafer, the lazy, and the undeserving." He concluded that the public authorities "have not done their work well, and are unsympathetic, [which] is a reason for alteration, but is no justification for all the quack remedies that neurotic Christians and fanatical faddists, combining universal brotherhood with incompetence and good salaries, try to impose upon us."[27]

Although there were bitter differences over the respective roles of the voluntary and public agencies toward the deserving and undeserving, an issue of far greater long-term significance was the function of pension schemes in public policy. The receipt of a pension, and particularly a contributory pension, was the mark of thrift and providence. As the pension became recognized as a right, public assistance became more clearly defined as a discretionary grant for those who could not qualify for a pension.[28] The Majority of the 1909 Commission opposed the existing noncontributory old age pension. Eligibility was dependent on an income test, prior conduct, and the previous nonreceipt of assistance. The Majority maintained that these pensions encouraged pauperism and "the decrease of filial duty."[29] The Minority, although not going so far as advocating universal pensions for the aged, supported the liberalization of the program. "Conduct" was still to be considered a prerequisite, but previous relief was not to serve as a disqualification. The Majority recommended that medical assistance should be organized for the working class on a voluntary subscription basis. They also favored a contributory invalidity insurance to provide some income during illness. For the Minority this was no substitute for a state medical service with a range of tax-supported services from "searching out disease" to "preventing either recurrence or spread of disease."[30] In providing for the ill and the aged the Minority were more willing to abandon the reward of merit for a more simply administered universal scheme.

The Majority and Minority agreed on the use of trade union out-of-work benefits as the foundation of unemployment insurance. Both considered the trade unions the most effective mechanism for administering unemployment insurance and advocated public subsidies of trade union funds. Neither viewed the receipt of benefits as a reward for membership in a trade union fund, although both recognized the value of trade unions in stabilizing employment. The Majority saw the insurance benefits as an inducement for skilled laborers to organize themselves into unions.[31]

The General Right to Support

There was no totally unqualified acceptance of the right to support, although several proposals incorporated the principle to a large degree. Charles Booth's universal noncontributory old age pensions would have provided a guaranteed income to all aged. The establishment of a national system of poor relief, as urged by Disraeli and the Tory socialists, would have broadened the base and liberalized the administration of assistance.[32]

The right to support indicated recognition of the responsibility of society for the economic welfare of its members. Poverty and the other ills of men were the result of social rather than individual forces. Although there were differences of opinion among the Liberal reformers, the settlement leadership and the Christian Socialists, and the Fabian Socialists and the radical labor leaders about the responsibility of society, the conditions of the poor were believed by all to be due to a large extent to external circumstances.

Orthodox economists like Alfred Marshall questioned the justice of the market distribution of wages and suggested that the advantage of the "buyers" of labor was the result of the pressure of hunger, which forced labor to sell its skill at a low price.[33] The Fabians were, of course, even more critical of the maldistribution of wealth. The Webbs pointed to "huge incomes . . . which bear no relation whatever to the relative capacity of the manufacturers or traders concerned, or to the amount of work that they perform."[34] These incomes were a reflection of what the Webbs termed parisitic industry, "which," they said, "habitually takes more out of its workers than the wages and other conditions of employment enable them to repair,—still more, if the effect of the employment is to deteriorate both character and physique of successive relays of operatives."[35]

The right to support was also strengthened by the growing belief that wealth was the result of social effort and could not be related entirely to any specific individual account. The generality of society should receive its appropriate share. Thus, Henrietta Barnett—no radical—spoke of the "right use and distribution" of wealth as the proper concern of society.[36] But even among such groups as the settlement leadership, who supported the concept of social wealth and social responsibility, there was great resistance to recognizing the right to social support. Like the Charity Organisation Society, the settlements feared that recognition of this right would pauperize the poor. The settlement leadership, therefore, turned social responsibility into other channels. Along with many contemporary reformers, they interpreted the right to support as fundamentally a right to equal opportunity in the competitive economic market.

The right to support was interpreted still differently by Alfred Marshall. Apart from the question of social justice, Marshall favored broadening the responsibility of society from indigence to poverty generally. He reported to the Royal Commission on the Aged Poor in 1893:

While the problem of 1834 was the problem of pauperism, the problem of 1893 is the problem of poverty; that a man ought not to be allowed to live in a bad home, that extreme poverty ought to be regarded, not indeed as a crime, but as a thing so detrimental to the State that it should not be endured, and that everybody who, whether through his own fault or not, was incapable of keeping together a home that contributed to the well-being of the State, that person should, under the authority of the State, pass into a new form of life.[37]

Marshall did not find the return of taxes to previous taxpayers now in distress to be "specially distasteful." His interest in the coming generation convinced him that subsidies might even be necessary for families with wage earners.[38]

The Fabians and the trade union leadership took a clear stand on the right of support. They were least sympathetic to the able-bodied who made insufficient effort to find employment. All other groups requiring services or support were to receive them as needed. According to the socialist platform of the 1880s, the object of poor law reform was "to provide generously, and without stigma, for the aged, the sick, and those destitute through temporary want of employment, without relaxing the 'tests' against the endowment of able-bodied idleness."[39] The right to support for the able-bodied was to be implemented by the right to work. The able-bodied were to be removed from the poor law system and placed in the hands of national government agencies responsible for employment policy. Those who would not work were to be subject to the correctional system and to receive the benefits of a strict and harsh policy. The Fabians and the labor leadership would not tolerate those who exploited the labor of others and added nothing to the social wealth of the nation.

The Right to Opportunity

The right to opportunity was, except for the most intransigent followers of the old classical economics or the more recent social Darwinism, the most universally accepted principle. For conservative reformers like Lord Shaftesbury the right to opportunity was the only reasonable answer to the inequalities suffered by many at the start of their economic careers. Even radical socialists, though they considered it only a beginning and piecemeal reform, recognized the significance of equalization of opportunity. Liberals, Fabians, and all groups dissatisfied with the contemporary situation felt that the advantages of such necessities as education, health, housing, and culture should be shared by the total citizenry. The right to support had been seriously weakened by the alleged excesses of the Speenhamland era, and the right to work represented an inordinate interference with the economic system for all but the socialists.

The redistribution of some of the benefits of production, however, so that all might have the opportunity to exert to the maximum their capacity for achievement and gain their maximum rewards was acceptable to almost everyone.

The right to opportunity was the principal plank in the platform of reformers favorable to the basic structure of nineteenth-century society. It maintained the incentives of the competitive system, but by opening the game to more players on a fair basis it produced greater results for all involved. Further, it seemed the one sure answer to the socialists and others who maintained that the gains of the laissez-faire society were being shared by a narrower and narrower circle of the elect. By extending opportunity and foreseeing the passing away of the static lower classes, the moderate reformers believed that they had the answer to the inevitability of class opposition preached by the socialists, and of the crude struggle for existence of the social Darwinists.

The popularity of increasing opportunity was demonstrated by the reforms carried out in nineteenth-century England. The first attack was on child labor, which continued to be a major focus of concern throughout the century. Investment in the young and saving them from the demoralizing conditions of their own backgrounds were important steps toward social and economic democracy. Restrictions on child labor were enforced at the same time that educational standards were raised. Gradually women came to be included in the reformists' zeal, and eventually protection was afforded to male workers.

In the latter half of the nineteenth century the proposals of a variety of groups, from the Liberal-Labour faction of Joseph Chamberlain to the Marxist Social Democratic Federation, revealed the breadth of agreement in providing for the more disadvantaged. Progressive taxation was universally accepted as fundamental to all social programs. Extension of education, improved housing, and better factory conditions were pressed on all sides. The social services were broadly mapped out and to a great extent delineated in the preventive program of the Minority Report of the 1909 Commission. The settlement movement and the Christian Socialists gave much attention to the cultural and recreational aspects of life. Participation in political institutions on the local and national level was also emphasized. If the almost static condition of the poor law administration and the few rare and modest attempts at emergency employment measures are contrasted with the extent of these reforms, the direction of British welfare policy is clearly indicated.

The Right to Work

The last vestiges of mercantilist paternalism had been cleared away by the poor law reforms of 1834. For the independent laboring class and the growing trade union movement of the second half of the nineteenth century, any system of wage supplements or doles was as unacceptable as it had been earlier to the rising middle class. In 1893, Alfred Marshall stated before the Royal Commission on the Aged Poor:

> I do not think that the ablest and most far-seeing members of the working classes are at all blind to the great benefits which the poor themselves have derived from the firmer administration of the Poor Law since 1834, and the general tendency to replace lax and undiscriminating out-relief.[40]

> I hold there would be a large majority among the working classes in support of a stern administration of the Poor Law in cases of all people who do not deserve well.[41]

The working class had substituted the need for employment, the only respectable source of income for wage earners, for the middle-class emphasis on unrestricted trade and industry. The lower-class expectation of work had moral as well as economic overtones. The Evangelical movement had made great headway among workers, and for many work had become a religious and social duty. John Burns, the leader of the London dockers' strike of 1889 and spokesman for the unemployed, incorporated the Protestant ethic in his working-class code. "How can the honest worker," he asked, "be provided with work uncontaminated with pauperism's degrading taint and charity's demoralising aid?" Burns called "employment on useful work, the real and only antidote to all the ills that laboring flesh is heir to."[42]

Thus the provision of work at a living wage was the only acceptable alternative for needy employable persons. Any other policy would have subsidized both idleness on the part of the worker and parasitism on the part of employers. The Webbs and the labor movement saw public assistance and the social services as a bounty to employers who did not pay adequate wages or maintain standards high enough to support independently their own labor supply.[43] In addition, all this resulted in a tremendous waste of social resources.

The confusion of work with the welfare or assistance system was as abhorrent to the socialists and the labor leadership as it had been to the 1834 Poor Law Commission. The Minority Report of the 1909 Commission recommended a national employment program unrelated to the public assistance structure. Work was not to be a form of relief but a significant contribution to the well-being of society. The Minority did not view favorably the emphasis on employing the aged and handicapped.

So long as there are young and healthy unemployed, it cannot be expected—it cannot even be desired—that the less efficient should fill the places to the exclusion of the more efficient. Insofar as aged men, and partially incapacitated men, are found among those in distress from Unemployment—and this is to some slight extent the case—the problem is one of how best to maintain them in their old age and partial invalidity—not how to get them again into industrial employment for which other men, also compulsorily idle, are more fitted.[44]

Parasitic employees were to be tolerated no more than parasitic employers. In later years the Fabians were somewhat apologetic about their early fervor. Sidney Webb remarked in 1920 that among the shortcomings of the Fabian approach in 1889 was the absence of a plan for the "noneffectives" and the idea that society was, or "ought to be, composed entirely of healthy adults, free from accidents and exempt, if not from death, at any rate from senility."[45]

The public assistance system, certainly as it served the able-bodied, was regarded by socialist reformers as an evil of the laissez-faire economy. While the "principle of collectivism" was necessary for the organization of industry, the socialists denied its application to the "distribution of relief—a *role* which Socialists would contend the individualistic system and method of industry has forced upon 'the State.'" For the "able-bodied idler," the "criminal department of the State" was the appropriate resource.[46]

The enforcement of the right and responsibility of work, according to the Fabians and their followers, depended on organizing the economy to make maximum use of the labor supply. During their earliest period the Fabians believed that recurrent unemployment could not be controlled in a capitalist society. The Minority Report's proposals for smoothing out the cycles of unemployment reflected a modification of this view. Through public planning it would be possible to arrange for continued employment even in a basically individualistic society.[47]

The Fabians made all policies subservient to the efficient use of the productive forces of the nation. Fundamental to Marxism was the exploitation of labor and the appropriation of labor value by the capitalist, but Fabian socialism had no such class partisanship—idlers and producers could be found in all classes, and efficiency was to the advantage of all. The more rational economy predicated on the growing involvement of government in industry included a more regulated use of the labor force. In 1887 the Fabians, considering remedies for unemployment, paralleled proposals for public works and nationalization with the conscription of the labor force.[48] The Webbs were critical of the compulsory treatment of the idle in the Majority Report, but the Minority proposals were, if anything, more stern.

Central to the Fabian scheme for the unemployed generally were residential colonies where the unemployed would help support each other cooperatively by the exchange of their products of labor. Such colonies would be the beginnings of communal and national enterprises and would eventually reduce the sphere of private business by their greater efficiency.[49] The labor leader John Burns opposed the colony plan on humanitarian grounds. Labor colonies, said Burns, would remove laboring men from the social milieu, and man is "a gregarious animal and loathes separation or isolation from his fellows."[50] Burns found little to distinguish the labor colonies from the detested poor law casual wards.

The specific proposals of the Fabians and the Majority for guaranteeing employment did not differ so much in type as in degree. The idea of a National Labour Exchange that would relate the supply of labor to the needs of the labor market had general approval in all quarters. More fundamental differences involved the actual provision of work when there was a surplus of labor in the private market. Both the Minority and Majority of the Poor Law Commission considered the problem of public works. During the twenty years prior to the Commission there had been an almost continuous history of municipal works. The Majority were extremely wary of such programs. Apart from their criticisms of the efficiency of these undertakings, the Majority feared that the practice of municipal relief work would "lead to a recrudescence of the evils so ably described by the Royal Commission of 1832. . . . Even now there are signs that among the casual labourers, encouraged and subsidised by the Unemployed Workmen Act, there is arising precisely that spirit of dependence and demoralization which was so rampant in 1832."[51]

The Majority of the Commission recommended that such municipal works be of the shortest possible duration. Only in periods of "exceptional and protracted distress" and "for a strictly limited period during the earlier years of the reforms" would the Majority countenance the establishment of public works.[52] The Minority had no such compunctions about the role of public works. They recommended that the national demand for labor be regularized over a ten year period by a plan for public works adjusted to the oscillations of the business cycle.

The Webbs were particularly concerned about the effect of substandard labor—"the physically or mentally diseased" and "the constitutionally inefficient"—on the labor market. They proposed withdrawing these groups entirely from the competitive labor market to avoid having the total labor force threatened by standards established for inferior workers. They recommended that special types of unskilled work, "Poor Law occupations," be provided, such as agricultural and sewage employment. In special noncompetitive industries those workers would not lower the bargaining position of other workers and would not undermine the morale of the more efficient. Finally, by manning the least skillful occupations with the least fit, more capable workers would be released for greater contributions to the national welfare.[53]

The Majority of the Poor Law Commission, except for its limited acquiescence to emergency public works, limited the role of government's provision of employment to the regular functions performed by the state. The Minority viewed government as the great stabilizer of employment and recommended that public departments, national and local, adjust their demands, when possible, to the conditions of the labor market. Government contracts should be held for periods when there was slack pressure for labor.

The Majority and the Minority members of the Commission were in substantial agreement on other types of programs for the able-bodied unemployed. While the Minority proposed that day training and residential colonies be under the Ministry of Labour, the Majority incorporated them in the public assistance organization. Both provided for some kind of work as routine practice in giving aid to the able-bodied. In some cases the recipient might work or undergo retraining while at home; in others, he might be expected to join a residential labor colony. Finally, for persistent offenses—neglect of family or refusal to work—detention colonies were to be established.

Conclusion

During the nineteenth century the three philosophies of economic security vied for priority—support, opportunity, and work. By the first third of the century the right to support had been nullified to a large extent both by the immediate failure to institute an efficient program and by the conflict between societal support and the dominant ethos of the competitive laissez-faire society. As long as work was recognized as the only legitimate source of income for most members of society, acceptance of responsibility by the state for the provision of employment would have clashed with the ideology of laissez-faire in much the same way as the right to support.

The Industrial Revolution was not long on the scene before its harmful effects were recognized. Among the most disquieting of these were the degrading conditions to which the lower classes were subjected. Apart from clearly humanitarian concerns, the limitations of the poor prevented their free and equal participation in the competitive economy and restricted the growth and health of the whole society. Thus, the right to opportunity became the chief goal of reform. The conditions of the poor could be bettered by improving opportunity without directly interfering with the economic market, as would have occurred had social responsibility for support or work been accepted.

The insufficiency of this policy still left the issues of support and work unresolved. Economic recessions at the end of the nineteenth century emphasized the instability of the labor market and the consequent lack of economic security in the normal employment situation. Those imbued with the principles of 1834 tried to avoid any enlargement of public responsibility; on the other hand, those influenced by socialist doctrine were willing to accept intervention in the productive system to guarantee stabilization of income from employment.

The advocates of greater equalization of opportunity through reforms in education, housing, health, and industrial conditions were still faced with the problem of economic security. Fundamentally, the right to opportunity was directed toward future generations and depended for its success on the healthful development of the children of the present generation. But could those children have expanded opportunities if society were indifferent to the economic security of their parents? Thus, the right to opportunity entailed a reconsideration of society's responsibility for support and work.

11

America in the
Nineteenth Century

VAST changes occurred in the United States during the latter half of the nineteenth century. The First World War marked the United States as a principal world power and symbolized the culmination of an era of major social and economic developments. The revolution from a predominantly rural and agricultural economy to an urban, industrial society proceeded at an increasingly rapid pace throughout the nineteenth century. Despite the opening of enormous areas in the West, the steady growth of urban centers resulted in an almost equal distribution of the population between urban and rural areas by the beginning of World War I. In 1840 the population was a little over 17 million and almost 90 percent rural; in 1910 it was about 92 million, of whom nearly half were settled in urban communities. The population as a whole had increased five and a half times, the urban population almost forty times.

The largest part of this growth and change took place after the Civil War. The victory of the Union forces was the victory of industrial and urban interests over the agricultural and rural slave economy of the South. In 1790 the total population of the country was almost evenly divided between the South and the North. By 1870 the population of the South was a third of the whole and was matched by both the Northeast and the North Central regions. The normal increase in these two regions was accentuated by the great influx of European migrants and their concentration in the urban industrial sections of the North.

The industrialization of America, as compared to England, was started and completed later and created less havoc with the existing social and economic structure. By the time of the colonization of America, British mercantilist policy emphasized commercial and industrial goals. American industrialization was primarily a phenomenon of the last three quarters of the nineteenth century.

The social and economic life of America underwent significant changes in the nineteenth century. The ideal of Jeffersonian democracy, which had struggled against Federalist economic nationalism, was no longer a realistic force on the American scene.[1] The myth of the Jeffersonian small democratic community still lingered on; in the latter part of the century Bryce found much to remind him of the neighborliness and social equality noted by de Tocqueville in earlier years. But the rapidity of change toward a commercial and industrial society was much too great in the closing decades of the century to permit any illusions about the direction America was taking.

The frontier, believed to be an endless source of opportunity, no longer existed by the end of the century. Cheap land and cheap money had been the eternal panacea of the debtor and poorer classes. Rather than the "working class," as Europe's workers viewed themselves, America's workers had considered themselves on the road to becoming small landholders, merchants, and capitalists. The drying up of available lands and the monopoly and exploitation of the natural resources by large corporations removed the last basis for optimism on the part of the ordinary man. "Go West, young man" had epitomized the spirit of the age of enterprise; but vigor and ambition alone no longer made the difference between success and failure. In the future, circumstances would limit the opportunity of both the enterprising and their less venturesome neighbors.

The growth of great business organizations extending from industry to agriculture further limited the sphere of individual action. The merchant adventurer was replaced by a complex combination of corporate interests. The barriers to passing from employee to employer became more fixed. Although this had been increasingly true over a long period of time, the "shock of recognition" became sharper toward the end of the century. The large entry into the United States of the most economically deprived European immigrants supplied a continuing reservoir of unskilled labor as well as the foundation of a truly urban working-class population. Between 1850 and 1900 the proportion of foreign born in the population increased from less than 13 percent to 18 percent.

The shifts in the economy, in the nature of the population, and in the means of livelihood were brought to the fore by the several long and serious industrial depressions prior to World War I: 1857–1858, 1873–1879, 1893–1897, 1907–1908. The Haymarket riot and the Homestead and Pullman strikes clearly announced a new era of industrial conflict. They were far different from those famous earlier struggles of the post-Revolutionary period, Shays' and the Whiskey Rebellion, and presaged the growing and continuing conflict between organized labor and large industry.

The complex and highly unpredictable modern economy exacerbated the problem of economic security for large masses of men. Urban living meant crowding and unhealthy conditions, but on the other hand, it brought continually rising standards and costs of consumption. For the simplicity and thrift of rural and small town life was substituted the complex of goods and services of the urban community. There were substantial increases in average wages throughout the post-Civil War period, but they did not necessarily indicate an increase in real wages.[2] In 1869 the Special Commission of the Revenue reported:

The aggregate wealth of the country is increasing, probably, as rapidly as at any former period; yet it does not follow that there is the same increase in general prosperity. The laborer, especially he who has a large family to support, is not as prosperous as he was in 1860. His wages have not increased in proportion to the increase in the cost of living. There, is, therefore, an inequality in the distribution of our annual product.[3]

The distribution of the national product became of increasing concern because it revealed the widening gap between the rich and the poor. Whatever the trend in average wages, there remained large sections of the population who had insufficient means to support themselves independently according to the minimal standards of urban life. Following Booth's survey of London, several American studies attempted to assess the prevalence of poverty in America. One such study in 1904 estimated that one fifth of the industrial population and one tenth of the remainder of the country lived in poverty.[4]

Poor health, business crises, large families, industrial accidents, and other factors that reduced income and increased normal expenditure threatened the way of life of the lowest wage earners. Employment opportunities for women and children had greatly expanded, and the changing mores of family life and the emancipation of women made such work acceptable. The wages of women and young people augmented the inadequate earnings of men, but new problems were created that threatened the stability of family life.

The roots of modern American economic security policy were in the post-Civil War era, when the growing industrial and commercial society caused serious problems for the economic welfare of the population. By the end of the nineteenth century the quasi-supports of rural and family life had given way, just as the earlier status systems that survived the Industrial Revolution in England finally crumbled in the post-Napoleonic era. The widespread development of the state boards of charities in the second half of the century signified the need for some more organized system of welfare than had been required in the preceding period. The United States had been able to stave off giving serious attention to the question of economic security for a half century longer than the British, but by the end of the nineteenth century it could no longer be wholly avoided. Solutions were not quick in coming, and even when recognized they were resisted and at best reluctantly accepted.

The latter half of the nineteenth century and the first decade of the twentieth was a time when the major problems of modern economic security were defined rather than settled. They remained to be worked out slowly during the better part of the twentieth century. As Commager has commented:

The great issues of the nineties still commanded popular attention half a century later; the seminal minds of that decade still directed popular thought. Problems of isolation and internationalism, of laissez faire and government planning, of the causes and cures of panics, the contrasts of progress and poverty, the humanizing of urban life, the control of business and the rights of labor, the place of the Negro and the immigrant in society, the improvement of agriculture and the conservation of natural resources, the actualization of democracy into social security—all these things which had monopolized public interest in the nineties, seemed no less urgent in the 1930's and 1940's.[5]

The American view of the problem of economic welfare was quite different from the British. The differences followed from both historical and contemporary factors. The contrasting experiences of the Industrial Revolution in both countries have already been mentioned. For England it was a cataclysmic experience, and in its wake came the uprooting of the remnants of the former social system and the expansion of unhealthy and unwholesome industry in urban areas. The impact in America was less noticeable. The concentrations of population were not so great; on the whole, people were better distributed. The effects of commercialism and industrialization were not striking enough to arouse the bitterness of a Carlyle or the disgust of a Ruskin. Their counterparts, the American Romantics, were relatively optimistic and asserted merely the classic response to materialism rather than shock at the despoilment of their own world.

Optimism was a continual tonic on the American scene. The American political economists had rejected the pessimism of English scholars like Malthus and Ricardo. Americans, remarked Myrdal, "criticized the British classics with arguments which at that time would have been hardly possible in any other social setting."[6] Believers in natural law, Americans always interpreted it as the good intentions of Providence in their behalf. Later, both scholars and the general public were exuberantly attracted to Herbert Spencer's social Darwinism because Spencer supplied a rationale for their belief in their own limitless destiny. A people who believed that the world was on their side could hardly be expected to be concerned seriously about a few economic dislocations.

In contrast to England, there was neither acceptance of class position by the poor nor recognition of responsibility by the rich. It was not until the late nineteenth century that the concept of stewardship of wealth espoused by Carnegie and other wealthy industrialists provided a rationale for paternalism on the American scene. The migration of the lower classes to America broke their ties with established social patterns and put an end to their expectations of help from the upper classes. England's Speenhamland policy would have been foreign to both upper and lower classes in America, although the example of Speenhamland was used to restrict further the already meager relief programs. The poor in America considered themselves merely impoverished entrepreneurs, not a dependent class. Opportunity, not support, was their goal. As Lincoln said,

"When one starts poor, as most do in the race of life, free society is such that he knows he can better his condition; he knows that there is no fixed condition of labor for his whole life."[7]

Much energy in the closing years of the nineteenth century was given to maintaining the reality and the belief of America as the land of opportunity. Bigness in business and industry was deprecated, and monopoly was restricted. It was not, as Lincoln said earlier, "any war upon capital"; rather, "we do wish to allow the humblest man an equal chance to get rich with anybody else."[8] The right to acquire wealth should not be limited to the few. The Homestead Act, which opened government lands to smallholders, was the American counterpart to British concern about the poor laws.

Although the urgency of poverty was less in America than in England, there were other issues that at times tended to camouflage the problems of economic need. The struggle between the advocates of "hard" and "soft" money turned the question of distribution of wealth into a problem of currency. The abolitionist zeal invested in the slavery issue absorbed the attention of many liberals who would normally have been concerned about the poor. The reaction to the new wave of immigrants in the post-Civil War period displaced attention from other pressing social and economic problems on the domestic scene.

The spread and diversity of the American population resulted in more local than national policy and little broad consensus on major issues. The Constitution was framed to balance parochial and national interests, but in action it seemed to favor the former at the expense of the latter. It is not surprising that local autonomy in economic welfare far outlasted local control in England and that local autonomy in America became a principle and virtue in itself. Local relief and settlement were viewed as important in the struggle of the localities to maintain their integrity against engulfment by larger forces. The issue of local taxes supporting local citizenry was important, but local relief also maintained the right of local exclusiveness inherited from early New England.

Radical thinking reflected the complex social pattern of American life. There were no distinctive schools of thought, no strict adherence to theoretical or ideological positions. More reforming than revolutionary, American radicals might span as broad a range of concepts as the practical and immediate solution of Henry George's land tax or the romantic utopianism of Bellamy's planned society. While both had an important impact on the American scene, neither's influence resulted in specific change or the establishment of a firm reform or radical movement.

The end of the nineteenth century was marked by a sharp renewal of reform activity. The mantle of Jeffersonianism, Jacksonianism, and Populism fell upon the loosely organized Progressive movement. From the last decade of the nineteenth century to America's entry into the First World War, members of the liberal wings of both major political parties as well as reformers and radicals of a variety of shades and opinions attempted to bring change to the industrial scene. They supported labor and antitrust legislation, the protection of natural resources, the rooting out of corruption and inefficiency in local government, city planning and tenement reform, the reorganization of the tax system, and programs for the underprivileged—the poor, women, children, and immigrants.[9] The Progressive movement was the widespread response of America to the emerging problems of industrialization, urbanization, and concentration of wealth and power. Unlike earlier Populist movements, which smacked of democratic Jeffersonianism, the Progressives sought to remedy the difficulties of society through effectively organized government intervention. Their thinking, platform, and actions laid the foundation for the reforms of the later twentieth century.

12

Ideologies: The Nature of Man and Society

Romanticism

FROM its beginnings individualism had been one of the outstanding characteristics of American society. The frontiersman, the pioneer, the trader, the farmer, the hunter, the mariner were all figures who stood for the triumph of the individual over nature and the settled way of life. In the nineteenth century there arose in America, as in Europe, a new movement to reawaken faith in the dignity of man and his unlimited potential.

Romanticism in America reflected the greater optimism and confidence in American society and the heightened sense of individualism stemming from Calvinism and Puritanism. Man was at the center of the universe; his intuition and his judgment were the measure of the good; and the perfectability of man's nature in God's image was the core of life. Romanticism sought to recover the inner essence and purity of man from the corruption wrought by the conventions of society. The Romantic ideal did not necessarily require a total rejection of society and might even take the form of establishing a society that fulfilled the belief in the sacredness of the individual. On the other hand, it might emphasize man's uniqueness through denial of society, which could only conflict with man's goal of transcending the immediate, the petty, the material.

British and American Romanticism indicated the relative emphasis of the nations on individual as against social factors. Both were greatly influenced by Hegel and the German Romantics, and the leading figures of the British and American movements kept in close contact. Carlyle found more in common with Emerson than with John Stuart Mill, his British contemporary who tempered rationality with Romanticism. The major difference between the two schools, however, was the American concentration on individualism and the British on the social organism. British Romantics, such as Carlyle and Ruskin, were not unconcerned about the spiritual nature of man, but they felt that the spiritual and social natures arose from each other and in harmony rather than in the conflict present in their contemporary society. Thus, British Romantics participated directly in the reform of society through Christian socialism, the settlement movement, and socialism itself. Even Marx's *Communist Manifesto* is a Romantic document in its protest against the bourgeois society that had destroyed the spirit of previous social systems.

The American Romantics emphasized the unique aspects of individualism. Individualism demanded that the independence and separateness of the individual be obtained at all costs. Thoreau epitomized this point of view, and his thinking, though not his behavior, was shared by the leading New England transcendentalists. Even Emerson and the more socially oriented of the group did not visualize a society of interdependent members. As Ralph Barton Perry has remarked, the transcendentalists were "an elite . . . primarily concerned with their own elevation of mind."[1] Humanitarians in the full sense they were not. Emerson complained bitterly of the people's slowness in learning the lesson of self-help. Society was full of "infirm people, who incessantly summon others to serve them."[2] "A sympathetic person is placed in the dilemma of a swimmer among drowning men, who all catch at him, and if he give so much as a leg or finger they will drown him."[3]

Like the English Romantics, the American transcendentalists were reformers, but the nature of their reform was different. They spoke out against the inequities of their day—slavery, the treatment of the insane and the blind, the exploitation of the working population, and the inhumanity of prisons. They did not, however, have any fundamental philosophy about social change because they neither concentrated on constructive social action nor shared a spiritual concern for the common good. Brook Farm, the retreat of the transcendentalists, was an exclusive fellowship of the initiated who sought a common withdrawal from society as Thoreau had individually. English Romantics, such as William Morris, also organized utopian communities, but their emphasis was not exclusively individual and personal. They were rather ventures in cooperative living to reestablish the bonds of earlier, simpler, and assumedly healthier societies.

The British Romantics worked with the lower classes to civilize and socialize them. Producers' and consumers' cooperatives were formed; education was extended to the working classes; and the university settlements acted to reawaken the social and cultural vitality of the slum population. This sharing with the lower classes, this faith in the honest workingman, was not part of American Romanticism. Only perhaps in Whitman does American Romanticism lose its cloak of New England parochialism and become a broadly social and democratic gospel.

We shall, it is true, quickly and continually find the origin-idea of the singleness of man, individualism, asserting itself, and cropping forth, even from the opposite ideas. But the mass, or lump character, for imperative reasons, is to be ever carefully weigh'd, borne in mind, and provided for. Only from it, and from its proper regulation and potency, comes the other, comes the chance of individualism.[4]

I know nothing more rare, even in this country, than a fit scientific estimate and reverent appreciation of the People—of their measureless wealth of latent power and capacity, their vast, artistic contrasts of lights and shades—with, in America, their entire reliability in emergencies, and a certain breadth of historic grandeur, of peace or war, far surpassing all the vaunted samples of book-heroes or any *haut ton* coteries, in all the records of the world.[5]

Other leaders of American Romanticism in the middle of the nineteenth century rejected the materialism of industrial and commercial society, but provided little to replace it but a refined and sensitive individualism. For the American Romantic there was no golden era to look back upon. For the British Romantic there was a period that preceded the onset of industrialism, an era of simple craftsmen and yeomen and established social patterns. The American Romantic, not having experienced the social chaos of a newly industrialized society, was shocked primarily by changing values—the landgrabbing pioneer, the union workman, the pushing small capitalist—and he revolted against popular democracy and the crass expectations that he believed had been introduced by the common man.

Romanticism in America was part of the dominant philosophy of individualism. Rejecting the selfish materialism and competition growing up about them, the Romantics substituted an enlightened and benevolent but more introspective, self-sufficient, and isolating individualism. In America the philosophy of individualism emphasized by the transcendentalists was spread by such diverse figures as Sumner and the social Darwinists and Horace Mann and the followers of the pedagogical principles of Pestalozzi and Froebel. In each, the individual became the center of focus, and the social scene remained in the shadows. The Romantic belief in self-fulfillment and the Spencerian concept of evolution were combined in the learning psychology of children. The free play of the child was a wholesome preparatory exercise of the impulses necessary in the struggle for survival.[6] Freedom to develop naturally was the ideal of the Romantic educator as well as of the social Darwinist.

Social Darwinism

The individualism of the American Romantics concentrated on self-fulfillment, but the individualism of the social Darwinists was necessary for the achievement of social goals. Freedom of individual action was required for social advancement, for social evolution was dependent on gradual progress toward the better society through the unhampered action of its members. The process of evolution promised that individual freedom would favor the fittest over their rivals, and those most capable of adapting themselves to the demands of their environment would produce the better society.

Spencer, and Sumner, his principal American apostle, elaborated an individualism more in accord with the pattern of American thought than the mystical Romantic notion of the "Great God Self." Social Darwinism recognized the individual as the key to the competitive game to which society was committed. The successful were those whose marks of achievement were clearly discernible by the prizes awarded.

Nevertheless, the Romantic ideal of the self and the Spencer-Sumner competitor shared more than the mere reference point of individualism. To many of the Romantics the successful leader symbolized the Romantic spirit. Hero-worship was common among the Romantics, and Carlyle's "captain of industry" was endowed with both Romantic and social Darwinist qualities. The mixture of robber baron, successful entrepreneur, and steward of wealth might have shocked Emerson's sensitivities, but by the end of the nineteenth century it was identified with the Romantic myth.

American Romantics and social Darwinists were on common ground in their praise of self-reliance. For English Romantics self-reliance was a quality of the leader, but his followers were permitted the luxury of dependence. The Tory socialism of Disraeli and the young England movement were systems of interdependence on the feudal model. The American Romantic, however, made self-reliance a universal tenet, and each man had the obligation to achieve maximum independence.

Herbert Spencer's absorption with liberty and freedom from state controls was almost fanatical or certainly seemed so on the British scene, but in America, Sumner was at least as extreme in his interpretation of individualism and freedom from constraint. His *What Social Classes Owe to Each Other* was a virulent denunciation of any attempt to make the individual responsible for the well-being of others. Yet Sumner did not seem out of place in nineteenth-century America, as Spencer did in England even earlier. The appeal of social Darwinism in America far outweighed its popularity in England. As a social doctrine, social Darwinism summed up and gave scientific approval to many of the beliefs already present in American society.

Social Darwinism provided a rationale for the present reward system and its continued operation. By maintaining that those who currently succeeded were in effect the most capable, the social Darwinists merely pointed to the justice of contemporary society. Rewards were not controlled by random or chance factors but were distributed according to the fitness of the competitors. As Andrew Carnegie so aptly stated, "What men call luck, is the prerogative of valiant souls."[7] Carnegie and other wealthy entrepreneurs offset any doubts they might have about the rightness of their favored position by preferring to view themselves as the stewards rather than as the absolute possessors of God's gifts.

The assumptions of hereditary differences underlying social Darwinism provided a strong foundation for an individualistic competitive society. Any effort to change the current distribution of wealth through private benevolence or state action would result in the misuse of wealth and the continued presence of inferior stock. While Galton, the British psychologist, studied hereditary genius, the American psychologists Dugdale and Goddard followed the life histories of two families with an extraordinary incidence of social problems and concluded that hereditary defects accounted for their high rate of pauperism, disease, and immorality. At the end of the nineteenth century these were considered by many to be the prototypes of the dependent classes.

Malthus had come to these conclusions almost a century before, but Americans had been unwilling to accept his pessimistic doctrine at the time. Helping the poor was short-sighted, Malthus pointed out, because it only took from the deserving and perpetuated the cancer of dependency. Now Sumner and other leading social philosophers and students of heredity espoused the scientific validity and social wisdom of Malthus' position. They added, however, an important element in keeping with the optimism of American society—the continuous improvement of man and society through natural evolution. This satisfied even the charitable and socially minded who found in social Darwinism a basis for continued faith in the perfection of man. Charles Loring Brace, the noted nineteenth-century child-welfare leader, saw "the law of natural selection affecting the moral history of mankind, as well as the physical. Evil must die ultimately as the weaker element, in the struggle with good."[8]

American reaction to psychological research on heredity was, however, far different from English reaction. Despite the comfort that belief in innate characteristics gave some, the subject was too intimately connected with basic American values to permit a consensus based solely on the findings of academic research. Americans were too "practical" to surrender their belief in the success of opportunity because of some complicated psychological studies. After Dugdale and Goddard's study the nature-nurture problem received more and more scholarly attention, but the more the research, the less conclusive the answer. Much skepticism arose about the possibility of obtaining any objective scientific findings, and the issue devolved frequently into an ideological struggle influenced by the social implications of emphasizing either heredity or environment. The confusion and conflicts in the scientific world only served to decrease the faith of the general public in research and affirmed its faith in practical knowledge.

As in England, educators were influenced by the psychological research on ability and intelligence, but the ideal of education for all was already so firmly rooted that there was little chance of either resisting or even reducing the spreading system of secondary education. Education was not only the ladder toward individual achievement, but it was also the great instrument of socialization and acculturation in a society consisting of a relatively diverse and sparsely settled population with no lengthy cultural tradition. As early as 1849, Horace Mann, possibly the most influential force in American education, set its goal.

Under our republican government it seems clear that the minimum of education can never be less than such as is sufficient to qualify each citizen for the civil and social duties he will have to discharge; such an education as teaches the individual, the great laws of bodily health, as qualifies for the fulfillment of parental duties; as is indispensable for the civil function of a witness or juror; as is necessary for the voter in municipal and national affairs; and finally, as is required for the faithful and conscientious discharge of all those duties which devolve upon the inheritor of a portion of the sovereignty of this great Republic.[9]

Somewhat differently but still in the same vein, Emerson stated:

The poor man, whom the law does not allow to take an ear of corn when starving, nor a pair of shoes for his freezing feet, is allowed to put his hand into the pockets of the rich, and say, you shall educate me, not as you will, but as I will: not alone in the elements, but by further provision, in the languages, in sciences, in the useful and in the elegant arts. The child shall be taken up by the State and taught, at the public cost, the rudiments of knowledge, and at last the ripest results of art and science.[10]

In 1835, Michigan incorporated in its constitution the principle of universal public education from primary school to university. Other states had included the general principle of education even earlier. After the influential Kalamazoo decision of 1874 by the Michigan Supreme Court secondary education became recognized as a public responsibility throughout the country.

The concern with innate characteristics and eugenics did not directly affect educational philosophy, but there was a growing fear that the native stock would be diluted by the great numbers of immigrants coming to America from all parts of the world. Some of this fear may be attributed to the belief in the inferiority of certain peoples, whether on racial or cultural grounds. From the 1880s, American immigration policy became increasingly selective in admitting immigrants, particularly those considered "foreign" to the American people and their way of life. In the South, where the issue was not the immigrant but the native Negro population, policies of discrimination were clearly rationalized on the grounds of racial inferiority.

Freedom of Will

The American approach to freedom of will has always been complex and inconsistent. On the one hand, Americans subscribed to deterministic philosophies, and on the other, they rejected any notion that did not permit full freedom and hold individuals responsible for their own choices. Calvinistic religious doctrines had emphasized man's depravity, and predestination or selection was an essential part of New England Protestantism. Later, social Darwinism created or permitted a secular rationale for a deterministic view of the cosmos.

However much Americans leaned toward mechanistic influences, they were hardly sufficient for a people who so strongly emphasized individualism. In the land of opportunity the environment was friendly and fertile for endeavor, and the individual determined his own success or failure. Carnegie and his fellows might accept their own good fortune as the select, but they had worked hard to become the select. Survival of the fittest meant to them not so much that those who were more fit from the start survived, but rather that those who had become fit in the struggle succeeded. In general, it was believed that America was a monument to free will and ambition because it was not handicapped by the gross inequalities that in Europe prevented all from participating equally in the competition for success.

Toward the end of the nineteenth century there were some misgivings about equality of opportunity for all. Benjamin Kidd's reformulation of social Darwinism had much appeal. He softened the harshness of Spencer's survival theory by suggesting that all should be equipped to start the contest from relatively similar positions.[11] Through social legislation and altruism the poor would be prepared and motivated to take part energetically in the business of society and, incidentally, would adjure the salvation of socialism.

Those who favored this position recognized that care must be taken not to blunt the competitive edge. If wealth was the goal and educated will the means, society should strenthen the means but avoid tampering with the end. The incentive to free action must be maintained at all costs if the individual was to be pressed to employ his greatest energies. Wealthy philanthropists in the proper practice of stewardship of wealth demonstrated this philosophy. Finley Peter Dunne's Mr. Dooley had this to say about Carnegie's charity:

Befure another year, ivry house in Pittsburg that ain't a blast-furnace will be a Carnaygie Libry. In some places all th' buildin's is libries. If ye write him f'r an autygraft he sinds ye a libry. No beggar is iver turned impty-handed fr'm th' dure. Th' pan-handler knocks an' asts f'r a glass iv milk an' a roll. 'No, sir,' says Andhrew Carnaygie. 'I will not pauperize this onworthy man. Nawthin' is worse f'r a beggar-man thin to make a pauper iv him. Yet it shall not be sad iv me that I give nawthin' to th' poor. Saunders, give him a libry.[12]

For most people the cultivation of free will was integral to an individualistic and competitive society. This was not, however, the only view. William James, a strong advocate of man's voluntary nature, interpreted the will of the individual as an essential constituent of collective action. The natural behavior of individuals might be defined as preponderantly cooperative rather than competitive. Man's free will would then lead directly to socially useful acts rather than toward selfish ends that eventually and mysteriously became applied to the social good. Veblen rejected the hedonistic bent of classical and neoclassical economics and referred to such social instincts as "parental bent" and the "instinct of workmanship." He anticipated the triumph of the socially committed nature of man over his primitive impulses.

Except for a possible reversion to a cultural situation strongly characterized by ideas of emulation and status, the ancient racial bias embodied in the Christian principle of brotherhood should logically continue to gain ground at the expense of the pecuniary morals of competitive business.[13]

By the end of the nineteenth century the social orientation of man received strong support from the new field of social psychology. The idea of man as a rational animal making hedonistic choices was attacked. McDougall's theory of instinctive behavior as the basis of social action was popularly accepted in the early years of the twentieth century. From another side and of growing importance was the stress on environmental influences in the development of the individual. Dewey viewed adjustment or responsiveness to the environment as essential for understanding behavior. Giddings and especially Cooley concentrated on the social environment as a determinant of the individual, and Cooley tried to replace the sharply distinct concepts of man and society with a more unified view of man as a product of his primary group.[14]

Responsiveness to environment had been part of earlier theories, particularly social Darwinism. But the responsiveness was, at any moment in time, a one-way relationship of two discrete and constant bodies. The inability of man to adjust to the dominant environment indicated his inadequacy and failure. The growing fields of sociology and social psychology emphasized the dynamic interaction of man and his world and the difficulty of separating one from the other. The acceptance and application of this position to social and economic problems would make for radical changes in policies based on previous nineteenth-century assumptions.

Laissez-faire

The dominant note on the American scene during the latter half of the nineteenth century was faith in America's continued growth and prosperity as a commercial and industrial society. The social Darwinists had broadened the value of economic liberalism from material gain to cultural progress. Competition founded on individual self-interest had proved to be the social ideal. Not that Americans ever needed a theoretical justification for their practical success. Throughout its history America had accepted, rejected, or modified schools of economic thought as they reflected the truth of the American marketplace. The practical businessman, not the academic economist, set the theme for the American economy. Business leaders were the experts on economics. Impatient with abstract theory, they preferred to phrase their principles in the work-a-day axioms of *Poor Richard's Almanac.*

American economists continued to ignore European theorists such as Sismondi, Saint-Simon, Louis Blanc, Proudhon, and Marx who deviated from classical economics. American economic thought in the nineteenth century represented a combination of Adam Smith and John Stuart Mill infused with a weak version of marginal-utility theory.[15] There were a few radicals like Veblen, but they were not in the mainstream. Two of the most prominent of the orthodox economists of the latter part of the century were Francis A. Walker and John Bates Clark. They were among the few American economists recognized beyond the borders of the United States. Both started out with critical analyses of the status quo but ended confirming its virtues.

Walker, Superintendent of the Ninth Federal Census in 1870, originally supported state intervention to equalize the opportunity of labor. He did not favor such radical measures as unions and strikes but supported social legislation for education, sanitation, savings banks, factory conditions, and the employment of women and children. His attack on the classical wage-fund theory was an impressive contribution to the field of economics and helped sweep away that theoretical rationalization for low wages. Later, however, Walker reinterpreted the relative positions of capital and labor in terms of marginal-utility theory and maintained that labor was receiving a share of the total product greater than its contribution. Walker's formulation left the wage earner in no better a position than the original wage-fund theory did, and at the same time a more satisfactory rationale was provided to support the existing scheme of distribution. Walker finally concluded:

If competition be perfect, no question can be made of its result in an equable division of all burdens and diffusion of all benefits throughout the industrial society. . . .

Competition, to have the beneficent effects which have been ascribed to it, must be all-pervading and unremitting; like the pressure of the atmosphere of which we are happily unconscious because it is all the while equal within and without us, above and below us.[16]

Even the style was of the eighteenth century.

J. B. Clark's early criticisms of the contemporary scene had a Christian Socialist flavor. He objected to the classical emphasis on material self-interest and proposed as a substitute morally motivated behavior. Competition of the marketplace, he suggested, must give way to moral purpose under the aegis of government. He viewed society as organic rather than individualistic in structure and believed that a healthy economy depended on the resolution of the conflicts inherent in the classical model. By the beginning of the twentieth century, however, Clark had shifted to strong approval of the competitive system as the source of a just distribution of wealth and of maximum wealth for all. Under the competitive system, he maintained, both rich and poor would benefit, and although the distance between classes would continue to be great, the increased wealth of the poor would obviate any need for resentment or conflict.[17] The ideal of Clark, like that of most American economists, remained the free and fluid workings of the competitive market in which entrepreneur and worker were each responsible for his own welfare.

The conservatism of American economics received added weight from the numbers of economists recruited from the ministry. Among the best known and perhaps most influential was William Graham Sumner, who was also a pioneer in the field of sociology. Sumner held views similar to, though stronger than, Spencer's on most social questions. For Sumner, laissez-faire was the ideal and symbolized the abandonment of false sentimentality and dependency. Reliance on help from others was a form of primitive behavior and in the contemporary world generally resulted in the appropriating of others' just earnings. Democracy and equality depended on man accepting complete responsibility for himself. Social intervention could not balance the differences between individuals and classes. In fact, Sumner and his followers in sociology held that the customs, the folkways, the status quo were beyond man's direct influence. The most characteristic aspect of society was its static condition, which survived any "impetuous" efforts to upset its balance.[18] Change was a slow and mysterious process.

The most significant attack on laissez-faire in the nineteenth century came not from the socialists, who had little following, but from those who wished to restore laissez-faire. Dissatisfied with the growing corporate power, the reformers saw government as a counterbalancing force to monopoly. They proposed changing the rules of the game or making rules that would guarantee the small business an equal chance with the large in the competitive market. In other words, they hoped to curb the restrictions of big business on the freedom of competition through government action. Gradually the sphere of government intervention widened, particularly under the impetus of the policies of Theodore Roosevelt and Woodrow Wilson.

The doctrine of state intervention had a curious history during the nineteenth century. At the beginning of the century the Jeffersonian liberals opposed a strong and active government. Their ideal was the small community free from external and formal controls. On the other hand, the Hamiltonian Federalists' commitment to national policy relied on strong central government support. Public works, a national bank, and tariffs were all political measures for encouraging economic growth.

By the end of the century the tables had turned. Those who had been identified with Jeffersonian decentralization and individualism had shifted to viewing the state as their ally, while the big business interests were concerned about government's restrictive functions. Upon its founding under the influence of younger radicals like E. J. James, Simon N. Patten, Richard T. Ely, Henry C. Adams, and J. B. Clark, the American Economic Association established as its first principle, "the State as an agency whose positive assistance is one of the indispensable conditions of human progress."[19] A few years later when the old guard took over, this position was abandoned.

Although social reformers tended to favor the expansion of government's role, this was not invariably true. There was still a strong sense of individual rights and distrust of government even among those desiring a more socially just society. Edward Bellamy and Henry George, for example, two of the most popular reformers of the period, differed greatly about the functions of the state. George was in some ways as antagonistic to government action as the social Darwinists, and it should be recalled that even Spencer in his early years was dissatisfied with the private control of landed property. George merely wished to free society from the injustice of land monopoly, but he opposed any more regulatory function on the part of the state. As a result of his land reform, "an immense and complicated network of governmental machinery would be dispensed with. . . ." "Society would thus approach the ideal of Jeffersonian democracy, the promised land of Herbert Spencer, the abolition of government. But of government only as a directing and repressive power."[20] Bellamy, on the other hand, conceived of a society in which nothing was beyond the guidance of the central authority.[21]

The desire for practical achievement on the part of nineteenth-century Americans, as James Bryce, the acute British observer, noted, often overcame any abstract adherence to laissez-faire. Bryce found this particularly the case with the state legislatures, many of which were newly established and filled by men unencumbered by traditional political positions and ideas.

The new democracies of America are as eager for state interference as the democracy of Britain, and try their experiments with even more light-hearted promptitude. . . . Men are even more eager than in Europe to hasten on to the ends they desire, even more impatient of delays which a reliance on natural forces involves, even more sensitive to the wretchedness of their fellows, and to the mischiefs which vice and ignorance breed.[22]

The combination of increasingly complex problems and the desire for progress resulted in expanding the role of government. Attention was turned toward improving the existing government machinery. The Pendleton Act of 1883, which provided for a bipartisan federal Civil Service Commission as well as other improvements in personnel policy, has been termed the Magna Carta of civil-service reform.[23] The development of the commission form of administration generally, combining executive and judicial functions, furnished a flexible, speedy, and independent machinery to deal with many new problems. Reforms were also made in the financial structure of government, in modernizing taxing, budgeting, and accounting methods.

By the end of the century the question of social responsibility had come to the fore on the American scene. The mounting problems of the day led to an examination of contemporary conditions in the light of American ideals. Social reformers, labor leaders, liberal clergymen, and academic economists were evaluating the economy according to social and moral criteria. Among those criteria was the level of living society should guarantee its members. John R. Commons, the leader of the institutional economists, held that society must provide its members with a minimal foundation of subsistence. He considered public poor relief the modern equivalent of earlier systems of support under slavery and serfdom. Commons held more advanced views than most of his economist colleagues on the issue of social responsibility, and he was confused by some with the socialists. It was not unusual for advocates of such measures as income or inheritance taxes to be attacked as radicals, and social reform frequently became muddied by linking it with socialism. Although the reformers in general favored the existing economic system, their opponents often pictured them as seeking its complete disruption.

Such issues as minimal subsistence and the income and inheritance taxes reflected America's concern for its deprived or underprivileged—the underdog. Americans had no strict theoretical assumptions about the nature of distribution, but they did have difficulty understanding the existence of great disparities in wealth, especially when people had insufficient means to meet the most minimal standard of living. The idea of minimal subsistence reflected the growing wealth and the optimism of America; some considered it a relative standard in keeping with the continually rising level of American life. There were those who spoke of labor's right to a larger share of the social product. Horace Greeley, the famous antislavery journalist, wrote of "slavery at home" as encompassing the exploitation of one group by another, the "power over subsistence on the one hand, and of necessity, servility, and degradation on the other."[24]

As in England, one of the major forms of social responsibility was the development of opportunities for the underprivileged to improve themselves and enjoy the fruits of a better way of life. Opportunity was, of course, considered the basic ingredient of success in America. The problem was to give everyone relatively equal access to opportunity. Social legislation in the interests of women and children and the expansion of education strengthened the chances of the lower classes to take advantage of the available opportunities. The American settlement movement, like the English, was an important force for enlarging the outlook of the lower classes, and wealthy philanthropists like Carnegie and Rockefeller invested in cultural and educational programs for the masses.

The guarantees of minimal standards and opportunity for all were not forms of social responsibility that clashed to any degree with the fundamentals of the dominant laissez-faire society. More serious inroads were made by those philosophies that questioned the right of individual ownership and disposal of property. The idea of social wealth—the existence of wealth created by and rightly belonging to the whole of society—received little support in America, although it appealed to an active and important minority. Henry Demarest Lloyd, a fervent critic of big business, wrote in the last decade of the century:

The world, enriched by thousands of generations of toilers and thinkers, has reached a fertility which can give every human being a plenty undreamed of even in the Utopias. Between this plenty repining on the boughs of our civilization and the people hungering for it step the "corners," the syndicates, trusts, combinations. . . . Holding back the riches of earth, sea, and sky from their fellows who famish and freeze in the dark, they declare to them that there is too much light and warmth and food. They assert the right, for their own profit, to regulate the consumption by the people of the necessaries of life and to control production, not by the needs of humanity, but by the desires of a few for dividends.[25]

The most important advocate of social wealth was, of course, Henry George, with his single-tax program for absorbing the increment in land value. George was perhaps more popular in England and Europe than in America. While the single-tax program was too radical for America, George was too conservative for English and continental reformers who identified the concept of social wealth with socialism.

Socialism itself had little vitality in nineteenth-century America. Bellamy's *Looking Backward*, Ward's sociology, the vague platforms of the Knights of Labor, and the skepticism of a few academic economists represented America's surge toward a planned economy. By the end of the first decade of the twentieth century a Social Democratic Party had been formed, and Eugene Debs, its presidential candidate, received almost one million votes in the election of 1912. Meanwhile, a more radical breed of socialism had been founded in 1905 by the Industrial Workers of the World. But socialism never attracted the great mass of workers and union leaders who formed the backbone of the socialist movement in other countries. As the president of the University of North Dakota noted in 1912, there was a clear distinction between reform in America and the trend toward socialism in other lands:

> The nation is now attempting to find a way to preserve its republican character and to continue the maintenance of democracy. We have gone a long way since the creation of the Constitution and the establishment of the federal government, a long way from the view that things can be accomplished by letting them go their own way. Little by little regulation has come about; the theory of non-interference has been abandoned, and we are setting up here and there various types of governmental machinery to protect the interests of the common people. But this development which is to be seen at the present time is not going on in accordance with the socialistic view.[26]

Even the mildest efforts at government control were attacked, and Justice Holmes reminded his colleagues on the Supreme Court that the Constitution was not a paraphrase of Herbert Spencer.

In England the individualism and self-interest of laissez-faire was attacked on two fronts—by those who talked of social wealth and social planning and by those who emphasized the organic interdependence of society. Frequently both went together, but there was no necessary relationship, and the absence of a significant socialist movement in America did not in itself nullify efforts at conciliating the disparate forces in Amercan life.

One of the major sources of such effort was America's feudal nobility, the wealthy industrialists and businessmen. The paternalistic benevolence of the stewardship of wealth was substituted for the earlier feudal code. It was advocated by Romantics like Emerson and by hard-bitten entrepreneurs fully under the influence of the Protestant ethic. Emerson's "just chance" would come "from the concession of the rich, not from the grasping of the poor."[27] However, neither Emerson's nor Carnegie's conception of *noblesse oblige* could be the foundation of a truly interdependent society because they retained a highly individualistic core in accord with American values.

The industrialist stewards or philanthropists did not look forward to a community of personal fidelity but rather hoped for a working class that would render faithful service to the corporation. Trusteeship of wealth was not to be the foundation of more intimate relations between master and servant. At most, its goal was to make it possible for the more adept of the lower classes to follow in the footsteps of their benevolent masters. Given encouragement and opportunity, the more skillful worker or his child would rise into the class of the philanthropic benefactors and maintain the link between classes of a socially mobile society. In America the successful lower-class individual was the symbol of social cohesion.

Private philanthropy and voluntary activity were supplemented by the fast growing field of professional social work. The development of charity organization societies and settlements in England was closely paralleled by similar activities in the United States. The charity societies in America, like those in England, emphasized the value of personal relationships between the well-to-do volunteers and the poor being helped; but, like their English counterparts, they had difficulty in finding voluntary visitors to fill the role. Although British observers were impressed by the use of volunteers in America, American leaders like Mary Richmond were disquieted by the failure to engage the interest of the upper classes in aiding the poor through "mutually helpful acquaintance."

One of the most deplorable results of our changed ways of living in cities is that we are finding it more and more easy to hold and express the most approved views about poverty without maintaining any personal relations with poor people whatever. Unconsciously but very rapidly we have been slipping away from a deeply varied social experience, one in which rich and poor, landlord and tenant, employer and workman, trademan and purchaser, dwelt together "in visible relationship," into a stratified life in which our social relations are sadly impoverished.[28]

In other contexts Miss Richmond complained of the displacement of the volunteer by the professional worker. The professional symbolized the emphasis on scientific expertise and the decline of personal philanthropy. Whether there was ever any reality to Miss Richmond's romantic illusion about class relationships in America, the working people at the end of the nineteenth century were certainly not willing to accept paternalistic help.

The Christian Socialist and settlement movements contained richer possibilities for the building of a cohesive democratic society. As in England, Romanticism was closely identified with the Social Gospel of the churches and the practical activities of the neighborhood settlements in urban communities. Religious and paternalistic influences were, however, much less noticeable in America. The mixed national and religious origins of American city dwellers, their democratic sensitivities, and their emphasis on the practical and the scientific all led to a more secular and egalitarian spirit. It was the Romanticism of Whitman rather than of Carlyle or even Emerson. Whitman projected a faith in democracy and a distrust of class leadership. He accepted the earthy and the material in contrast to the Romantic concentration on the spiritual. For him the organic and cohesive society was a goal of the future, not a return to the past.

And, topping democracy, this most alluring record, that it alone can bind, and ever seeks to bind, all nations, all men, of however various and distant lands, into a brotherhood, a family. . . . Not that half only, individualism, which isolates. There is another half, which is adhesiveness or love, that fuses, ties, and aggregates, making the races comrades, and fraternizing all.[29]

The socialist element in the Society Gospel of America was not prominent. W. D. P. Bliss, one of the early leaders, criticized the power of business and pointed out that socialism followed from Christ's teachings. His program of municipalization of utilities, nationalization of transportation and communication, education, progressive taxation, and public works was similar to the British Fabians'. The core of American Christian socialism was not socialist, but reformist. Richard T. Ely, an economist and an intellectual leader in the movement, stood for the church taking the side of the laboring class, the regulation of utilities, factory legislation, and cooperatives.

The Social Gospel cut across all denominations. The famous papal encyclical on the conditions of the working class had been delivered in 1891. The more liberal Protestant churches—Unitarian, Congregational, and Episcopal—concerned themselves with fundamental social issues. In the years before World War I, Walter Rauschenbusch, Washington Gladden, Graham Taylor, and George D. Herron, among others, gave careful attention to the social and economic conditions of the time. These leaders of the Social Gospel movement attacked the existence of slums, inequalities of wealth, labor conditions, corruption in politics, and corporate power. The more fundamentalist Protestant churches continued to view reform as a personal rather than a social matter. Vice, intemperance, improvidence were, for them, the causes of individual and social problems. On the whole, however, the Social Gospel of the churches was not of major influence. As Commager concluded:

And it was, perhaps, . . . inevitable that a people who were complacent about their own achievements should not take too seriously the jeremiads of their preachers, a people whose standards were material should reject clerical warnings against the seas of avarice, covetousness, and pride, and a people who were careless should be content with gestures toward reform.[30]

The Social Gospel found a major voice in the settlement movement. The settlements spread quickly in the major cities of America, and, as in England, they expressed the urge of social service, the desire to share and improve the lives of the poor. The specific kinds of reform supported by settlement workers were many and varied from child labor to libraries. Jane Addams' description of the problems of urban life leading to the founding of Hull House in 1889 illustrates the motif of the settlement movement:

The social organism has broken down through large districts of our great cities. Many of the people living there are very poor, the majority of them without leisure or energy for anything but the gain of subsistence. They move often from one wretched lodging to another. They live for the moment side by side, many of them without knowledge of each other, without fellowship, without local tradition or public spirit, without social organization of any kind. Practically nothing is done to remedy this. The people who might do it, who have the social tact and training, the large houses, and the traditions and custom of hospitality, live in other parts of the city. The club-houses, libraries, galleries, and semi-public conveniences for social life are also blocks away. We find working-men organized into armies of producers because men of executive ability and business sagacity have found it to their interests thus to organize them. But these working-men are not organized socially; although living in crowded tenement-houses, they are living without a corresponding social contact. The chaos is as great as it would be were they working in huge factories without foreman or superintendent. Their ideas and resources are cramped. The desire for higher social pleasure is extinct. They have no share in the traditions and social energy which make for progress. Too often their only place of meeting is a saloon, their only host a bartender; a local demagogue forms their public opinion. Men of ability and refinement, of social power and university cultivation, stay away from them. Personally, I believe the men who lose most are those who thus stay away. But the paradox is here: when cultivated people do stay away from a certain portion of the population, when all social advantages are persistently withheld, it may be for years, the result itself is pointed at as a reason, is used as an argument, for the continued withholding.

Miss Addams then noted the limitations of paternalistic philanthropy in meeting these problems:

It is constantly said that because the masses have never had social advantages they do not want them, that they are heavy and dull, and that it will take political or philanthropic machinery to change them. This divides a city into rich and poor; into the favored, who express their sense of the social obligation by gifts of money, and into the unfavored, who express it by clamoring for a "share"—both of them actuated by a vague sense of justice. This division of the city would be more justifiable, however, if the people who thus isolate themselves on certain streets and use their social ability for each other gained enough thereby and added sufficient to the sum total of social progress to justify the withholding of the pleasures and results of the progress from so many people who ought to have them. But they cannot accomplish this.

For her, the settlement was a religious and social mission.

I believe that there is a distinct turning among many young men and women toward the simple acceptance of Christ's message. They resent the assumption that Christianity is a set of ideas which belong to the religious consciousness, whatever that may be, that it is a thing to be proclaimed and instituted apart from the social life of the community. They insist that it shall seek a simple and natural expression in the social organism itself.

Miss Addams said of the settlement point of view:

It must be grounded in a philosophy whose foundation is on the solidarity of the human race, a philosophy which will not waver when the race happens to be represented by a drunken woman or an idiot boy. Its residents must be emptied of all conceit of opinion and all self-assertion, and ready to arouse and interpret the public opinion of their neighborhood. They must be content to live quietly side by side with their neighbors until they grow into a sense of relationship and mutual interests. Their neighbors are held apart by differences of race and language which the residents can more easily overcome. They are bound to see the needs of their neighborhood as a whole, to furnish data for legislation, and use their influence to secure it. In short, residents are pledged to devote themselves to the duties of good citizenship and to the arousing of the social energies which too largely lie dormant in every neighborhood given over to industrialism. They are bound to regard the entire life of their city as organic, to make an effort to unify it, and to protest against its over-differentiation.[31]

The settlement movement in America faced the enormous complexity of the mixture of nationalities and cultures in American cities. While the English settlement gave primary attention to unifying the social class structure, the American settlement was plagued by the differences within the lower-class urban population itself. And the settlements' emphasis on local ties frequently limited the efficacy of cooperation involving broader areas. Despite this difficulty, the American settlement played a leading role in establishing an environment for the conciliation of diverse interests. The settlement provided the place where the industrial and social conflicts of the day might be discussed, even if a cooperative solution was not always achieved.

The American settlements rejected the paternalistic notion of the protection of the poor by the rich. Cooperation must be between equal partners, and Miss Addams supported the organization of trade unions as the means of workers obtaining a "more equitable distribution" and "more orderly existence."[32] On the other hand, the settlements did not accept conflict as natural but believed that the basis for cooperation between capital and labor was greater than the sources of conflict. Whenever class interest interfered with cooperative endeavor, that interest was morally and intellectually wrong. The settlement movement hoped to bridge the gap of social and economic conflict and establish a cooperative cohesive society. Democratic cooperation rather than paternalistic philanthropy or competitive struggle would lead to social welfare and progress.

In their day-to-day business the settlements were involved in the often bitter differences between capital and labor. Although they might see themselves in a neutral corner theoretically, practically their constituency was the poor, and the settlements aided the poor to achieve their goals in a democratic society. Even "the mother who sews on buttons for seven cents" must understand, said Jane Addams, that she "commits unwittingly a crime against her fellow-workers, although our hearts may thrill with admiration for her heroism, and ache with pity over her misery."

The maternal instinct and family affection is woman's most holy attribute; but if she enters industrial life, that is not enough. She must supplement her family conscience by a social and an industrial conscience. She must widen her family affection to embrace the children of the community.[33]

The mission of the settlements in the urban slums and the awareness of the gross inadequacies in the lives of the poorly paid industrial workers made the settlements spokesmen for labor and the poor.

Uniformity

Despite the heterogeneity of American life there were strong popular feelings against foreigners and their ways. During the colonial era the early settlers resisted "intruders" on economic and ideological grounds. The scattered and sparsely settled colonies felt that they could not tolerate those who might become an economic burden or might encourage religious differences. Deviation from the strict moral code of the New England colonies was especially cause for banishment.

During the following centuries there was a continuous incorporation of new immigrants, but resistance to foreigners was a recurrent theme in American life. The immigrant became the scapegoat for all the failings on the American scene. If the economy was in difficulty, it was the fault of the unskilled immigrant laborers who crowded the urban areas. Distinctions were made between the hardy early pioneer stock who bore the vicissitudes of the original settlements and the later immigrants who, it was alleged, exploited what already had been achieved in the hope of easy gains.

Popular resentment against the immigrant as a source of poverty, slums, and crime was given scientific support, albeit of dubious reliability, by early social statisticians. The immigrant, however, was not only the cause of much social pathology; in the eyes of the dominant groups he was also a troublesome advocate of foreign ideologies. The immigrant was identified with radical change, with socialism, with all un-American ideas. Dislike of the immigrant meant opposition to social legislation because it would benefit the immigrant population and because it was un-American in view of its identification with immigrant needs and desires. As Jane Addams commented:

There is no doubt that America has failed to make legislative provisions against those evils [unemployment] as other countries have done partly because the average citizen holds a contemptuous attitude toward the "foreigner" and is not stirred to action on his behalf. This may account for the fact that the United States has been so unaccountably slow in legislation designed to protect industrial workers.[34]

The East European immigrants of the latter part of the nineteenth century exemplified for many the unfit or the inferior species of the social Darwinists. The opposition to the foreigner was reflected in an antagonism toward urban life, which was identified with the immigrant. The city became synonymous with social problems and heterogeneity. There was a hankering after the good old days before the complications of urbanism and industrialism. Romantics like Emerson complained of the spiritual defilement in the wake of commercialism.

If the accumulated wealth of the past generation is thus tainted . . . we must begin to consider if it were not the nobler part to renounce it, and to put ourselves into primary relations with the soul and nature, and abstaining from whatever is dishonest and unclean, to take each of us bravely his part, with his own hands, in the manual labor of the world.[35]

The universal practice of the new child welfare agencies in the later nineteenth century was to gather the poor slum children in droves and send them wholesale to enjoy the spiritual and physical advantages of rural life.

During the closing decades of the century there was a strong agrarian reaction to the growth of large-scale business and industry. It was the struggle of rural America, the real foundation of the American ideal, against Wall Street, the symbol of the alien monster. The agrarian revolt was essentially conservative and rejected the surge of forces that conflicted with the illusion that America was a simple land of small independent farmers and tradesmen. Those efforts to resist the realities of American society resulted in the delay of the social reforms essential for a complex urban industrial nation.

Progress

Progress was the goal of nineteenth-century America, and there were many concrete signs to validate the faith of those who maintained that the key to progress was already in their hands. Dramatic changes were occurring; each decade showed vast improvements in the conveniences of life and the ease of transportation. Technology made enormous strides in the post-Civil War period. Even more impressive were the great growth of business structure and the concentration of capital and power in vast commercial enterprises. Profit became the symbol of progress for many, and progress became identified with the society in which profit was made.

Progress, however, had different meanings. There were those who believed in progress but did not accept the evidence of the advocates of laissez-faire. They were certainly not a major force in America in the nineteenth century. The dissatisfactions of the Romantics have already been mentioned. Theirs was largely a struggle over values, the materialism and conformity of the majority against the Romantic emphasis on individualism and spiritual and moral worth. In addition, the Romantics shared with other critics of the contemporary scene a sympathy for the underdog. Progress, to them, meant a better world for the weak and underprivileged.

Many of the New England Romantics and reformers were active in the struggle against slavery. Others were busy in philanthropic enterprises for the more humane treatment of the insane, the criminal, or the poor. The lot of the poor as contrasted to the prosperity of the wealthy was a major source of discontent. Henry George's *Progress and Poverty* graphically pointed to the contradictions of a society experiencing progress at the cost of its poor. The critics of the contemporary notion of progress increased as the century went on. Veblen acidly sketched the social and economic scene. Henry C. Adams and Edmund James, the Director of the Wharton School of the University of Pennsylvania, noted the failure of society to care for all its members. The first decade of the twentieth century saw the full flower of the muckraking movement of Lincoln Steffens, Ida Tarbell, Gustavus Myers, and Upton Sinclair. Hardly a sacred symbol of American life and progress was not held up for examination and ridicule.

By the end of the century there was a growing belief that progress had not necessarily resulted in rewarding the worthy. There was skepticism about those who advocated laissez-faire for the generality but aided special interest groups to use government for their own advantage. The dissatisfactions crystallized in demonstrations and strikes and in short-lived radical organizations like the Greenback-Labor Party and the Knights of Labor, but there was no real outlet for those who deviated from the dominant view of progress. The upper classes had not become involved in social reform as they had in Christian socialism and Fabianism in England, and the working classes had not developed a strong movement of their own.

The natural-law school of thought, whether represented by Adam Smith, Malthus, Spencer, or Sumner, had discouraged any scholarly interest in the reform of social conditions. Progress was a result of the unimpeded movement of natural forces, and the role of the scholar was to observe and formulate the laws of nature, not to suggest experiment or change. The truth of the social sciences would be revealed in the laws of society as the truth of physics in the workings of the physical universe.

Not until the last decades of the nineteenth century was there any significant reaction to the belief in natural law. In economics, sociology, psychology, philosophy, and jurisprudence a group of practitioners and scholars questioned the major tenets of natural law. For the normative principles of the natural-law adherents, they substituted a pragmatic-inductive approach. Trends or social events were neither taken for granted nor dismissed but were examined for their social consequences. Truth in this view was not an abstract principle, as among the followers of laissez-faire, but a reality subject to the test of application. The validity of any scientific or ethical assumption related to human behavior would be determined by its practical effect, not by its logical relationship to established law.

This criticism of the sacredness of natural law was followed by an acknowledgement of the role man might play in his own behalf. Under natural law man merely hoped to follow the paths determined by the rules of the universe. But the new skeptics could see no reason why man should not be a force in influencing the course of events. In economics Veblen, John R. Commons, Richard T. Ely, and Simon Patten and in sociology C. H. Cooley, Albion Small, Edward A. Ross, and Lester Ward were among the most prominent in laying the ground work for the new examination of social issues. Of them, perhaps most representative of the reaction against laissez-faire and the passive determinism of natural law was Lester Ward. Man, he believed, could shape his own destiny through intelligent and purposeful behavior. Progress and civilization were the product of such behavior, not the result of laissez-faire. Education and an improved standard of living would increase the possibility of all men to participate in the betterment of society as a whole. Ward rejected social Darwinism for its analogy between nature and society, and he vehemently opposed Spencer and his American disciples.[36] Of Sumner's *What Social Classes Owe to Each Other,* he wrote:

The whole book is based on the fundamental error that the favors of this world are distributed entirely according to merit. . . . Those who have survived simply prove their fitness to survive; and the fact which all biologists understand, viz., that fitness to survive is something wholly distinct from real superiority is, of course, ignored by the author.[37]

In the law, philosophy and practice were combined in the leadership of a new group of "social" jurists. Such eminent and influential lawyers and justices as Holmes, Brandeis, Cardoza, and Pound discarded the prevalent fixed and rigid constitutionalism and introduced a socially oriented pragmatism. The state and the courts, in their opinion, should not stand by but should protect the interests of individuals and the underprivileged generally in the increasingly unequal struggle against big business and giant organizations. Thus, progress became associated with clearly identifiable objectives to be achieved consciously and actively.

13

Labor, the Poor, and Poverty

The Labor Movement in the Nineteenth Century

ALTHOUGH labor was greatly affected by the changing ideologies of the nineteenth century, it had little part in their formulation. In the earlier part of the century the laboring population had not been sufficiently organized to influence policy in its own interest. The major political parties paid little attention to labor, and the short-lived workmen's parties before the Civil War were for the most part conservative themselves. Poverty and lower-class position were viewed as temporary conditions, and it was considered to be in labor's interest to maintain and support the competitive system, which would provide opportunity for all to become independent and wealthy.[1]

Even reformers who were concerned about the lower classes tended to concentrate on the issues affecting the more powerful and rich rather than on the problems of the poorer workers. Tariffs, monopoly, and currency, important in the struggle between the merchant industrial North and the agrarian South, were the major sources of controversy. Labor's role was to identify with one of the dominant groups while awaiting its rise to a more fortunate estate.[2]

The few radicals who thought along different lines rarely had any concrete proposals. They borrowed here and there from European ideas and applied them loosely to the American scene, but American labor had no philosophy of its own to contribute. Until the Civil War the issue of slavery monopolized the attention of radicals and reformers, and other issues tended to be overlooked. There was, however, some awareness of the deprivation in urban communities, which made Orestes A. Brownson remark that the slave's condition was generally superior to that of the wage earner in the North.

After the Civil War the organization of labor greatly expanded, but, on the whole, American labor gained no advantages comparable to what was achieved in England and Europe. Labor remained too weak to act independently, and its dependence on others greatly curtailed the extent of its demands. Government, the major instrument for reform in other countries, was not trusted by labor in the United States. Government power had been used against labor, particularly in strikebreaking. What social legislation had been passed was frequently so hedged by legislative and administrative safeguards as to be ineffectual. The courts were particularly unfriendly to social legislation and the efforts of organized labor, and reduced any advantages gained through these methods.

The decision of organized labor to concentrate on direct economic bargaining was both a cause and effect of labor's weak political position. Avoidance of the political arena meant dependence on the political organization of others and the absence of a politically oriented leadership.[8] Although significant changes occurred in labor organization during the later years of the century, there was relatively little shift in labor's ideological stand. In fact, the achievement of a stable and successful organization was accompanied by more rather than less acceptance of the status quo.

During the 1870s the foundation of an effective labor movement was laid. The great national railroad strike of 1877 was evidence of the growing strength of labor. Just prior to the 1870s the Knights of Labor was formed, and in the 1880s the American Federation of Labor was established. The Knights of Labor, as their title indicated, had a strong romantic inclination. They favored cooperative action rather than strikes and militancy, and their platform called for arbitration of disputes. They looked to political rather than economic pressure, and their proposals were a mixture of abstract demands for the proper distribution of wealth, reforms in the conditions of employment, and policies generally beneficial to the poor. Specifically, the Knights favored weekly wages, mechanics' liens, abolition of child labor, the eight-hour day, abolition of the national bank, and the provision of public lands for settlers. By 1886 the Knights had a membership of 700,000, but following the Haymarket affair they declined rapidly until there were only 100,000 members in 1890.[4]

The American Federation of Labor, in contrast to the Knights, eschewed the political arena and concentrated on achieving its goals through direct bargaining without governmental intervention. The Federation and its leadership accepted society as it was. Their purpose was not to reform society but to make the most practical gains for labor within the limits of the existing system. Labor would improve its position alongside and in partnership with business. By the beginning of the twentieth century, under the leadership of Samuel Gompers, the Federation numbered more than two million members.

The conservatism of the AFL reflected the general spirit of organized labor and its goals. The Federation's emphasis on organizing only skilled labor meant that the interests of the unskilled and the most poorly paid workers were not represented by the labor unions. The Federation's abandonment of even the vague idealism of the Knights was not compensated for by any other significant developments of a political or radical nature. While the Populists, the IWW, and the early socialist movement of Eugene Debs expressed more fundamental dissatisfactions, their relatively limited support indicated that neither labor nor any other major group of the population seriously expected economic reform.

Attitudes Toward the Poor

The growth of unionism helped elevate the position of labor and improve its image in its own and others' eyes. By the end of the nineteenth century concern about the growing power of big business created sympathy with the position of laborers and a realization that labor must be organized if it was to bargain effectively. Sympathy for the poor or the impoverished laborer was, however, slow in developing. It was difficult to reconcile the existence of poverty with the belief that anyone who was willing to work could make a living. The simplest solution was to condemn the poor as criminal, degenerate, wasteful, and immoral. The urban poor were the "dangerous classes," to their more well-to-do contemporaries, and were believed to be largely composed of foreigners.[5]

Horace Greeley, the journalist, was among the first influential Americans to understand the effects of the Industrial Revolution and to recognize that the poor were largely so as a consequence of the new economic order. In 1845 he wrote, "If I am less troubled concerning the Slavery prevalent in Charleston and New-Orleans, it is because I see so much slavery in New-York, which appears to claim my first efforts."[6] But, those whose business it was to be concerned with poverty—the officials of the charitable societies—were not of the same mind. Robert M. Hartley, a contemporary of Greeley and founder of the New York Association for Improving the Condition of the Poor, wrote in one of the Association's tracts:

Every able-bodied man in this country may support himself and family comfortably; if you do not, it is probably owing to idleness, improvidence, or intemperance. . . . You will gossip and smoke, neglect your children and beg, live in filth and discomfort, drink and carouse, do almost anything rather than work, and expect, forsooth, to be supported by charity.[7]

That was the conventional attitude of the charity workers, and it persisted until the end of the nineteenth century. Mrs. Josephine Shaw Lowell, the prominent lay leader of the New York Charity Organization Society, concluded that heredity accounted for much poverty. "We do not hesitate to cut off, where it is possible," she said, "the entail of insanity by incarcerating for life the incurably insane. Why should we not also prevent the transmission of moral insanity, as fatal as that of the mind?"[8] In 1893, Charles D. Kellogg, at one time secretary of the Philadelphia and New York Charity Societies, classified those needing employment "as for the most part shirkers of labor" and in the same category as "the vicious and those having resources sufficient to make beggary unjustifiable."[9] Under those circumstances it was logical for Mrs. Lowell to attack public relief as an attempt to give "the idle, improvident, and even vicious man . . . the right to live in idleness and vice upon the proceeds of the labor of his industrious and virtuous fellow citizen."[10]

As might be expected, the views of the charity leadership about the poor affected the treatment of their clientele. The literature of the societies was full of admonitions to visitors to avoid "patronizing" attitudes and to treat the poor as "equals," as "friends and neighbors." The continued and repetitive insistence on more democratic treatment certainly indicated the difficulty of its accomplishment. But by the end of the nineteenth century, even the charity movement could not overlook the growing importance of the labor movement. At the 1905 Conference of Charities and Correction a plea was made for cooperation between labor and philanthropy, and Mary Richmond, the most influential of the charity leadership, favored cooperation with labor in charitable undertakings because labor might be won over "to a sounder and less sentimental view of the pauper and his rights."[12]

The settlements looked upon labor and poverty from a different vantage point. The laboring classes as a whole were literally their neighbors and clients. The settlement was not a charitable or relief-giving agency. The settlement leaders attempted to distinguish the working classes from the clients of the charity agencies, not so much to degrade the latter as to give proper dignity to the former. By concentrating on the needs of labor rather than of the destitute the settlements played a part in raising the standards for all. "To confound thus two problems," said Jane Addams, "is to render the solutions of both impossible. . . . Working people live in the same streets with those in need of charity, but they themselves, so long as they have health and good wages, require and want none of it."[13]

By the first decade of the twentieth century urban unemployment was recognized as a normal phenomenon of a highly complex industrial society. The unemployed in the cities could not be explained by the failure of idle workers to take advantage of the opportunities in rural and frontier areas, for there was an influx into the cities of those desperately searching for work. Poor law officials began to understand the nature of unemployment and the function of relief and even to recognize that unemployed migrants were not all vagrants and loafers.[14]

The attitude of the labor movement toward programs for the poor was affected by the limited goals of organized labor and by its distrust of government intervention. As early as the depression of 1857 the jobless demanded the right to work and relief, but they did not follow up with any practical program. In the depression of 1873 a trade union meeting at Cooper Union in New York agreed on the plea of "work, not charity." At the same time demonstrations in major cities called for food, clothing, and shelter.[15] Meetings were held and strikes organized to improve the conditions of labor. The short-lived Marxist International Working

Men's Association endorsed a platform that illustrated the essentially reformist rather than revolutionary character of the American movement. It stated that government should provide employment at usual wages; it should advance money or food for one week to the unemployed and their families; and it should prohibit evictions for nonpayment of rent for six months.[16]

Although they rejected any radical position, during the depression of 1893 Gompers and the AFL supported government responsibility for supplying work when private industry failed to do so. At its 1893 convention the AFL resolved, "When the private employer cannot or will not give work, the municipality, the state or nation must."[17] The platform of Coxey's march on Washington also stressed public works, but there was little government response.

Although the general instability of economic life was growing more apparent, both trade unions and corporations sought ways of dealing with the problem on a limited and decentralized level. The depression of 1893 was the first in which the unions themselves had a significant role in providing unemployment relief. Mostly the wealthier unions in the skilled trades were involved. In New York City some 500 unions with 125,000 members paid benefits of over $500,000, the greater part of which was for unemployment.

At about the same time employer welfare plans were being organized. Scientific management tried to alleviate with personnel and welfare programs the industrial conflict that had marred the business scene in the late nineteenth century. Welfare measures would assure the loyalty of employees. American labor was susceptible to these overtures. Its own weakness and its middle-class aspirations made acceptable greater employer influence than was possible, for example, in England. The employer welfare programs grew slowly, however, and it has been estimated that by 1910 at most 8 percent of workers were covered, and the benefits were extremely limited.[18]

All these developments indicated the changing attitudes toward the poor and poverty. Economic need was no longer an emergency situation for many or a chronic condition of a maladjusted few. The concern with need was not limited to the charity societies and their voluntary workers or to the poorly staffed and administered public agencies. The poor and poverty were becoming a matter of general concern, and the solutions proposed suggested new social and economic approaches to the societal problem of economic security.

Causes of Poverty

During the latter part of the nineteenth century the search for the causes of poverty was as conscientiously carried on as at any time in history. There was a vast collection of opinions and theories on the phenomenon of poverty. The increasing rate of business crises helped sharpen awareness of the large numbers of impoverished. The continued presence of poverty in the land of opportunity and plenty drove home the need to examine the reasons for this paradox. The development of the social sciences aided by statistical measures, however crude, tempted scholars and others to seek more elaborate and complex explanations of social phenomena.

The employment of more scientific or at least more quantitatively refined techniques did not necessarily result in more accurate interpretations of the causes of poverty. At the 1886 Conference of Charities and Correction, Fred H. Wines, an outstanding state welfare official, attacked with verve and accuracy many of the statistical studies of the day. He remarked on the gullibility of the lay and learned public with regard to such studies and pointed out that causality in such complex phenomena as poverty and crime could not be attributed, as it frequently was, to single factors. Alcoholism was the favorite devil of the causation experts, but Wines' own examination of the evidence did not demonstrate that alcoholism had an appreciable effect on the incidence of crime. He wondered if much of the reporting of intemperance by criminals was not done to satisfy the preconceptions of the investigators.[19]

Somewhat later Amos Warner, Professor of Economics and Social Service at Stanford and a leading authority on social welfare, analyzed the difficulties of studies of the causes of poverty. He pointed out that the schemes of classification used overlapping categories, thus preventing a clear delineation of causes. Much case counting, he found, degenerated into a descriptive rather than analytical frame of reference and did little to clarify the underlying problems. Like Wines, Warner doubted that alcoholism was the major cause of dependency and maintained that long-term study rarely corroborated this emphasis. He concluded that more careful investigation would be needed before the true causes of poverty would be uncovered.[20]

The contemporaries of Warner and Wines confounded the problem of causation by also trying to assess the degree of guilt or personal responsibility. Most studies of dependency and other problems started from the assumption that immorality was a major factor and were more concerned with laying blame than with objective exploration. The popular approach was to find "scientific" justifications for established values and prejudices. How, asked Warner, can one validly differentiate between "misconduct" and "misfortune" in classifying causes?[21] Those who used the terms seemed to have no difficulty, but there was a vast difference in determining where the real responsibility lay.

Most studies were limited to the populations served by public and private charitable agencies and thus had little significance for the poor in general. An 1881 survey of charity organization societies under the auspices of the National Conference of Charities and Correction concluded that between 50 and 90 percent of poverty and crime was caused by intemperance.[22] In a study of Michigan almshouses, personal rather than environmental factors were found to account for 75 percent of the need for almshouse care.[23] Warner himself was inclined to place some credence in the reports that "misconduct" accounted for some 10 to 32 percent of poverty because of the consistency of this finding.[24] As the century came to a close, studies more and more emphasized environmental over individual causes of poverty. Even among personal factors those that were beyond the individual's control took precedence over those for which he could be held directly responsible.

The major catch-all for personal causes was heredity. Heredity was frequently referred to directly, but there were, no doubt, other factors attributed to heredity without explicit mention of the connection. An extensive survey of public almshouses in New York City and Brooklyn concluded that heredity was at the base of the idleness, improvidence, and drunkenness associated with poverty. In the 1890s studies by charity organization societies found that the "leading cause of incipient pauperism" was "weakness of childhood," and that, according to Dugdale's study of the Jukes, was the symptom of "hereditary pauperism."[25] In the minds of some pauperism was a kind of unique and unified characteristic that might be "transmitted entire" by heredity.[26]

The personal qualities generally associated with dependency, whether or not considered hereditary, were drink, ignorance, shiftlessness, inefficiency, sickness, physical and mental defects, immorality, and irresponsibility. Obviously these were not mutually exclusive categories. There was no agreed upon and defined terminology, although the factors noted above show up with persistent regularity in the studies and commentaries on dependency at the end of the nineteenth century. Further, as already mentioned, exact estimates were made about the relative importance of these causal factors.

How many personal or subjective factors were considered the fault of the individual rather than accidents of fortune? The heavy weighting of moralistic concepts used in classification schemes helped bias the findings in the direction of individual responsibility. A study at the beginning of the twentieth century classified such factors as shiftlessness, indolence, improvidence, intemperance, and sexual immorality as "direct" or "positive" causes, whereas sickness, old age, industrial conditions, poor food, insufficient wages, lack of education were "negative" or "indirect" causes of less importance.[27]

The search for moral weaknesses prevented any real objective evaluation of study data. In 1907, for example, a St. Louis voluntary agency client survey listed 17.8 percent of its cases as due to "defective character." The report of the study to the National Conference of Charities and Correction gave no information on the remaining 82.2 percent but concentrated on the relative significance of inefficiency, intemperance, improvidence, shiftlessness, immorality, ignorance, and stupidity in causing the dependency.[28]

There was a gradual shift from individual to social causation at the beginning of the twentieth century. The emphasis on unemployment itself as a significant phenomenon in relation to poverty was symptomatic of the changing point of view. However, considerable concern over intemperance and personal habits persisted. Edward T. Devine, a leader in charity reform, reported, "Lack of employment, which, at the time of application, is given in the great majority of instances as the reason for being in need, is usually found on inquiry to be due to some personal deficiency in the employee."[29] The *Chicago Tribune* commented as late as 1913 that people still "persist in looking upon joblessness as a reflection upon the individual whereas it is a reproach to the nation."[30]

Investigations of industrial conditions by state commissions played an important part in making clear that irregularity of employment was indigenous to an industrial society. In New York it was found that "at all times of the year in good times as well as in bad, wage-earners, able and willing to work, . . . cannot secure employment." Referring to the factors affecting employment, this investigation concluded: "These irregular causes of unemployment are constantly operating; they are necessary accompaniments of industrial progress. . . . We want to know not so much how many are without work, as how many *need to be* without work."[31] Even the conservative Josephine Shaw Lowell recognized that the unemployment of men in the depression of 1893 was "not due usually to moral or intellectual defects on their own part, but to economic causes over which they could have no control, and which were beyond their power to avert as if they had been natural calamities of fire, flood or storm."[32]

A large number of social factors were also suggested to account for the amount of dependency and poverty. Among those most frequently mentioned were poor housing, high interest rates, concentration of population, emancipation of women, child labor, old age, bad sanitary conditions, poor education, immigration, and war. The list of social evils was almost endless, and those who hypothesized social causes were frequently as dogmatic as those emphasizing individual factors. C. H. Cooley, a pioneer in social psychology, stated confidently in 1896, "With the greater part, abnormality appears to be social, not organic, and could therefore have been prevented by a good environment."[33]

Perhaps the single most widely accepted cause of dependency was the relief system itself. Throughout all periods the assistance program had been considered responsible for the encouragement of need and dependency. This assumption was the foundation of the English poor law reform of 1834. The charity organization societies in England and America attempted to abolish public outdoor relief as the most monstrous of evils. Their leadership spoke of the need for careful screening and cautious relief, but in fact, as Mary Richmond once obliquely stated, they preferred no public relief.[34]

Fear of the consequences of relief was, of course, closely related to the belief in the defective character of the recipients. For it was either those who were, or were not far from being, improvident, shiftless, immature, and irresponsible who would use relief as a substitute for honest endeavor, not the "worthy" clients of the voluntary bodies. This continued fixation of the effects of relief was offset to some extent by the recognition of poverty as a general phenomenon affecting large sections of the population and related to the social and economic conditions of society. Poverty itself was examined as a cause, rather than a result, of individual and social breakdown. There were at least beginning attempts to view poverty and dependency objectively and scientifically rather than subjectively and moralistically.[35]

14

American Economic
Security Programs

The Organization of Assistance

ALTHOUGH the dominant philosophy of nineteenth-century America favored laissez-faire and personal responsibility, the growing complexity of social and economic life resulted in a corresponding increase in social intervention. Governmental action, while obviously present in many functions of society, was still a subject of controversy in the field of social welfare. By Woodrow Wilson's term the broad welfare role of government was finally established, but that was the aftermath of a half century of struggle and resistance following the Civil War.

As late as the 1880s, when the consequences of industrialization were recognized, Americans were still wrangling over the issues that had faced the English Poor Law Commission of 1834. In the period directly after the Civil War economic security measures were largely limited to the sporadic programs of local public and private charity. By the beginning of the twentieth century consideration was being given to a wide variety of approaches to the problem of economic insecurity. In addition to the established programs of public relief and private charity, such proposals as a minimum wage, public works, and social insurance, to mention a few of the more prominent, were receiving serious attention. The maturing of economic security policy in America, as elsewhere, was symbolized by the extent to which economic security was no longer identified with poor relief.

Economic assistance in the United States after the Civil War was provided by a loose collection of organizations and services, both public and private. In no sense could it be compared, for example, to the English system of poor relief in terms of thoroughness of coverage and definiteness of responsibility. In America there were still communities that did not accept responsibility for assistance, and each wave of unemployment resulted in a temporary patchwork of programs to tide workers over the immediate crisis. For a large part of the nineteenth century differences about public or private control, indoor or outdoor relief, and personal service or material aid were obstacles to the development of any unified or effective assistance program.

In the less settled areas the traditional approaches of auctioning off the destitute to the lowest bidder and binding out the idle and vagrant continued. Most commonly present was the undifferentiated almshouse containing a mixed population of children, aged, sick, and able-bodied. Not only were these various groups with varying needs housed in the same institutions, but there was often no physical separation of one from the other. During the last quarter of the century advances were made in classifying institutions and separating out the populations needing specialized care. This was a major function of the new state charity boards, which established their own institutions for the feebleminded, the insane, the sick, the aged, and the delinquent and also subsidized other public and private institutions receiving state charges.

The able-bodied, the potentially employable who fit into none of the growing categories of the institutionalized population, were the most complex problem for the public and private authorities. Despite the increasing mobility of the population, the practice of local responsibility for relief remained strong. While the local areas rarely provided any regular assistance for their own able-bodied unemployed, they were singularly careful in refusing aid to migrants seeking employment in their areas. During periods of depression mobile laborers were treated like tramps and vagrants and sent back to their communities of settlement. New York complained that some 7000 paupers had been sent by Massachusetts, many of whom did not belong in New York.[1]

To what extent the able-bodied needy received any help from local assistance programs is difficult to estimate because there is little reliable knowledge of the aid provided. Accurate records of the numbers in institutions and those receiving relief in the community were not kept. Even as late as the depression of 1893 it was impossible to obtain a valid picture of the numbers unemployed and needing assistance.[2] As for the care of the able-bodied generally, Frank B. Sanborn of the Cornell faculty and a leader in the field of charity summarized the situation in 1890, "That mythical class the 'able-bodied poor,' are scarcely found in this country in public establishments, except for a few months in the cold season, when the number of employments, both for men and women is considerably reduced by Nature herself."[3] And at such times it was more than likely that a work test was administered to separate the "work-shy" from the "really" impoverished.

The major tests for the public relief system were the depressions that occurred with increasing frequency after the Civil War. Great numbers of unemployed required subsistence, and the large metropolitan centers, particularly, were faced with situations for which they were totally unprepared. In these emergencies the outdoor-relief rolls swelled, and a series of helter-skelter measures were hastily thrown together. The limited capacity of the public agencies and the extraordinary demands of the times generally resulted in private philanthropy bearing a major burden. Public help to the unemployed usually consisted of temporary relief in kind: food, lodging, and clothing. Sometimes work relief was provided, or larger efforts were made, such as New York's public works program of 1894, when some 2000 laborers were employed with a weekly payroll of $30,000.[4] During that time seventeen other cities introduced programs of subsistence gardening for their unemployed.[5]

The inability of the regular public assistance system to meet the crisis of unemployment was demonstrated by growth of emergency relief committees during every depression. These committees, generally under the sponsorship of the private charity societies toward the end of the century, coordinated the efforts of the established agencies and the emergency programs. They were by no means always effective, because the problems faced were often beyond the limited capacities and conservative policies of the private agencies.

The public agencies were hindered in developing more effective programs of their own by the determination of the voluntary agencies to force the public agencies to abandon the provision of outdoor relief. During the last quarter of the nineteenth century many of the major cities, including New York, Brooklyn, Baltimore, Philadelphia, and Washington, withdrew public outdoor assistance. In New York City only $50,000 out of $1,800,000 spent on assistance in 1903 was for outdoor aid.

Alongside the public system a vast network of nongovernmental or private philanthropy grew up. The voluntary agencies considered relief one of their major functions and vied with the public agencies for sole responsibility for administering relief to persons in their own homes. Similar efforts had taken place in England also, but the public system had become so entrenched by the end of the nineteenth century that even the Majority of the 1909 Commission could not hope to make more than minor changes in the functioning of the public programs.

In the years immediately preceding the Civil War private relief societies grew, and they played a prominent role in providing emergency help. The coordination of private effort, which plagued the charity organization movement from the 1880s on, was already a problem in the first part of the century. The New York Association for Improving the Condition of the Poor was established in 1843, and similar societies with the goal of organizing charity arose in other large cities during the following decade; but the times were not ready for a coordinated approach to philanthropy.

During the years before the charity organization movement there was a vast increase in charitable bodies. The Civil War provided many opportunities for service to soldiers, veterans, and civilians. Independently and in cooperation with the local authorities, the private charities had formed the backbone of much regular and emergency community relief. The charity organization societies, starting with Buffalo in 1877, were not set up to provide an additional source of relief but to coordinate existing efforts and reduce the alleged wasteful use of relief. In their first twenty-five years a few charity organization societies provided relief, but their main functions were coordination, friendly visiting, investigation, registration, the encouragement of thrift societies, and the support of such urban reforms as housing and sanitation.

The charity organization societies emphasized the separation of relief and personal service. Relief, although a necessity, was an obstacle to the goal of client independence, which was to be achieved through personal service. The foremost enemy was, of course, public outdoor relief, and by 1900 the charity societies had succeeded in inducing twelve of twenty-one cities with a population of over 200,000 to give little or no outdoor relief. Boston remained the major eastern city that stood out against the campaign of the societies to abolish public outdoor relief.[6] In reviewing the Brooklyn experience, where the public function had been placed in the hands of a private relief society that had reduced the average family relief grant to $1.54 a year, the committee of the Boston board of overseers commented laconically that if the grants could be reduced to $1.54, "and that if only this amount stands between them [the poor] and independence, it would be desirable for Brooklyn to give up private relief entirely."[7]

Despite their struggle against public outdoor aid and their efforts to keep their own services free from the contamination of relief, the charity societies themselves succumbed to the provision of assistance. By 1904 half the societies gave relief from their own funds, and no new society subscribed to the no-relief policy. The societies responded to the need for adequate relief in the communities they served and to the expectation of the public that something more than service was required to justify public support. Perhaps most important, however, was the realization that relief-giving would continue, and if the societies were to be influential, they must themselves control the giving of assistance. The relief function was to be entrusted to the societies' professional workers, who would "understand the subordinate part which relief must take in the work of restoring a needy family to normal conditions, and will not neglect the more arduous lines of effort. Without the high standard of service no degree of division of functions will result in successful restorative work."[8]

The charity organization movement spread rapidly. By 1895 there were 100 societies, and ten years later, 150. The influence of the charity societies, however, went beyond their immediate organizations. The charity organization leadership dominated the National Conference of Charities and Correction, and discussion of public programs more and more gave way to the affairs of private charities. After 1900 there was a noticeable decrease in consideration of assistance programs at the Conferences, and attention concentrated on the organization of charity societies and on the skill and training of their workers.

These advances in the organization of the private field were not unparalleled by developments in the public field. On the state level, the number of state boards of charities increased rapidly after 1863, when Massachusetts established the first board. By the 1890s some twenty state boards had been organized. Most had only advisory or supervisory powers with few functions beyond reporting to the state executive or legislature, but they laid the groundwork for the later state departments of welfare. Somewhat slower in development were the municipal boards and departments that sprang up in Washington, Baltimore, Philadelphia, Kansas City, Cincinnati, and Los Angeles prior to World War I. These bodies were part of the general trend toward sounder administration in municipal and state government.

Major Issues

The Provision of Assistance

There was a large and influential public who believed that the evils of material aid far outweighed its benefits. The attack of public aid and the support of private charity was largely based on the assumption that assistance would be used more sparingly by the private societies. Mary Richmond approvingly quoted Edward Denison of the English charity movement: "Every shilling I give away does four-pence worth of good by helping to keep their miserable bodies alive, and eight-pence worth of harm by helping to destroy their miserable souls."[9] For Mary Richmond, the first professional Secretary of the Baltimore Charity Organization Society, relief conflicted with independence, and though she and her colleagues tolerated society's humanitarianism, they did not weaken in their opposition to financial assistance.[10] The General Secretary of the Associated Charities of Cincinnati stated as one of the "two cardinal principles, which are so generally accepted among systematic thinkers on matters pertaining to almsgiving as to need no argument . . . for their defense: That almsgiving is *per se* injurious to the recipient, and must be accompanied and followed by some treatment as an antidote." His second cardinal principle was that public relief is "generally evil" and should give way to private effort.[11]

In their condemnation of relief the charity workers and others employed the traditional argument of the pauperizing effects of material aid. As one of the voluntary leaders stated, relief serves to weaken the character, to excite the gambling spirit, the recklessness and extravagance which came of chance gains; but it does not give the quiet and peace, the power to live for worthier objects than mere physical support, which an assured income supplies, while it also destroys all the incentives to activity, energy, and industry which are usually supplied by the struggle to "make a living."[12]

The charity leaders also found in Romanticism a rationale for their criticism of assistance. Economic aid was wrong because it emphasized—overemphasized—man's material nature; "man is a spiritual being, and, if he is to be helped, it must be by spiritual means."[13] Miss Richmond lamented that even the early techniques of the charity societies had been influenced by "economic data."[14] The opponents of relief also borrowed liberally from the social Darwinists. Mrs. Lowell had mentioned the felicitous effect of individuals struggling for a livelihood, and Reverend Gurteen described the evolution of the individual from independence through "involuntary poverty" to "confirmed pauperism" by the route of charity.[15] Charity's responsibility for the increase in "inferior stock" must also be considered, it was pointed out.

Those who attacked relief during the last decades of the nineteenth century were convinced that it was a force for individual and social degeneration. If relief was to be made acceptable, it must benefit the "children of misfortune" rather than the "children of degradation." This distinction was fundamental, and there were doubts whether it could be accomplished by any program of assistance. At the National Conference of 1878 the question was posed whether any agency, public or private, could successfully discriminate between the really needy and the chronic paupers. Studies during the latter part of the century tended to emphasize the number of "unworthy" individuals receiving aid. In 1887, Charles D. Kellogg reported on 28,000 cases aided by the charity organization societies throughout the nation and estimated that only 10 percent were deserving of continuous relief and 27 percent of temporary relief. Forty percent, he concluded, needed work rather than relief, and 23 percent were definitely ineligible for any help.[16]

Seth Low, the prominent and public-spirited Mayor of New York and President of Columbia University, summed up the dilemma.

Some are worthy; some are unworthy. How can the worthy poor, who need perhaps but a little help to tide them over the evil day,—how can the worthy poor in our large cities be helped without being permanently harmed? And what is to be done for the unworthy, and how is it to be done, without encouraging others who are still independent to seek, in preference to the hard-won and meagre support which honest independence gives, the aid which seems so easy to obtain, but which is so demoralizing?[17]

The answers varied. Some felt, as did the influential Mrs. Lowell, that the principles of England's poor law reform of 1834 were still sound. The poor should not be coddled; relief should be made painful to the point of punishment. Others thought that the nature of the present administration could be reformed so that the dangers of relief might be mitigated, if not avoided. In contrast to those who would develop harsher standards were those who saw the answer in providing more adequate relief.

There was some concern about the effect of relief on wages. The charity organization leadership sharply criticized relief being used as a supplement to inadequate wages. Miss Richmond favored direct confrontation of the employer in the case of low wages.[18] She could see no reason why, on an individual basis, employers could not be influenced to pay appropriate wages. Still influential was the argument of the classical economists wedded to the wage-fund theory, who maintained that aside from encouraging idleness relief decreased the total amount available for wages.

The spokesmen for economic assistance were either fewer or less vocal than its critics. The advocates of relief were in a more sensitive position because they were in principle supporting practices that had many real difficulties and that conflicted with many widely held beliefs. From the point of view of abstract rights, the economist John R. Commons had pointed out that individuals could expect of society, as a personal right, a minimal guarantee of subsistence, but this was hardly a generally accepted philosophy at the time.[19] Men like Edward T. Devine and Leo A. Frankel, leaders of voluntary charities, turned to the social causes of economic insecurity as a justification for society's providing assistance to the needy. It was society's failure that resulted in poverty, and that failure must be balanced by social provision, said Frankel. Devine viewed relief-giving as the normal function of an industrial society in which the individual's welfare was dependent on so many complex factors.[20]

The proponents of assistance shared some of the fears of relief of its opponents, but on balance they tended to minimize the dangers. Devine thought that greater evils ensued when people were left without adequate living standards. There must be a clear definition of responsibility because uncertainty was disastrous.[21] Frederic Almy, the Director of the Buffalo Charity Organization Society, agreed with Devine's emphasis on the necessity for material aid and openly advocated what many of the societies were already quietly doing, i.e. the provision of assistance by the charity societies.[22] Mary Richmond strongly attacked this position at the National Conference of 1911. While she maintained that relief was a "neutral" thing—neither good nor bad intrinsically—she did not favor the charity societies combining personal service with relief-giving because she was afraid the latter would overwhelm the former.

The emphasis on relief brings us a support subject to the law of diminishing returns, while the emphasis on cure assures us a public increasingly willing to go the whole distance. Relief, in other words, is a very good servant, but a bad master.[23]

The advocates of more rather than less relief believed that there was much more poverty than was accepted by the critics of relief. They thought, too, that material need must be met by material aid if people were to be helped. They did not view as realistic the tendency of some of the charity leadership to minimize material aid in favor of personal service. The President of the Society of St. Vincent de Paul in New York reported:

The visits of encouragement and advice do far more than material relief, but all people interested in charity realize that entering a house with a book and pencil for information, must be accompanied by material help to be effective. It is the old story. "Advice very seldom or never is appreciated on an empty stomach."[24]

Jane Addams, like the English settlement workers, criticized the charity organization concentration on the pauperizing effects of assistance. "I have not that great fear of pauperizing people which many of you seem to have," she stated.[25] She deprecated the virtues the charity workers stressed and pointed out that man should be evaluated on more than his thrift and his economic independence.

Now the settlement does not ignore, I hope, those virtues; but it does not lay perpetual and continual stress upon them. It sees that a man may, perhaps, be a bit lazy, and still be a good man and an interesting person, who cares for lectures and holds opinions.[26]

The Administration of Assistance

To a great extent the bodies given the responsibility for administering assistance would determine its fundamental nature. Thus, there was much controversy about where the assistance function should be lodged. Even many of the charity organization societies that had avoided relief-giving at the start recognized the inevitability of some program of relief and preferred to be active participants rather than passive observers. By the 1890s the private agencies had taken the leadership in the assistance field either directly through their own provision or by inducing the public authorities to turn over their functions to private societies. On the whole, the leaders of private societies dominated the scene even when public functions were maintained in public hands. Even the recipients often saw the public system as secondary to private effort. Julia Lathrop gave the following description of the situation in Cook County, Illinois:

It is here, of course, that much private charity supplements the county's efforts, or rather that the county's provision is accepted when all the resources of private charity and neighborly aid have been exhausted. Indeed, one may as well admit in starting, that the capacious bosom of the county is sought with much reluctance, even by the population of which we speak; and while this population represents the last degree of social submergence, the county is in turn its *dernier ressort*.[27]

The period between 1890 and the beginning of the First World War was the high-water mark of the private agencies in the field of assistance. The local and state public welfare departments were barely established, and the private agencies had not yet turned their attention to the psychological aspects of adjustment. However, there was a continuous and bitter struggle between those favoring public or private assistance. The missionary fervor of the early leadership of the charity organization movement lent at times a fanatical spirit to the conflict.

One of the principal objections to the public administration of assistance was the low opinion held of local and state government. James Bryce said of the state legislatures:

Though not of themselves disposed to innovation, [they] are mainly composed of men unskilled in economics, inapt to foresee any but the nearest consequences of their measures, prone to gratify any whim of their constituents, and open to the pressure of any section whose self-interest or impatient philanthropy clamours for some departure from the general principles of legislation. For crotchet-mongers as well as for intriguers there is no such paradise as the lobby of a State legislature. No responsible statesman is there to oppose them, no warning voice will be raised by a scientific economist.[28]

But the corruption and inefficiency of state government was minor compared to the political chicanery of the big cities. The chief target of the new muckraking literature of the early 1900s was the city boss and the rottenness of local government. In this political jungle public assistance was not considered merely another corrupt department but was believed the source of corruption since public assistance funds were alleged to be the political treasury. Constant attention was directed to the issue of political influence at the National Conferences of Charities and Correction during the last quarter of the nineteenth century. The Reverend Francis Wayland, Yale professor and author of one of the most popular texts on political economy, stated at the 1878 Conference:

Official aid sooner or later degenerates into personal favoritism or outright corruption. The designing and persistent applicant, however unworthy, receives the largest proportion of assistance, and the timid or easily discouraged is thrust aside.[29]

In the following year, the Report of the General Committee on the Prevention of Pauperism stated:

City government in the United States, at all events in our larger cities, is a failure. . . . The statesman who can tell how to govern large cities well, with universal suffrage, will render a service to his country that will rank with that of Washington who founded and of Lincoln who saved it. . . . Cities are dominant in this government; and our most imminent danger now is from the vice and crime and pauperism to which this abominable misgovernment leads.[30]

In commenting on the indoor-outdoor relief controversy, Thomas F. Ring of Massachusetts remarked, "As far as I can remember, when a city has abolished public outdoor relief, the cause is more in the dishonesty of the officials than in the giving of the aid itself."[31] The concern about politics in welfare became so great that the National Conference of Charities and Correction established a standing committee on Politics in Charitable and Correctional Affairs.

The situation was not, however, entirely hopeless. The centralization or consolidation of administration in the local authorities was a step toward greater efficiency. Experienced administrators of public programs were aware that welfare budgets would eventually fail to receive support if the public continued to question the honesty of their administration. The trend toward civil service had also helped eliminate one of the major causes of corruption in city government. It was even suggested that the criticisms leveled against the public welfare services might be true of any large organization with insufficient personnel, even the universities.[32]

The large-scale, bureaucratic public system was seen as an advantage by some. Stanton Coit, active in settlement and trade union work, considered the public system the most effective environment for the performance of charitable functions.

It is to be deeply deplored that . . . the people who started the Charity Organization Society were tainted with laissez-faire doctrines and extreme individualistic theories. They did not see that the organization and unification of all relief agencies and methods cannot possibly be brought about by private efforts. The results of years of work by the Charity Organization Society may be swept away in one season of unusual distress by sentimentalists and by newspaper advertising schemes for relieving the poor. Scientific philanthropists will some day learn that charity organization is a distinctive municipal function. Who but the city can prevent the dispensing of free bread, and can limit the relief of each agency to a given district, so that there shall be no waste or overlapping? Who but the city can gather, week by week, full and accurate statistics of the unemployed? . . . Who but the city can compel every agency to follow careful methods to avoid fraud?[33]

The dependability of government income was certainly a strong argument in favor of public programs. Through taxes the support for public welfare would be more adequate and reliable than the fluctuating funds of the private charities. As early as 1868 the Massachusetts Board of State Charities answered the question of the need for public aid by stating that public programs would be required "until private charity has been taught to relieve distress with the same speed and certainty that is seen in the best forms of public almsgiving."[34] There were those, however, who opposed the public provision for those very reasons. They saw taxation for relief as an unjust burden on the industrious in favor of the idle. Voluntary giving was considered morally preferable to taxes, and there was the complaint that taxation relieved the wealthy and philanthropic of their sense of responsibility for the poor. Finally, and this was the main criticism, a public fund was believed to give the recipients the impression that they had a right to assistance, which, in turn, made the poor complacent and subjected the fund to unlimited demands.

The advocates of public responsibility held opposite views on these issues. For them, taxation was a more just system of financing because its mandatory nature resulted in payment according to ability rather than whim. If the poor did see relief as a right, that was appropriate because it was the state's responsibility to see that all individuals had a minimal standard of living. There were differences as to the standard, but even those who favored a low standard based on the 1834 principle of less eligibility could see no reason why it was not enforceable by the public agencies.

The supporters of public programs emphasized their relative responsiveness to democratic controls. In addition to the usual procedures of democratic government, public agencies were required to give a full accounting of their expenditures, a practice few private agencies followed. In answer to those who maintained that public aid resulted in an impersonal relief by hardened officials, it was pointed out that not everyone approved of the personal and paternalistic approach of the charity societies. Some, particularly in the labor movement, criticized these agencies for their "inquisitorial" tactics and their identification with the status quo responsible for poverty and unemployment.[35]

The gradual swing from private to public domination in the field of economic security was part of the general trend toward the increasing role of government on all fronts. Despite Julia Lathrop's harsh criticism of public assistance in Cook County, she maintained that "there is no finer conception in the world as it is, than of a system of public charities."

Such a system sets aside the egotistical Oriental sanction for charity and replaces the almoner's personal effort "to acquire merit" by the state's solemn acknowledgment of its responsibility for its feeblest member. Instead of the capricious gifts of the individuals, we have the unfailing reservoirs of the commonwealth; instead of the uncertainty of individual interest, we have, in theory at least, the unflagging devotion of the state to a great humanitarian service accepted by it as a necessary function of government.[36]

Methods of Assistance

For the charity organizations helping the poor was a personal service, and whatever interfered with the helping relationship must be sacrificed.

They were convinced that the provision of relief itself was an obstacle to curing dependency, and when relief was necessary, they favored informal rather than organized help. Aid from one's family, friends, neighbors, and others with whom there was personal contact was preferable to relief from any agency.[37] If personal influence were properly used, the charity organization leadership thought, relief societies might well be superfluous.[38] Robert T. Paine of Boston found that prohibiting the friendly visitors of the charity societies from giving aid was part of the "great discovery" of training gentlemen and lady visitors to help families to help themselves.[39] Miss Richmond pointed out that anything that "relieves people of any share of just responsibility toward relatives, friends, fellow church-members, employees, or less favored acquaintances . . . checks charity."[40]

The American charity workers emphasized the healing value of the friendly touch, and, like that of their English counterparts, their emphasis reflected more the influence of Romanticism than scientific theory. If anything, the Americans greatly expanded the practice of personal service and were more inclined to rely exclusively upon it. If the charity leadership's criticism of public agencies was based only on the lack of sufficient and well-trained personnel, the problem would not have been insurmountable. But the major and insuperable limitation, in the minds of the voluntary leaders, was that a formal and bureaucratized system could never develop the informal relationships necessary for real help.

At the beginning of the charity organization movement voluntary visitors were to be guided by the following precepts:

The best means of doing the poor good is found in friendly intercourse and personal influence. The want of money is not the worst evil with which the poor have to contend; it is in most cases itself but a symptom of other and more important wants. Gifts in alms are, therefore, not the things most needed—but sympathy, encouragement, and hopefulness. . . . The starting-point of all really useful work is a genuine neighborly interest in those whom you seek to serve. They must be approached as beings of the same flesh and blood, and therefore kinsfolk.[41]

Similar appeals were made almost a quarter of a century later.

It [the charity organization movement] prevents waste, duplication, imposition, and fraud, and instills the new and higher ideals of charity, educates the public judgment and conscience, and welds the public and private charitable instinct into an intelligent fabric of human usefulness, sheltering worthy poverty against both misfortune and temptation, and teaching the divine truth that we are our brother's keeper, and that by personal service alone can our sacred duties to humanity be discharged.[42]

The problem of restoring the unsuccessful person to an industrial basis and of helping him to make a success of his struggle for self-support presupposes a moral force. No visitor can hope to advise or influence such a struggling person unless he or she has moral power and earnestness.[43]

It requires vivid imagination to realize that the hand-to-hand ministration of neighborly kindness is a blessing to both giver and receiver, that it not only averts the pangs of hunger but brings courage to the despondent, strengthens the weak, enriches the lives of all concerned, and makes for self-respect and moral integrity. Contrast this with the over-reaching deceitfulness on the one hand, and suspicion on the other, which so generally characterize public-relief work, and one cannot doubt that in so far as public relief supplants personal charity it is an unmitigated evil.[44]

Finally, as Mary Richmond so wistfully stated:

If it were only possible to take all the well-to-do of our city—all who possess a certain standard of right living—and possible to place them in natural friendly relations with the less fortunate and less disciplined—think what a different city this would be. Through all the alleys and byways, through all the miles of wretched common-place and squalor, into every miserable semblance of a home, it would bring a new standard of decency, order, and self-control, a new hope and expectancy, to which the poor would slowly but surely rise.[45]

As in England, the actual voluntary participation of the dominant and well-to-do in the interests of the poor was far from satisfactory. An observer of charity in the West complained in 1902 that the societies' functions were largely limited to investigation and routine tasks rather than positive, personal help.[46] Even in the cultivated East similar complaints were heard. Charles Kellogg of the Philadelphia Society maintained that "not until the churches awake with enthusiasm to caring for our less fortunate neighbors in the wise and helpful good Samaritan spirit will there be sufficient attention brought to bear upon the mass of poverty to have appreciable effect."[47] Frederic Almy of Buffalo, whose society had a high reputation in England for its program of home visiting, remarked bitterly:

In our best charity organization societies an agent is apt to have the care of not less than two hundred or three hundred families, and as has been suggested, the volunteer support is usually frail and inadequate. "Not alms, but a friend," like many creeds, is more easily said than lived up to.[48]

The major problem for the early charity organization societies was poverty and dependency. The spirit of their approach was inherent in the purpose of "repressing mendicancy," which was frequently incorporated in their title. The societies avoided the "wholesale" approach—general programs dealing with large groups—for the individual or "retail" approach. Although the societies participated in preventive campaigns for better housing and sanitation, the personalized treatment of the poor was for them the most significant means of preventing and treating dependency.[49] Despite the vagueness of their theories and the doubtful effectiveness of their practical efforts, the charity organization societies had a lasting impact on poor relief policy. The lack of a well-organized public service and the prestige of the leaders of private philanthropy often encouraged the belief that the goal of public policy was the achievement of the ideals of private charity.

Outdoor Relief

The controversy over outdoor relief was affected by the general attitude toward any public relief program and by the belief that any help provided in the community must be especially supervised and individually administered, conditions possible only under the private agencies. Outdoor relief had been officially abandoned at the beginning of the nineteenth century, but it continued in practice. After the Civil War the increasing incidence of economic crises led to the expansion of community emergency programs. However, outdoor relief continued to be the subject of most concern for critics of public assistance. Even the usually liberal Edward T. Devine maintained that the provision of outdoor relief should be entrusted only to the private charities.[50]

Public outdoor relief was viewed as the major source of political corruption and dependency. As in earlier periods, it was alleged that outdoor relief bore most responsibility for giving the impression that there was a social responsibility for support. Outdoor relief was thought to lower wages by supplementing substandard wage scales and to prevent the control and discipline necessary for constructive assistance.

The advocates of outdoor relief under public auspices pointed to the fact that aid in the community was more economical than institutional relief. Per capita costs were shown to be a great deal lower for persons and families maintained on outdoor relief than for those in the almshouses. Remaining in the community provided the possibility of partial support from employment, whereas indoor relief required total support from public assistance funds. Outdoor relief, it was stated, continued family life intact while almshouse care resulted in the breaking up of the family. The maintenance of family unity became a more telling point as the twentieth century wore on and the close relationships between children and parents became the cardinal principle of social welfare. During the nineteenth century and the beginning of the twentieth century the mass shipment of children from urban slums to rural areas, with almost indiscriminate foster placement, was common practice among children's agencies.

The best argument in favor of outdoor relief, however, was supplied by the nature of the existing institutions. The demoralizing character of the almshouses provided advocates of outdoor relief with sufficient evidence against institutional care. One superintendent of the poor with thirty-two years of experience in public relief stated, "I have come to the conclusion that a very poor home, in the world's estimation, is better for a child in the end than institutional life."[51] In the minds of many observers, there was little question that despite the problems of outdoor relief, it was superior to almshouse care.

If the unfortunate experience of the almshouse and institutional care generally was to be avoided, then relief in the community must be given even when able-bodied adults were in the home. It was around the needy able-bodied and their families that the controversy centered most strongly. It was proposed at the 1890 National Conference that "no one should be provided with indoor relief who has physical strength, and is able by industry and sobriety to earn even a scanty subsistence,"[52] but that position was not widely held in charitable circles. However, many believed that the able-bodied would choose to rely on relief if they and their families were not made exceedingly uncomfortable. Mrs. Lowell stated the popularly held view:

That the community cannot afford to tempt its members who are able to work for a living to give up working for a living by offering to provide a living otherwise; and that public relief must be confined to those who cannot work for a living, and the only way to test whether they can or cannot is to make the living provided by the public always less agreeable than the living provided by the individual for himself, and the way to do this is to provide it under strict rules in an institution.[53]

At the 1899 National Conference the Committee on County and Municipal Charities recommended that able-bodied husbands be separated from their families and placed in workhouses and that after deduction of living expenses the remainder of their earnings be sent to their families for support.[54] The dominant view at the end of the nineteenth century was that public outdoor relief was more injurious than institutional care and that outdoor relief for the able-bodied was the most disastrous of all. Only under the carefully controlled policies of the private agencies was outdoor relief at all feasible, and even there service rather than relief was the central motif.

Work Relief

Work relief was the most frequently considered method of assisting the able-bodied as an alternative to, or in combination with, other forms of relief. As a test of need and industriousness, work was often a formality attached to indoor or outdoor relief. On the other hand, relief might be given as the compensation for a job provided by the public assistance authority as a substitute for direct relief or almshouse care.

It was not always easy to distinguish work relief from emergency employment in periods of depression. Generally speaking, work relief differed from public works by the nature of the employing authority, the pay provided, the kinds of employment undertaken, and the persons eligible for employment. Work relief was usually administered by public or private assistance agencies. Salaries were generally computed on the basis of subsistence needs rather than on wage rates. Even if the basic scale approximated regular wage rates, the amount of work and the total pay only met relief standards. The jobs were mostly unskilled and were intended to absorb the maximum number of displaced unskilled workers. Employment was ordinarily dependent on eligibility for relief.

Work relief was provided by public or private bodies in some degree during all the depressions after the Civil War. This was, of course, not a new development, since work had been part of early poor law policy and had been incorporated in many private charitable undertakings. Before the Civil War the Association for Improving the Conditions of the Poor had been active in work relief, and other agencies carried on similar programs. The depression of 1893, however, represented the first extensive use of work relief, known as "made work," to alleviate unemployment. On the whole, work-relief programs had little success during the nineteenth century in meeting economic need or providing employment, but despite its limitations work relief continued to have ardent advocates.

Although Mary Richmond attacked work relief as an example of ineffectual mass measures, work-relief plans were particularly appealing to those who viewed unemployment as an individual or personal problem.[55] Relief in the form of work was certainly not considered a restorative to the economy in the nineteenth century, but it was considered to have a rehabilitative effect on individuals without work. Work relief would separate the truly indigent from the chronically idle and might even cure some of the latter who were hard put enough to undergo the rigors of work discipline. For the others it would help maintain their sense of independence and attachment to the labor market, which was threatened by the acceptance of any aid. It was hoped that work relief might even result in the development of new habits and skills of work.

Experience with work relief during the last quarter of the nineteenth century led many to criticize its value or at least the manner of its administration. The New York Association for Improving the Conditions of the Poor opposed the City of Boston's work-relief program with the classical argument of Daniel Defoe some two centuries earlier.

What more has been effected by all this special array of machinery and effort, than to divert work from one channel through which it was employing the poor into another channel, through which it is accomplishing a like purpose? In other words, what more has been done by this well-meant movement than to monopolize an amount of work for the special benefit of certain [workers], to the injury of others equally needy and deserving.[56]

The effect of work relief on the labor market had always been of great concern. The principle of least eligibility, or conditions inferior to the labor market, was generally applied to punish those dependent on the community's resources and to avoid competing with regular jobs. As was stated in 1895:

It must be decidedly underpaid in order not to attract those who already have work at half-time, or who have otherwise disagreeable work. The whole must be so unattractive as to guarantee that, when other work can be had, the laborer will seek it.[57]

Jane Addams disagreed with the prevalent policy and resigned from the Chicago street-cleaning committee. She maintained that the payment of lower wages in work relief threatened the basic wage scale. "I insisted," she said, "that it was better to have the men work half a day for seventy-five cents, than a whole day for a dollar, better that they should earn three dollars in two days than in three days."[58]

Work relief had other difficulties beyond wage policy. The work projects themselves were frequently poorly conceived and poorly managed. Only a fraction of those needing work were employed, and since need rather than skill was the major criterion for employment, those employed had little to contribute to the projects. The period of employment was short, rarely as much as two weeks a month. The irregularity of the work and its inefficiency and wastefulness hardly met the goals of those recommending work relief as a morale-building exercise. There was also conflict over the demands of the workers for pay in money and the practice of the relief agencies of giving grocery orders or payment in kind. This irritated the workers and certainly did not permit work relief to simulate a normal work experience.

By the beginning of the twentieth century there was growing skepticism about work relief and an increasing awareness of its problems. In 1911 a New York State Commission examined the experiences of New York, Massachusetts, England, and Germany and concluded by opposing work relief as a public policy.

The provision of public work for the sole purpose of caring for the unemployed has almost always proved disastrous. In periods of great emergency such provision is often necessary, but all experience seems to show that its administration is fraught with great difficulties and the relief which it affords is paid for in widespread demoralization.[59]

Even those more sanguine about work relief suggested drastic reforms, although there were often conflicting recommendations because of the desire to satisfy employment and relief goals. Reforms were proposed in the regularity of work, its supervision, and the skills to be employed. Much attention was given to the possible municipal planning of employment, and not only by radical thinkers. For example, at the 1895 National Conference of Charities and Correction one speaker commented:

One proposition stands strong and clear. It is that, if the municipal or local authorities have work that must be done at some time, such as park improvement or road-making or public building, it is especially well that this be given through regular contractors or otherwise at the period of hard time. . . . This is by no means a concession to the cry of the socialists that the State should supply work to all who need it. Far from it. This is but using the State aid in preserving social equilibrium, so that the highest individualism, which includes the individual well-being of the poor as well as of the rich, may have free play.[60]

Amos Warner, after a full consideration of the principles of scientific charity as applied to work relief, concluded:

In the last analysis, we must agree, the problem of the unemployed is industrial, not charitable; and in as far as every philanthropic person is himself a citizen and a worker, he will be engaged in the effort after an economic solution.[61]

Other Economic Security Measures

The first consistent distinction between poverty and pauperism in public welfare policy occurred in the first decade of the twentieth century. The separation of public works from work relief and the recognition that there were two separate fields of action—"the charitable" and "the economic"—indicated this new approach.[62] In the sphere of economic welfare the emphasis shifted to the social and economic conditions affecting the general well-being in contrast to the former preoccupation with the unique individual characteristics making for failure. Concern was broadened to the larger population with low income levels who, while not in immediate need or directly dependent on charitable aid, were constantly threatened by economic crises. Priority was given to programs preventing the conditions resulting in need and dependency. The contrast between the old and the new approach was illustrated by the 1911 report of the New York State committee on unemployment.

Although the normal development of our industrial system makes this unemployment necessary and inevitable, the State of New York assumes no responsibility towards the able-bodied unemployed. No organized attempt is made to prevent suffering and degeneration among those who have to act as reserves in our industrial army. Only when the unemployed have become sick, disabled, and pauperized, when they apply for admission to a charitable institution, or when they become homeless and criminal and are arrested for vagrancy or breaking the law—only then do our public authorities take any notice of them. While foreign governments are devising and establishing agencies to prevent unemployment as far as possible and to provide against the degradation of those who have to be unemployed, our State is content to allow the idleness to have its full effect. Instead of helping the unemployed to remain or become self-supporting, our policy is, to establish State and philanthropic institutions to take care of them when they are no longer able to provide for themselves.[63]

The increasing emphasis on such constructive measures as employment bureaus, social legislation, and social insurance widened the gap between those concerned with the menace of pauperism and those concentrating on the prevention of poverty. The philosophies, the principles, and the programs of the two groups differed sharply. Although efforts were made to maintain some unity, the energies, interests, and knowledge of those engaged in the "wholesale" and "retail" approaches were directed along divergent routes. The private charity societies and the public assistance agencies continued to struggle with the problem of individual failure, and on the the other side there grew up a host of commissions and agencies dealing with such issues as industrial safety and compensation, old-age pensions, and child labor. The establishment of a Committee on Standards of Living and Labor at the National Conference of Charities indicated the growing trend toward social reform. The 1911 report of the Committee discussed minimum wages, workmen's insurance, vocational education, working hours, legislation for women and children, occupational safety, and disease. Florence Kelley of the National Consumers League was chairman, and others reporting were Jane Addams and Dr. Alice Hamilton of Hull House, A. J. McKelway of the National Child Labor Committee, Paul Kellogg of the *Survey,* and Louis Brandeis. While this group was considering broad social measures affecting the total population, the chairman of the old Committee on Families and Neighborhoods, representing the traditional point of view stated, "This National Conference of Charities and Correction is endeavoring to . . . take adequate care under right idealism, of those classes which are failures under our political and industrial constitutions."[64]

The administration of relief and personal service were the primary concerns of those concentrating on the "failures." Beyond this they aimed to encourage the poor to develop habits of thrift that would help to maintain them both during employment and in times of crisis. The establishment of thrift societies and banks accepting small deposits were encouraged to induce thrift and protect the savings of the working class. It was hoped that they would protect the poor from the inhuman exploitation of loan companies. Benevolent societies frequently arranged for loans to the indigent at low rates of interest and pressed for legislation to prevent unethical loan practices. The emphasis on thrift also led to the advocacy of insurance under public and private auspices. Attempts were also made to educate the poor in the problems of family budgeting and economy.

Such measures as vocational training, employment bureaus, and the establishment of day nurseries for working mothers were supported by the old charity leadership and by the new social reformers. As early as the 1830s private charities had organized free and reduced-fee employment agencies for low-income workers.[65] In 1911 the recommendations of the New York State Commission were almost exclusively directed to the establishment of public employment offices.[66] Employment offices ceased to be viewed as a function of charitable agencies and were recognized as a normal institution in an economy marked by high labor turnover and difficulty in matching men and jobs. By 1900 there were twelve state employment offices, and the number was tripled in the next ten years.[67]

Public works, like employment bureaus and vocational training, had a lengthy history of public and private support. Despite approval in principle, there had been little actual provision of employment. As late as 1894 the Mayor of New York City replied to a petition of unemployed workmen:

It is not the purpose or object of the City government to furnish work to the industrious poor. That system belongs to other countries, not to ours. We can't tear down the City Hall so as to furnish work for the unemployed.[68]

By the end of the century, however, public works had become a more generally accepted responsibility of municipal and state governments, although the distinction between work relief and public works continued to be vague. In 1895 public works were undertaken in Massachusetts by 21 of 30 cities and 13 of 41 larger towns.[69] Consideration was given in a state study to labor colonies where cooperative projects would make the unemployed self-supporting and to municipal factories where the city would provide employment in idle plants. Neither of these proposals was considered practical at the time. The 1911 New York State Commission recommended public employment at strategic times to keep the economy in balance. There was growing support for public works by labor, emergency aid societies, and experts on the problems of unemployment, but strong opposition continued from politicians, conservative business-men, and others identified with the principle of laissez-faire.[70]

Direct participation by public authorities in the economy was one of the more controversial issues. Of relatively greater acceptability was leg-islation to guarantee more adequate wages and increase the possibilities of private employment. Labor also favored a shortened working day to spread the available employment.[71] Legislation proceeded slowly along both lines. Early laws affecting hours and wages were generally limited to women and children and tended to be largely ineffective.

Women and children, in contrast to men, were considered to require the protection of the state. Men were viewed by the courts as entirely capable of settling their employment demands in free bargaining. In the famous Lochner case of 1905 the Supreme Court nullified a ten-hour day for bakers on the grounds that such statutes are "mere meddlesome in-terferences with the rights of the individual."[72] Public action in favor of male workers in these years was largely limited to government employ-ment. Even the unions were not entirely favorable to government inter-vention because many preferred direct bargaining to legislative action.

The impetus for reform and social legislation came from many sources. Although the American Federation of Labor as a body did not support legislation, some individual unions actively supported it. Organi-zations like the National Child Labor Committee, the National Consum-ers League, the American Association for Labor Legislation, and the General Federation of Women's Clubs played an important role, par-ticularly as outlets for women interested in social reform. Jane Addams, Florence Kelley, and others worked to influence both organized charity and social work in the direction of social legislation. Their approach dif-fered markedly from the charity organization movement, and they formed the backbone of the Progressive movement. As Florence Kelley stated in her discussion of minimum wages:

A generous estimate of the people so afflicted [incapable of full self-support] based upon long, careful study gives, however, a maximum of three in a hundred of our population. . . . But it is with vastly more than three in a hun-dred of the population, that we are concerned in this conference year after year. Upon us there is forced the slow, reluctant recognition of a third cause of poverty, which was hidden from our predecessors. We cannot longer escape the knowledge that there is no more efficient cause of wholesale destitution in the United States than industry.[73]

She concluded, "Let us take courage and make known, especially to the legislators, that from this day forth charity declines to attempt the impossible, to make good the social deficit created by insufficient wages."[74]

Social insurance of various types was the most radical innovation among American economic security proposals, and it was hardly acted upon prior to the First World War. Social insurance had already made substantial progess in England and Germany before it became a serious issue in America. The first discussion of insurance at the National Conference of Charities and Correction occurred in 1905 and was centered about the German scheme for workmen's compensation. At this meeting, apart from Florence Kelley and one or two others, most participants opposed any form of pension on the grounds that they were socialistic and paternalistic, interfered with individual liberty, would not reduce but would rather increase relief by encouraging higher standards, and would affect foreign trade by raising the American cost of production. Reference was also made to the alleged excesses of the veterans' pensions as illustrative of the weaknesses of any pension program.

The pension or insurance issue was complicated by the confusion between noncontributory pensions and income-conditioned grants, such as those for widows and veterans, and benefits in return for premiums paid by employers and employees, such as workmen's compensation and unemployment insurance. In general, the early opposition tended to concentrate on noncontributory pensions. In addition to the arguments already noted, pensions were attacked because they lessened personal responsibility, took from the thrifty and gave to the indolent, weakened family responsibility, and depressed wages. Further, as a state dole supplementing wages, some critics felt pensions would permit employers to pay less than a living wage. The charity organization societies, which by principle opposed any "wholesale" method of dealing with poverty, were particularly disturbed by the possibility of pensions being accepted as a right and by the absence of any personal service for pensioners. This opposition specifically centered around proposals for widows' pensions.[75]

The support for some predictable and efficient scheme of economic support, whether contributory or otherwise, grew rapidly. By 1908 the representative of a large private insurance company who attacked public insurance largely on grounds familiar to the supporters of Spencer and Sumner received a poor reception at the National Conference of Charities and Correction.[76] By 1912 the Conference's Committee on Insurances recommended workmen's compensation, unemployment insurance, and old age insurance, and those recommendations were incorporated in the Progressive Party platform.[77]

The coverage of insurance was constantly expanded to include additional risks. Proposals were made for insurance to provide for sickness, invalidity, death, and retirement. The most significant and controversial of the early measures were pensions to be paid mothers at the death of the family breadwinner. These noncontributory pensions were to make possible the maintenance of family life, despite the loss of the husband's income, when children were in the home. Widows' pensions followed from the emphasis on family life as the appropriate environment for children and the growing recognition that child placement was not so simple or successful a procedure as was at first believed. The nation as a whole was becoming more aware of its responsibility for the welfare of children. The first White House Conference on Children, held in 1909, and the establishment of the Children's Bureau three years later, symbolized the nation's interest in the healthy development of its young.

The alternative to widows' pensions, apart from the possible breakup of the home, was child labor or the irregular support of public and private charity. As Gertrude Vaile asked, "When the father dies why should a good mother have to depend upon the alms of her more fortunate neighbor?"[78] As for child labor, Jane Addams employed the same argument the Webbs used when she accused the community of taking advantage of the low wages of "parasitic" industry to the detriment of its child population. A similar situation prevailed when the mother was forced into employment to maintain her family at the death of her husband.[79]

There was still opposition to widows' pensions, particularly from some of the charity organization leadership, who saw in the pensions another breach in their struggle against public outdoor relief. Edward T. Devine, formerly Secretary of the New York Charity Organization Society and Director of the New York School of Social Work, attacked the pensions as tax-supported relief, not insurance, "as embodying no element of prevention or radical cure . . . , as an insidious attack upon the family, inimical to the welfare of children and injurious to the character of parents."[80] Mary Richmond spoke of the "funds to parents" as a "backward" step—"funds to the families of those who have deserted and are going to desert!"[81] Mothers' pensions were seen as a subsidy to immorality and a discouragement of private charitable effort. Within private philanthropy, however, such leaders as Frederic Almy of Buffalo and Homer Folks of the New York State Charities Aid Association were willing to risk experimenting with public pensions for families with children. The first statewide mothers' pension laws were enacted in 1911, and within a decade most states had such measures.

The idea of workmen's compensation for industrial injuries had a much longer history than mothers' aid, but effective legislation was passed about the same time. Previously workers had had the opportunity to collect from their employers in court if negligence of the employer could be proved. For most of the nineteenth century, workers had found little effective redress for their injuries from the courts. Gradually legislation was secured to protect the rights of employees. Workers could no longer sign away in a blanket fashion their right to collect damages. Suits in the case of the death of the employee were recognized, and the common law limitations on employer responsibility were narrowed.

A series of public studies of employer liability at the beginning of the twentieth century pointed up the major weaknesses of workmen's compensation. Recovery was difficult and inadequate and was the source of much friction between employers and their workers. Although some earlier attempts at state regulation had been made, the first effective state legislation for workmen's compensation began in 1911, and by 1913, twenty-two state laws had been passed.[82]

Old-age pensions, which in England had been provided separately from poor relief at the end of the nineteenth century, did not receive important consideration in the United States prior to World War I. Special groups, such as soldiers, nurses, firemen, policemen, and civil servants, had made some progress on their own. In the 1880s California provided for grants to public or private agencies caring for persons over sixty. This was repealed within a dozen years because of the expense and inefficiency of its administration.[83]

The first serious modern consideration of public old-age pensions occurred in 1907, when Massachusetts appointed a commission to study the problem, but no action was taken. The first state law was passed by Arizona in 1915 but was declared unconstitutional. Progress toward pension schemes, both contributory and noncontributory, had already been made in some industries by the last quarter of the nineteenth century, particularly in railroads. By 1908, seventy-two railroads employing almost one million workers had old-age pension plans, and manufacturing concerns were also expanding their programs.[84]

Unemployment insurance, also a major part of foreign social security systems, made no progress in the United States until somewhat later. The first state measure was introduced in Massachusetts in 1916, but it was not until 1932 that the first act was passed. As with old-age pensions, the major advances during this period were made by private plans. Out-of-work plans by trade unions went back to the first half of the nineteenth century, but they were never adequate to meet the needs of unemployment, particularly during the widespread depressions toward the end of the century. By 1908 only ten out of 530 local unions paid any benefits. A unique plan for its time was an unemployment scheme jointly sponsored by employers and unions in the wallpaper industry. Its purpose was to counteract the seasonal nature of the trade and may be viewed as an early attempt at a guaranteed annual wage.[85]

Administrative and financial responsibility were major issues in the development of social insurance. Prior to World War I, government, employers, and unions acted as sponsors, and generally sponsorship and financing went together, although in workmen's compensation there was a trend toward government control with financing remaining the employer's responsibility. Employers began to recognize the value of social benefit schemes. Twentieth-century firms searching for ways to establish loyalty and attachment of workers found welfare benefits a useful device. Pensions, from the employer's point of view, kept employees from leaving and decreased the tendency to strike. They provided incentives to satisfactory performance because loss of job reduced or removed pension rights. On the one hand, pension benefits encouraged remaining with the same firm, and on the other, they made possible the retirement of the elderly and inefficient.[86]

The growing interest of unions and companies in insurance was paralleled by the increasing recognition by government of its responsibility for the economic security of its citizenry. Louis Brandeis clearly pointed to government's welfare function:

If the government permits conditions to exist which make large classes of citizens financially dependent, the great evil of dependence should at least be minimized by the state's assuming, or causing to be assumed by others in some form, the burden incident to its own shortcomings. . . .

The manufacturer who fails to recognize fire insurance, depreciation, interest and taxes as current charges of the business, treads the path to bankruptcy. And that nation does the like which fails to recognize and provide against the economic, social and political conditions which impose upon the workingman so large a degree of financial dependence.[87]

As the twentieth century went on, government became more and more active in social insurance. This involved both direct participation and the supervision of programs sponsored by other bodies. The expansion of government's role did not lead to a decline in the interest of other organizations in the insurance field.

The financing of benefits was perhaps the most controversial of the issues facing social insurance. If benefits were to be provided without contributions from the insured, it was argued, the consequences would be worse than public assistance since insurance involved a right never really recognized in public relief. Compulsory universal public insurance involving contributions from the insured were criticized, however, as interfering with the right of the individual to make his own choice while at the same time suggesting a public duty "to pension all worthy citizens."

The conflict between individual and social responsibility was not easily resolved. During the years which followed, the differences became polarized around whether social insurance should resemble a private insurance policy or a social security measure. Frederick L. Hoffman, a statistician of the Prudential Life Insurance Company, compared the "American" and the "Bureau of Labor" definition of insurance.

Social insurance in the American sense may be said to comprehend all efforts, methods and means to provide, in conformity to insurance principles, a sufficient pecuniary protection to wage-earners and others in moderate circumstances against the economic consequences of industrial accidents, disease. . . .

The Bureau of Labor definition as presented by Mr. Hoffman was:

The methods of organized relief by which wage-earners or persons similarly situated and their dependents or survivors, become entitled to specific pecuniary or other benefits on the occurrence of certain emergencies. The right to these benefits is secured by means of contribution from wages, or by the fact of the insured person's employment, or by his citizenship or residence in the country.[88]

While there was some overlapping in the two approaches, the emphasis on equity according to "insurance principles" in the first and on adequacy according to need and social standards in the second assured continuing differences.

Indirect Measures

In addition to the measures planned directly to affect income by providing employment, setting wage standards, or giving assistance, there were great areas of policy that indirectly affected economic security. From its earliest history the state had been a partner in the economic development of the nation. Intervention by government to ensure the prosperity of the country took many forms, from canal building to territorial expansion. Although all such policies had some effect on economic security, the tariff, currency, and taxes were considered particularly significant for low-income groups and were the source of much political conflict. In fact, during the nineteenth and early twentieth centuries those measures received more popular attention than the programs dealing specifically with economic security. The duties on foreign goods, the value of the dollar, and the distribution of the cost of government were viewed as having the greatest significance for economic welfare.

The tariff in early America had been supported as the protector of infant industry. In time, however, both farmers and urban labor came to see in the tariff a measure affecting their own interests. Low tariffs were considered a threat to American wages and employment because they permitted foreign goods to flood the American market. On the other hand, as President Cleveland maintained, protection gave "immense profits" to special groups at the cost of the general population, who paid for the protection of these groups through high consumer prices. This conflict was not settled during the nineteenth century because all attempts at tariff reduction were defeated.

In the currency struggle the low-income groups found themselves allied with one of the most powerful interests in the country. Since the Revolution the poor merchants, farmers, and workers in America had viewed currency as their cause. In debt or without fixed wealth, they believed that a cheapening of the dollar would enrich them at the expense of the creditor or capital-holding classes. In the early years of the Republic it was the national bank that symbolized hard money; at the end of the nineteenth century it was the gold standard and Wall Street. Free coinage of silver became the rallying cry of the agricultural and working classes against the financial and manufacturing interests of the East. The politically active Farmers' Alliance, the People's Party, and the American Federation of Labor endorsed free silver. In the election of 1896 the silver interests dominated the Democratic Party, and Bryan, with his famous allusion to the "cross of gold," became their candidate. The discovery of vast silver mines in the West supplied the additional strength of the silver mining companies interested in raising the value of silver. They were able to make only relatively small gains, however, and the adherents of cheap money finally lost their struggle with the passing of the Gold Standard Act of 1900. By that time, however, new reserves of gold as well as other measures to expand the currency had removed much of the grounds for concern about the scarcity of currency.

The era of modern taxation in the United States may be dated from the passing of a 2 percent tax on incomes above $4000 during the Cleveland administration in 1894, although an income tax had been used occasionally in earlier periods. The income tax provided a large and secure resource for government and had the additional advantage of being related to the ability to pay of the taxpayer. The Cleveland bill was drawn up to gain Populist support for the general revenue measures of the Democrats and was an attempt to shift some of the tax burden to the more wealthy. The Supreme Court declared the act unconstitutional as a "direct" tax to be apportioned according to population, not wealth. There was a strong reaction to the Supreme Court decision, and agitation continued until the Sixteenth Amendment authorizing a federal income tax was adopted in 1913.[89]

In the following periods economic security policy grew in both directions—measures for the direct distribution of income to those in need and measures affecting the total economy for the benefit of low-income groups. In time, both types of measures became facets of a unified national policy concerned with the general welfare.

Part IV

TOWARD THE WELFARE STATE

15

Introduction

IN both England and the United States the period after World War I was marked by a greatly intensified concern with national economic policy. Although the United States had never fully embraced free trade, on the one hand, or had made substantial progress toward a system of social insurances, on the other, as had the British before the war, similar tendencies were noticeable in both countries. Foreign and internal policy was clearly geared to the national interest, and government took an increasingly energetic role in promoting the national welfare. The sphere of private control remained substantial, but less and less decision-making was left to the casual interplay of the free market. This recrudescence of mercantilism or neomercantilism has been noted by commentators on the growth of British and American national policy.[1] The expansion of government activity for national welfare has obscured the lines between measures clearly related to the economic security of the population and other programs of government. This does not signify, however, that the goals of national policy have of necessity been congruent with the social and economic welfare of the great mass of the population, as the widespread use of the term "welfare state" has at times implied.

By the beginning of the twentieth century there had already been a strong commitment by government to social and economic reform, particularly in England and some of the European countries. The United States had moved more slowly in this direction, and the federal government had been especially cautious in directly sponsoring programs affecting the well-being of the citizenry. In the period of Theodore Roosevelt and Woodrow Wilson, however, the foundation for broad federal intervention was established. The major impetus to hastening the pace of government action during the twentieth century were the two world wars and the intervening depression. Between the beginning of World War I and the conclusion of World War II there were only brief periods when the United States and Britain were not involved in meeting critical foreign and domestic situations. World War I was the first major national effort of the United States as an industrial power, and the experience left its mark for future attempts to meet national crises. The planning and regimentation established during the war provided a pattern for coping with emergencies as well as an orientation generally toward planning for the nation's problems. In addition, modern mass wars involving the total population, whether in a civilian or military capacity, have resulted in the development and rationalization of governmental programs for the whole of society that have continued beyond the emergency period. In general, social and economic standards have been raised in response to the war needs, and they have continued to act as universal goals of social policy.[2] As a result of the British experience in World War II, Professor Titmuss stated:

It was increasingly regarded as a proper function or even obligation of Government to ward off distress and strain among not only the poor but almost all classes of society. And, because the area of responsibility had so perceptibly widened, it was no longer thought sufficient to provide through various branches of social assistance a standard of service hitherto considered appropriate for those in receipt of poor relief—a standard inflexible in administration and attuned to a philosophy which regarded individual distress as a mark of social incapacity.[3]

The planning function of the state was greatly extended because of the growing complexity of society and its institutions during the twentieth century. The increasing complexity of organized industry, agriculture, and labor required that government at least play the role of the accomodator of the diverse social and economic forces in the nation. Beyond the concentration of power in the hands of private interests and the need for representation of the general public interest were the many problems of communication, transportation, and urbanization and of the conservation of human and natural resources with which society was faced. In England the rise of the Labour Party after World War I indicated that the demand for improvements in the standard of living for the population at large was a political issue of the first priority, and the forums of government were to be increasingly occupied with its solution. While labor in the United States had avoided direct political action, after the depression of 1929 it became more intimately involved with politics and in the support of programs of social legislation; and, as in England, the economic conditions of a greater proportion of the population were affected by government policy.

Before the 1930s the major support for social legislation in America came from such private organizations as the American Association for Labor Legislation, the American Association for Old-Age Security, the National Child Labor Committee, and the National Consumers League. The labor unions, under Samuel Gompers' leadership, preferred to emphasize the gains to be made by union action and collective bargaining rather than legislative reforms. Strong unions rather than the state were considered to be the source of strength for labor. Even after the unions gave their support to governmental welfare programs, they continued to press for social security benefits through private pension plans with industry. By 1960, 22.6 million active workers or 45 percent of the population employed were covered by private company retirement plans. Collective bargaining agreements accounted for two out of three workers covered. The greatest number of these plans were effected after the establishment of the federal insurance programs in 1940.[4] Even larger numbers of workers have been covered under collective bargaining agreements for health and other benefits such as life insurance.[5] Thus American labor has in recent years placed major emphasis on social welfare or fringe benefits in industrial contracts, and those benefits have supplemented, or been a substitute for, some of the state programs relied upon by British workers.

Occupational schemes are, however, of growing prevalence in the United Kingdom. There has been relatively greater coverage of salaried workers at higher income levels than among workers in lower-wage groups. It has been estimated that in 1964 eleven million employees were covered by occupational pension schemes. Of them, approximately seven million were in private employment. Of the total eleven million, some four and a half million were persons who had contracted out or substituted an occupational pension scheme for the government's graduated retirement scheme. Expenditures on occupational pension plans amounted to 3.3 percent of payroll in the United States as compared to 1.85 percent in Britain in 1960. Average expenditure on fringe benefits relative to payroll was higher for companies in the United States. This has been particularly influenced by health insurance, which is a widespread private benefit in the United States but which because of the National Health Service has tended to appeal only to the better-off members of the community in Britain.[6]

During the post-World War II period both the United States and the United Kingdom have increased their public social welfare expenditures, which include health and welfare services as well as income security programs. The British have devoted a much higher proportion of their national income to social security expenditures. In 1956–57, for example, 11.9 percent of the national income of the United Kingdom was spent for these purposes as compared to 6 percent in the United States.[7] Apart from increasing standards and proliferation of programs, the size of income maintenance expenditures has been heavily influenced by the growing proportion of aged in both Britain and America.

In 1963 those over retirement age, i.e. men over sixty-five years and women over sixty years, constituted 11 percent of the population in the United States as compared to 15 percent in the United Kingdom. In 1940 the comparable proportions were 9 and 11 percent. The proportion of aged in the United Kingdom is not only larger but has also been rising at a more rapid rate during the last two decades. The proportion of dependent population—aged and children under fifteen—has increased, however, more sharply in the United States over the same period. In 1940 children and aged combined were 34 percent of the population as compared to 33 percent in the United Kingdom. In 1963 they accounted for 42 percent of the American and 38 percent of the British population. The overall population increase in the United Kingdom has been small in comparison to those of the United States and other western European nations. Between 1938 and 1958 the population of the United Kingdom increased by 9 percent, while that of the United States increased by 34 percent.[8]

While these population trends are significant, they do not in themselves indicate an impoverishment of, or greater drain on, the nation's economy. Increases in the labor force and in the productivity of labor may result in a growth in the gross national product that may more than compensate for the proportions of children and aged in the population. The increasing numbers of women, particularly married women, in employment has been an important source of growth in productivity. Between 1956 and 1961 the British labor force increased by 0.4 percent and average productivity by only 2.5 percent despite a high rate of investment in capital per worker.[9] Relative to other countries the increase in per capita gross national product in the United Kingdom since World War II has been small. Between 1938 and 1957 the per capita gross national product in the United States improved at twice the rate of the United Kingdom's although since 1950 the rates have been relatively equal.[10]

In both countries there has been considerable concern about the growth of the national product during the past decade. The rate of growth in many of the countries of western Europe has far outdistanced the rate in the United States and the United Kingdom.[11] Apart from the interest in growth as an indicator of general economic health, growth has been related to current specific social and economic problems. The maintenance of England's relatively high standard of living has been considered dependent on a continuously rising rate of economic expansion. In the United States a substantial degree of unemployment has been attributed to an insufficient rate of economic growth.[12] America's Council of Economic Advisors and England's National Economic Development Council have both emphasized goals for expansion of the economy.[13]

Since World War I substantial progress has been made in the standard of living of the United States and the United Kingdom when such factors as per capita income, housing, nutrition, infant mortality, and general health care are taken into account. However, those gains have not been universal, and specific parts of the population have not shared to any extent in the general prosperity of the post-World War II era. This disparity has been particularly noticeable in the United States, where a relatively high rate of unemployment has persisted despite the general level of prosperity. Except for a brief period the unemployment rate has remained between 4 and 6 percent since 1950,[14] while the British rate has, on the whole, fallen below 2 percent.[15]

Compared to the period between the wars, the unemployment rate in both countries has been phenomenally low. In his famous Report of 1942 Beveridge assumed an average unemployment rate of 8.5 percent and in his 1945 study of employment he set as a goal a rate of 3 percent.[16] Those were radical assumptions in view of the period prior to World War II, when the British rate varied between 10 and 22 percent, and the American rate rose briefly to 11.9 percent in 1921 and ranged between 14 and 25 percent from 1931 to 1940.[17] This lengthy period of unemployment in Great Britain was somewhat mitigated by the already established system of social insurance, which, in addition, was supplemented by a variety of other measures. In America the public relief system was expanded, and a vast series of temporary programs were introduced. It has been estimated that between 1933 and 1940 the numbers receiving direct public income in the United States ranged from 10 to 22 percent of the population. Indirect measures and aid in kind would have greatly added to this number.[18] The gross national product per capita in the United States declined from $857 in 1929 to $590 in 1933.[19] In the United Kingdom per capita income fell after the war and continued to decline until the 1930–1932 period.[20] The changes were not, however, so violent as in the United States.

During the long period of unemployment in Britain it was clear that the economic crisis did not affect equally all wage-earning groups. There was even a rise in average wage rates during the depression, but the actual increase was not spread over the total population. Although there was a gradual improvement in the standard of living after World War I, there were large groups of chronically unemployed whose standards dropped.[21] This was especially observable in the variations in economic conditions between such regions as Wales and the Southeast of England. This phenomenon of differential access to the opportunities and advantages of society even within the working-class population gained increasing significance in America after World War II. Here despite general prosperity a large block of the population did not share in the greater available wealth.

The major social trends that prior to World War I were associated with the need for expansion of economic security measures continued with increased impetus. More and more families lived in urban areas and were dependent on the complex industrial employment market for their living. By 1920 the majority of the American population lived in urban areas. By 1950 more than three fifths of the population were urban residents.[22] From 1910, when almost a third of the working force was in agricultural occupations, the absolute numbers and proportion declined rapidly until in 1950 about an eighth were employed in farmwork.[23] In Great Britain only 5 percent of the work force was engaged in agriculture, forestry, or fishing in 1951,[24] and about a fifth of the population lived in rural areas.[25] Thus, greater proportions of the working population have been affected by changes in the industrial economy and have been influenced by such technological advances as automation.

On the other hand, in both England and the United States there has been growth in the service industries and· in salaried and professional personnel generally. The careers of persons engaged in these occupations have tended to be more stable, less responsive to short-term economic trends and to shifts in methods and service of production. In the United States the number of white-collar workers approximately doubled, while the number of manual workers increased by less than 50 percent between 1920 and 1950.[26] In Great Britain professional personnel increased by 55 percent as compared to an overall increase of 16 percent between 1931 and 1951.[27] While there has been greater stability in these occupations, those in such employment have tended to be more conscious of the need for insurance, and it has been administratively more feasible to provide them protection against the risks of modern society.

Noticeable throughout the industrial era the changes in family and community life weakened the supports provided by earlier systems of association. The family unit became a narrowly defined "nuclear" one, and ceased to be an umbrella for the several generations incorporated in previous periods. The heightened sense of individualism among the members of these smaller families tended to restrict the extent of their interdependence. The swift pace of cultural change loosened the bonds among family members and neighbors. Mobility, both social and geographical, impeded the establishment of firm roots and firm relationships.

While the changes have had disintegrating consequences for the established social system, they have also released strong forces for the fulfillment of democratic ideals in both countries. In the United States the major focus of change since World War II has been related to racial equality. In England, where a more structured system of class was inherited from the nineteenth century, there has been a gradual narrowing of the gulf between classes and an opening of opportunities previously restricted to the more privileged classes.[28]

A combination of higher standards and expectations, changing social and economic forces, and a reorientation of the role of government has led to a vast development of economic security policy in the period after World War I and especially after the depression of the 1930s.

16

Social and Economic Planning

THE major impetus to economic security developments in the years following World War I came from the increasing attention given to social and economic planning. Planning, and particularly government planning, despite vigorous and vociferous opposition, was found more and more acceptable in the postwar climates of Britain and America. The comprehensive manner of conducting modern warfare and the seriousness of the postwar depression period, as already mentioned, were influential in popularizing the notion of planning. Other forces, however, less dramatic, laid the groundwork for social and economic planning in society. The growing sense of social responsibility, the increasing disillusionment with laissez-faire, and the developing awareness of the complexity of modern society supported the belief that some planning was necessary if society was to function effectively.

Social Responsibility

The emergence of social responsibility in both Britain and America, though similar in many respects, occurred through different routes, which account in large measure for the divergent pace of social planning in the two countries. In Britain, with its long tradition of responsibility inherited from the feudal and mercantilist periods, the social emphasis toward the end of the nineteenth century was a renewal of earlier obligations under modern social, economic, and political circumstances. The hiatus in the recognition of public responsibility was relatively short even if measured by the time elapsing between the two great Poor Law Commissions of 1834 and 1909. In America there was at best a weak tradition of social responsibility based on the remnants of colonial poor law. These reflected more the early settlements' efforts to discourage and punish dependency than recognition of community responsibility. The growth of social responsibility thus represented a relatively new phenomenon in an environment of individualism and contract norms. Despite these differences however, the development of social responsibility in both countries had many common ideological roots.

The view of society as an organic system, complex and interdependent, was fundamental to the assumption of broader functions by society with respect to its members. To varying degrees the ideas were gaining currency that society was a whole and that the welfare of individuals could not be separated from the condition of the collectivity and, in turn, that the whole relied on the health of its elements. This was not a new concept of the nature of society, but its prevalence was indicative of its acceptance in spite of the potential conflict between collective action and the individualistic ideologies of western society.[1] The importance of the concept of an interdependent society was emphasized in 1938 by Harold Macmillan, a leading Conservative and later Prime Minister:

The individual has sacrificed his position as an independent producer. He has, as it were, pooled his economic fortune with other members of society. He has become to a greater extent part of society. The individual units of which society is comprised have been knit closer together in a greater mutual dependence. The relations of society and the individual have thus been changed, and the question arises, what new responsibilities should be undertaken by society towards the individual and what new duties and obligations the individual must undertake in return.[2]

More recently an even stronger rationale was presented by another Conservative spokesman:

Individuals are not in fact isolated from each other. They exist and always have existed in society. They belong to societies not because their primitive ancestors at some point resolved to form a community but because they are so constituted as to make it impossible for them to survive outside society. Their thought, inseparable from the language in which it is expressed, is largely a social product. They receive from society more than they give to it, and what they give and what they receive are not easily distinguished. They are born with obligations arising out of society and with needs which can only be satisfied within it. Individual wills, unchecked by society, are a succession of self-contradictory desires which can be made consistent with each other only by the discipline of social relations. Society is natural. Government does not create it, it sustains it.[3]

Although in America there have been differences among radicals and conservatives about the phrasing and implementing of the organic concept of society, there has been no effective rejection of the notion from the period of the New Deal. Even the modern adherents of old-fashioned liberalism stress the interdependence of man. "Of all people," wrote Elliott Dodds speaking for British Liberals, "Liberals are most conscious of this fact [the complexity of the social system], and accordingly they are better described as 'personalists,' aiming to make men responsible as well as self-directing, stressing their interdependence as much as their independence."[4] Similarly Walter Lippmann in America starts from the premise of the complex nature of the division of labor in modern society.[5] Both Watson and Lippmann have been challenged by the evident intricate interrelationships in society, and while they seek solutions of an independent order, they have accepted a great deal of regulation and planning. It is, in fact, Lippmann's thesis that the "fallacy" of nineteenth-century liberals was their failure to appreciate the degree to which laissez-faire was dependent on the institutions of law and the structure of the state.[6]

The conception of society as a complex web of relationships received much support from the rapidly developing fields of psychology and sociology. The study of society revealed more and more the patterned and interlocking system of social institutions. Society was a social system maintained in delicate balance by the interaction of its parts. Analogies, albeit more sophisticated than in earlier times, were drawn between biological organisms and social systems. The concept of equilibrium was employed in functional analysis to represent the abstract model of homeostasis in biology. Thus Talcott Parsons, the prominent American functional sociologist, has referred to the concept of equilibrium as a:

fundamental reference point for analyzing the processes by which a system either comes to terms with the exigencies imposed by a *changing* environment, without essential change in its own structure, or fails to come to terms and undergoes other processes, such as structural change, dissolution in a boundary-maintaining system (analogous to biological death for the organism), or the consolidation of some impairment leading to the establishment of secondary structures of a "pathological" character.[7]

The delineation of the basic functional attributes or "imperatives" of any social system followed from consideration of the functional relationships of specific institutions to the whole. Anthropological studies of primitive cultures supported the notion of a society in which each aspect of the culture had a recognizable role in maintaining the integrity of the whole.

Human behavior was seen as primarily a response to external stimuli and as conditioned, controlled, or heavily influenced by the culturally available solutions. The human being was the product of his environment, and his environment was the social system studied by the sociologists. The concept of man as a social animal was extended from his being generally gregarious and dependent on society for his existence to his being the creature of society. Learned behavior was socially patterned, not fortuitous. Individual personality became, in the eyes of the social psychologist, the unique locus of the surrounding social determinants. Such concepts as role, status, class, authority, power, values, norms, and reference groups were recognized social phenomena accounting for the varieties of behavior in society.

Even the classical Freudian personality traits were linked with the cultural milieu. The diversity of class and ethnic personality types was explained by differing environmental expectations and their effect on instinctual drives for gratification. Sociological and anthropological research directly contributed to Freudian knowledge. A number of community studies in depth documented the process through which attitudes, expectations, and ways of life generally arose. Ecological data on social life paralleled earlier epidemiological studies of health conditions and reaffirmed the lesson of social responsibility. Even economists considered the possibility of changes in expected behavior under different cultural norms in contrast to the universal assumptions of earlier classical theory.[8] By the 1960s such phenomena as delinquency and poverty were being accounted for by sociologists as subcultures generated by dysfunctional aspects of the dominant society. For some, at least, that helped explain the presence of poverty in a society of affluence. Whether poverty was directly transmitted by society or was a more subtle response to the conditions of life, the essence was still in social causation.

Lawrence K. Frank, a pioneer in social health, aptly symbolized the new emphasis when he spoke of "society as the patient." He pointed to the individual's "almost complete dependence upon the group life" and the movement in contemporary society toward a "reinstatement of the ancient doctrine of group responsibility." Frank predicted the transition from individual to "cultural responsibility" as "another great step forward in human life." He concluded, "Until the culture makes the conservation of human values the dominant theme, the individual cannot, or will not, find fulfillment."[9]

Social causation and social determinism had replaced the emphasis on individual morality that had dominated the era of the Protestant ethic, the period from the Reformation to the decline of laissez-faire at the end of the nineteenth century. Whether the nature of man himself had changed, as was indicated by Riesman's "other-directed" and Whyte's "organization" man, or whether the new social sciences were providing merely a more complete view of man's ultimate nature, never before had man been so completely viewed as a social animal.

The scholarly analysis of man's social nature was paralleled by an expansion of the attention given social values in society generally. Such concepts as social good, social risks, social protection, social justice, social policy, and the public interest were the moral and political equivalents of the terminology of the behavioral sciences. Individual faults and guilt, the coin of early Protestanism, gave way to social problems and social risks. In addition to the social determinants of man's behavior, man was no longer held solely responsible for his own destiny. His rationality had been impugned by a variety of studies and theories purporting to demonstrate his primarily emotional character. Man was found to be a "complex creature of impulse and passion and emotional preference who occasionally directs his irrational desires to some intelligent end. Reason is but the umpire among often unruly and conflicting impulses."[10] If man was essentially or substantially irrational, then social rationality and social responsibility must compensate for his childlike impulses.

Society shouldered or shared the blame for a number of the vicissitudes that had heretofore been considered the responsibility of man and his close, primary group. The concept of social risk implied that society bore responsibility for what happened to any of its members as contrasted to efforts to establish individual fault or guilt. The social system was too complex to determine the legal or moral responsibility of its members for events that could be predicted with almost statistical regularity. As the Supreme Court of the United States said of workmen's compensation, "The liability is based, not upon any act or omission of the employer, but upon the existence of the relationship which the employee bears to the employment because of and in the course of which he has been injured." As the Court pointed out, its point of view rested "upon the idea of status, not upon that of implied contract."[11]

The emphasis on the individual that had pervaded nineteenth-century social work was giving way to measures of social protection, which, although no less individually oriented in their consequences, conceived of the individual as a member of a social class, making a social contribution, and entitled to social consideration. This consideration, although humane in intent, was neutral in its operation. Remedies for social ills were sought, and those suffering from present difficulties were treated without assessing guilt. The belief that generosity of treatment was an encouragement to antisocial behavior continued to be a major source of conflict. But, from the time of Lloyd George in Britain and Woodrow Wilson in the United States, though the pace varied, there was a continuous movement toward providing social defenses for individual welfare.

The protective function of society, most clearly evident in social legislation, combined support for the weaker and less favored elements in society with a concern for conserving human resources. Human values were juxtaposed to property values. The protection of the underdog had a broader base than the field of social legislation. Protection of the underdog included farmers and small businessmen in America struggling against the growth of monopoly. It was generally apparent that all members of society were not equally matched in the competitive marketplace and before the law, and society attempted to rectify the balance.[12] The establishment in the United States of administrative tribunals or commissions to adjudicate matters of economic conflict and to represent the public interest indicated the significance of such matters.

The concepts of equity and adequacy, used to distinguish between the principles of private and social insurance, were useful in clarifying the nature of social legislation and protection. Equity was an abstract emphasis on justice or equality of treatment, whereas adequacy incorporated such values as social minimum and need by which individuals were brought to a state of equality through society's contribution.[13] Whereas equity protected property values, adequacy overlooked property or equity from investment in the interests of social justice. Justices like Cardozo and Brandeis were particularly influential in replacing the abstract concepts of law with recognition of the social and economic factors affecting the public interest.

The growing dominance of the public interest reflected the changing nature of individual property rights. The doctrine of public interest threatened the sacredness of property, which was inherited from the laissez-faire period. The public interest permitted modification of the rights of property and the redistribution of its gains for social purposes. Liberals in America, such as Lippmann and Berle, recognized the flexible nature of property. In describing property as a "phenomenon of culture" Berle stated, "Its value depends, not on itself, but on the flow of economic life, that is, on motion and turnover. Stop the motion, and its value disappears." He finally asks, "What quality of it can fairly be called 'private'?"[14]

Thus, Henry George's views of the previous century were now representative of a large segment of liberal opinion. The line between private property and social wealth was still rigidly held by many in theory, but it had become much fainter in practice. Progressive income and other taxes provided government with a large share of the national income to be used for social purposes. An increasing proportion of wealth was directed toward social goals. Intervention into what were once the inviolable realms of private property was rationalized not only by the social nature of wealth but also by the constructive effect of intervention on the increase of private wealth. Early laissez-faire proponents like Adam Smith and Jeremy Bentham might have agreed to more social intervention but for their belief that it would have reduced the total amount of available wealth. Modern economic doctrine, following Keynes, gave the state responsibility for encouraging economic expansion through a variety of techniques, including fiscal policy. Bentham's dilemma of the conflict between the security of private property and the equalization of wealth was to some extent, at least, solved by their assumed compatability.

This position has been strongly held by John Kenneth Galbraith, who favors a realignment of investment of America's wealth between the public and private sectors to solve the problem of "social balance."

It will be clear that to a remarkable extent the requirements for the elimination of poverty are the same as for social balance. (Indeed a good deal of case poverty can be attributed to the failure to maintain social balance.) The myopic pre-occupation with production and material investment has diverted our attention from the more urgent questions of how we are employing our resources and, in particular, from the greater need and opportunity for investing in people.[15]

It is not surprising that Galbraith began his chapter on social balance with a quotation from Tawney on "collective provision."[16] The regulation of investment and the nature of Galbraith's social goals have more in common with socialist planners such as Tawney than with any modern inheritors of the mantle of classical economics. Without conforming to any school of thought, the modern economist concerned with contemporary practical problems has frequently suggested pragmatic solutions that implicitly involve assumptions of social wealth, social goals, and the public interest to the curtailment of strictly private values.

The expansion of social responsibility has been paralleled by a reexamination of the nature of individualism and its relationship to social responsibility. On the whole, the earlier conflict between the expansion of social responsibility and the rights of the individual had been resolved, although there still remained a small group, principally Hayek, Friedman, Machlup, and von Mises, who supported the cause of strict individualism. The crisis of individualism in America came during the great depression, and the solutions of the advocates of individualism had been found wanting. There had already been strong trends away from orthodox individualism in England prior to World War I, but in America the period between the war and the depression was still dominated by individualism and laissez-faire thinking.

The restoration of prosperity in America after the brief depression of 1920 and 1921 strengthened faith in the traditional social and economic values. Men such as Viner, Dickinson, and Garver advocated laissez-faire economics with renewed vigor. There was a speedy relaxing of the controls that had been developed during the War. The return to normalcy advocated by President Harding signified a rejection of even the few measures of social responsibility that had been accepted in the early years of the century. The proponents of laissez-faire saw economic individualism as the basis of all human rights; without economic freedom, all other freedoms were meaningless. This was the position of Herbert Hoover, the last of the prosperity era presidents.[17]

The defense of economic freedom was shared by business and labor during this period. American labor had not adopted a position of radicalism or reform, which led the British trade union movement to lend its support to the rising Labour Party. Right up into the depression American labor and industry were equally critical of any limits on the freedom of economic action. In 1931 the president of the National Association of Manufacturers and the president of the National Industrial Conference Board still stressed individual responsibility and the inevitability of natural law. As Magnus W. Alexander of the Conference Board stated, "Fundamentally, . . . the responsibility for providing against the unforeseen but none the less certain hazards of life, I submit, rests in our democracy with the individual."[18] Labor leaders made similar statements, and the position of Gompers of the American Federation of Labor in 1916 represented labor up to the 1930s.

When you recommend an investigation of social insurance it shall be with the understanding that the rights of the workers and the freedom secured by the workers shall not be frittered away by a patch upon our social system and that under that patch there shall not be a germ that shall devitalize the American citizenship and take away from them the vital principles of freedom of action and the exercise of their normal activities and their higher and best concepts of human welfare combined with freedom . . . As I live, upon the honor of a man, and realizing the responsibility of my words, I would rather help in the inauguration of a revolution against compulsory insurance than submit. As long as there is any spark of life in me I will help in crystallizing the spirit and sentiment of our workers against the attempt to enslave them by the well-meaning siren songs of philosophers, statisticians and politicians.[19]

The clear symbol of the spirit of the times was the abandonment by the Protestant churches generally of whatever stance they had previously taken on the Social Gospel. Fundamentalism and its concern with individual and personal morality became dominant. The energies of the churches were absorbed in correcting individual sin, and the struggle over

Prohibition signalled the churches' removal from social and economic issues. The emphasis on saving individual souls as against social concerns reflected not only the belief that the social order was no business of the church but also the general satisfaction of the church leadership with the current state of things. The churches' response to the rise of atheistic Communism in Russia was to identify Christianity with economic individualism.[20]

Even during the 1920s, however, the counterforces had already set in. Laissez-faire as a viable economic policy and laissez-faire as a guarantee of individual freedom came under attack. In the era of prosperity there were critics who maintained that at its best the laissez-faire economy failed to satisfy the needs of the economy as a whole. Various industries and regions of the country had suffered badly, and the economy benefited some at the expense of others.[21] The system's failure to be self-adjusting was demonstrated on theoretical grounds even while the depression was supplying empirical confirmation.

Probably the most prominent and influential of the modern critics of laissez-faire policies was the British economist Keynes. His attack on Say's law, the assumed self-adjusting equilibrium of the economy, was effective in demolishing one of the major supports of the natural system of classical and neoclassical economists. Others, like Hobson in England and J. M. Clark in the United States, were skeptical of the orthodox theory that the process of production creates the necessary demand for its own consumption. William Trufant Foster and Waddill Catchings, two American economists, came to much the same conclusion at the time that Keynes was formulating his own analysis. Keynes, however, made a full-scale analysis of the weaknesses of equilibrium theory and at the same time provided a rationale for the continuance of the capitalist economy. Keynes himself supported the idea of laissez-faire after the necessary adjustments were made for keeping the system in balance. His name, however, has been primarily identified with his policy recommendations, which, though leaving much to the "free play of economic forces," stimulated far-reaching government activity.[22]

By Keynes' time, Say's emphasis on the equilibrium between production and demand had been transferred to the relationship of full employment and demand. Keynes pointed out that demand left to itself would not guarantee full employment. Private interests and public ends did not naturally coincide; in fact, they might well be in opposition. Full employment could be maintained only by a rationally planned approach involving the "artificial" development of demand through encouraging the propensity for consumption and investment. Whatever the acceptance of Keynes' underlying theoretical assumptions, his continued popularity has rested on his seminal role in directing British and American society away from the simple dogma of economic individualism into more sophisticated economic policy.

Keynes' formulations were in accord with the needs of the times and with the thinking advanced by some of the less orthodox economists. The growing consciousness of business cycles brought on by the depression, which followed the war in England and came a decade later in America, provided the setting for innovations in national economic policy. Earlier beliefs about the appropriateness of laissez-faire were giving way. For example, J. M. Clark responded to the fear that intervention would threaten the general prosperity by stating that there was no "definite assurance . . . that the net result [from a full adherence to laissez-faire] would be to make us richer in the aggregate instead of poorer."[23] It was not only a question of distribution but a failure to develop the full economic potential of society.[24]

Berle and Means, in the tradition of Veblen, Commons, and Mitchell, examined the institution of modern business and found that it had changed radically. The flexibility of earlier periods, when business was relatively small and simple in operation, no longer held. With the concentration of capital in the modern corporation, the economy must be organized to meet a wholly new set of circumstances.[25] Like Tugwell and other economists of the period, Berle and Means concluded that planning for the nation as a whole was essential to the health of society. By the 1960s, Berle, no longer ahead of his times, could state complacently, "It [laissez-faire] has been completely displaced as an infallible god, has been substantially displaced as universal economic master, and increasingly ceases to be, or to be thought of as, the only acceptable way of economic life."[26]

While laissez-faire was being demolished as the final economic truth, its connection with the whole gamut of individual freedom was also being questioned. There was a growing recognition that the liberties of laissez-faire provided no foundation for individual action in modern society.

The assumption that economic liberty and social and political democracy were one and the same was no longer considered valid. Liberals were criticized for placing themselves in the position of tying the economic and the social so closely together that they thwarted desirable social reforms by supporting the status quo on the economic scene.[27]

In the second decade of the century economic institutions were beginning to be examined under the light of pragmatism. As Roscoe Pound, the eminent Dean of the Harvard Law School, wrote:

I am content to see in legal history the record of a continually wider recognizing and satisfying of human wants or claims or desires through social control; a more embracing and more effective securing of social interests; a continually more complete and effective elimination of waste and precluding of friction in human enjoyment of the goods of existence—in short, a continually more efficacious social engineering.[28]

The economic system was not an end in itself but a means to man's welfare, and as a means to man's welfare the organization of the economy under a philosophy of laissez-faire was considered wanting. It failed to supply the social supports necessary for man to achieve his full individual potential.

Acceptance of the social foundation of individual action was more and more in evidence as the twentieth century went on. Governments in England and America, whatever the party in power, continued the established policies of social legislation. Some set the limits of social support more narrowly, but on the whole all would agree with Mary Follett that social legislation was in support of individualism, "because it is legislation for the individual."[29] This position was clearly stated by contemporary British Liberal leadership: "We argue that Welfare is actually a form of Liberty inasmuch as it liberates men from social conditions which narrow their choices and thwart their self-development as truly as any governmental or personal coercions."[30] Some twenty years earlier Harold Macmillan of the Conservative Party had said in much the same vein, "We are seeking to discover what *is* the minimum basis of material welfare and security that man must enjoy if he is to maintain his physical efficiency and increase his liberty."[31]

In 1934 Franklin Roosevelt stated in a message to Congress:

Among our objectives I place the security of the men, women and children of the Nation first. This security for the individual and for the family concerns itself primarily with three factors. People want decent homes to live in; they want to locate them where they can engage in productive work; and they want some safeguard against misfortunes which cannot be wholly eliminated in this man-made world of ours.[32]

In that message, Roosevelt spelled out one of the basic rationales for the modern state's responsibility to the individual.

Security was attained in the earlier days through the interdependence of members of families upon each other and of families within a small community upon each other. The complexities of great communities and of organized industry make less real these simple means of security. Therefore, we are compelled to employ the active interest of the nation as a whole through government in order to encourage a greater security for each individual who composes it.[33]

The natural state of the social Darwinists and the earlier classical economists was replaced by the complexity of a "man-made" environment. The simple environment, around which the social Darwinists had developed their model of the competitive struggle for existence, was also seen as the source of man's needs. The growth of urban industrial society removed man's ready access to the supports available in less advanced cultures. Modern society must provide substitutes for the cooperative, security-giving aspects of nature. The resources provided by society, rather than weakening and threatening the individual, according to this point of view, were in reality only restoring the earlier freedoms that civilization had eroded.[34]

The term *social security* paralleled the concept of psychological security, which had already become popularized. It was recognized that the individual needed limits and supports if he was to be healthy psychologically. The ideal of the totally independent individual, which had pervaded eighteenth- and nineteenth-century political economy was viewed as an unnatural construct. Man was not dependent on others merely because of the division of function noted by Adam Smith. This only provided the basis for a contract society built around the atomistic exchange of the marketplace. Survival in the purely physical sense had been enlarged by the psychologists and social psychologists to include the development of emotional and personality qualities considered characteristically human; these depended on an intimate and protective relationship of the individual with his social environment.

Social legislation and social security measures were the economic counterparts of the growing field of mental health. As J. M. Clark perceptively remarked:

Economists have obviously departed far from the attitude, prevalent a generation ago, which condemned any encroachment on the customary range of things that individuals were supposed to do for themselves, as contrary to the principles of our system. C. H. Cooley long ago disposed of the idea that the way to develop effective capacity for decision-making is to impose on everyone complete responsibility for all the decisions that affect his interests.[35]

For Clark, as well as for others, the major problem was finding the proper balance between social and individual responsibility. While the necessity for some system of social supports has had almost universal acceptance in the realm of practical policy-making, there have been differences about the extent of the system and, conversely, the degree to which the individual should be required to be accountable for himself.

Much of the emphasis on individual responsibility has been in the tradition of nineteenth-century liberalism. The need for social intervention has been weighed against the assumption that any extension of social protection compromises the goal of maximum individual responsibility. As Professor Peacock, the British economist, stated:

The ultimate object of a Liberal society is surely to persuade individuals to recognize their social responsibilities and to carry them out themselves. A social policy which accepts it as axiomatic that individuals are totally unfit to live up to these ideals is adopting what must always appear to Liberals a counsel of despair.[36]

A related and perhaps stronger concern for maintaining individual responsibility comes from the reaction against what is viewed as the elimination of the individual in the mass society dominated by the bureaucratic state. Some of this reaction reflects Herbert Spencer's thinking, with its emphasis on individual incentive and fear of state intervention. E. H. Carr, for example, has referred to the need of finding "the ultimate and final sanction to replace the [former] ultimate sanction of hunger—the economic whip of the old dispensation."[37]

The *laissez-faire* view of wages as the price of labour has long been tempered by the principle of a minimum wage adjusted to need, by family allowances and by social insurance; differences of remuneration originally designed to provide an incentive for the most intelligent and most industrious have been increasingly ironed out by the incidence of a highly progressive income tax; and the whole structure has now been overlaid by the structure of the welfare state in flat contradiction with the original design of the edifice.[38]

The failure of modern society to resolve adequately the problem of individual commitment has been aggravated, in Carr's opinion, by the substitution of "mass democracy" for "individualist democracy" and of the "cult of the strong remedial state for the doctrine of the natural harmony of interests."[39]

To men like Carr and Peacock in England or Lippmann in America, concern with the effect on the individual of the growth of the welfare responsibilities of society does not represent a desire to return to the golden era of nineteenth-century laissez-faire. All recognize the inequities of that period, but they hope to salvage the major values of an individualistic society. They have accepted some limited social reform as the foundation for a society of individual responsibility, but they have insisted on maintaining as much independence as possible from an organized system of social intervention.

This point of view has received considerable attention recently from a group of liberal economists and others in Britain and has been reflected on the political scene in controversies over the nature of the welfare state. *Crossbow,* a Conservative publication, has been a major forum for discussion of returning much of welfare to private control. In agreement with the American economist, Milton Friedman, it has been suggested that the present compulsory membership in governmental schemes financed by universal taxation be modified to allow maximum freedom of choice of social services.[40] While not all would go as far as Friedman in abolishing compulsory retirement programs, there has been much consideration given to transferring to the competitive market and consumer choice what have grown to be recognized as traditional state services in education, health, and social security.

Those opposed to the present system of social security insist, apart from philosophical objections to "paternalistic" bureaucratic controls, that the current programs are anachronistic in societies of affluence. While they are possibly attuned to the need for sharing resources in societies of scarcity, the growth of personal income has made realistic a reliance on mechanisms for individual choice. It is maintained that the psychology of the depression era has continued to influence the planning of social welfare at a time when conditions have changed so radically as to require a considerable reorientation of social policy. The proponents of more private control deny that sufficient real poverty exists to make rational universal social welfare programs. The effect, as they see it, has been state compulsory planning of personal income rather than what might have been the earlier goal of redistribution. Instead of transfers between rich and poor, they maintain, there are merely transfers of individual income from one period of life to another, and the programs satisfy the needs of neither the rich nor the poor. It has been "equal treatment of people in unequal situations." As Arthur Seldon has stated the case:

Equal benefits for people with unequal need is a mockery of equality; it is discrimination against the needy. It distributes bread to people with cake and denies a second loaf to those with only one.[41]

The advocates of choice would, in general, limit public programs to public assistance or some other program like the negative income tax, which discriminates between the needy and the remainder of society and only provides for the former. Beyond that, they would either induce or oblige individuals to make further arrangements for their own security with nongovernmental bodies or leave wholly to the discretion of the individual the problem of insurance and savings.[42] This point of view has received some endorsement from the Conservative Party. In its 1965 statement of aims the Party favored the expansion of the national assistance function and at the same time the reduction as far as possible of the state pension scheme in favor of "occupational or similar pensions on top of the State basic pension."[43]

Although the balance between individual and social responsibility has been critically examined from the traditionally liberal point of view, this issue has also received attention from those more favorable to social planning and collective responsibility. For them, the problem is not the potential conflict between individual rights and social controls but the maintenance of maximum opportunity for individual choice as an integral part of the supporting system of governmental responsibility.

A universal public system of social security and social welfare has been integral to the social planning of those favoring the state's commitment to a fundamental role in social policy. The optimistic denial of poverty by those who would drop the present insurance structure has not been shared by the supporters of a more effective measure of the current programs. They have pointed to the presence of a sizable population with less than a decent standard of living and have been concerned about what appears to be a growing inequality alongside the affluence of modern society.[44]

Withdrawal from the public insurance systems in favor of private planning has been seen as a dangerous course. While it has been recognized that occupational pension schemes have been expanding, doubts have been raised about their continued rate of growth and their selection of favorable risks. The stability of the private insurance funds, the continuing rights of workers shifting employment, and the ability of private funds to adjust to rising costs of living have also been questioned.[45]

Apart from differences about the nature and degree of poverty and the capacity of private insurance, other social policy issues have centered about the effect on the economy and society generally of substituting private for public control of insurance. On the one hand, the funds of the public insurance systems have been seen as important instruments of public policy, and on the other, the growth of capital in the hands of private insurance companies has been viewed as giving extraordinary financial power to bodies outside democratic controls.[46]

The Institute of Economic Affairs' surveys indicating a sizable interest by the public in private pensions and services[47] have been questioned by some on technical grounds, while others have been skeptical of the surveys' policy implications. It has been argued that the complex field of economic security and welfare services cannot be effectively adapted to consumer choice on the private market. It has also been suggested that some of the assumptions underlying the pressure for change are ill-founded. For example, it has been stated that the population, including the middle classes, have not felt "degraded" and are not "in revolt against the Welfare State"[48] but that reliance on private arrangements might aggravate class distinctions.[49]

The advocates of a public and universal system of welfare have not been blind to its weaknesses. Richard Titmuss in a much quoted statement wrote:

Many of us must also now admit that we put too much faith in the 1940s in the concept of universality as applied to social security. Mistakenly, it was linked with economic egalitarianism. Those who have benefited most are those who have needed it least.[50]

More recently he has said, "It is time we returned to consider their roles [housing and social security] afresh and with new vision. Perhaps we might then entitle our journey 'Ways of Extending the Welfare State to the Poor'."[51] Among measures of this nature the Labour Party has included income guarantees but not as a substitute for the whole of the public social security program as has been suggested by some critics of universal welfare programs.[52]

There has been increasing concern on the British welfare scene about the rigidities of the welfare structure that make it less responsive to changing and diverse needs.[53] This lack of sensitivity to "users' wants, feelings, and expectations" has been attributed by one sympathetic critic to the failure to outgrow the "lower-class" traditions of the social services.[54] From this point of view, it is not a question of too much social responsibility but of the manner of its implementation. Brian Abel-Smith has outlined three fundamental questions for increasing the area of individual decision-making for "consumer sovereignty."

First, there is the question of how much compulsory redistribution of purchasing power is required—between income groups, between those who currently have family responsibilities and those who have not, between the young and the old, and between those at work and those unable to work. Second, there is the question of how much of this redistribution should take the form of cash allowances and how much the form of free or subsidised services in kind. Third, there is the question of whether all or the bulk of the service facilities should be publicly owned and organized.[55]

The issue of choice in welfare has focused attention on the role of the consumer in the welfare mechanism. Consideration of consumer choice represents a new phase in the maturation of social welfare that heretofore has often been administered as if the consumer could not be trusted to make decisions or as if the programs themselves could not be organized on other than an undifferentiated mass basis. The opponents of the current system have viewed governmental monopoly as a rigid obstacle to any democratic controls and have placed their faith in the subtle workings of the competitive economic market. The advocates of the state system have been of the opinion that placing social welfare on the economic market will neither achieve this result nor guarantee any modicum of security for all. In turn, they believe that the state mechanism can be adapted to the needs of the citizenry both individually and collectively.[56]

Cooperation and Control

By the end of World War I laissez-faire had all but been abandoned as the ideal of political economy.[57] Economists still identified themselves with the classical school, such as Milton Friedman and Lord Robbins among contemporary economists, and while economists of classical bent were more favorable to laissez-faire, pragmatism rather than rigid orthodoxy was the order of the day. Conservative American economists like Fred M. Taylor and E. W. Kemmerer among others favored social legislation early in the century and approved the transfer of surplus wealth for the health and welfare of the less fortunate in society.[58] The cause of laissez-faire received support not so much from economists as from practical men of business and politicians who had only a crude notion of economic theory but whose loyalty was based to a large extent on a belief in the magic of free enterprise.

While the individualistic competitive model of society failed to meet the needs and satisfy the goals of the postwar world, there were few in America who offered a viable alternative. In England the Labour Party was definitely committed to reforming the social and economic order. In America socialist doctrine had failed to draw sufficient support to become a significant political movement. Radicalism and social reform movements were probably less influential during the 1920s than at any time since the Civil War, but even during the depression years the socialist parties in America never achieved significant strength.

The interest of the churches in Social Gospel, though largely stilled in the United States during the 1920s, continued to stress more cooperative relations in society. The Catholic Bishops' Program of 1919 set the general pattern of Catholic social goals. Without upsetting private property, the Bishops hoped to solve the conflict between workers and employers by allowing workers some share of company ownership and management. They did not favor state ownership. Similar proposals were made by the Social Action Department of the National Catholic Welfare Council.[59]

During the 1930s the Social Gospel movement achieved a more prominent place in Protestant and Catholic circles. Catholic leaders emphasized industrial partnership between employers and employees. Society was viewed as an organism with the welfare of the whole as its goal. Private ownership was not attacked, but social responsibility and social justice were to replace selfish individualism. The unit of cooperation was seen as relatively small—the plant or an occupational group—and such units were to act as intermediate links between the individual and the vast and impersonally complex state.[60] The Catholic Worker movement begun by Dorothy Day in the early 1930s had much of the original flavor of the social settlements.

The Protestant churches had their conventions and their committees on social action, which enunciated socal doctrine. They, too, were opposed to "irresponsible individualism," profit as the motive of the economy, and competition as the means to wealth. Although they stressed cooperative relationships, there was greater acceptance among some Protestant groups of government intervention and even ownership.[61] The Federal Council of Churches in its 1932 "Social Creed" stressed the need for social planning and control in the nation's economy. The more radical wing of the Protestant churches leaned toward planned socialist society. Reinhold Niebuhr, one of the most influential Protestant theologians, denounced the old idealism of the Social Gospel and its belief in voluntary cooperative reform as unrealistic and pressed for radical reform.[62]

But, neither radical change nor the development of a cooperative system occurred on the American scene. Radicalism had never gained a strong foothold in America, and the movement for cooperation also failed to draw support. Although the 1930s was more ready for change than previous decades, the emphasis on cooperation under the aegis of the churches had little influence on a primarily secular society. Labor and industry were not prepared to replace the present structure of their relationships. Both had moved toward large bureaucratic organizations that militated against industrial cooperation on a local or informal level. Large-scale business and national unions arranging contracts for all the workers in an industry would soon become the pattern of employer-labor relations. While there were some agreements on profit-sharing, organized labor on the whole preferred to press its demands independently in collective bargaining rather than in partnership with management.

Sporadic attempts to revive the idea of industrial democracy as well as democratic industrialism have continued. In 1959 the Conservative Political Centre in Britain published *Everyman a Capitalist*, a proposal for a "share-owning democracy." Similarly, in America it has been maintained that industry is a community or social venture because of the widespread nature of stock ownership. A Conservative spokesman some ten years earlier had suggested the establishment of formal "constitutions" in industry that would replace "open conflict" and obviate the need for labor unions, which, it was stated, "exist to bargain not to cooperate."[63]

As a historian of Catholic social action in America has concluded, the movement for cooperation remained a religious ideal with little secular influence.

Although neither capital nor labor showed any real interest in industrial partnership, Catholic social workers continued to insist on its adoption, fortified as they were after 1931 with *Quadragesimo anno* and its plan to invest the co-partnership principle with public authority. The vocational group plan was not adopted—in fact it was sharply criticized—but it provided an ideal in the light of which Catholics estimate the strength and shortcomings of all reform measures in the industrial field.[64]

The romantic ideal of a cooperative society has received little encouragement in either England or America. The major economic forces have been powerful enough to represent their own interests in situations of competition or conflict. In America the concentration of big business led to antitrust legislation to prevent the growth of monopoly and the destruction of competition. However, attempts to curtail the expansion of large corporations were half-hearted and ineffective. It was recognized that while free competition was an abstraction, large-scale organization was the order of the day, and government was almost powerless in discouraging the amalgamation of business into larger and larger units. A variety of corporate devices were invented to evade the letter of the law, and only the most outrageous and open flouting of the principle of competition was challenged.

The tacit acceptance of bigness was not entirely due to acquiescence to its inevitability. Although competition was praised as the basis of a free society, it was also seen as a source of waste and unnecessary conflict. There were even those who favored industry having the recognized right to organize and develop agreements for controlling competition. President Hoover opposed such action as threatening the maintenance of the free American economy.[65] During the New Deal, however, until the Supreme Court's decision on the National Recovery Act, there was widespread development of industrial agreements under the voluntary codes sponsored by the National Recovery Administration.[66]

In Great Britain similar developments took place. If anything, the merging and concentration of industry was more acceptable. The absence of a Jeffersonian tradition favoring small enterprise and the greater concern about social and economic waste provided a more favorable climate for large organization. The British, on the whole, were more impressed with the greater advantages of rationalizing industrial production and distribution than with the disadvantages of imperfect competition.[67] Mechanisms for policing the growth of monopolies were set up relatively late in Britain and were armed with only limited controls. As in the United States, where enforcement procedures were more clearly defined, the concentration of business was little affected.

Large-scale labor organization, as already noted, paralleled the development of mammoth industry. The concept of industrial democracy or partnership, which so appealed to John Stuart Mill and others in the nineteenth century, had made little progress. In England and in the United States, particularly after the founding of the Congress of Industrial Organizations (CIO), the bulk of union membership was found in a small group of unions covering the major industries. The fact that labor and management had become large impersonal bodies, however, has not limited the breadth of their negotiations. In protecting the interests of its members the modern union has been concerned with almost every aspect of industry. In most respects the union has been involved in as many issues of company management as would be the case in industrial partnership, but the conditions of bargaining have reflected positions of conflict rather than cooperation.

The demands of social responsibility, on the one hand, and the failure of laissez-faire to meet the expectations of society, on the other, resulted in a search for new solutions. The gap between technological advance and society's ability to manage those achievements for its own ends was noted on all sides. The lag between the social and material culture was emphasized by sociologists.[68] Man had not created social instruments equal to the task of coping with the increasing complexity of social and economic problems and the conflicts arising from the opposing interests of powerful groups and organizations. The issues became more critical as society accepted responsibility for providing a floor or social minimum for its members or for sharing generally in their social and economic risks. In addition, both the domestic and foreign situation required that problems be viewed as national issues rather than from a limited local or sectional perspective.

The major solution offered to correct the contemporary social and economic deficiencies was planning. Planning had been the favorite tenet of the English Fabians, and they had helped permeate British society with the logic of rationally ordering its resources. Although planning had at first been primarily a socialist goal, it became increasingly popular with other groups after World War I. For example, Arthur Pigou, Marshall's neoclassic successor at Cambridge, recognized the need for intervention to promote the welfare of the citizenry as a whole.[69] The Conservative leader Harold Macmillan stated in the thirties that to achieve the minimum level of income established by Rowntree "a carefully planned economic policy which takes into account all the likely repercussions of each single step proposed"[70] would be required.

The return of the Conservatives to power in 1951 disappointed some of their supporters when it became apparent that they were not ready to remove or even to reduce considerably the framework for state planning and intervention introduced by the previous Labour government.[71] In fact, rather than deprecating planning the Conservatives have since defended themselves against the possible criticism that they are not enthusiastic for and capable of effective planning. One Conservative leader, for example, has vehemently affirmed this position by stating as his cardinal principle, "Increase the planning powers of the central government and exercise those which it enjoys."[72] While the two major parties in Britain may differ on goals and strategy, the concept of state planning itself has been recognized as an essential platform for receiving popular support.

In the United States planning continued to be a controversial issue. The sociologist Lester F. Ward and the economist Simon Patten had been early advocates of planned social change—society making rational choices in its own behalf.[73] Since the 1920s a wide range of Americans representing many fields have shown an ardent interest in planning. In a series of volumes John Dewey, the philosopher, laid the foundation for social planning. He examined man's potential for change, criticized old-fashioned individualism, and indicated the value and methods of organized collective effort for the common good.[74] Historian Charles Beard emphasized the historical necessity of planning.[75] Rexford G. Tugwell, an economist, was particularly active in supporting the need for a managed economy.[76] George Soule,[77] Herbert Croly, and Paul H. Douglas all sought the advantages of planning and coordination without eliminating freedom of action. Some, like Stuart Chase, the Reverend Harry F. Ward, Lincoln Steffens, and the writers Edmund Wilson and John Dos Passos, were influenced by state planning in European nations. They and others provided the intellectual leadership that prepared the background for the first major American experiment in social planning during the Roosevelt administration.

Planning in the United States and Great Britain has combined the techniques of control and cooperation. On the whole, American and British governments have relied on indirect inducements and persuasion rather than on direct controls of the social and economic life of the nation. Even when direct controls have been expanded, they have often been seen as temporary expedients in periods of crisis, such as wartime, and have been abandoned when no longer considered necessary. Although both governments have engaged in direct intervention in the economy through regulatory measures, subsidies, and public enterprises, the major tools of government have been fiscal and monetary policy. Through its own budget and its control of monetary and credit conditions, government has played a decisive role in economic affairs. These measures have affected the general market, but they have not replaced the decision-making powers of those participating in the market.[78]

A major strategy of government planning in the United States and England has been the use of government's prestige in influencing economic behavior. The government has attempted to carry out its policies by providing information about the state of the economy and publicizing its goals as well as by direct appeals to the parties involved and arbitration of disputes. Often lacking the power and frequently reluctant to use the power when available, British and American governments have assumed an underlying harmony between public and private interests and a willingness on the part of private interests to play a publicly cooperative role.[79]

Planning in the United States and England has had largely a pragmatic basis. Planning developed as an *ad hoc* activity of the state to satisfy unmet needs and to remedy social and economic problems, and it has continued to reflect this pragmatic origin rather than any integrated approach to a planned society. The variety of government agencies involved and particularly the autonomy vested in local authorities often result in government intervention reflecting cross-purposes and interests rather than a centrally determined, monolithic policy. Since World War II, however, the institutionalization of government responsibility for the economic welfare of the nation has been demonstrated by the annual reports of the Council of Economic Advisers in the United States and the reports of the National Economic Development Council in the United Kingdom.

Planning, as Myrdal pointed out, has become a regular, if not always acknowledged, function of government.[80] The variety of forces that have accelerated the pace toward a society of social responsibility have also resulted in the investment in government of the role of rational planner for the needs of the citizenry. More and more, government has been expected to provide the stability necessary for the sound development of individual and private interests, and governments have accepted the function of implementing rational foresight for the welfare of society.

17

Goals of Social Policy

THE social policy of modern industrial states has been so greatly oriented to the economic welfare of the nation that there have been few public issues that could not be interpreted as relevant to the economic security of the population at large. Within the welter of foreign and domestic matters, however, there have been several interrelated goals more directly identified with economic security. Those goals, shared by the United States and Great Britain, have included maintenance of the economic stability of the nation, promotion of full employment, expansion of the economy, elimination of poverty, and improvement of human resources. Governments have varied in the extent of their direct involvement in the achievement of these goals, but there has been little question of their responsibility in the final analysis for the well-being of their citizenry. The nature of modern social policy has been defined not so much by the uniqueness of specific goals as by their combination and their underlying philosophy. Thus modern policy bears some striking similarities to the status principles of the mercantilist era, but the contemporary values of social equality and individual worth have made for essential differences. It would be difficult to apply the term "welfare state" to the combination of social and economic policies of any previous period.

Stability

Stabilization of the national economy, although the most complex and encompassing of goals, has been the most generally recognized responsibility of government. In England the Webbs had promoted a scheme of balancing public and private investment, which was incorporated in the Minority Report of the 1909 Poor Law Commission.[1] In America the experience of the depression of 1929 was a major influence in directing the power of the state toward guaranteeing economic stability. The depression dramatically demonstrated the inability of the private sector to eliminate significant cyclical trends. As late as 1933 the eminent labor economist Leo Wolman thought that despite the evident failure of private business in establishing the basis for economic stability, there was little chance of effective governmental action.[2] By 1935, however, Herbert Hoover spoke of government mitigating the booms and slumps of the business cycle;[3] and he had attempted during his period of office, albeit ineffectively, through such programs as the Reconstruction Finance Corporation to use government credit for countercyclical purposes.

By the end of World War II there was little doubt in England and the United States about government's stabilizing functions, and many of Keynes' suggestions that had been rejected as radical in the previous decades became part of orthodox governmental policy. In the United States the Employment Act of 1946 anticipated the development of a "national economic policy to promote maximum employment, production and purchasing power."[4] In England a similar formal commitment was made in the 1944 White Paper, *Employment Policy*.

The continuous surveillance of and regular intervention in the economy, when considered necessary, have distinguished modern governmental policy from the intermittent and conditional programs of earlier periods. Even the governments that most strongly favored the freedom of the competitive market have accepted their institutionalized role as guardians of the national economy.[5] The postwar period in Great Britain has been described as an attempt at government "management of the economy."[6]

There has been a vast variety of measures available to government for stabilization of the economy. They have expanded greatly since the nineteenth-century emphasis on public works and public contracts to smooth out the periods of depressed private activity. While fiscal and credit policies have been the mainstays of the British and American governments, there have been few domestic or foreign policies that have not been related directly or indirectly to the goal of stability. It is noteworthy, for example, that when Wolman weighed the stabilizing function of the social insurances in 1933, he concluded that the role of insurance was fundamentally support of the needy, while a quarter of a century later the Rockefeller Reports emphasized the proven effectiveness of insurance in stabilizing the economy.[7]

Stabilization of the economy in itself does not imply an improved level of living, as does full employment or the reduction of poverty. However, one of the major goals for economic welfare in modern society has been security from the irregularities of the market economy. Early in the century the British economist Arthur Pigou viewed the diminishing of the "variability" of the national dividend, particularly the part "accruing to the poor," as increasing the economic welfare of the whole society.[8] Apart from its direct consequences, however, stabilization in modern economies has had additional significance. Stabilization has not been a static concept; its achievement has generally depended on a dynamic economy involving high levels of productivity, demand, and employment. Thus stability in the United States and England has been closely correlated with the other major goals of social policy.

Full Employment

Since the end of World War II the rate of unemployment or conversely the degree of full employment has been the most consistently used measure in appraising the state of the nation. The employment rate has acted as the single most accepted barometer of national health in contrast to earlier periods, when other economic indicators were given primary attention. As already noted, the maintenance of full employment as a national goal was reflected in the British White Paper of 1944 and the American Employment Act of 1946. In both countries economic policy has been tailored to the goal of full employment, and no government, particularly in the United States where the rate of unemployment has been relatively high, has been indifferent to its political implications.

This emphasis on full employment signified a growing belief that the business recessions responsible for periods of abnormally low employment could be mitigated and that even the normal rates of unemployment could be influenced to obtain an optimum employment situation. The idea that the rate of employment was responsive to planned intervention in a predominantly privately controlled economy has gained popularity only recently. "Inevitable" was the term most widely used in the 1930s to describe the recurrent fluctuations in employment. Abraham Epstein summarized the position of many concerned with the problem.

While the present depression has been the most severe and the most extensive of all our crises, it must be remembered that unemployment is no temporary or occasional phenomenon. Even in the active years of 1920, 1923 and 1926, the estimated minimum unemployment in the United States was 5.08 per cent, 5.23 per cent and 5.25 per cent, respectively, of the total non-agricultural wage-earners. Unemployment is as inherent in the industrial process as the machine which helps to produce it. It is the inevitable concomitant of the factory system and our acquisitive social order.[9]

But the practical experience of the depression as well as the permeation of new ideas made for a willingness to experiment with the previously sacrosanct private economy. Socialist critics put capitalism on the defensive about the recurrence of severe unemployment, and even its supporters questioned the need for the instability of the employment market. Of these, as noted, the most influential was Keynes, who considered the "failure to provide for full employment" the major fault of current society. In his general rejection of the notion of natural balance in the economy, he specifically attacked the idea that the "level of employment consistent with equilibrium" in the economy would be "equal to full employment." He maintained:

The effective demand associated with full employment is a special case, only realized when the propensity to consume and the inducement to invest stand in a particular relationship to one another. This particular relationship, which corresponds to the assumptions of the classical theory, is in a sense an optimum relationship. But it can only exist when, by accident or design, current investment provides an amount of demand just equal to the excess of the aggregate supply price of the output resulting from full employment over what the community will choose to spend on consumption when it is fully employed.[10]

The concept of "design" was slow in being accepted, but it eventually counterbalanced the belief in inevitability or natural law inherited from previous generations.

With attention being given to full employment, the subject of employment itself has received more careful examination. In the United States, census data on employment began in 1940. British data were available from the end of World War I in relation to unemployment insurance. In both countries data from earlier periods were not comparable and had to be adjusted for trend analysis. Even contemporary statistics, however, have frequently failed to measure adequately the employment picture.[11] In addition to unemployment as generally recognized, there have been large quantities of underemployment and concealed unemployment not taken into account. In attempting to define what full employment involves, it has become clear that there have been many situations that simulate full employment and that must be carefully distinguished before the concept of full employment itself may emerge. Thus the full participation of individuals in the labor market has been limited by partial employment, underemployment, or disguised unemployment,[12] even where there appears to be no lack of employment.

Although full employment has been identified with several goals, it has generally signified that satisfactory job opportunities are available for all those able and willing to work. Satisfactory job opportunities are assumed to include appropriate utilization of the capacities of those employed under conditions of acceptable employment.[13] There have been differences of opinion about when such a situation obtains in a country. For example, Beveridge has argued that there should always be more vacant jobs than persons seeking employment.[14] Others have maintained that an excess of jobs is inflationary and that a balance between available employment and those seeking jobs is the optimum state.[15] It has been recognized that even under optimum circumstances there will still be some unemployment due to friction in the industrial market. Beveridge, despite his insistence on an excess of employment opportunities, estimated that an unemployment rate of 3 percent would account for normal frictional shifts and the continuous readjustments of workers and jobs, and this has frequently been accepted as a reasonable goal for full employment.[16]

The stress on full employment in contemporary Britain and America has represented a combination of traditional and modern values. In earlier eras and in less technically advanced countries productivity and morality were considered closely related. The survival of the community was dependent on the efforts of all, and idleness was a threat to the survival of an economy of scarcity. In the minds of some today, idleness would have no damaging effect,[17] and there have been a variety of proposals for providing income unrelated to industry and freed from the deterrents and controls heretofore considered necessary.[18] There has been still greater concern, however, about the wastage of unemployment and idleness and about the gains that could be achieved through full use of the labor force.[19]

Although Great Britain has enjoyed relatively full employment since the war, there has been dissatisfaction with the productivity of the labor force. The National Economic Development Council has recommended that both the pool of available manpower and the rate of individual productivity be increased.[20] Because of its less favorable employment situation, the United States has emphasized the expansion of opportunities for employment, but it too has been conscious of the need to "reduce the barriers that deny us the full power of our working force."[21]

While the economic advantages of full employment have received much attention, there has been growing concern about the psychological and social significance of work in modern society. Since earlier societies were faced with clear economic requirements, there was little reality in posing the question of work versus leisure. Modern societies do have the choice, and there has been a tremendous expansion of leisure opportunities in wealthy industrial nations. It is noteworthy, however, that neither in the United States nor in Great Britain has there been any serious consideration of the reduction of employment beyond what the limitations of the labor market may impose. The emphasis on full employment has indicated that employment continues as the preferred source of income, and national policy has concentrated on providing income through the employment market rather than through the alternate economic security mechanisms that developed so rapidly between the depression of the 1930s and the end of the war. It is also significant that the great advances in pensions and other benefits since World War II have been attached to wage-related income.

Some of the emphasis on work has reflected earlier values about the importance of work to man's well-being, but there have also been other, more recent assumptions about the nature of employment. The period of the Great Depression left lasting impressions about the social and psychological consequences of lengthy unemployment. Absence of work lowered dignity and pride and destroyed morale.[22] Studies like *Men Without Work*[23] in England and *Citizens Without Work*[24] in the United States documented the ill effects of unemployment. The United States Committee on Long-Range Work and Relief Policies, at the end of the depression, recommended that government, if necessary, must provide work. In its report, the Committee concluded:

In the last resort we do not face a choice between a painful and a painless social policy. The risks and costs of the policy of public provision of work must be set against the risks and costs of doing nothing. We believe that the social costs of prolonged idleness and denial of participation in the normal productive life of the community are so great as to overshadow the social and economic costs incidental to the provision of work by government.[25]

The right to work has received more and more recognition as unemployment has been attributed to the failure of social policy. The public provision of work has been avoided, but indirect stimuli to employment have been regularly used. While the right to opportunity has been emphasized, as in the Economic Opportunity Act of 1964 in the United States, opportunity has meant more than a vague equalization of cultural advantages. Opportunity has come to mean the obligation of society to provide employment, not merely the preparation of the individual for the employment market. The original Full Employment Bill (S.380), introduced in the United States Congress in 1945, stated:

All Americans able to work and seeking work have the right to useful, remunerative, regular and full-time employment, and it is the policy of the United States to assure . . . sufficient employment opportunities to enable [them] . . . freely to exercise this right.[26]

The success of programs has been judged by the numbers absorbed in employment, not by the numbers educated or trained. A measure most frequently used to depict the lot of disadvantaged groups in society has been their invidious position with regard to employment. The modern test of democracy has been its willingness and ability to make equal employment available for all its citizenry.

Gunnar Myrdal and Margaret Mead, as well as others, have pointed to the focal importance of employment in providing meaningful activity in contemporary society.[27] Both the individual's sense of self-respect and the status accorded him are largely dependent on occupation. Recent research has indicated the effects of periods of unemployment on the individual's sense of membership in society.[28] The influence of employment on self-image and the value system of workers has also been described.[29] Thus from a variety of points of view the policy of full employment reflects major norms of British and American life.

Apart from employment as the means or source of other satisfactions there is the satisfaction to be obtained directly from the employment itself. As Beveridge stated, "Idleness is not the same as Want, but a separate evil, which men do not escape by having an income. They must also have the chance of rendering useful service and of feeling that they are doing so."[30] Employment is not merely any form of work that provides a wage. This concern with the value of work for itself is reminiscent of the Romantic reaction against the loss of artistry and the drabness of nineteenth-century industry. J. A. Hobson suggested a revision of the classical assumption that all labor must be painful and consumption its compensation. Pains and pleasures alike are found in all production and consumption. The productive activities like those of consumption can be the source of healthy and vital growth processes although there are wide variations in the creative satisfactions available in industry.[31]

The meaning and satisfaction of employment have been demonstrated by the reluctance of many to accept retirement even when not faced with financial pressures. Studies of employed populations have also indicated that work is more than a means to an end and is "a source of interesting, purposeful activity and . . . intrinsic enjoyment" although workers of lowest skill and status have tended to see employment as being almost entirely for the purpose of gaining wages.[32] Galbraith has suggested that laborious or tedious labor must be distinguished from intellectually satisfying occupations. There has been a decreasing need for the former and an expansion of the latter, and for Galbraith the goal of social policy is to substitute for painful employment the growth of "interesting and rewarding occupation."[33]

For a variety of reasons, from immediate concern with national defense and productivity to basic assumptions about the role of work, full employment has been the foundation of current economic security. Income from employment has been the primary source of income, and eligibility for substitute income from social insurance in the United States and Britain has been determined by previous or present relationships to the employment market. There is in current policy a sensitive balance between the amount of available employment and the adequacy of the insurance fund. The solvency of social security is dependent on the existence of a condition of relatively full employment.[34]

Expansion of the Economy

The goal of maximum production has been largely synonymous with the goals of full employment and maintenance of economic stability. The justification for the emphasis on productivity has changed greatly from the period when both Britain and the United States were suffering from economies of scarcity. But productivity has continued to receive support along the traditional lines of earlier eras. Increased productivity has been looked upon as a good in itself, as a measure of a society's greatness, and as a guarantee of its strength in international competition and conflict. In the United States a constantly improving standard of material living has been the ideal of progress and has made for continuing attention to productivity.

According to the marginal utility assumptions of the neoclassical economists, consumer demand would provide a less and less urgent stimulus for goods as need was increasingly satisfied. This has not, however, proved to be the case. The consumer demand schedule has demonstrated an amazing flexibility, and the expected satiation point has not been approximated. Whatever the validity of any concept of natural or basic needs reflecting essential economic wants, civilization has documented the psychological and social dimensions of consumer behavior.[35] Veblen's acerbic analysis of "conspicuous consumption" in western society has been paralleled by anthropological studies of primitive communities.[36] Despite the dissatisfaction of some, like Galbraith,[37] with the irrationality of consumer expectations and their influence on productivity, social values appear to have as much effect as dire want in maintaining the pressure for increased goods.

The emphasis on productivity has, however, received support from other sources in the modern economy. A healthy rate of expansion of the gross national product has been linked with the overall prosperity of the country and has been considered a key to full employment. The slow rate of growth of the American economy has been held responsible for the existence of poverty and unemployment even though most are enjoying a high level of living.[38] In his 1964 Economic Report, President Johnson said he regarded the "achievement of the full potential of our resources—physical, human, and otherwise—to be the highest purpose of governmental policies next to the protection of those rights we regard as inalienable."[39] He looked forward to a "free and growing economy which . . . generates *steady and rapid growth in productivity*—the ultimate source of higher living standards—while providing the new skills and jobs needed for displaced workers."[40] An expanding economy was viewed as essential to the solution of all the basic economic problems of society.

The British concern with expansion of the economy has stemmed, as noted, from dissatisfaction with the limitation placed on the resources of the nation by the slow growth of the economy as compared to those of other European nations. While full employment has been one of the major goals of growth in the United States, its relative accomplishment in the United Kingdom has not necessarily resulted in optimum economic performance. The maintenance of officially reported full employment has ceased to be a sound indicator of the state of the economy.[41] In America the question has been how can an expanding economy ensure full employment, whereas in England the issue has been the attainment of economic expansion under conditions of full employment. Among the objectives of the National Economic Development Council in 1962 was "to consider together what are the obstacles to quicker growth, what can be done to improve efficiency and whether the best use is being made of our resources."[42] In evaluating progress in 1964 the Council noted the small amount of additional labor available and stated that "the main challenge of the programme for faster growth is to the ability to increase output per man at a faster rate than previously."[43]

In America, as Galbraith has commented, increased production has not been valued for itself alone but also for its remedial effects on the economic "tensions," "anxieties," and "privations" of society.[44] A substantial rate of growth would, according to its advocates, entail the full use of the nation's resources and provide employment and a higher level of living for all. Approaches to poverty that do not affect production are viewed as unrealistic or having a "stultifying" effect on the rich potential of society.[45] But if economic growth in modern industrial societies is to have the desired consequences, it cannot merely be generally stimulated but must have specific direction to achieve the desired results. The assumptions of natural law no longer hold, and stimulating the economy without specifically including the participation of the already disadvantaged groups has been held to provide no guarantee against their continued poverty. As President Johnson told Congress in his 1964 Economic Report, "We cannot and need not wait for the gradual growth of the economy to lift this forgotten fifth of our Nation above the poverty line."[46] Beveridge and others who emphasize the importance of increasing production have stressed as a corollary the improved distribution of goods and services among the population.[47]

Despite the opinion of skeptics and those who would reconsider the social goal of material progress in contemporary life, expansion of the economy with the maximum use of productive resources has remained a key focus of Britain and America. Rates of expansion have been credited with being among the most important measures of national health. Even critics of the emphasis on productivity have praised its increase as influential in reducing dissatisfaction. The availability of abundance, it is believed, has distracted attention from differences in wealth that in societies of scarcity make crucial distinctions in standards of living. Thus, much of the bitterness and strife due to the invidious distribution of limited resources is considered avoided under conditions of relative affluence. Increased productivity has been seen as an influential force in avoiding the conflicts prevalent in the twentieth century over the distribution of wealth.

The importance of work in western society has also provided a significant rationale for an expanding economy. On the one hand, it helps guarantee a state of full employment, signifying an opportunity for all to have an independent income. On the other, it indicates that even with advancing automation there will be a contributory function for all in society. For although American and British society may have reached the point when increased production in itself has diminishing value and society may be able to support greater numbers without requiring their contribution, work continues to have primary social and psychological meaning for the members of society. As currently organized and with contemporary values, neither Britain nor America has overlooked the noneconomic functions of work. While there has been much talk about leisure, it has often been viewed more as a threat than a contribution when separated from the structure and discipline of work. But the social consequences of full employment have not yet received the attention given to its economic implications.[48]

The Elimination of Poverty

The elimination of poverty has been among the most dramatic and popular of the goals of social policy. Beveridge's "abolition of want" and President Johnson's "war on poverty," although almost a generation apart, symbolize the determination of contemporary British and American society to rid themselves of poverty. This determination reflects a moral discomfort with the existence of poverty, a conviction that poverty can be eliminated, and an awareness of the debilitating effects of poverty on the state of society as a whole.

Dissatisfaction with the presence of poverty in British and American society occurred well before the twentieth century. Nineteenth-century economists, including Malthus, Ricardo, and Mill, gave sympathetic attention to the problem, but their deference to natural law resulted in giving the impression of the inevitability of poverty. Natural law, however, not only accounted for the existence of poverty, but those who identified natural law with "the good" assumed poverty had a positive and useful function for the economy.

By the end of the First World War, the abandonment of laissez-faire and the growing responsibility of government for and intervention in economic affairs made poverty a matter of national policy. Even those who did not support an active economic role for the state recognized that the existence of poverty could not be disregarded. In 1928, President Herbert Hoover, optimistically foreseeing the end of poverty in America, declared:

One of the oldest and perhaps the noblest of human aspirations has been abolition of poverty. By poverty I mean the grinding by under-nourishment, cold and ignorance, and fear of old age of those who have the will to work. We in America today are nearer to the final triumph over poverty than ever before in the history of any land. The poorhouse is vanishing from among us. We have not yet reached the goal . . . but . . . we shall soon with the help of God be within sight of the day when poverty will be banished from this nation.[49]

In 1911 the Webbs, radicals in their time, wrote of destitution as representing the "moral failure of the community as a whole."[50] They pointed to the obligation of society to provide the conditions for the healthy growth of its citizens. Over fifty years later an American Secretary of Health, Education and Welfare introducing the Economic Opportunity Act of 1964, known as the "poverty program," stated:

The most basic reason for declaring war on poverty is a moral one. The belief that each individual should have the opportunity to develop his capacity to the fullest is the very foundation of this Nation and its institutions.[51]

Between the Webbs and the act of 1964 there was a rapidly growing sense of social failure at the presence of poverty. Much of this was related to the belief that poverty was unnecessary, that society had the resources to abolish poverty. During the depressions following the First World War it was clear that the suffering was not universal, that only some bore the brunt of the crisis, and that despite widespread poverty the economy had rich unused and untapped resources. Like Harry Hopkins, Franklin Roosevelt's chief welfare administrator, many reacted with indignation to the conditions of the poor. Poverty was not the necessary price of a competitive economy. As Hopkins stated:

I have never liked poverty. I have never believed that with our capitalistic system people have to be poor. I think it is an outrage that we should permit hundreds and hundreds of thousands of people to be ill clad, to live in miserable homes, not to have enough to eat; not to be able to send their children to school for the only reason that they are poor.[52]

Poverty was not inevitable, but even if people were poor there was no reason why they should have to live under conditions generally associated with poverty. Thus the task was a dual one: the prevention of the unstable and low incomes that make for poverty and the alleviation of poverty by improving the standard of living of low-income groups. As the condition of the poor came to be viewed as one of the major sources of continuing poverty, these goals became interrelated, although they have often been treated separately.

Poverty as a social disease passed on from generation to generation has received much attention in the United States. Despite the generally high level of the economy since World War II, the presence of a sizable proportion of the population (variously estimated between 20 and 40 percent[53]) with inadquate incomes and large numbers dependent on public assistance brought the most serious attention to the problem of poverty since the 1930s. Studies of the poor indicated that poverty was associated with particular characteristics such as race, education, sex of head of household, occupation, and place of residence.[54]

Much attention has gone into identifying the demographic aspects of poverty, but there has been equal or even greater concern with understanding the significance of poverty in an affluent society. Michael Harrington's *The Other America* was influential in popularizing the idea that there were pockets removed by poverty from the mainstream and deprived of the opportunity of benefiting from the growing wealth of society. This "two nation" view of American life has received much support from sociological studies of the culture of poverty—the attitudes, traditions, values, and methods generally that the poor have developed to adjust to the problems of life. Poverty was found to have a two-pronged effect: the families of the poor, because of their own cultural and aspirational levels, limited the potential of their members; and society confirmed those limits by providing unequal access to socially approved satisfactions and goals.[55]

The circularity of this relationship between society and the poor has been examined particularly with regard to education, which many consider the major channel for socialization and social and economic mobility. Morgan and his colleagues found that the amount of education of children was affected by the education, income, and occupation of their parents.[56] Similar results were reported by Lansing[57] and Iffert,[58] who found that the education and income level of parents had an important influence on aspirations, plans, and achievement of college education. Hollingshead[59] and Sexton[60] examined the effect of lower-class status on the educational experience in elementary and high schools and found that the schools reinforced the deprivation of these youngsters. Other studies have attempted to delineate those aspects of the school culture that discriminate against children from lower-income groups and thus artificially limit their potential for achievement.[61]

The cleavage between the poor and the majority culture and the inaccessibility to the poor of society's major institutions for bridging the gap and preparing them for social participation have been found in all areas. The housing and health standards of the poor have been markedly inferior.[62] In mental as well as physical health, the higher rate of disorders of those of lower socioeconomic status has been associated with, among other factors, the more limited availability of treatment resources.[63] The U. S. Public Health Service has reported, on the basis of household surveys, that the amount of medical and dental attention received by a family was a function of family income.[64] There are indications that in the United Kingdom a similar class difference has occurred in the use of health resources.[65]

In general, it has become more apparent in both the United States and Britain since World War II that the problem of poverty and the poor requires special treatment. The raising of the general level of living or the expansion of social resources for all has not necessarily affected the well-being of the lowest socioeconomic groups of the population. Their smaller share of the economy as a whole has been paralleled by a similarly limited share of the institutions for the reduction of the consequences of poverty.[66]

The individual and social consequences of poverty have been viewed as interrelated in modern society. It has been assumed that the social, political, and economic ramifications of poverty are so serious that poverty cannot be evaluated in individual terms. Economically, the existence of poverty has been seen as curtailing the total wealth of society. The reduced productive capacity and consumer market represented by the poor has been one of the major problems of domestic policy. In effect, modern society cannot afford poverty as, for example, the mercantilist era could because a surplus of needy laborers was considered a valuable national resource. The social Darwinist conflict between the welfare of the poor and the survival of the fittest or the good of society no longer received serious consideration. Pigou, an important link between the old and the new, accepted the superiority of the wealthy but questioned the social Darwinist assumption of opposition of interests between the poor and society and maintained that improving the condition of the poor was of benefit to the nation as a whole.[67] In addition to the "multiplier" effects of individual poverty on the total economy, the social and political threat of poverty has been foremost in the minds of policy-makers. As Abraham Epstein stated succinctly, the insecurity of the wage earner "endangers the very existence of the social order. No society which exposes the majority of its members to such grave and continuous hazards and injustices can endure for long."[68]

The emphasis on the social consequences of poverty has been associated with a more objective and impersonal view of the phenomenon of poverty as a whole. There has been a trend toward recognizing poverty as the result of social and economic phenomena beyond the fault of the individual. Even when individual factors have been stressed, they have not been viewed so much as moral shortcomings as manifestations of social problems. Their treatment or correction has been considered the responsibility of society.

While there has been continued attention to case poverty,[69] major concern has centered around the limitations of an economic system that has failed to provide adequately for many of its members. Among Keynes' contributions was the concept of involuntary unemployment, i.e. unemployment due to the absence of work rather than to the refusal to work. Earlier classical economists had assumed that apart from temporary frictional conditions there would always be a balance between jobs and labor as long as the latter did not refuse to work at the market wage. Keynes rejected this notion and pointed to the absolute scarcity of employment that arose under typical patterns of economic activity.[70] Others, such as Beveridge and Rubinow, stressed that the failure to make a living was largely impersonal. The causes, said Rubinow, "must be found in the fluctuation of business, not in his [the worker's] mental capacity or dexterity. These are fixed rather than variable factors."[71]

Although some of the characteristics reported to be connected with poverty have been of a remediable type, e.g. poor education or health, there has been much evidence that limited economic opportunity or resources have affected particular groups of the population, such as youth, the aged, women, nonwhites, or farmers. The problem thus has been seen as requiring a full approach to those factors in the economy responsible for the low income of large segments of the population. Leon Keyserling has maintained:

An assault upon poverty not interwoven with the attack upon these other problems would focus excessively upon a purely "case-work" or "welfare" approach which sought to make poverty a bit less oppressive, or lose itself in a few dramatic situations of no great nationwide import, instead of building an economic environment in which massive poverty would find no place.[72]

The focus on structural difficulties in the economy as the source of unemployment and inadequate income emphasizes the maladjustment of the labor supply to the needs of the job market in a way that symbolizes the modern, objective approach to questions of poverty. In previous periods the gap between the demands of industry and available labor would have been largely interpreted as the unwillingness of workers to expend the necessary effort and foresight to satisfy the requirements of employment. It was assumed that as long as employment was available, nothing but a penchant for idleness explained the worker's failure to be employed. Thus almost all poverty was an individual problem. However, the modern concept of structural unemployment has fixed on the relative lag in labor skill that occurs in a rapidly changing society. It is not a question of moral or psychological reform, but of a program which defines the needs of industry and maintains a realistic relationship between these needs and the skills of wage earners.[73]

The trend toward the acceptance of social responsibility for the presence of poverty has thus been paralleled by the seeking of causes and remedies within the larger social environment. Although there had been a gradual movement in this direction from the middle of the nineteenth century, the experience of both Britain and the United States in the Great Depression after the First World War provided the greatest impetus for viewing poverty as a social rather than an individual issue. The widespread unemployment affecting many who could not conceivably be classified as lazy or dependent, the valiant efforts to find work, the evident disrupted state of the economic system, and the common sense of frustration and lowered standards, all influenced a sharp turn toward major institutional reforms in society.[74] The Social Security Act in America and the Beveridge Report in England, both encompassing major advances in the organization of economic security, were direct outgrowths of the preceding period. The extension of the insurance concept of risk to the major contingencies affecting the security of the individual neutralized or avoided the question of fault or individual guilt. In effect, the incidence of certain contingencies occurred with sufficient statistical regularity that it was more realistic to plan objectively for them as normal social phenomena than to establish unique responsibility in individual situations.

Some of the change toward a more objective or impersonal treatment of poverty was influenced by the greater sophistication about social and economic causation generally. The nineteenth-century approach of singling out and weighing the factors responsible for the condition of poverty had lost popularity. It was recognized that poverty was too complex for such crude analysis and that the interrelationship of causal elements was too great for the identification of specific responsible agents. The tendency of the social sciences to speak in terms of correlations rather than causes has been indicative of modern research. This has been paralleled on the applied or program level by the abandonment of earlier overambitious attempts to root out the causes of poverty, whether individual or social. Instead, much attention has been given to dealing with limited but controllable aspects of the problem or employing empirically some alleviative strategies.

This new approach has also reflected changing values in society. During the nineteenth and early twentieth centuries the search for causes generally resulted in assigning a heavy proportion of the blame to the individual and in applying deterrent and punitive or, at best, paternalistic methods of treatment. The increasing pressures toward democracy, however, particularly with regard to the rights of the lower classes, made anachronistic any invidious treatment of the poor. The goal was the dignity of objective service to all.[75] Even the case treatment of poverty became more and more founded on a professional and scientific code in contrast to earlier stress on moral and personal influence.[76] There still, of course, remained sizable programs linking the treatment of poverty with reform of the individual, but the bulk of the programs were more general in nature and related to the larger social and economic context.

The primary goal for the elimination of poverty has been the guarantee of some minimum absolute standard of living to all individuals and families, although during the period since the Second World War there has as well been some consideration of poverty as measured by the relative standard of income distribution within society. The concept of a minimum, whether measured by absolute or relative standards, has been, as J. M. Clark has stated, based on the "principle that effective freedom, or opportunity, includes command over the material means necessary to make adequate use of it."[77]

The goal of a national minimum was strongly supported in Great Britain by the Minority Report of the Poor Law Commission of 1909, but it was not until the Beveridge Report that the goal was fully elaborated for implementation. Similarly the American social security system attempted to guarantee "a minimum income adequate for a decent living."[78] But the philosophy underlying both the British and American social security programs limited their role to interruption or loss of earning power and other special circumstances. In general, they provided a subsistence base in times of need and left the broader question of adequate living standards to be decided by earnings from employment. One of the principles of social security has been to provide benefits at a level low enough not to compete with the employment market, and in turn, it has been expected that that level will be supplemented by income from other sources to achieve a relatively adequate standard of living.[79]

The concept of a social minimum has, however, expanded beyond the originally conceived philosophy of social security. Government's function in eliminating poverty has come to reflect the view that society should be concerned with establishing a reasonable standard for all, not merely a minimal base in response to particular risks or in periods of crisis. The poverty line thus has been interpreted as the level of living beneath which the rights of individuals to participate in a democratic society are no longer protected. In attacking poverty, society has taken responsibility for supporting a particular way or standard of life. As the Committee on Long-Range Work and Relief Policies stated in 1943, the goal is "to ensure to all our people the widest possible measure of access to the essentials of the good life."[80]

Studies of poverty in England were undertaken by Arthur Young and Sir Frederick Eden in the eighteenth century, but the modern era of poverty research began with the classical surveys of Charles Booth and Seebohm Rowntree at the end of the nineteenth century. In the 1930s, Rowntree conducted a second survey of York and attempted to draw some comparisons between the two periods. During the Great Depression there was a relatively large amount of research on the condition of the unemployed and the poor in the United States and England. More recently, the awareness of continuing pockets of poverty in the United States despite the general prosperity has stimulated studies on the nature and extent of poverty.

Most surveys and analyses of poverty have set some point or income level to define poverty, although there has been a tendency to use two standards for indicating dire poverty and a more liberal standard of need. Society can, in effect, select its ultimate standard for income distribution while at the same time it sets immediate goals for poverty reduction. For example, Rowntree had two classes "below the minimum":

Class A included families whose income was 10s. below standard, and Class B, families with incomes less than 10s. below standard.[81] The 1962 Conference on Economic Progress in the United States used the Department of Labor's "modest but adequate budgets" for city workers' families as its baseline. Poverty was defined as a family income of $4,000, or two thirds of that budget, and a "deprivation level" was established to account for those falling between the standard and the poverty line.[82] Other studies have used different standards. Morgan and his colleagues selected a budget used by the voluntary Community Council of Greater New York.[83] The Social Security Administration has preferred the Department of Agriculture's economy food plan as the foundation of its estimate of poverty.[84] In addition to low current income, some studies have required evidence of continuing inadequacy for their definition of poverty in order to exclude families suffering from temporary deprivation. But the inclusion of long-term factors in these surveys did not result in important changes in the estimates of poverty. It would seem that few of the poor had assets that indicated that their current income was not representative of their general position.[85]

Despite differences of definition, most studies on the American scene have suggested that approximately 20 percent of the population fall into the poverty class. Herman Miller of the Bureau of the Census has suggested that instead of seeking an absolute cut-off point, the fifth of the population with the lowest income be considered in need. "As incomes go up," he concluded, " 'needs' also go up—evidently in such a way as to leave a large proportion of the population at substandard levels."[86] He pointed out that in 1951 the lowest fifth had incomes below $2000 as compared to $2900 in 1960. The 1960 income was not the 1951 income adjusted for rising prices. If so, the difference would be almost halved.[87] In contemporary Britain, Brian Abel-Smith and Peter Townsend using National Assistance standards concluded that 14.2 percent of the population had incomes of less than 40 percent above assistance standards.[88]

Miller's approach has raised the question of whether, in societies where physical subsistence needs are met, relative differences are not the most significant measure of poverty. Galbraith has denied that concern about inequality plays a major part in modern western states. Among other reasons, he has maintained that the concentration on increased production with dividends for all has replaced the attention to uneven distribution of earlier scarcity societies.[89] The argument for relative standards rests on the assumption that for practical purposes standards have become so fluid that no definition of need, no matter how broad, satisfies the ever-changing expectations of modern life. Poverty thus represents deviation from social and economic norms. Comparative poverty, as I. M. Rubinow pointed out, "has led more often to social change than has absolute poverty."

Luxuries become comforts, comforts become necessaries; and repeated emphasis of the fact that in comparison with civilizations of the past or more backward contemporary cultures the poor in the United States now enjoy what would have constituted unusual luxuries a thousand or even a hundred years ago may lead to an entirely barren conception of the problem of poverty as an aspect of distribution of wealth. Thus an increase in perceived poverty is a phenomenon particularly characteristic of American life during periods of so-called prosperity.[90]

The establishment of a national minimum itself has represented one aspect of the process of equalization when its fulfillment has meant the transference of wealth from the rich to the poor.[91] For some, however, the conflict between poverty and democratic opportunity has been primarily identified as the conflict between economic inequality and democracy. In both Britain and the United States the twentieth century has been an era of extending democracy into the social and "economic unequals" in contrast to periods in which "justice becomes the rule of the stronger, liberty the law which the stronger allow. The freedom that the poor desire in a society such as this is the freedom to enjoy the things their rulers enjoy. The penumbra of freedom, its purpose and its life, is the movement for equality."[92] Crosland, the British economist and Labour Member of Parliament, agrees with Galbraith on the smaller importance of relative differences with a general rising standard of living, but he has emphasized the need to reduce inequality of income "in order to create a more just and democratic society."[93]

The rationale for narrowing the income gap between rich and poor, however, preceded the relatively recent stress on democratic values. Its antecedents go back to the early Utilitarians, the marginal utility theory of the late nineteenth century, the new welfare economics, and Keynesian theory in the twentieth century. At each point in this evolution of the argument for equalizing income a new defense was added or an old contradiction removed. Bentham had accepted the virtues of greater equality of incomes but had feared that any move toward equalization would threaten the security of economic interests and thereby disturb the total production of wealth.

At the end of the century economists like Alfred Marshall cogently discussed the greater value or satisfaction received by the poor from additional units of wealth as compared to the rich. Although by this time the redistributive effects of taxes had become acceptable, any more concerted policy was viewed as dangerous to the free flow of the economy. The new welfare economics, with Pigou as its pioneer, concentrated on the problem of improving the welfare or satisfaction of society. Accepting the premise of marginal utility theory that wealth is of greater satisfaction to the poor, Pigou minutely analyzed the effect of various sorts of transferences upon the total welfare of society. He examined such assumptions as the possible conflict between increasing the share of the poor and enlarging the national dividend, and developed a system of principles for intervening in the natural system of the economy in order to encourage maximum satisfaction.[94]

For Keynes the income of the poor and the interests of the total economy had become synonymous. He was critical of the "arbitrary and inequitable distribution of wealth and incomes." While recognizing the motivation behind disparities of wealth, Keynes found no economic justification for inequality and noted that, in contrast to earlier opinion, inequality actually impeded the growth of national wealth.[95] Since the marginal propensity of the poor to consume is greater than that of the rich, redistribution of wealth in favor of the poor would have greater overall effect.

There has, of course, been strong dissent from the theoretical prescriptions of those favoring redistribution. Redistribution toward equality of income has implied that all have relatively equal capacities for the enjoyment of income and that interpersonal comparisons can be made in assessing the effect of redistribution policy. The critics of equalization question these assumptions. They have maintained that there may be inherent differences that make for different capacities for satisfaction and that the nation's welfare is not merely a simple addition of individual states of satisfaction.[96] The positive effect of redistribution on aggregate consumption has also been examined critically, and differing conclusions have been drawn with regard to the specific conditions under which income redistribution takes place.[97] Still others have questioned the fundamental tenet of the neoclassical contribution to welfare economics, i.e. the relationship between income and welfare. It is their belief that the strength of desire expressed in consumer expenditure is no measure of satisfaction.[98] Finally, the age-old issues of incentive and reward have been raised as deterrents to any rigorous approach to equalization of income. A. A. Berle, for example, has written:

Neither the Founding Fathers nor the American economic system was so stupid as to assume that men should remain equal through life. The industrious should go farther than the idlers; men of integrity should outpace rascals. All, through their own efforts and in accordance with their own moral and intellectual capacity, should settle their inequality by achievement and result.[99]

It is apparent that the controversy about equalization of income will hardly be settled in the arena of science. Apart from the unsettled state of the relevant fields of economics and psychology, major questions still remain in the area of values. The concept of welfare itself, around which redistribution has been centered, is heavily value-laden. But as we have already noted, equalization of income has been an integral part of the extension of the democratic ideal, and that will probably play a more significant role in determining the extent of equalization than abstract questions growing out of the theory of welfare economics.[100] The pressure toward equalization in both the United Kingdom and the United States appears to have gone only so far, at present, in eliminating gross inequalities, largely through the establishment of minimum standards of living.

The saliency of the issue of equalization of income may to some extent be gauged by the scholarly attention in recent years, in both England and the United States, to the subject of income distribution. The study of income distribution is exceedingly complex and consists of two fundamental parts, the nature of the original distribution of income and the effect, if any, of any redistributional operations in altering the original distribution. Not only is the basic research fraught with difficulties, but since the goal is often the trend in income distribution, there is the problem of comparison over time when the essential variables may have been defined and measured differently. In the opinion of R. M. Titmuss, these problems have made questionable many of the British attempts to plot the direction of income distribution.[101] Similarly Lampman, in the United States, has suggested that seemingly reduced inequality may reflect changing types of wealth and definition of income units rather than real differences.[102]

On the American scene Kuznets and others have examined the changing share of the top income groups, the upper 1 percent and 5 percent of the income range.[103] Generally a lessening concentration of wealth at the very top of the income scale has been reported, but assuming that is valid, it does not indicate the way this wealth was shared among the remainder of the population. Others have analyzed both ends of the income scale. Selma Goldsmith, for example, found a shift from upper to lower income groups between 1935 and 1950. Most of that occurred, however, between 1941 and 1944. The shift over the whole period was extremely small.[104] Herman Miller also noticed that changes in distribution occurred during the war period of 1939 to 1945 and interpreted that as a special rather than a general trend.[105]

In Britain, too, there probably occurred a leveling of incomes during the war, but the general trend has been open to a great deal of disagreement. There has been a general impression of greater equalization, which was supported by studies indicating a narrowing of the range of both pre-tax and post-tax incomes.[106] However, as Professor Titmuss has carefully documented, a host of statistical problems and social changes must be accounted for before confidence may be placed in these conclusions.[107] In addition to differences about the distribution of income, there have been disagreements about trends in the ownership of capital.[108] The relatively higher ownership of net capital by skilled manual workers in America has been contrasted to the situation in Britain.[109] It is the distribution of property rather than income that has disturbed some critics on the British scene.[110]

Even more complex than assessing the distribution of original incomes has been the question of what happens to the original distribution as a result of taxation, social insurance and other financial benefits, and the social services generally. Do the benefits result in a net gain to the lower-income groups and thus effectively increase their incomes at the expense of the more wealthy and reduce the gap betweeen high and low initial incomes? To achieve any reliable answer requires taking into account a great variety of phenomena. Although the effects of government policy prior to redistribution are generally not considered in studies of redistribution, government policy cannot be considered neutral in its consequences for initial income. In examining possible benefits or losses the whole of the system must be taken into account. Redistribution occurs not only as a result of social welfare programs but also reflects government policy in taxes and occupational benefits.[111] Nor can it be assumed that the social services always act in the direction of equalizing income differences. Welfare transfers may benefit all equally, may operate within rather than across income groups, may transfer individual income over risk periods, or may even favor the wealthy under certain circumstances.

Thus, Morgan has emphasized the extent to which transfer payments, viewed by some as making a significant contribution to lower-income groups in the United States, have represented transfers over time from earning to retirement years rather than transfers between income levels.[112] The regressive nature of the social security taxes in the United States and in Great Britain have been criticized.[113] Cartter, when comparing Britain and the United States in the immediate pre- and postwar periods, concluded that in contrast to the United States, Britain had both tended toward greater equality in initial incomes over this period and also toward more redistribution in the direction of equalizing differences.[114] I. M. D. Little, assessing the period immediately following, between 1950 and 1960, concluded that there was some slackening of the earlier use of fiscal policy for purposes of redistribution until 1960, when changes in tax policies and food subsidies represented a more marked retreat.[115] Probably the clearest trend in both countries has been the failure of social income, whether insurance or assistance, to keep pace with the changing income structure or even, in many cases, to maintain its earlier value. This has been a particular hardship for the lowest-income groups, who are most dependent on such income. In addition, many of the services in kind, such as housing, health, and education, have frequently been of greater benefit to the more well-to-do than to the very poor.[116]

18

Economic Security Policies
and Measures

The Role of Social Income

ECONOMIC security measures have focused on two major policies: (1) the establishment of conditions ensuring an adequate and stable livelihood from the normal economic market, and (2) the regularization or institutionalization of those forms of substitute and supplementary income considered essential for meeting the minimal standards of society. The attention given to the primary sources of income is a relatively contemporary phenomenon. Not since the mercantilist era has state policy been concentrated so strenuously on the provision of sufficient and continuous income from employment. Nineteenth-century reform in Britain and the United States was oriented not to the economic but to the social conditions the lower classes suffered as a result of their limited economic means. The early part of the twentieth century was spent in reviving and strengthening the emergency system of assistance measures eroded during the period of laissez-faire.

The state's concern with full employment, a stable and expanding income, and the elimination of poverty has involved government in an elaborate series of economic interventions. With some exceptions, however, government did not take direct responsibility for either providing employment or determining wage scales. The private economy remained the fundamental source of control with government engaged in providing an optimum environment for utilizing the income derived from employment. In both Great Britain and the United States legal minimum rates were established in certain industries, but the major influence on workers' incomes has been the collective bargaining between unions and management. The public nature of negotiations and the principles and issues underlying them have made the union contract, particularly in large industries, a quasi-public instrument with widespread influence on wage scales. Those contracts have introduced a basis of stability into the income structure by their long-term nature and their resistance, as Arthur F. Burns has observed, to downward adjustments in periods of declining business activity.[1] While governments have combatted inflationary tendencies, unions, on the other hand, have increasingly protected their members by agreements incorporating wage increases relative to the cost of living.

In general, union agreements in both Britain and the United States have moved toward giving the wage worker the job security previously associated only with salaried work. Arbitrary dismissals from employment have been curtailed and more continuity of work and wages guaranteed. In the United States progress has been made toward an annual wage, and a minimum weekly wage has been established in many industries in both countries.[2] Thus although government plays an important role directly and indirectly in influencing business conditions and union-management negotiations, the decisions affecting the income security of employees during their employment years, and to some extent beyond, are made primarily within the nexus of the private economy. Employment remains the keystone of income security. The two major systems of income security, other than wages, for low-income groups, social insurance and occupational pensions, have clearly work-connected benefits. The only categories of persons both in the United States and Britain who have been generally accepted as recipients of non-work-related benefits have been those incapable of self-support through labor, e.g. children, the aged, and the disabled, although many such benefits are related to some wage base.

The income supports of the social welfare system had become institutionalized by the 1940s in the traditional means-tested public assistance and the contributory social insurance. However, alongside these in the United Kingdom and other nations, there developed a new form of aid—

social assistance. Such programs as the family allowances provided a universal form of state subsidy with the dignity of insurance but without the requirement of contribution. In effect, the state accepted the responsibility of sharing the contingency of the additional costs of family life regardless of need or work history, the rationales of the previous income security measures. Thus far the United States has not adopted any programs of the social assistance type. In addition to orthodox assistance and insurance, it has relied on preferential income tax treatment for large families, the aged, or handicapped, but the exemption from taxation has often failed to benefit the lowest-income groups relative to their greater need.

A much broadened concept of the social assistances has recently received attention in both Britain and the United States. The guarantee of a social minimum has been given precedence over the formulation of assistance and insurance policy. Although such advocates of a publicly guaranteed minimal income as Lady Rhys-Williams in England and Milton Friedman and Robert Theobald in the United States differ in broad social philosophy as well as in the details of their income plans, they have in common the establishment of a minimal income standard applicable to the total population whose benefits would not be dependent on any of the specific eligibility criteria in current programs.[3] Although the various plans for a guaranteed social income incorporate independently earned income as a fundamental part of individual income, the share of socially provided income is institutionalized beyond the emergency character of the public assistances, the special categories of the social assistances, and the self-insurance assumptions of social insurance. Social wealth replaces or at least absorbs a major share of the responsibility for income security previously attached to individual earning power.

The changing role of social income was noted by I. M. Rubinow and Seebohm Rowntree in the 1930s. Rubinow questioned whether those receiving relief could be considered poor if, despite their dependency, "the standards of health and comfort are decidedly above those prevailing in the community at large."[4] Rowntree estimated that the social services contributed eighteen times as much on the average to working-class families in 1936 as in 1901.[5] The increasing importance of redistributed income aggravated the historic concern with loss of incentive and dependency.

Twentieth-century welfare economists and social security specialists followed the classical tradition of "less eligibility" in devising systems of social support that would not compete with the labor market. Pigou classified governmental transferences as those "which differentiate against idleness and thriftlessness," those "which are neutral," and those "which differentiate in favor of idleness and thriftlessness."[6] The low flat benefit of the Beveridge plan was only to provide "the minimum income needed for subsistence."[7] Low benefits would encourage continuance in the labor market for immediate income and would also require that current income be viewed as a resource for the future since the minimal social security base could hardly be considered adequate in meeting most contingencies. As Beveridge stated:

The State in organising security should not stifle incentive, opportunity, responsibility; in establishing a national minimum, it should leave room and encouragement for voluntary action by each individual to provide more than that minimum for himself and his family.[8]

Currently, the National Assistance Board's policy of the "wage stop" maintains a differential between the level of assistance and earned income.

Similar principles have been espoused on the American scene. Edwin Witte, among the most influential architects of the Social Security Act, considered the goal of social security to be "a necessary minimum income as a protection against the worst economic consequences of the personal hazards of life."[9] Rubinow, while skeptical of the "exaggerations of Freudian psychology" about dependency needs, stressed positive incentive in recommending less than restoration of full wage loss through social insurance.[10] Lewis Meriam, a less ardent advocate of social welfare generally, consistently raised the question "whether a government should make relief standards approximately as high as the standard which is attained by fully employed workers in the lower-wage brackets."[11] He also opposed social insurance benefits beyond a minimum standard of need. "After need has been relieved," he asked, "should not persons be dependent on their own activities and upon their own thrift and savings?"[12] In 1943 the Congressional Committee on Long-Range Work and Relief Policies, staffed by experts on social security, recommended that social insurance be the basic income-support program in the United States but warned that there must be safeguards against people preferring socially provided income to work.[13] Although the original British insurance systems were flat benefits and the United States has a modified scaling of benefits to previous income, both reflect the policy of maintaining a sizable gap between social benefits and earned income.

The distinction between socially provided and individually earned income, whose importance so impressed the pioneers of social insurance, has become less clear in the evolution of economic security programs. The foundation of social insurance was the relationship of contribution to benefit, the encouragement of thrift through both the experience of insurance and the need for supplementation from private resources, and eligibility through earnings from employment. With these principles social insurance seemed to be the ideal measure for demonstrating social responsibility without threatening individual obligations in a contract-oriented society.

There were, however, gradual though marked shifts from the earlier belief that a public insurance system modeled on private insurance would adequately meet the economic security needs of modern society. The large numbers in Great Britain and the United States who continued to receive public assistance as their total means of support or as supplementation of insurance benefits indicated that much social income evaded the carefully defined limits of the social insurances. More fundamentally, the nature of social insurance itself changed.

The private investment principle of equity, the fixed relationship between the amount of contribution and benefit, qualified from the start, gave way to the concept of social equity. Contribution was not the governing factor in benefits so much as were the differing needs of the beneficiaries. That was particularly apparent in the American system with its short period required for eligibility, the benefits allotted dependents and survivors, the arranging of the insurance formula in favor of lower-income groups, the exempting of periods of low earnings from the wage record affecting benefits, and the establishment of minimum and maximum benefit limits. A comparable situation has existed in the United Kingdom. The Phillips Committee, for example, reported that the difference between the accumulated contributions from 1926 and capital value of a pension in 1954 for a single man and a married man with a wife of the same age were respectively £700 and £1,440.[14]

The significance of social income was heightened by changing attitudes toward saving in contemporary society. As the importance of consumption to the stability of the economy was emphasized, the virtues of thrift were less apparent. Spending was an almost patriotic duty, and public policy was oriented toward maintaining the purchasing power of the lower income groups with the greatest propensity for spending.[15] The vast expansion of consumer goods through mass production, the stimulation of demand through improved marketing techniques, and the ease of acquisition through purchase on time, encouraged full use of current income and the commitment of future income. The assumption that social insurance would have merely the role of meeting minimal needs was based on a belief that there would be widespread supplementation from individual savings. This, however, did not prove to be valid.[16] In the United States approximately two thirds of aged couples and four fifths of other aged beneficiaries of OASDHI in 1962 had less retirement money income than was required to meet the Bureau of Labor standards for "modest but adequate" living.[17] Retirement income, defined as "all income from reasonably permanent sources" other than OASDHI benefits, amounted to less than $150 in almost half the beneficiary couples and two thirds of nonmarried beneficiaries.[18] Similarly, a survey of savings in Britain found few liquid assets among the low-income population.[19] Generally there has been found to be a high correlation between income and assets.

The relatively small income from interest, dividends, rents, and private pensions, as well as the reliance of many social insurance recipients in England and the United States on supplementation from public assistance, indicate both the lack of personal resources and the central role social insurance has come to play in the lives of most people.[20] During lengthy periods of interrupted earnings and retirement social insurance income has become the major source of support, not an emergency guarantee against the possible failure of private prudence as was frequently conceived in earlier planning. For this as well as other reasons there has been a trend for social insurance to provide a higher proportion of the beneficiaries' cost of living. In 1959 the British modified their flat-rate retirement scheme by supplementing it with graduated contributions and benefits according to earnings. The scheme took into account the existence of extensive occupational pension plans by permitting the substitution of an employer's plan.[21] Similar "earnings-related supplements" are contemplated for unemployment and sickness benefits. The maximum has been fixed at 85 percent of earnings.[22]

In the United States, although the social insurances were originally conceived as graduated plans reflecting income differences, failure to improve the programs or even to keep up with the rising trends in income has resulted in a reduced proportion of average income being returned at retirement and even less during unemployment. The demand for health insurance as part of retirement benefits has been motivated by the failure of retirement income to be sufficient to meet the health expenses of the aged and may, therefore, be considered a device for increasing total insurance income. Thus far, despite the extensive growth of occupational benefit plans, with few exceptions, there has been no attempt to relate them to the public system.[23]

The trend toward an increasing role for social income in the total of personal disposable income has not been due entirely to concern for individual welfare. Inadequate distribution of income is a threat to the total economy. The social minimum, in the near future, will not be equated entirely with a standard of individual living requirements, no matter how liberal, but will partly depend on a standard defined as necessary for society to meet its social, economic, and political goals. The acceptance of an expanded role for social income has conflicted with a great host of inherited prejudices and economic ideas. Joan Robinson, for example, in recommending that the unemployed be permitted a liberal limit for their own earnings without losing eligibility for public relief, commented:

It follows that regulations calculated to prevent him from doing himself any kind of good are harmful to him and not beneficial to the rest of society, while regulations that deprive him of the dole on a slight pretext are deleterious to the rest of society as well as himself. The administrative complications involved, the strong moral objections to scroungers, felt by workers as well as by taxpayers, and the difficulty of preventing employers from obtaining an illicit subsidy, may be regarded as sufficient justification for such regulations. But their economic effects can only be harmful.[24]

The belief persists that public money will be preferred to private earnings unless the former is measurably more inadequate and uncomfortable to obtain. Despite the changed views of man, society, and work since the beginning of the nineteenth century, the pleasure-pain concept of the psychology of that era has remained in economic thinking. There has been little reliable research on the subject, but the limited evidence available casts much doubt on the "propensity to be supported in idleness."[25] The persistence of the belief in man's inclination toward economic dependence is another illustration of Galbraith's concept of "conventional wisdom" where "because economic and social phenomena are so forbidding . . . and because they yield few hard tests of what exists and what does not, . . . the individual . . . may hold whatever view of this world he finds most agreeable or otherwise to his taste."[26]

Without necessarily denying the proposition of assistance and dependency, some economists have balanced it against, or given more weight to, other assumptions and values. Galbraith, for example, has suggested a graduated unemployment compensation depending on the amount of general unemployment. As unemployment increased and the availability of jobs clearly was limited, compensation would rise to approximate the normal wage with a "surviving difference" as "the continuing concession to the Puritan principle that leisure should be less amply rewarded than work."[27] Galbraith has not been impressed with the arguments of those concerned about deliberate idleness but has pointed out that "in a world where production is no longer urgent we can obviously view an increase in voluntary idleness with some equanimity."[28] On the other hand, he recommended his scheme for increased compensation during periods of high unemployment because of its countercyclical consequences.

The guaranteed-minimum-income schemes of Lady Rhys-Williams, Milton Friedman, and Robert Theobald, all have work-incentive components. Under Lady Rhys-Williams' "Social Contract" the individual would either be employed or would accept suitable employment unless he wished to forego the benefits.[29] In the Friedman plan a person with no, or reduced, individual income would receive only a proportion of the allowed exemptions and deductions in contrast to those with income.[30] Theobald would also provide a higher income to those with greater private earnings.[31] It is noteworthy that Friedman and Theobald, like Galbraith, in adjusting to conditions of affluence and abundance in American society have been less rigid than Lady Rhys-Williams, who in 1943 made employment an essential part of her program. Friedman, though in most respects a nineteenth-century liberal, remarked casually that "like any other measures to alleviate poverty it [his plan] reduces the incentives of those helped to help themselves."[32] Theobald's proposal is founded on the goal of breaking the "job-income link" in a society of automation and abundance in which the necessity of employment income for all, in his opinion, has irrational social and economic consequences.[33]

In both Britain and the United States the minimum-income guarantee has earned support from persons and groups with otherwise widely divergent views on social and economic matters.[34] The income tax strategy of PAYE, it has been suggested in the British Conservative publication, *Crossbow,* should be supplemented with RAYN—"Receive As You Need."[35] This is, in effect, a negative income tax and has been criticized as entailing some of the unpleasant connotations of the historical means test. Advocates of the negative income tax maintain that such consequences can be easily avoided and that earlier responses to the means test are no longer a reality in contemporary society.[36] The negative income tax has also been criticized as being administratively unwieldy, particularly for short-term interruptions of income. An alternative suggestion has been the "universal demo-grant" paid to all regardless of need. This, it is maintained, would be more egalitarian in benefiting all equally, would have less effect on incentive, and would be less complex to administer.[37] The normal income tax would act as the readjustment and redistribution mechanism.

Despite the continued emphasis on earned income and the connection between earned income and social security income, there have been strong indications that social or redistributed income will have a growing significance in British and American society, as well as other welfare-oriented nations. The relationship between work and income will become less clear as the economic function of work changes and as new social goals come to the fore in societies of abundance. On the other hand, Eveline Burns' warning must also be taken into account:

For I cannot believe it would be a healthy, or a viable, society if only a small portion of the potentially active population was involved in, and rewarded for, something called "work," while the rest lived on the guarantee in idleness, even if it is called "leisure."[38]

The Responsibility for Economic Security

The trend toward social and economic planning, the recognition of national interdependency, and the growing significance of social or redistributed income under the aegis of the state, have been paralleled by a shift from individual and primary group responsibility to the responsibility of larger and more formal units. The nineteenth-century model of the charity organization societies has largely been reversed. Reliance on the goodwill and charity of family, friends, and neighbors has given way to the obligations of higher levels of government and negotiated benefits between organized labor and management. With increasing mobility and the growth of large complex urban centers, the patterns of family and community have been drastically altered. The supports previously provided have altogether disappeared or have become so negligible as to be relatively minor supplements to the government-sponsored system of economic security.

The transition to state responsibility for economic security began early on the British scene and was practically completed by the time American society accepted the significant participation of the central government. The earliest poor laws provided for the sharing of financial responsibility when parishes were unable to support their own poor. Gilbert's unions at the end of the eighteenth century were the first major amalgamations of poor law authorities. The amalgamations continued sporadically until after 1834, when, under Chadwick's leadership, the Poor Law Commission pressed forward energetically with the incorporation of parishes into unions. In addition to the merging of the poor law authorities into larger units, there was also from this time the continuous presence of a national administrative board concerned with poor law policy. In 1929 the famous poor law guardians were abolished, and their duties were taken over by the largest of the local authorities, the counties and the county boroughs. Finally in 1948 the public assistance system came wholly to be a central government function. The Determination of Means Act of 1941 had already narrowed the area of enforceable family responsibility.

The central government's direct involvement in economic security policy had, however, antedated its responsibilities for assistance by some forty years. In 1906, Parliament made the first national contribution to the relief of poverty arising from unemployment. Two years later a national system of old-age pensions was established. In 1911, Lloyd George's government enacted the first major British insurance for sickness and unemployment. In 1925 insurance was extended to cover old age and death. During the depression following the First World War Parliament provided "extended benefits" to those whose unemployment insurance eligibility had run out, and later Treasury grants were made to the local authorities for continued aid to the unemployed. In 1937 the Unemployment Assistance Board removed the unemployed from the jurisdiction of the local authorities, and in 1944 a Ministry of National Insurance was created.

The evolution of economic security from a private to public responsibility and from a local to federal function was considerably slower in the United States. Although there were significant advances on the state and municipal level, the depression of the 1930s found the dominant leadership of the country approaching the crisis with much of the attitude of the charity organization societies of the nineteenth century. A few years before the depression Herbert Hoover had sharply criticized the growth of government responsibility.

It is the failure of groups to respond to their responsibilities to others that drives government more and more into the lives of our people. And every time government is forced to act, we lose something in self-reliance, character, and initiative. Every time we find solution outside of government we have not only strengthened character but we have preserved our sense of real self-government.[39]

Personal responsibility was still considered the foundation of economic security, but when it failed, the most appropriate alternatives were local and voluntary action. The continued opposition of the voluntary social work leaders to widows' and other pensions was indicative of the fear of relieving individual need by public measures. The abandonment of public outdoor relief in many of the largest communities of the nation at the end of the nineteenth century demonstrated the weak foundation of even local government aid and presaged their incapacity when major crises arose.

At the start of the depression, in 1929, there was no state responsibility for local relief, and although the majority of states had special assistance programs for mothers, the aged, and the blind, only a fraction of these programs extended any significant aid to the needy. The federal government and the nation as a whole turned to what were considered the only proper and effective measures to combat the spreading poverty: greater effort on the part of the individual poor, community sharing and cooperation, private philanthropy, and the voluntary initiative of the business leadership. Matthew Woll, vice president of the American Federation of Labor, attacked the notion that government should be considered the appropriate instrument for meeting the nation's economic ills. In 1931 Woll stated:

Industry cannot go to Congress and get this salvation. Industry must work it out within itself. But, if industry does not work it out for itself and within itself, if industry stands with a frozen back to the wall and with a brain paralyzed in the face of a new condition, then the masses in their desperation may be expected to turn to a Congress made responsive by the ballots of enraged people, demanding abdication of private interests in favor of the state. That will be a resort fraught with the direst consequences, probably unable to survive, prey to abuse and chicanery, but accepted because there is no other way open.[40]

Private charities expanded their efforts, and by 1931 they were spending between eight and nine million dollars per month on relief. The rate dropped off rapidly, however, and it became clear that the private charities, even if subsidized by government funds, could not accomplish the job.[41]

A sharp increase in public spending and direct administration of relief occurred. By the end of 1932 it was estimated that 88 percent of expenditures for assistance came from public funds. An increase of almost 9 percent in public expenditures occurred between September and October, 1932 as compared to a drop of 25 percent in private outlay.[42] The depression was the critical turning point in the recognition of public responsibility for economic security in the United States. Within a short period of some half-dozen years, not only was public commitment firmly established, but both the state and federal governments took a major share of what was previously primarily, if not exclusively, a local function.

The states and the federal government moved into emergency relief, work relief, and public works. Not all of those roles were to have lasting effects. The Social Security Act of 1935, however, committed the states and the federal government to a continuing responsibility for the special categories of public assistance and social insurance. Many of the states also assumed more active roles with respect to the general assistance population, previously relegated almost entirely to the localities. Perhaps the most far-reaching shift was the federal government's sponsorship of old-age insurance. This placed the federal government in the forefront of the most universal of all social security programs. Within a short time this program was expanded to include benefits for dependents, survivors, and disabled workers. Since its inception, OASDHI has also acted as the focus of all major proposals for health insurance. Recently public funds have accounted for about 85 percent of all expenditures for organized income maintenance and welfare services, and three fourths of those funds have come from the federal government.[43]

These changes, while marked on the American scene, have had a relatively short history when compared with the evolution of public programs in other western nations. As might be expected, there have still been sporadic twinges of the nerves that lead to the paths of personal and local responsibility. In twenty-six states general assistance continues to be administered by local political jurisdictions, and in seventeen states the funds come from local taxes. Except for sixteen states, the remainder draw their general assistance funds from a combination of state and local sources. In view of the localities or the states or both having full financial responsibility and in view of the common belief that availability of relief encourages migration, more than four fifths of the states have residence requirements limiting eligibility for assistance.[44] Even with federal participation in the public or categorical assistances, a similar proportion have settlement restrictions.

The anachronistic notion of society as a collection of isolated communities with static populations has been the ideological base of residence laws. Its counterpart in family life is the assumption that the structure and functions of the American family are essentially as they were in the pre-industrial and pre-urban era. The consequence has been, as with settlement, the continuation of earlier policies that attempted to focus responsibility within the primary group. In nearly every assistance jurisdiction there are policies and procedures for the maintenance of family responsibility. They are frequently overlooked in practice and often cost more to administer than any possible gains in reducing assistance payments. Apart from the assumed but not demonstrable preventive force of such measures, there remains the belief that reforming laws of relative responsibility to conform with contemporary family life would not merely recognize the realities of the present scene but would also give tacit official approval.

Notwithstanding these legacies of Elizabethan policy, the trend toward a broader view of public responsibility has been clear. The expansion and extension of the federal assistance categories have greatly narrowed the populations dependent on local or general relief. Although residence requirements have been permitted in the federally subsidized programs, they have been restricted by the federal limits, and there have been indications of national impatience with state residential policies.[45]

Perhaps a more significant, though less obvious, barometer of the shift toward full societal responsibility for economic security has been the financing of social insurance. In 1954 federal loans were provided to states with insufficient reserves in their unemployment insurance funds, and "extended benefits" were made possible under the Temporary Federal Unemployment Compensation Act of 1958 for the unemployed who had exhausted their benefits. The establishment of a permanent nation-wide system of reinsurance, federally funded, has received much support.

The financing of old-age and survivors' insurance originally included the possibility of general tax subsidies when the contributory fund was inadequate. This was soon dropped, but the principles underlying the financing of social insurance indicate its broad national character. Although initially conceived by many as a public form of private insurance, the redistributive character of social insurance conflicted with the equity principle of private insurance. More fundamental differences, however, occurred around the long-term funding resources of social as compared to private insurance. The OASDHI program was not long in operation before it was recognized that it would be unwise to accumulate sufficient funds to pay all future benefits to members of the system. The program has rather relied on the potential of future income to guarantee currently incurred obligations.[46] From this point of view, social insurance has introduced an intergenerational issue in redistribution by raising the question of the appropriate apportionment of cost between the present and future citizens of the nation.[47] This is an issue that would hardly have entered the minds of those who originally conceived of the insurance as a device for enforcing individual thrift and responsibility.

The most radical change in the pattern of economic security during the period after the Second World War was represented by the increasing importance of employee-benefit plans. In 1949 expenditures from these plans amounted to 8 percent of the total of public and private expenditures for income maintenance and welfare services. By 1962 benefits had increased five-fold and were more than 11 percent of the total.[48] If health expenditures are included, employee-benefit plans provided benefits totaling $9.8 billion in 1962.[49] It has been estimated that by the end of 1962 benefit plans covered 111 million workers and their dependents under some form of health insurance, 52 million under life insurance, and 23 million under private retirement plans.[50] Not only have the contributions and benefits increased sharply, but the plans, in contrast to their early beginnings in company paternalistic policy,[51] have become a solidly institutionalized part of the economic negotiations between workers and management. They have also, like social insurance, escaped from the narrow confines of being viewed essentially from the principle of employer liability, and have become part of the larger context of social security.

Industrial responsibility has revived some of the earlier status concepts suppressed during the era of laissez-faire. The employer has recognized the value of industrial plans in encouraging the attachment of workers. Fringe benefits have acted as a binding force for continuity and good will in employment. But workers have looked upon fringe benefits and employer participation in social benefits as rights connected with their general employment rather than as sources for gratitude and loyalty to particular employers.

The Nature of Economic Security Programs

The expanding economic role of the state has left few matters affecting the economic welfare of the citizenry about which government is indifferent. The programs considered below will be those designed for the provision of income outside of the normal workings of the economic market. However, it need not be emphasized again that although there has been a vast growth of this function, there has, relatively speaking, been more attention in recent decades to the creation of those conditions which strengthen the normal market and obviate the pressures for alternative action. Programs for economic growth and stabilization and general anti-recession measures have reduced the reliance on the traditional pattern of income maintenance. To a large extent these older programs have been reexamined in the light of the more positive philosophy of modern political economy and have been incorporated within its framework. Broad preventive and stabilizing features have shared and, in some cases, overshadowed the attention previously given solely to programs for individual and family welfare. For example, the 1964 Report of the President's Council of Economic Advisors recommended as the "strategy against poverty": accelerating economic growth, fighting discrimination, improving regional economics, rehabilitating urban and rural communities, improving labor markets, expanding educational opportunities, encouraging job opportunities for youth, improving the nation's health, promoting adult education and training, and assisting the aged and disabled.[52]

Thus, income maintenance measures formerly marked by their response to emergencies and unanticipated situations have changed through the reduction of such occurrences and through the recognition of the regularity of some risks and the institutionalization of the mechanisms to deal with them. Contemporary economic security programs may be classified as (1) the broadly preventive, promotional, and restorative; (2) the formally supplementary and supportive; and (3) the critical and provisional. Earlier emphasis on the last has shifted to the first two, and even the unique and unexpected have been considered contingencies to be prepared for.

Direct Benefits

The evolution of direct money benefits from public charity to social security has been one of the most striking features of economic security policy. The transition from private to public programs of assistance had not necessarily involved a change in the philosophy of providing aid. Until the beginning of the twentieth century, in both England and the United States, the similarity of the principles of the private and public welfare leadership made possible the relinquishing of public programs to private control. The increasing sense of democracy and the rising status of the lower classes in the twentieth century resulted in new expectations of the role of government in economic support as well as in other aspects of public responsibility. For the paternalism of earlier policy there would be substituted the objectivity, impartiality, and justice of the modern state. Public aid was not to be considered a personal favor to be repaid by gratitude and subservience.[53]

To meet those objectives, benefits would be required to satisfy criteria radically different from the former public and private systems of aid. If the program was to recognize and respect the social equality of beneficiaries of public welfare, it must not subject them to the demeaning experience of soliciting aid and relying on the discretion of the officials in charge. Eligibility for help must be conditional only on meeting a formally established series of regulations, and the amount of aid must follow some prescribed formula. The benefit must be adequate to prevent demoralization. Finally, the program must cover a large enough part of the population so that it would not become identified with the status of the poorest and most unfortunate elements of society.

The type of program most suited to these expectations at the end of the nineteenth century was social insurance. The various systems were a radical departure from public relief and combined the virtues of thrift and foresight on the part of the individual with the business-like ideal of contractual obligation on the part of the state. Although the contributory or private insurance model was identified with the desired goal from the start, it was recognized by some of the pioneers that the concept of social insurance did not require any particular method or source of financing. The collective bearing of risk rather than the individual premium-benefit relationship was considered the mark of social insurance.[54] The social insurance systems, with their increasing stress on adequacy as against equity, came to function clearly as mechanisms for redistribution.

While social insurance moved toward being a privileged form of assistance largely supported by ear-marked wage taxes, the old forms of assistance took on some of the features of insurance. In England the new National Assistance Board tried to avoid the stigma of the old poor law authorities by administering its responsibilities as objectively and formally as possible. Eligibility and benefits were clearly defined, and the potential for influence and control of recipients through the social services was placed in the hands of other bodies. In the United States types of assistance had not evolved as far in the direction of insurance, but they had made considerable progress. The efforts to replace relief with pensions for such select groups as widows, the aged, and the blind culminated in the federal public assistance categories. They were not so liberal as their opponents in the charity organization societies had feared or as their advocates, who referred to them as "definite forms of social insurance,"[55] had hoped. They were by no means unconditionally administered, but they were a distinct change from the pattern of local relief. Federal standards, financing, and encouragement as well as state participation removed much of the degrading and deterrent aspects of general assistance.

Even the requirement of money payments in the federal categories removed some of the stigma and limitations of relief previously associated with aid-in-kind.[56]

The term *noncontributory pension* used in early descriptions of American old-age assistance programs no longer applies, but it indicates the assumed gulf between them and the traditional forms of relief. The development of social insurance, however, turned attention to the contributory pensions as the preferred approach to modern income security. In Great Britain noncontributory, means-tested pensions distinct from national assistance have been provided for the blind and the aged. The main shift from the contributory principle has occurred in the family allowances, which are administered routinely to all British families according to the number and age of the children. The risk is shared through tax funds as in public assistance, but the unconditional nature of the grant resembles social insurance. Thus far, no similar program has been introduced in the United States; nor have the British expanded their tax-supported allowances, although there are those who have advocated its substitution for the present insurance for the aged.[57]

The trend toward income benefits of the predictable unconditional kind is indicated by the changing proportions of benefits in insurance as compared to assistance. In 1944–45 total benefits under assistance in the United States were approximately five sevenths as large as insurance. In 1962–63 insurance expenditures were almost five times as great as those of assistance. In terms of fixed dollars, per capita social insurance expenditures had increased by 242 percent between 1949–50 and 1963–64 as compared to 39 percent in assistance.[58] The increasing proportion of federal funds in total assistance expenditures also indicates that more benefits are being provided under the relatively more standardized categorical assistance programs than under the local relief programs.[59]

The effort, on the one hand, to reduce the population who were the responsibility of local relief and, on the other, to set up a precise definition of the risks to be handled in the new assistance and insurance programs resulted in a proliferation of income-benefit programs for specific groups. In the United States there were special or categorical assistance programs for the aged, the blind, and families with dependent children, and to these have been added the permanently and totally disabled. Old-age insurance was expanded to include dependents of the aged and disabled and retired individuals and their dependents, but on the whole social insurance in the United States, like assistance, has proliferated into separate and specific programs. Unemployment insurance, workmen's compensation, and temporary disability insurance, although catering to a common population, are administered independently. Only by concentrating on the risk rather than on the person, it would seem, could these programs avoid the paternalism and subjectivity of the traditional relief practices.

The postwar growth of insurance and allowances or programs with no means test, in contrast to assistance, has not been so spectacular in the United Kingdom as in the United States. In 1949–50 assistance was about one sixth, and in 1963–64 it was about one seventh the size of insurance and family allowances.[60] Because of the relatively long history of insurance prior to the National Assistance Act, it did not demonstrate the initial growth rate of American insurance over the same period, and it is possible that both countries may stabilize with similar proportions of assistance to insurance. On the other hand, national assistance has, on the whole, been more acceptable to the British as an institutionalized part of the economic security function of society. Administered more as a social than a public assistance, it may continue as a flexible extension of the insurance system. This trend toward greater institutionalization of the British social security programs has been indicated by their integration into single, unified measures for insurance and assistance respectively. While the American programs have expanded coverage by delineating additional contingencies for which, by principle, society accepts responsibility, the amalgamation of programs in Britain suggests that economic security itself has become a more firmly grounded principle.

The transition in Britain and the United States from charitable relief to objectively administered assistance and insurance has been marked by a change in the nature of the population served. Eligibility for the early relief programs was limited to the most needy, those with least status and most easily patronized. The experience of the post-World War I depressions, when large sections of the previously "respectable" population became dependent on relief, did much to democratize the assistance programs. Insurance and social allowances were, however, the major wedge in reforming the spirit of government economic provision. In addition to their own specific nature, those programs incorporated within the economic security function of government the total population without class distinction. The universality of social insurance, with benefits going to the rich as well as to the poor, lent support to a neutral and business-like administration. The failure of insurance benefits to meet adequately the needs of those covered and the consequent resort to assistance also tended to affect the administration of the latter; for it was clear that insurance beneficiaries requiring supplementation from assistance could not be considered improvident as a class when their presence on assistance was largely a reflection of the state's failure to provide an adequate insurance program.

The emphasis on unrestricted money payments in modern social security programs has also supported the sense of freedom and equality of the recipients. In former periods the recipients were either directly supplied with goods by the assistance authorities or limited in their choices to particular suppliers or specific kinds of commodities. Although there still remain some reminders of earlier practices in local relief in the United States in such programs as the food stamp plan, both philosophically and administratively the controlling of the recipient's choice through the provision of commodities instead of income has been found anachronistic. The provision of money in assistance programs in the United States has not in itself wholly protected the client against official interference with his use of income. The controversial nature of freedom of choice in spending public assistance grants has been indicated by the Public Welfare Amendments of 1962 in the United States, which permitted a limited number of payments in the Aid to Dependent Children program to be made to third parties and stressed official responsibility for seeing that payments were used appropriately. In England a different position was taken by the Ministry of National Insurance when criticisms of the use of family allowances were made by the general public and the voluntary children's societies. In effect, as the Ministry stated, the allowances were the families' and were to be used as they saw fit.

Allowances are paid, not for particular children, but for the benefit of ordinary families with two or more children, in order to lessen the financial disadvantages at which such families are placed in relation to single persons and childless or one-child families.[61]

A more complex problem has been created by the balance between direct money payments and the provision of housing and other social services for low-income groups. To what extent should society subsidize low-income units by making certain essentials available to them below normal market cost? Should emphasis be placed rather on guaranteeing an adequate income for the purchase of these essentials or their desired substitutes on the open market? This is part of the total question of the balance between individually disposable income and socially determined choices, which will affect the planning generally for welfare services in British and American society.[62] However, the principle has gradually emerged that inadequate or low income in itself should not be used as the basis for restricting control over the use of income.

Work

Historically the two most fundamental components of economic security policy have been the provision of direct income and opportunity for work. Public policy has fluctuated over the centuries since the Elizabethan Poor Law, which gave the parishes responsibility for finding or providing work for the indigent able-bodied. In some periods the state has at most taken only indirect interest in the employment of the needy or has viewed the work provided not as a source of income but as a punitive measure to discourage eligibility for direct aid. At other times, such as the 1930s in the United States, work was an essential part of all public relief policy. In general, government has incorporated the provision of work in economic security policy through work-relief or the furnishing of work to those on assistance, public works or the stimulating of general employment directly through public contracts, the maintenance of a sound employment market through the influence of indirect economic measures, and the training and placement of those who have difficulty in finding employment.

During the depression of the thirties the New Deal government of Franklin Roosevelt engaged in a vast program of public works and work-relief. Apart from the traditional reasons given for the preference of work to direct assistance, the massive nature of unemployment and the inadequacy of the assistance system made for emphasis on a national program of work. The federal government expanded the pump-priming activities that had begun during Hoover's presidency. Through its own activities and loans and grants to the states and localities, the federal government increased its share of total construction financing from 3.4 percent in 1930 to 35.6 percent in 1935.[63] A second and more spectacular role of the federal government was the development of programs for directly employing the unemployed needy. Prior to 1935 federal funds had been provided for relief and work-relief. After 1935 the federal government accepted responsibility for programs affecting only the employable needy. At their maximum effectiveness such programs as the National Youth Administration, the Civilian Conservation Corps, and chiefly the Works Progress Administration provided employment for about a third of the unemployed.[64]

Those programs and the federal government's involvement in them were the source of much controversy. On the one hand, they were considered wasteful and politically inspired, but, on the other, they were viewed as maintaining the morale of the unemployed and making a contribution to the national wealth.[65] Whatever their strengths and limitations, they were organized on a scale and in a manner far different from the local work-relief programs that preceded and followed the depression of the thirties. By World War II the federal government had greatly curtailed its employment policies, and after the war other types of measures were relied on to stabilize the economy and ensure a high level of employment. Government has, of course, been increasingly involved in employment through the expansion of its own functions and services. Although the influence of government expenditures on the employment market has been clearly recognized, those expenditures have not been specifically related to the provision of employment.

Direct intervention in employment has not, however, been completely abandoned. During the postwar recessions public works were always one of the alternatives considered for supporting the economy.[66] In the early 1960s a series of public works and employment acts were passed by Congress: the Area Redevelopment Act of 1961, the Public Works Acceleration Act of 1962, the Manpower Development and Training Act of 1962, the Vocational Education Act of 1963, and the Economic Opportunity Act of 1964. They represent the most active intervention of government in employment since the early years of the New Deal era and indicate the extent to which employment is regarded as the responsibility of government. This new legislation implies the right of all to employment and tries to correct those circumstances that have limited the opportunities of particular segments of society. The legislation of the early 1960s is the response of an affluent society to the invidious conditions that have kept some from enjoying the wealth of all. In the period immediately after the war it was assumed that prosperity would be evenly spread and that any limits could be eradicated by accelerating the total economy. The acts of the sixties are among the remedies for "the Other America."

Generally the acts provide for training and work for those who have difficulty finding employment. Those living in depressed areas, those whose skills have become obsolete, unemployed fathers, needy persons, and young people are specifically referred to in the several pieces of legislation. They are to be provided with training, retraining, work experience, and employment opportunities. Loans to local authorities and private businesses, technical aid, and public works are to increase directly the available employment and enhance the opportunities for community development and economic growth. One of the most striking features of this body of legislation is the concentration on dealing objectively with those features that seem responsible for the deprived conditions of individuals and communities. There is no attempt to discover, punish, or leave to their fate the "guilty" parties but rather to change the factors associated with poverty.

The emphasis on preparation for, and provision of, employment is a unique feature of contemporary American social policy.[67] It indicates the extent to which economic security is viewed as related to increasing individual income from employment. Compared to England and other industrial western nations, the United States has given considerably more attention to work training. While it is true that there has been a higher rate of unemployment in the United States, it is also true that the wealth and resources of the United States have made possible the tolerance of a higher rate. It is also noteworthy that the goal of full employment has not been paralleled by any national policy of spreading or sharing the scarce opportunities for employment. In fact, there has been much resistance among political leaders to the shortening of the work week or any measures that might affect individual productivity. The rewards for labor have depended on a market-oriented economy and have not been incorporated in or related to any scheme of social provision.

Until recently, government-sponsored vocational training schemes in Britain have been largely limited to the disabled and to veterans of the armed forces. The main responsibility for training below the professional level rested with the particular trades and industries involved. Youth employment service, variously administered, has existed since the early part of the century to provide vocational information and guidance to young people and help them find and adjust to suitable employment.[68] A major difference between the United States and Britain has been the relative emphasis by the United States on stimulating incentive, capacity, and opportunity for individual success on the open job market. The Economic Opportunity Act of 1964 and the war on poverty generally have represented strategic efforts to rectify the imbalances in employment opportunity for special groups of the population. In Britain there has been growing concern about the "manpower gap," and the government has proposed to increase training facilities and to encourage workers to move to jobs of greater priority to the economy.[69]

The British have invested far more of their resources and for a longer period of time in programs for protecting individuals against the exigencies arising from inadequate employment income. The experience of the British with work-relief programs prior to the twentieth century had dulled their enthusiasm for the kinds of emergency work programs that were developed in the United States during the depression of the thirties.[70] Instead they relied heavily on the system of unemployment benefits that was first established before World War I. When the insurance foundation of these benefits proved inadequate to finance continuing unemployment, the principle of insurance was modified and extended to cover the unanticipated length of the depression. The Beveridge Report of 1942 assumed an average rate of unemployment of 8.5 percent as compared to the then current operating assumption of 15 percent. The Beveridge Report stated, "The Plan for Social Security provides benefit for a substantial volume of unemployment."[71] In addition to preparing for a large volume of unemployment, the Report recommended that there be no limit to the duration of unemployment benefits as long as the insured person maintained his eligibility.[72] The National Insurance Act, however, provided for normal benefits of thirty weeks and extra benefits up to nineteen months, with a possible extension for those who had exhausted their statutory right. This extension was dropped in 1953 since such contingencies failed to materialize.[73] Present plans, however, provide for a standard benefit period of 312 days.[74]

The American approach to unemployment insurance illustrates sharply the differences in philosophy between the United States and Great Britain about the relative roles of redistributed or social insurance income and income from employment. Of the two major kinds of social insurance established by the Social Security Act of 1935, unemployment insurance has been the less well endowed and generous in its benefits. Dependent on state administration and almost everywhere financed by employer contribution, most unemployment compensation funds can meet only short-run unemployment at a small proportion of average wage. During recent years, with federal subsidies, some of the states have provided a maximum of three fourths of a year's benefits during severe recessions. Only a handful of states have made any provision for unemployment or lack of income due to illness. Compared to OASDHI, with its federal administration and constantly rising scale of benefits, unemployment compensation has made substantially no progress since 1935, and its benefits are considerably smaller in proportion to average wages than at the time of its origin.

There has been no lack of awareness of the weakness of the unemployment insurance system. On the state level, the failure of state funds to meet any long-term crises has become an almost classical situation. On the federal level, apart from emergency measures to meet the depletion of state funds, there have been a variety of proposals for setting unemployment compensation on a sounder basis. The lack of constructive action, particularly in view of several serious recessions since 1935 and a generally high unemployment rate, has been clearly underlined by the effort and resources invested in programs to eliminate unemployment through advancing opportunities for competing in the job market. The security of sounder insurance has had little appeal against the romantic notion of unlimited opportunity for all. As President Johnson stated in signing the Economic Opportunity Act:

Our American answer to poverty is not to make the poor more secure in their poverty, but to reach down and to help them lift themselves out of the ruts of poverty and move with the large majority along the high road of hope and prosperity.[75]

Rehabilitation

The emphasis in the public programs on individual opportunity and achievement for increasing employability and employment has also been reflected in the income maintenance programs for the needy. Individual change is seen as a major force for reducing economic dependency. Although only a relatively small proportion of those on assistance in the

United States have the potential to be self-supporting or, for reasons of family responsibility, are in a position to be, rehabilitatve services in programs of public assistance have received much support and have greatly expanded. The primary objective of the 1962 amendments to the Social Security Act was "the provision of services to help families become self-supporting." According to the Department of Health, Education, and Welfare, the amendments would enable the states "to provide incentives that will result in a reduction in the need for continued public assistance," and recognize "the importance of rehabilitation in helping welfare recipients to be able as a minimum to care for themselves, and in many cases to become self-supporting."[76]

The public assistance programs in the United States have reflected the individualism of American life since the colonial era. The individualism of the Puritan colonial settlers and the Jeffersonian democrats, which set the pattern for a limited assumption of public responsibility, was followed by the Romantic psychology of the early charity organization societies and the Freudian psychology of the later family agencies, both relating dependency to pathology. The original concern with dependency on purely economic grounds was now strongly reaffirmed with the sanctions and prestige of the new field of mental health. Thus, even when the causes of dependency have been considered to be social, there has still remained a strong belief that the process of change or rehabilitation must be centered on the individual. There has been a great proliferation of diagnostic literature on the problems and clinical typologies of the poor. Earlier classification by moral categories has given way to social and psychological classifications, equally oriented to the task of treating dependency.[77] Only through rehabilitation of the individual directly, it has been assumed, can he be motivated toward self-fulfillment. The individual has been considered the source of change in American public assistance programs even when the techniques for change stem from the group or the community.

The Public Welfare Amendments of 1962 gave great impetus to the rehabilitation services of the states by generous federal subsidies to their programs and to the training of professional personnel.[78] The grants were more liberal than the matching of state funds for purely economic assistance. The individual or case emphasis of public assistance was evidenced by the assumpton that "to increase the supply of adequately equipped public welfare personnel" would "reduce the need for and the cost of public assistance programs." The states had held this philosophy even prior to federal encouragement, and many, either through their own organization or through private bodies such as the Community Research Associates, had undertaken to apply modern casework rehabilitative techniques to assistance clients. The seriousness of the federal government's approach was demonstrated by the separation of public assistance from social insurance and the establishment of a Welfare Administration that would combine an emphasis on services with public assistance. This clearly indicated that the latter were not to be confused with the objectively administered social insurance systems.

The establishment of the poverty program under the Office of Economic Opportunity and with a leadership far outside the public assistance and social work fields (although the goals and the clients of public assistance and the poverty program have much in common) has been particularly significant on the American scene. The traditional public assistance stress on dependency has been highlighted by the poverty program's effort to avoid the case approach by making accessible general opportunities for training and employment and by emphasizing citizen and community participation in the planning and administration of the local programs. The poverty program under the Economic Opportunity Act has been related to the wide variety of factors and circumstances that have given rise to inadequate income for large segments of the population. The demographic characteristics on which the public assistance categories were based, e.g. aged, blind, children, and disabled, have been broadly useful classifications for case services. On the other hand, the Economic Opportunity Act and other major legislation in the poverty program have focused not on population groups but on broad measures for removing the major obstacles to obtaining appropriate employment.

In Britain the basic public assistance program, under the National Assistance Board created by the act of 1948, has reflected the goal of abolishing the stigma of relief previously associated with local poor law administration. The responsibility of the Board has been the provision of economic assistance in the most constructive fashion. This has not involved the Board in viewing the recipient as a client in the American casework sense of the term or in providing a set of services for the total adjustment of the recipient and his family.[79] Economic need has not been seen as necessarily associated with other problems requiring the Board's attention, nor is it the philosophy of the Board that the provision of assistance can be more effectively accomplished by, or gives the right of, more intimate involvement in the lives of those assisted. In one of its earliest reports the Board stated:

The people receiving assistance from the Board are . . . in the main competent to manage their affairs and differ from other people only in the point of income. There is, for example, no reason to suppose that the 700,000 old people who depend in whole or in part on assistance are less able to manage their affairs than many of the 6,000,000 old people whose resources make it unnecessary for them to seek assistance. The primary business of the Board is to ensure that people applying to them have a sufficient income, and have it in the majority of cases with as little trouble and inconvenience to themselves as possible. Considering the large number of people wholly or partly dependent on assistance this is in itself no small task.

The recipients of assistance include, of course, a proportion of people who need a watchful eye kept over them. The fact, however, that a minority need special attention is no reason for departing from the general principle that people who do not need such attention should not have it forced on them.[80]

That does not mean that assistance is offered in an unsympathetic fashion, but the Board's officers are limited in their function. They are advised that they may "allow a fairly lengthy interval to elapse between visits . . . if three important conditions are fulfilled."

The first is that proper care should be taken to pick out the cases where more frequent visiting is required. . . . The second consideration is that the visiting should be done by officers who have the art of seeing points of difficulty or possible difficulty. . . . The third consideration is that the recipients should feel sufficient confidence in the goodwill and helpfulness of the Board's officers to take the initiative in approaching them on all needful occasions, and as regards this the Board hope that the necessary confidence is being built up in the only possible way, that is by consistently courteous understanding and helpful behaviour on the part of officers.[81]

When more personal services are required, the Board's officers rely primarily on the resources of other agencies in the community.

The British and American approaches to public assistance illustrate essential differences in their perspectives on social support. By 1909 the advocates of the Minority Report of the Royal Commission on the Poor Law had already organized a strong campaign for placing public assistance on an objective basis. Economic need, in their opinion, reflected the economic limitations of society, not willful dependency or personal inadequacy. The paternalistic controls identified with the old poor law and the new methods of the voluntary charity organization societies were gradually abandoned in favor of a neutral bureaucratic administration. It was not a simple and smooth transition, and as Barbara Wootten has noted, the "determination" to explain poverty by "the quality of the poor" survived into the 1930s, when "anybody who, for whatever reason, might be unable to support himself or herself, or to maintain a family by his (or her) own legitimate efforts was liable to be labelled 'sub-normal'."[82] Nor has the situation been completely resolved. The Conservative Party suggested in 1965 that state economic programs be limited to the needy and that such aid be coupled with greater efforts at rehabilitation. It was proposed that the Ministries of Health and of Pensions and National Insurance be merged into a new Department of Health and Social Security. The National Assistance Board would be replaced by an organization "closely associated with" the new Department, and it would have the "positive duty of seeking out those needing help."[83]

In America the trend has been generally in the other direction. After abandoning their functions to the private charities in many areas at the end of the nineteenth century, the public agencies in reestablishing their role in assistance sought in large measure to emulate the professional case approach of the voluntary field. While there has been criticism of this trend on administrative, philosophical, and therapeutic grounds,[84] there has been insistence, within the public assistance system, on treating economic need as a pathological or potentially pathological condition.

Some tendencies toward a drawing together of the British and American approaches have, however, been noticeable. The National Assistance Board has expanded its direct rehabilitation efforts for special groups of recipients requiring more prolonged service.[85] More attention has been given to the Board's own training courses to help its officers "in the acquisition of the skill and of the insight and understanding of human behaviour called for by their often delicate duties, particularly with people whose personalities are in some way abnormal."[86] In America the emphasis on diagnostic classification of assistance recipients has been coupled with the goal of differential caseloads indicating the need of, and potential for, more intensive treatment. Consideration has also been given to the general problem of distinguishing between the more objectively and more personally administered services and of developing a rationale for the appropriate separation and combination of the services and the clinical approach.[87]

On the whole, the British have emphasized external change and social reform as the major tools for rehabilitation, and they have viewed the social services and particularly socially supplied income somewhat differently from the Americans. Improvement in economic and social conditions has in itself been considered to have the potential for increasing the individual's capacity for adjustment. For American economic security programs there has always been, at least implicitly, the intervening variable of the individual personality and its dependency needs.

Although more intervention in the lives of public assistance recipients has been tolerated in the United States, the goal in this as in other public welfare programs has been the strengthening of the individual to compete successfully as an individual in a competitive culture. In British society, on the other hand, there has been a greater expectation of socially productive behavior. While the individual's adjustment has been considered a personal matter, his failure to carry out his share of the total social responsibility has not been readily accepted. When the individual fails in his socially defined obligations, the welfare system has provided itself with sterner measures for enforcing social demands. The National Assistance Board, for example, has "reestablishment" centers for those men who have not shown sufficient responsibility in maintaining themselves and who may be referred to the center for its disciplined training instead of receiving a money grant.[88]

The numbers assigned to the reestablishment centers have been small,[89] but the idea of the training center has not been limited to those requiring direct economic assistance. The local authorities have provided intermediate housing for families whose standards do not meet the expectations of public housing. Such housing is below the usual level of housing, and the families are given guidance and supervision in preparation for their transfer to more adequate accommodations.[90] Training centers have also been established for mothers who have difficulty managing their households and providing proper child care. Mothers, if they are willing to attend, in most instances are referred by voluntary organizations or local health authorities, but the Home Office has had an arrangement with the Salvation Army for mothers convicted of neglect who must reside in the Army's center as a condition of their being placed on probation.[91] Thus, in principle, the use of compulsory measures for the rehabilitation of those not fulfilling their social obligations has been considered more appropriate on the British welfare scene than in the United States. This suggests that there is greater clarity of standards, less willingness to tolerate asocial behavior, and more readiness to exercise formal methods of social control.[92]

Conclusion

THE study of the development of economic security policy since the sixteenth century has involved tracing the ebb and flow of the many systems of ideas and ideologies that influenced the changing shape of social policy. The underlying theme has been shifting balance between the concepts of status and contract that have dominated British and American society since the period of mercantilism. While both societies have many traditions in common and have been continuously influenced by their political, economic, and cultural interaction, the similarities in their economic security policies have frequently been more superficial than real. The English poor law, the common ancestor of both systems, followed different paths and incorporated unique emphases as it was adapted to the particular cultures of the two countries.

Although British and American policy apparently had the same roots and diverged in time, this has not actually been the case. Up until the Civil War there was nothing that could seriously be called American public welfare, whereas the British already had a firmly established poor law system. During the latter part of the nineteenth century American public welfare first began to set the foundation for its future growth. Only towards the twentieth century, as the social and economic developments of the two nations converged, did the earlier traditional values come to the fore and result in a greater correspondence of solutions to the problem of economic security. It was then that the "reality" of industrial society, which had become increasingly clear in England during the latter part of the nineteenth century, crystallized in America, and the dominant notions of laissez-faire ceased to maintain their hold.

The logic of a competitive society gave way as abundance replaced scarcity. Poverty was no longer inevitable, and the moral sanctions that supported industriousness and thrift were less meaningful when human labor became less important to productivity, and consumption became vital to balancing the ever-increasing productive capacity of industry. The modes of distribution of a laissez-faire society were no longer adequate to meet the demands of the complex industrial world. The irregular and sketchily organized techniques of both public and private charity were incapable of solving the problems of a society that could not tolerate the severe economic crises that appeared to be endemic to advanced industrialism.[1]

Out of this conflict between the old ideology of laissez-faire and the realities of society emerged a new set of solutions or at least a radical reorientation of the old. The changing economics intermingled with social and political reform provided the background of that diffuse and pragmatic phenomenon not too aptly termed the welfare state. The welfare state was the evolutionary reaction of the western democracies to those conditions that resulted in more cataclysmic change in other societies. Its very eclectic and amorphous style reflected the culture of the societies in which it took root. The economic requirements of the industrial era were tempered by the humanitarianism, rationality, individualism, and social and political democracy that were the traditional heritage of British and American society.

The development of the welfare society has permitted the resolution to a large degree of the conflict previously believed inherent in the concepts of status and contract. The earlier dichotomy between a society in which the individual's interests were subordinated to his membership in the whole and a society in which the whole gave way to the interests of the individual was no longer necessarily tenable. The former abstract notions of natural law and human nature, the stumbling blocks to imaginative social reform, had lost much of their magical appeal, and in their place there was a gradual proliferation of the rights of man and the goals of social justice. The erratic paths of British and American societies have led toward the merging of those aspects of status and contract compatible with the ideals of individual freedom and social responsibility in this era.[2] This, however, is the beginning, not the culmination of the effort to create an approach to welfare suitable to contemporary society. The welfare state, for both Britain and America, has heralded a vast complex of social and economic issues and problems requiring new policies, strategies, and techniques.

NOTES

Notes

Introduction

1. Quoted in William Ashley, *An Introduction to English Economic History and Theory*, 4th ed., London: Longmans, Green, 1920, I, Pt. 2, 341
2. Ferdinand Tonnies, *Fundamental Concepts of Sociology*, trans. Charles P. Loomis, New York: American Book, 1940.

PART I

Chapter 1

1. R. H. Tawney, *Religion and the Rise of Capitalism*, New York: Mentor, 1947, p. 34.
2. Eli F. Heckscher, *Mercantilism*, London: Allen & Unwin, 1935, II, 316–24.
3. F. J. Fisher, "Commercial Trends and Policy in Sixteenth-Century England," *Essays in Economic History*, ed. E. M. Carus-Wilson, London: Edward Arnold, 1954, I, 152–72.
4. Heckscher, *Mercantilism*, II, 273–85.
5. Jacob Viner, "Power Versus Plenty as Objectives of Foreign Policy in the Seventeenth and Eighteenth Century," in *The Long View and the Short*, Glencoe: Free Press, 1958, pp. 277–305; Heckscher, *Mercantilism*, I, 17.
6. Erich Fromm, *Escape From Freedom*, New York: Farrar and Rinehart, 1941, p. 93.
7. Thomas More, *Utopia*, New York: Appleton-Century-Crofts, 1949, p. 34.
8. John W. Allen, *A History of Political Thought in the Sixteenth Century*, New York: Dial Press, 1928, pp. 151–52.
9. Edmund Whittaker, *A History of Economic Ideas*, New York: Longmans, Green, 1940, pp. 367, 374, 419.
10. J. W. Gough, *The Social Contract*, 2d ed., Oxford: Clarendon Press, 1957, pp. 138–39.
11. More, *Utopia*, p. 54.
12. Heckscher, *Mercantilism*, II, 297.
13. Margaret James, *Social Problems and Policy During the Puritan Revolution*, London: Routledge, 1930, p. 281.
14. Quoted in ibid., pp. 344–45; also see Edgar S. Furniss, *The Position of the Labourer in a System of Nationalism*, New York: Kelley & Millman, 1957.
15. Quoted in James, *Social Problems and Policy*, p. 272.
16. Quoted in E. Lipson, *The Economic History of England*, 6th ed., London: Black, 1956, III, 262.

17. More, *Utopia*, pp. 9–10.
18. Ibid, p. 25.
19. Lipson, *Economic History of England*, III, 5.
20. Quoted in James, *Social Problems and Policy*, p. 275.
21. Quoted in Joseph Dorfman, *The Economic Mind in American Civilization*, New York: Viking, 1946, I, 9.
22. E. A. J. Johnson, *Predecessors of Adam Smith*, New York: Prentice-Hall, 1937, Ch. 13, discusses the importance of inventiveness and manufacturing skill, but it is unlikely that these characteristics were applied to the general laboring population.
23. Quoted in Daniel J. Boorstin, *The Americans: The Colonial Experience*, New York: Random House, 1958, p. 156.
24. See H. R. Trevor-Roper, *Archbishop Laud*, London: Macmillan, 1962.
25. More, *Utopia*, p. 41.
26. *New Atlantis*, in *Ideal Commonwealths*, ed. Henry Morley, New York: Colonial Press, 1901, pp. 117–18.
27. *Oceana*, in *Ideal Commonwealths*, p. 316.
28. Quoted in Heckscher, *Mercantilism*, I, 267.
29. Robert Crowley, *The Select Works*, ed. J. M. Cowper, London: Trubner, 1872, pp. 156–57.
30. Francis Hutcheson, *A System of Moral Philosophy*, London, 1755, I, 321–22.

Chapter 2

1. Quoted in Sidney and Beatrice Webb, *English Poor Law History*, Pt. I, in *English Local Government*, London: Longmans, Green, 1927, pp. 82–83.
2. E. Lipson, *The Economic History of England*, 6th ed., London: Black, 1956, II, pp. xxx, 330; W. Cunningham, *The Growth of English Industry and Commerce in Modern Times*, Cambridge: Cambridge U. Press, 1925, p. 49; S. and B. Webb, *English Poor Law History*, Pt. I, p. 43.
3. Lipson, *Economic History of England*, II, p. xvii; Edward P. Cheyney, *A History of England*, II, London: Longmans, Green, 1926, 261–62.
4. Margaret Gay Davies, *The Enforcement of English Apprenticeship 1563–1642: A Study in Applied Mercantilism*, Cambridge: Harvard U. Press, 1956, p. 7.
5. This analysis is based on the documents in *Some Early Tracts on Poor Relief*, ed. Frank R. Salter, London: Methuen, 1926.
6. Ibid., p. 101.
7. Ibid., p. 125.
8. Ibid., pp. 13–14.
9. Ibid., pp. 107, 110.
10. Ibid., pp. 93–94.
11. Ibid., p. 102.
12. Ibid., p. 54.
13. Ibid., p. 55.
14. Ibid., p. 5.
15. Ibid., p. 71.
16. Ibid., p. 7.

17. Ibid., p. 77.
18. S. and B. Webb, *English Poor Law History*, Pt. 1, pp. 396–401; R. H. Tawney, *Religion and the Rise of Capitalism*, New York: Mentor, 1947.
19. Margaret James, *Social Problems and Policy During the Puritan Revolution, 1640–1660*, London: Routledge, 1930, pp. 283–84.
20. Quoted in R. H. Tawney and Eileen Power, eds., *Tudor Economic Documents*, London: Longmans, Green, 1924, I, 335.
21. Ibid., I, 360.
22. Ibid., I, 355–57; Davies, *Enforcement of English Apprenticeship*, pp. 2–3.
23. Tawney and Power, *Tudor Economic Documents*, I, 340–41.
24. Quoted in E. M. Leonard, *The Early History of English Poor Relief*, Cambridge: Cambridge U. Press, 1900, pp. 147–48.
25. Quoted in Tawney and Power, *Tudor Economic Documents*, I, 361.
26. Quoted in Leonard, *Early History of English Poor Relief*, p. 72.
27. Quoted in ibid., p. 147.
28. Quoted in S. and B. Webb, *English Poor Law History*, Pt. 1, p. 97.
29. Leonard, *Early History of English Poor Relief*, p. 225.
30. S. and B. Webb, *English Poor Law History*, Pt. 1, p. 84.
31. Quoted in Sir George Nicholls, *A History of the English Poor Law*, New York: Putnam's, 1898, I, 288–89.
32. Quoted in Tawney and Power, *Tudor Economic Documents*, I, 343.
33. Quoted in A. E. Bland, P. A. Brown, and R. H. Tawney, *English Economic History*, New York: Macmillan, 1919, p. 342.
34. Quoted in Lipson, *Economic History of England*, III, 259.
35. Quoted in ibid., II, pp. cvi–cvii.
36. Quoted in Heckscher, *Mercantilism*, II, 166.
37. Leonard, *Early History of English Poor Relief*, pp. 199 ff.
38. Ibid., p. 125.
39. Ibid., p. 111.

Chapter 3

1. Quoted in Robert W. Kelso, *The History of Public Poor Relief in Massachusetts*, Boston: Houghton Mifflin, 1922, p. 31.
2. Quoted in Joseph Dorfman, *The Economic Mind in American Civilization*, New York: Viking, 1946, I, 81.
3. Quoted in Richard B. Morris, *Government and Labor in Early America*, New York: Columbia U. Press, 1946, p. 64.
4. The extent of the impact of indentured servants may be judged by the fact that in three months in 1709, 1,838 indentured servants came to Philadelphia alone and represented almost every type of trade. (Philip S. Foner, *History of the Labor Movement in the United States*, New York: International Publishers, 1947, p. 23.)
5. Morris, *Government and Labor in Early America*, p. 45.
6. Quoted in ibid., p. 59.
7. Morris, *Government and Labor in Early America*, pp. 4–11.
8. Quoted in Dorfman, *Economic Mind in American Civilization*, I, 42.

9. E.A.J. Johnson, *American Economic Thought in the Seventeenth Century,* London: P. S. King, 1932, pp. 31–32.
10. Quoted in Marcus W. Jernegan, *Laboring and Dependent Classes in Colonial America, 1607–1783,* Chicago: U. of Chicago Press, 1931, p. 196.
11. Quoted in David M. Schneider and Albert Deutsch, *The History of Public Welfare in New York State,* Chicago: U. of Chicago Press, 1938, I, 61.
12. Quoted in ibid., p. 62.
13. Dorfman, *Economic Mind in American Civilization,* I, 101.
14. Johnson, *American Economic Thought in the 17th Century,* pp. 107–08.
15. Quoted in Kelso, *Public Poor Relief in Massachusetts,* p. 98.
16. Schneider and Deutsch, *Public Welfare in New York State,* I, 23.
17. Quoted in ibid., I, 24.
18. Quoted in ibid., I, 47.
19. Quoted in ibid., I, 47.
20. Jernegan, *Laboring and Dependent Classes in Colonial America,* p. 182.
21. Kelso, *Public Poor Relief in Massachusetts,* p. 114.
22. Morris, *Government and Labor in Early America,* p. 15.
23. Schneider and Deutsch, *Public Welfare in New York State,* I, 22.
24. Johnson, *American Economic Thought in the 17th Century,* p. 31.

Chapter 4

1. Quoted in Dorothy Marshall, *The English Poor in the Eighteenth Century,* London: Routledge, 1926, p. 206.
2. Marshall, *English Poor in the 18th Century,* p. 248.

PART II

Chapter 5

1. Arnold Toynbee, *Lectures on the Industrial Revolution of the Eighteenth Century in England,* London: Longmans, Green, 1927, p. 67.
2. Sir William Ashley, *The Economic Organization of England,* London: Longmans, Green, 1914, p. 139.
3. Toynbee, *Industrial Revolution,* p. 106.
4. Dorothy Marshall, *The English Poor in the Eighteenth Century,* London: Routledge, 1926, pp. 182–83.
5. Quoted in M. Dorothy George, *London Life in the Eighteenth Century,* London: Kegan Paul, Trench, Trubner, 1925, p. 318.
6. Quoted in Harry Elmer Barnes and Howard Becker, *Social Thought from Lore to Science,* Boston: D. C. Heath, 1938, p. 367.
7. David Hume, "An Enquiry Concerning the Principles of Morals," in *Hume Selections,* ed. Charles W. Hendel, Jr., New York: Scribner's, 1927, pp. 216–19.
8. See particularly, Glenn R. Morrow, "Adam Smith: Moralist and Philosopher," in J. M. Clark et al., *Adam Smith, 1776–1926,* Chicago: U. of Chicago Press, 1928, pp. 156–79.

9. *Adam Smith's Moral and Political Philosophy*, ed. Herbert W. Schneider, New York: Hafner, 1948, Ch. I, Pt. I, sec. I, p. 73.

10. Ibid.

11. Ibid., p. 74.

12. Ibid., Introd., sec. III, p. 54.

13. Ibid., Introd. sec. II, p. 39.

14. Ibid., p. 40.

15. Ibid., Pt. 2, sec. II, p. 117.

16. Ibid., Pt. 2, sec. II, pp. 124–25.

17. Adam Smith, *The Wealth of Nations*, New York: Modern Library, 1937, p. 14.

18. *Adam Smith's Moral and Political Philosophy*, Ch. I, Pt. 2, sec. II, p. 125.

19. Hume, "An Enquiry Concerning the Principles of Morals," in *Hume Selections*, p. 217.

20. *Adam Smith's Moral and Political Philosophy*, Ch. I, Pt. 2, sec. II, p. 117.

21. Charles Parkin, *The Moral Basis of Burke's Political Thought*, Chicago: U. of Chicago Press, 1956.

22. A. V. Dicey, *Lectures on the Relation between Law and Public Opinion in England during the Nineteenth Century*, London: Macmillan, 1924, p. 401.

23. Maldwyn Edwards, *John Wesley and the Eighteenth Century*, London: Allen & Unwin, 1933, pp. 180–82.

24. Quoted in Mary Gladys Jones, *Hannah More*, Cambridge: Cambridge U. Press, 1952, p. 158.

25. Reinhard Bendix, *Work and Authority in Industry*, New York: Wiley, 1956, p. 17.

26. Wellman J. Warner, *The Wesleyan Movement in the Industrial Revolution*, London: Longmans, Green, 1930, pp. 122–35, 148–50, 174, 208–09.

27. G.D.J. Cole, *A Short History of the British Working Class Movement*, London: Allen & Unwin, 1927, I, 130.

28. R. H. Tawney, *The Acquisitive Society*, New York: Harvest, 1948, p. 11.

29. Quoted in E.A.J. Johnson, *Predecessors of Adam Smith*, New York: Prentice-Hall, 1937, p. 297.

30. David Hume, *Writings in Economics*, ed. Eugene Rotwein, Madison: U. of Wisconsin Press, 1955, pp. 23–24.

31. Ibid, p. 13.

32. Smith, *Wealth of Nations*, p. 625.

33. Jeremy Bentham, *Jeremy Bentham's Economic Writings*, ed. W. Stark, New York: Burt Franklin, 1952, I, 113.

34. Hume, *Writings in Economics*, p. 15.

35. Ibid., p. 17.

36. Smith, *Wealth of Nations*, p. 81.

37. Ibid., pp. 78–79.

38. *The Works of William Paley*, New York: D. Longworth, 1811, III, 67.

39. Ibid., III, 95.

40. Ibid., III, 50.

41. "A life of labour, such, I mean, as is led by the labouring part of mankind in this country, has advantages in it which would compensate all its inconveniences. When compared with the life of the rich, it is better in these important respects: It supplies employment, it promotes activity. It keeps the

body in better health, the mind more engaged, and, of course, more quiet. It is more sensible of ease, more susceptible of pleasure. It is attended with greater alacrity of spirits, a more constant cheerfulness and serenity of temper. It affords easier and more certain methods of sending children into the world in situations suited to their habits and expectations. It is free from many heavy anxieties which rich men feel; it is fraught with many sources of delight which they want." ("Reasons for Contentment," addressed to the Labouring Part of the British Community, *The Works of William Paley*, Philadelphia: J. J. Woodward, 1835, p. 499.)

42. T. R. Malthus, *An Essay on Population*, London: J. M. Dent, 1914, II, 168–73.

43. "Labour, like all other things which are purchased and sold, and which may be increased or diminished in quantity, has its natural and its market price. The natural price of labour is that price which is necessary to enable the labourers, one with another, to subsist and perpetuate their race, without increase or diminution." (*The Works of David Ricardo*, London: John Murray, 1881, p. 50.)

44. See Nassau W. Senior, *An Outline of the Science of Political Economy*, New York: Farrar and Rinehart, 1939.

45. Bentham, *Economic Writings*, ed. Stark, I, 115–16.

46. Jeremy Bentham, *A Fragment on Government*, ed. Wilfred Harrison, Oxford: Blackwell, 1948, p. lxv.

47. Patrick Colquhoun, *A Treatise on Indigence*, London, 1806, pp. 7–8.

48. Ibid., p. 234.

49. *The Reports of the Society for Bettering the Condition and Increasing the Comforts of the Poor*, 4th ed., London, 1805, I, 2.

50. Malthus, *Essay on Population*, I, 16.

51. Sir Frederic Morton Eden, *The State of the Poor*, ed. A. G. L. Rogers, New York: Dutton, 1929, p. 92.

52. Smith, *Wealth of Nations*, p. 82.

53. Joseph A. Schumpeter, *History of Economic Analysis*, New York: Oxford U. Press, 1954, p. 558,

54. Malthus, *Essay on Population*, II, 12.

55. Ibid., II, 254.

56. Quoted in Jones, *Hannah More*, p. 152.

57. Colquhoun, *Treatise on Indigence*, p. 148.

58. Ibid., p. 80.

59. Ibid., p. 261.

60. *The Reports of the Society for Bettering the Condition and Increasing the Comforts of the Poor*, I, 4.

61. Smith, *Wealth of Nations*, pp. 15–16.

62. Leslie Stephen, *The English Utilitarians*, London: Duckworth, 1902, II, 83.

63. John Plamenatz, *Mill's Utilitarianism*, Oxford: Blackwell, 1949, Ch. I.

64. *The Reports of the Society for Bettering the Condition and Increasing the Comforts of the Poor*, I, 3.

65. Chalmers' scientific understanding was relatively sophisticated for his day. On the one hand he castigated philanthropists and legislators who sought grand solutions while overlooking the "particulars," and the result was "utter futility." On the other hand, he was equally critical of the mere col-

lectors of facts. "If in former times the tendency was to proceed on principles without facts—as if to keep at the greatest possible distance from this error, the incessant demand now is for facts without principles. And so our empirical statesmen would commit questions of the most momentous import into the hands of mere collectors and empirics like themselves." He than pleads for "sound theory" against the fashionable tendency of collecting meaningless statistics. (*Chalmers on Charity,* ed. N. Masterman, Westminster: A. Constable, 1900, pp. 2–4, 12–13.)

66. Bentham, *Economic Writings,* ed. Stark, I, 224–25.
67. K. B. Smellie, *A Hundred Years of English Government,* 2d ed., London: Duckworth, 1950, Ch. 3.
68. Malthus, *Essay on Population,* II, 143.
69. Sir Edwin Chadwick, *An Article on the Principles and Progress of the Poor Law Amendment Act,* London: Knight, 1847, pp. 14–15.
70. Hume, *Writings in Economics,* pp. 21–22.
71. Quoted in J. L. and Barbara Hammond, *The Town Labourer,* London: Guild Books, 1949, II, 127.
72. Quoted in Robert Kiefer Webb, *The British Working Class Reader,* London: Allen & Unwin, 1955, p. 135.
73. Quoted in George, *London Life in the 18th Century,* pp. 271–72.
74. Smith, *Wealth of Nations,* p. 86.
75. Eden, *State of the Poor,* p. 2.
76. Lionel Robbins, *Robert Torrens and the Evolution of Classical Economics,* London: Macmillan, 1958, pp. 235–36.

Chapter 6

1. *Report from His Majesty's Commissioners for Inquiring into the Administration and Practical Operation of the Poor Laws, 1834,* London: W. Clowes, 1835, p. 127.
2. T. R. Malthus, *An Essay on Population,* London: J. M. Dent, 1914, II, 190–91.
3. Sir Frederick Morton Eden, *The State of the Poor,* ed. A.G.L. Rogers, New York: Dutton, 1929, pp. 92–93.
4. David Ricardo, *Principles of Political Economy and Taxation,* ed. E.C.K. Gonner, London: G. Bell, 1908, p. 83.
5. Quoted in Sir George Nicholls, *A History of the English Poor Law,* New York: Putnam's, 1898, II, 261.
6. Quoted in Sidney and Beatrice Webb, *English Poor Law History,* in *English Local Government,* London: Longmans, Green, 1927, Pt. 2, pp. 10–11.
7. Marian Bowley has maintained that the wage fund theory did not mean to economists a "fixed" wage fund. (*Nassau Senior and Classical Economics,* New York: A. M. Kelly, 1949, p. 284.) However as John Galbraith has noted, "Although the truth rarely overtakes falsehood, it has winged feet as compared with a qualification in pursuit of a bold proposition. The iron law, in its uncompromised clarity, became part of the intellectual capital of the world." (*The Affluent Society,* New York: Mentor, 1958, p. 34.)

8. Bowley, *Nassau Senior,* p. 243.
9. Quoted in ibid., p. 245.
10. Quoted in ibid., p. 291.
11. Quoted in ibid., p. 244.
12. Max Beloff, *Public Order and Popular Disturbances,* London: Oxford U. Press, 1938, p. 155.
13. Mark Blaug, in two articles, "The Myth of the Old Poor Law and the Making of the New," and "The Poor Law Report Reexamined," *Journal of Economic History,* xxiii, 2 (June 1963), 151–84, and xxiv, 2 (June 1964), 229–45, has made a careful analysis of the variety of assumed effects of the Speenhamland policy, i.e., demoralization of working class population, wages, rents, decline of yeomanry, burden on ratepayers. Blaug found no evidence to substantiate the influence of Speenhamland on any of these factors. Other forces than Speenhamland were found to be primary, and Blaug concluded that it was low wages that led to Speenhamland rather than Speenhamland resulting in low wages.
14. The Webbs (*English Poor Law History,* Pt. i, p. 183) point out that standards of allowances had fallen by as much as one-third between 1795 and 1830.
15. Modern analysis of population growth has not supported the assumption that the birth-rate showed a spectacular increase during the period of Speenhamland. Rather it appears that there was a dramatic increase in the number of live births and in longevity rather than in the total number of births. (J. H. Clapham, *An Economic History of Modern Britain,* Cambridge: Cambridge U. Press, 1926, i, 54–56).
16. John Weyland, *A Short Inquiry into the Policy, Humanity and Past Effects of the Poor Laws,* London, 1807, p. 94.
17. Ibid., p. 141.
18. A. W. Coats, "Economic Thought and Poor Law Policy in the Eighteenth Century," *Economic History Rev.,* xiii, 1, (August 1960), 39–51.
19. Nicholls, *History of the English Poor Law,* ii, 86.
20. Ibid., ii, 90.
21. For an interesting discussion of this evolution, see Georg Rusche and Otto Kirchheimer, *Punishment and Social Structure,* New York: Columbia U. Press, 1939, pp. 94–95.
22. The opinion of the court in a case at the time was, "There can be no doubt, however, that it is the primary duty of overseers to find employment for the poor, if possible." (Cited in Sir Gregory A. Lewin, *A Summary of the Laws Relating to the Government and Maintenance of the Poor,* London: William Benning, 1828, p. 217).
23. Sir Edwin Chadwick, *An Article on the Principles and Progress of the Poor Law Amendment Act,* London: Knight, 1837, p. 15.
24. Ricardo, *Political Economy and Taxation,* p. 83.
25. Ibid., p. 86.
26. Bowley, *Nassau Senior,* p. 293.
27. *Report of the Poor Law Commissioners, 1834,* p. 36.
28. Ibid., p. 37.
29. The Webbs present evidence which refutes the common impression that

rents were in fact "swallowed up in rates." (*English Poor Law History,* Pt. 2, p. 3.) The reader is again referred to Blaug's excellent analysis of the effects of poor law policy. See n. 13.

30. *First Annual Report of the Poor Law Commissioners for England and Wales,* London: W. Clowes, 1835, p. 11.
31. *Report of the Poor Law Commissioners, 1834,* p. 34.
32. Chadwick, *Poor Law Amendment Act,* pp. 56–57.
33. J. L. and Barbara Hammond, *The Village Labourer,* London: Guild Books, 1948, ii, 38.
34. Charles D. Brereton, *An Inquiry into the Workhouse System and the Law of Maintenance in Agricultural Districts,* 2d. ed., Norwich, 1825, p. 68.
35. M. Dorothy George cites improvements along these lines in the reform of the system of petty magistrates, the police, and local government generally. (*London Life in the Eighteenth Century,* London: Kegan Paul, Trench, Trubner, 1925.)
36. *Report of the Poor Law Commissioners,* p. 18.
37. Ibid., p. 37.
38. Ibid., p. 41.
39. *Report of the Poor Law Commissioners, 1834,* p. 123.
40. S. and B. Webb, *English Poor Law History,* Pt. 1, p. 476.
41. Quoted in Nicholls, *History of the English Poor Law,* ii, 118.
42. Quoted in G. M. Trevelyan, *Lord Grey of the Reform Bill,* 2d. ed., London: Longmans, Green, 1952, p. 253.
43. Quoted in S. and B. Webb, *English Poor Law History,* Pt. 2, p. 37.
44. Nicholls, *History of the English Poor Law,* ii, 186–87.
45. *Extracts from the Information Received by His Majesty's Commissioners as to the Administration and Operation of the Poor Laws,* London: B. Fellowes, 1833, p. 1.
46. Nicholls, *History of the English Poor Law,* ii, 203–04.
47. Chadwick, *Poor Law Amendment Act,* p. 24.
48. J. L. and B. Hammond, *Village Labourer,* pp. 119–29.
49. *Extracts from the Information as to the Administration and Operation of the Poor Laws,* pp. 250–51.
50. Ibid., p. 261.
51. Nicholls, *History of the English Poor Law,* ii, 75.
52. Malthus, *Essay on Population,* ii, 225–34.
53. George, *London Life in the 18th Century,* pp. 301–03.
54. Colquhoun, *Treatise on Indigence,* pp. 136–37, 252–54.
55. Ibid., pp. 119–20.
56. Nicholls, *History of the English Poor Law,* ii, 70.
57. Ibid., p. 98.
58. Ibid., pp. 175–76.
59. S. and B. Webb, *English Poor Law History,* Pt. 2, p. 38.
60. Malthus, *Essay on Population,* ii, 224–25.
61. Ibid., ii, 239–42.
62. Nicholls, *History of the English Poor Law,* ii, 110.
63. *The Reports of the Society for Bettering the Condition and Increasing the Comforts of the Poor,* i, 27.

64. William H. Beveridge, *Voluntary Action*, London: Allen & Unwin, 1948, p. 23.
65. Malthus, *Essay on Population*, ii, 242–43.
66. Ibid., ii, 243.
67. Quoted in Nicholls, *History of the English Poor Law*, ii, 176.
68. Ibid., ii, 192–93.
69. There was some controversy about the abandonment entirely of outdoor relief. While some of the Commissioners, both in the inquiry and in the later administrative commission, certainly opposed all outdoor relief, the recommendations of the Commissioners leading to the Act of 1834 excluded the able-bodied alone from outdoor relief.
70. Thomas Gilbert, *Considerations on the Bills for the Better Relief and Employment of the Poor*, London, 1787, p. 41–42.
71. *Report of the Poor Law Commissioners, 1834*, pp. 7–8.
72. S. and B. Webb, *English Poor Law History*, Pt. 1, p. 426.
73. Colquhoun, *Treatise on Indigence*, p. 242.
74. *Report of the Poor Law Commissioners, 1834*, pp. 99–100. The Webbs point out that in addition to these reasons the Commissioners must have been aware of the great objections which would have been raised to substituting a vast new national bureaucracy for the entrenched local system and its personnel. (S. and B. Webb, *English Poor Law History*, Pt. 2, p. 75.)
75. *Report of the Poor Law Commissioners, 1834*, pp. 99–100.
76. *Poor Law Amendment Act, 1834*, sec. 15. The functions of the Board follow closely Bentham's proposals for a Minister of Indigence Relief, and were probably influenced by Bentham's disciple, Chadwick.
77. Nassau Senior, one of the Commissioners, wrote: "I felt a strong objection to leaving the question untouched, being convinced that the present Settlement Laws greatly aggravate the existing evils, and add materially to the difficulties of improvement. But I was much tempted by the proposal of substituting nothing for the abolished heads of settlement." (Quoted in Bowley, *Nassau Senior*, p. 304.)
78. S. and B. Webb, *English Poor Law History*, Pt. 1, p. 426.
79. *Report of the Poor Law Commissioners, 1834*, p.147.
80. Ibid., p. 147.
81. C. J. Ribton Turner, *A History of Vagrants and Vagrancy and Beggars and Begging*, London: Chapman & Hall, 1887, pp. 251–52.

Chapter 7

1. Louis M. Hacker, *The Triumph of American Capitalism*, New York: Simon & Schuster, 1940, pp. 94–95; Karl Holl, *The Cultural Significance of the Reformation*, New York: Meridian Books, 1959, pp. 89–90.
2. Hacker, *Triumph of American Capitalism*, pp. 103–04.
3. John B. McMaster, *A History of the People of the United States*, New York: D. Appleton, 1895, iv, 522.
4. John A. Krout and Dixon R. Fox, *The Completion of Independence*, New York: Macmillan, 1944, pp. 373–74.
5. John R. Commons et al., *History of Labour in the United States*, New York: Macmillan, 1921, i, 155.

6. Quoted in ibid., 1, 193.
7. Mary Beard, *The American Labor Movement,* New York: Macmillan, 1931, p. 42.
8. Quoted in David M. Schneider and Albert Deutsch, *The History of Public Welfare in New York State,* Chicago: U. of Chicago Press, 1938, 1, 133–34.
9. Quoted in ibid., 1, 127.
10. Robert W. Kelso, *The History of Public Poor Relief in Massachusetts, 1620–1920,* Boston: Houghton Mifflin, 1922, pp. 128–32.
11. See Benjamin J. Klebaner, "The Myth of Foreign Pauper Dumping in the United States," *Social Service Rev.* xxxv, 1 (September 1961), 302–09.
12. Cecil Woodham Smith, *The Great Hunger,* London: Hamish Hamilton, 1962.
13. Philip S. Foner, *History of the Labor Movement in the United States,* New York: International Publishers, 1947, p. 66.
14. Edward C. Kirkland, *A History of American Economic Life,* 3d. ed., New York: Appleton-Century-Crofts, 1951, p. 324.
15. McMaster, *People of the U. S.,* iv, 493.
16. Quoted in Foner, *Labor Movement in the U. S.,* p. 98.
17. See Benjamin J. Klebaner, "Poverty and its Relief in American Thought, 1815–1861," *Social Science Rev.* xxxviii, 6 (December 1964), 398.
18. Alexander Hamilton, John Jay, and James Madison, *The Federalist,* New York: Modern Library, 1937, No. 10, pp. 55–56.
19. Ibid., No. 51, p. 337.
20. Charles A. Beard, *An Economic Interpretation of the Constitution of the United States,* New York: Macmillan, 1939.
21. Quoted in Charles A. and Mary R. Beard, *The Rise of American Civilization,* New York: Macmillan, 1930, p. 494.
22. Thomas Paine, *Rights of Man,* New York: Heritage Press, 1961, p. 161.
23. Elie Halevy, *The Growth of Philosophic Radicalism,* Boston: Beacon Press, 1955, p. 128.
24. Ibid., p. 126.
25. Quoted in C. and M. Beard, *Rise of American Civilization,* p. 456.
26. See Ralph Barton Perry, *Puritanism and Democracy,* New York: Vanguard Press, 1944, p. 170; also Krout and Fox, *Completion of Independence,* p. 150.
27. Quoted in Joseph Dorfman, *The Economic Mind in American Civilization,* New York: Viking, 1959, 11, 505.
28. Noah Brooks, *Henry Knox,* New York: Putnam's, 1900, pp. 194–95.
29. Quoted in Dorfman, *Economic Mind in American Civilization,* 11, 606.
30. Ibid., 11, 550.
31. For a discussion of the similarities between the scientific and "moral diagnosis" of poverty in America, see Perry, *Puritanism and Democracy,* pp. 302–04.
32. Quoted in Foner, *Labor Movement in the U. S.,* p. 98.
33. Quoted in Schneider and Deutsch, *Public Welfare in New York State,* 1, 211–12.
34. Ibid, 1, 212.
35. McMaster, *People of the U. S.,* iv, 527–28.
36. Schneider and Deutsch, *Public Welfare in New York State,* 1, 219.
37. Klebaner, "Poverty and Relief," pp. 383 ff.

38. Quoted in Schneider and Deutsch, *Public Welfare in New York State*, I, 216.
39. Klebaner, "Poverty and Relief," pp. 390 ff.
40. Dorfman, *Economic Mind in American Civilization*, II, 397.
41. Quoted in Foner, *Labor Movement in the U. S.*, p. 97.
42. Anthony Trollope, *North America*, New York: Harper, 1862. p. 218.
43. Quoted in Kelso, *Public Poor Relief in Massachusetts*, pp. 124–25.
44. Quoted in Schneider and Deutsch, *Public Welfare in New York State*, I, 169.
45. Ibid, I, 169–70.
46. Margaret Creech, *Three Centuries of Poor Law Administration: A Study of Legislation in Rhode Island*, Chicago: U. of Chicago Press, 1936, pp. 105–06.
47. McMaster, *People of the U. S.*, IV, 524–25.
48. Quoted in Dorfman, *Economic Mind in American Civilization*, II, 558.
49. C. and M. Beard, *Rise of American Civilization*, I, 495–96.
50. Commons et al., *Labour in the U. S.*, I, 83.

Chapter 8

1. Royal Commission on the Distribution of the Industrial Population, *Report*, Cmd. 6153, London: HMSO, 1940, p. 42.
2. Ibid., Table 1, p. 22.
3. Ibid., Table 2, p. 23.
4. See Joseph A. Schumpeter, *History of Economic Analysis*, New York: Oxford U. Press, 1954, pp. 548–49.
5. J. H. Clapham, *An Economic History of Modern Britain*, Cambridge: Cambridge U. Press, 1932, II, 388.
6. See S. E. Finer, *The Life and Times of Sir Edwin Chadwick*, London: Methuen, 1952.
7. Clapham, *Economic History of Modern Britain*, II, 153.
8. Henry Sidgwick, *The Principles of Political Economy*, 3d ed., London: Macmillan, 1901, p. 396.
9. Alfred Marshall, *Principles of Economics*, 8th ed., New York: Macmillan 1920, p. 131.
10. Ibid., p. 229.
11. Ibid., p. 65.
12. Ibid., p. 65, n. 1.
13. Ibid., p. 140.
14. Ibid., p. 136.
15. Talcott Parsons, "Marshall in Relation to the Thought of his Time," *Qtly. Journal of Economics*, XLVI (November 1931; February 1932), 101–40; 316–47.
16. John Stuart Mill, *Principles of Political Economy*, London: Longmans, Green, 1917, pp. 361–84. Mill in his later years recanted the wage fund theory.
17. Marshall, *Principles of Economics*, pp. 229–30.
18. See Sidney and Beatrice Webb, *Industrial Democracy*, London: Longmans, Green, 1901, pp. 644–45; for more recent criticism, see Charles Gide and Charles Rist, *A History of Economic Doctrines*, 2d ed., New York: D. C. Heath, 1947, p. 498.

19. Marshall, *Principles of Economics*, pp. 705, 715.
20. Ibid., p. 230.
21. See Parsons, "Marshall in Relation to the Thought of His Time."
22. Marshall, *Principles of Economics*, p. 309.
23. Ibid., p. 212.
24. Ibid., p. 3.
25. Schumpeter, *History of Economic Analysis*, p. 947.
26. Marshall, *Principles of Economics*, pp. 2, 664.
27. See James Mill, *Analysis of the Phenomena of the Human Mind*, London: Longmans, Green, Reader and Dyer, 1869, I, 119–20.
28. J. S. Mill, *Autobiography of John Stuart Mill*, New York: Columbia U. Press, 1944, p. 192.
29. Quoted in Pauline Gregg, *A Social and Economic History of Britain*, London: George C. Harrup, 1959, p. 518.
30. Quoted in I. L. Kandel, *History of Secondary Education*, London: George C. Harrup, 1931, p. 348.
31. Victoria Hazlitt, *Ability*, London: Methuen, 1926, p. 2.
32. J. J. Findlay, *The Foundations of Education*, London: U. of London Press, 1925, I, 20–21.
33. Kandel, *History of Secondary Education*, p. 373.
34. See L. S. Hearnshaw, *A Short History of British Psychology, 1840–1940*, London: Methuen, 1964, p. 61.
35. Gregg, *Social and Economic History of Britain*, pp. 70–71.
36. J. S. Mill, *Autobiography*, p. 78.

Chapter 9

1. W. Stanley Jevons, *The State in Relation to Labour*, London: Macmillan, 1894, p. 14.
2. Ibid., p. 171.
3. See Sir William Beveridge, *Voluntary Action*, London: Allen & Unwin, 1948, p. 307 *n.*
4. Crane Brinton, *English Political Thought in the Nineteenth Century*, London: Ernest Benn, 1954, pp. 189–90.
5. Marshall stated, "The drift of economic science during many generations has been with increasing force towards the belief that there is no real necessity, and therefore no moral justification for extreme poverty side by side with great wealth. The inequalities of wealth though less than are often represented to be, are a serious flaw in our economic organization." (Alfred Marshall, *Principles of Economics*, 8th ed., New York: Macmillan, 1920, pp. 713–14.)
6. Henry Fawcett, *Pauperism: Its Causes and Remedies*, London: Macmillan, 1871, p. 155.
7. Herbert Spencer, *Social Statics*, New York: D. Appleton, 1897, p. 261.
8. Fawcett, *Pauperism*, pp. 6–7.
9. Marshall, *Principles of Economics*, p. 48.

10. Henry Sidgwick, *The Principles of Political Economy*, 3d ed., London: Macmillan, 1901, p. 23.
11. Marshall, *Principles of Economics*, p. 48.
12. Jevons, *State in Relation to Labour*, p. 8.
13. Marshall, *Principles of Economics*, pp. 41–42.
14. Jevons, *State in Relation to Labour*, p. 8.
15. John Stuart Mill, *On Liberty*, New York: Appleton-Century-Crofts, 1947, p. 9.
16. Henry Sidgwick, *The Elements of Politics*, 4th ed., London: Macmillan, 1919, pp. 36–37.
17. Ibid., p. 146.
18. Ibid., p. 161.
19. See A.J.M. Milne, *The Social Philosophy of English Idealism*, London: Allen & Unwin, 1962.
20. Thomas Hill Green, *Works*, ed. R. L. Nettleship, London: Longmans, Green, 1888, III, 373.
21. Richard Hofstadter, *Social Darwinism in American Thought*, Boston: Beacon Press, 1955, p. 100.
22. Marshall, *Principles of Economics*, p. 130.
23. Quoted in Brinton, *English Political Thought in the 19th Century*, p. 197.
24. G.D.H. Cole, *Socialist Thought, Marxism, and Anarchism: A History of Socialist Thought*, London: Macmillan, 1954, II, 388–89; M. Beer, *A History of British Socialism*, London: Allen & Unwin, 1940, Pt. 2, p. 259.
25. G. D. H. Cole, *The Second International: A History of Socialist Thought*, London: Macmillan, 1956, III, Pt. 1, 184.
26. Royal Commission on the Poor Laws, *Majority Report*, Cd. 4499, London: HMSO, 1909, pp. 49–50, 311, 318.
27. R. H. Tawney, *The Webbs in Perspective*, London: Athlone Press, 1953, p. 7.
28. Margaret Cole, *Beatrice Webb*, New York: Harcourt, Brace, 1946, p. 219.
29. S. E. Finer, *The Life and Times of Sir Edwin Chadwick*, London: Methuen, 1952, p. 3.
30. G.D.H. Cole points out that in their early period the Fabians were "apostles of efficiency more than of brotherly love." Only later (after 1909), under Beatrice Webb's influence, did the Fabians become "the leading proponents of the 'national minimum standard of civilized life.'" (*Socialist Thought*, III, Pt. 1, 203.)
31. Sidney and Beatrice Webb, *Industrial Democracy*, London: Longmans, Green, 1901, p. 774.
32. Ibid., p. 767.
33. Ibid., p. 771.
34. Ibid., pp. 774–75.
35. Sidney Webb, "Historic," in Bernard Shaw, et al., *Fabian Essays*, Jubilee ed., London: Allen & Unwin, 1948, pp. 53–55.
36. Bernard Shaw, "Preface to 1908 Reprint," in *Fabian Essays*, p. xxxviii; Sidney Webb, "Introduction to 1920 Reprint," in *Fabian Essays*, pp. xxiv ff.
37. Sidney Ball, "The Moral Aspects of Socialism," Fabian Tract No. 72, 1896; Sidney Webb, "The Difficulties of Individualism," Fabian Tract No. 69,

1896 (All Fabian tracts are published by The Fabian Society, London). Also Sidney Oliver, "Moral," in *Fabian Essays.*

38. Sidney and Beatrice Webb, *The Prevention of Destitution,* London: Longmans, Green, 1912, p. 2.
39. Ball, "Moral Aspects of Socialism," p. 19.
40. S. and B. Webb, *Prevention of Destitution,* Ch. 3.
41. Royal Commission on the Poor Laws, *Minority Report,* London: HMSO, 1909, p. 1172.
42. Ibid., p. 1175.
43. S. Webb, "Introduction to 1920 Reprint," in *Fabian Essays,* pp. xxii–xxiii, and "Historic," p. 32.
44. Una Cormack, *The Welfare State,* London: Family Welfare Assoc., 1953.
45. Beveridge, *Voluntary Action,* p. 307 *n.*
46. Ball, "Moral Aspects of Socialism," p. 19.
47. Beatrice Webb, *Our Partnership,* New York: Longmans, Green, 1948, p. 468.
48. William Temple, "The Christian Social Movement in the Nineteenth Century," in *Christian Social Reformers of the Nineteenth Century,* ed. Hugh Martin, 2d. ed., London: Torch Library, 1933, p. 12.
49. John Stuart Mill, *Principles of Political Economy,* London: Longmans, Green, 1909 p. 754.
50. Ibid. p. 754.
51. Ibid., p. 756.
52. J.A.R. Pimlott, *Toynbee Hall,* London: J. M. Dent, 1935, pp. 12–14.
53. Helen Bosanquet, *Social Work in London, 1869–1912,* New York: Dutton, 1914, pp. 22–23, 25; and C. S. Loch, *Charity Organisation,* 2d ed., London: S. Sonnenschein, 1892, p. 250.
54. Loch, *Charity Organisation,* p. 9.
55. Quoted in H. de B. Gibbins, *English Social Reformers,* London: Methuen, 1892, p. 223.
56. Ibid., p. 165.
57. Henrietta Barnett, *Canon Barnett,* London: John Murray, 1921, p. 638.
58. Henrietta Barnett, "Passionless Reformers," in *Practicable Socialism,* ed. Samuel and Henrietta Barnett, 2d ed. London: Longmans, Green, 1894, p. 89.
59. H. Barnett, *Canon Barnett,* p. 622.
60. Ibid., p. 575.
61. F. C. Montague, *Arnold Toynbee,* Baltimore: Johns Hopkins U. Press, 1889, pp. 18–19.
62. Helen Bosanquet, *The Strength of the People,* New York: Macmillan, 1902, p. 44.
63. Ibid, p. 18.
64. Loch, *Charity Organisation,* p. 11.
65. C. S. Loch, "Some Controverted Points in the Administration of Poor Relief," in *Aspects of the Social Problem,* ed. Bernard Bosanquet, London: Macmillan, 1895.
66. C. S. Loch, *Charity and Social Life,* London: Macmillan, 1910, p. 386.
67. H. Dendy, "The Industrial Residuum," in *Aspects of the Social Problem,* p. 83.

68. H. Bosanquet, *Social Work*, p. 102.
69. H. Bosanquet, *Strength of the People*, p. 39.
70. H. Barnett, "Passionless Reformers," in *Practicable Socialism*, p. 90.
71. S. Barnett, "University Settlements," in *Practicable Socialism*, p. 165.
72. Ibid., p. 166.
73. Loch, *Charity and Social Life*, p. 475.
74. Ibid., 475, n. 1.
75. H. Bosanquet, *Strength of the People*, p. 55.
76. J. A. Hobson, *John Ruskin, Social Reformer*, Boston: Dana Estes, 1898, pp. 174–75.
77. Loch, *Charity and Social Life*, pp. 368–69.
78. Ibid., pp. 366–69.
79. Ibid., p. 443.
80. Ibid., pp. 352–66.
81. Canon and Mrs. S. A. Barnett, *Towards Social Reform*, New York: Macmillan, 1909, p. 12.
82. Quoted in L. L. Price, *Political Economy in England*, 6th ed., London: Methuen, 1910, p. 196.
83. H. Barnett, "What Has the Charity Organisation Society To Do With Social Reform?" in *Practicable Socialism*, p. 214.
84. S. Barnett, "Town Councils and Social Reform," in *Practicable Socialism*, p. 102.
85. Ibid., p. 103.
86. Quoted in Beer, *British Socialism*, Pt. 3, p. 179.
87. Quoted in R. P. Anschutz, *The Philosophy of J. S. Mill*, Oxford: Clarendon Press, 1953, p. 40.
88. John Herman Randall, *The Making of the Modern Mind*, Boston: Houghton Mifflin, 1940, pp. 451–53.
89. Quoted in Hobson, *John Ruskin*, p. 202.
90. Quoted in Pimlott, *Toynbee Hall*, p. 42.
91. Loch, *Charity and Social Life*, pp. 370–71.
92. Ibid., p. 412.
93. B. Bosanquet, "The Duties of Citizenship," in *Aspects of the Social Problem*, p. 23.
94. H. Bosanquet, *Strength of the People*, p. 335.
95. Loch, *Charity and Social Life*, p. 371.
96. H. Bosanquet, *Social Work*, p. 53.
97. Loch, *Charity Organisation*, pp. 82–83.
98. Ibid., p. 84.
99. H. Barnett, *Canon Barnett*, p. 704.
100. Philip Lyttelton Gell, "The Work of Toynbee Hall," in *Arnold Toynbee*, p. 61.
101. Ibid., p. 59.
102. Ibid., p. 61.
103. Sir John Gorst, " 'Settlements' in England and America," in *The Universities and the Social Problem*, ed. John M. Knapp, London: Rivington, Percival, 1895, p. 9.
104. Ibid. p. 9.
105. H. Barnett, *Canon Barnett*, p. 658.

Chapter 10

1. Thomas Mackay, *A History of the English Poor Law*, New York: Putnam's, 1900, III, p. v.
2. Ibid., pp. 525 ff, 599–601.
3. Royal Commission on the Poor Laws, *Majority Report*, Cd. 4499, London: HMSO, 1909, pp. 219–32.
4. Ibid., p. 219.
5. Ibid., p. 221.
6. Ibid., p. 222.
7. Ibid., p. 52.
8. Ibid., p. 227.
9. Ibid.
10. Ibid., p. 228.
11. Ibid., pp. 15–22.
12. Ibid., pp. 16, 42–43.
13. Barbara Wootten, *Social Science and Social Pathology*, London: Allen & Unwin, 1959, p. 43. See also Samuel Mencher, "Newburgh: The Recurrent Crisis of Public Assistance," *Social Work*, VII (January 1963), 3–11.
14. *Majority Report*, p. 33.
15. Ibid., p. 43.
16. Ibid., p. 43.
17. Ibid., p. 161.
18. Ibid., p. 178.
19. Mackay, *English Poor Law*, III, 229.
20. *Majority Report*, p. 232.
21. Mackay, *English Poor Law*, III, 499 ff.
22. "The Abolition of Poor Law Guardians," Fabian Tract No. 126, 1906, p. 21.
23. Ibid., p. 22.
24. Alfred Marshall, *Official Papers*, London: Macmillan, 1926, p. 214.
25. Ibid., p. 211 ff.
26. Bernard Shaw, "Socialism for Millionaires," Fabian Tract No. 107, 1901, pp. 7–9.
27. John Burns, "The Unemployed," Fabian Tract No. 47, 1893, p. 7.
28. *Majority Report*, p. 165.
29. Ibid., p. 178; See Geoffrey Drage, *The Problem of the Aged Poor*, London: A. and C. Black, 1895, Pt. 2, Ch. 1, for an excellent summary of the variety of positions on state pensions.
30. Royal Commission on the Poor Laws, *Minority Report*, London: HMSO, 1909, p. 1224.
31. *Majority Report*, p. 420. The Webbs were wary of the emphasis given insurance. Except in extraordinary cases, the Webbs did not see insurance as performing a preventive welfare function—their major interest—and thought that the movement for insurance distracted from the goal of more fundamental reform. (Sidney and Beatrice Webb, *The Prevention of Destitution*, London: Longmans, Green, 1912, Ch. 7.)
32. Mackay, *English Poor Law*, III, 268, 461 ff.

33. Alfred Marshall, *Principles of Economics*, 8th ed., New York: Macmillan, 1920, pp. 335–36.
34. Sidney and Beatrice Webb, *Industrial Democracy*, London: Longmans, Green, 1901, p. 677.
35. Ibid., p. 767, n. 1.
36. Henrietta Barnett, "The Poverty of the Poor," in *Practicable Socialism*, ed. Samuel and Henrietta Barnett, 2d ed., London: Longmans, Green, 1894, p. 28.
37. A. Marshall, *Official Papers*, pp. 244–45.
38. Ibid., p. 202.
39. Sidney Webb, "Historic," in Bernard Shaw et al., *Fabian Essays*, Jubilee ed., London: Allen & Unwin, 1948, p. 51.
40. A. Marshall, *Official Papers*, p. 199.
41. Ibid., p. 216.
42. Burns, "The Unemployed," Fabian Tract No. 47, 1893, pp. 5–7.
43. S. and B. Webb, *Industrial Democracy*, p. 767, n. 1.
44. *Minority Report*, p. 1171.
45. Sidney Webb, "Introduction to 1920 Reprint," in *Fabian Essays*, p. xxii.
46. Sidney Ball, "The Moral Aspects of Socialism," Fabian Tract No. 72, 1896, pp. 5–6.
47. S. Webb, "Introduction to 1920 Reprint," in *Fabian Essays*, p. xxii.
48. G.D.H. Cole, *Socialist Thought, Marxism, and Anarchism: A History of Socialist Thought*, London: Macmillan, 1954, II, 406.
49. Annie Besant, "Industry under Socialism," in *Fabian Essays*, p. 144.
50. Burns, "The Unemployed," Fabian Tract No. 47, 1893, p. 18.
51. *Majority Report*, pp. 394–95.
52. Ibid., p. 664.
53. S. and B. Webb, *Industrial Democracy*, pp. 784–89.

Chapter 11

1. See Vernon L. Parrington, *Main Currents in American Thought*, New York: Harcourt, Brace, 1930, II, 61.
2. Alfred H. Conrad, "Income Growth and Structural Change," in *American Economic History*, ed. Seymour E. Harris, New York: McGraw-Hill, 1961, pp. 55–56.
3. Quoted in Louis Hacker, *The Shaping of the American Tradition*, New York: Columbia U. Press, 1947, II, 733.
4. Robert Hunter, *Poverty*, New York: Grosset & Dunlap, 1904, pp. 350–51.
5. Henry Steele Commager, *The American Mind*, New Haven: Yale U. Press, 1950, p. 54. Commager, speaking generally of the similarity of America and Britain, states: "But the inheritance was highly selective and the impact of environment uneven. Institutions—notably those of a political and judicial character—suffered only minor modifications, but the modification of social organization was so profound as to suggest a departure from the normal course of evolution, while the psychological modification was nothing less than revolutionary." (ibid., p. 4.)

6. Gunnar Myrdal, *The Political Element in the Development of Economic Theory,* Cambridge: Harvard U. Press, 1954, p. 148.
7. Quoted in Parrington, *Main Currents in American Thought,* ii, 154.
8. Ibid.
9. See Roy Lubove, *The Progressives and the Slums,* Pittsburgh: U. of Pittsburgh Press, 1962.

Chapter 12

1. Ralph B. Perry, *Characteristically American,* New York: Knopf, 1949, p. 45.
2. Ralph Waldo Emerson, *Emerson,* ed. Eduard C. Lindeman, New York: Penguin, 1947, p. 158.
3. Ibid., p. 60.
4. Walt Whitman, "Democratic Vistas," in *Democracy and the Gospel of Wealth,* ed. Gail Kennedy, Boston: D. C. Heath, 1949, p. 16.
5. Ibid., p. 18.
6. Gardner Murphy, *An Historical Introduction to Modern Psychology,* 2d ed., New York: Harcourt, Brace, 1930, pp. 282–83.
7. Quoted in Ida M. Tarbell, *The Nationalizing of Business,* New York: Macmillan, 1936, p. 114.
8. Quoted in Richard Hofstadter, *Social Darwinism in American Thought,* Boston: Beacon Press, 1955, p. 16.
9. Quoted in I. L. Kandel, *History of Secondary Education,* London: George C. Harrup, 1931, p. 441.
10. Quoted in ibid., p. 450.
11. Ibid., pp. 99–104.
12. Finley Peter Dunne, "The Carnegie Libraries," in *Democracy and the Gospel of Wealth,* p. 112.
13. Quoted in Hofstadter, *Social Darwinism,* p. 143.
14. See Murphy, *Modern Psychology,* Ch. 18.
15. Joseph Dorfman, *The Economic Mind in American Civilization,* New York: Viking, 1946, iii, 258; Vernon L. Parrington, *Main Currents in American Thought,* New York: Harcourt, Brace, 1930, iii, 104–05; Joseph A. Schumpeter, *History of Economic Analysis,* New York: Oxford U. Press, 1954, pp. 801–02.
16. Francis A. Walker, *The Wages Question,* New York: Henry Holt, 1891, pp. 158, 163; Dorfman, *Economic Mind in American Civilization,* iii, 101–10; Parrington, *Main Currents in American Thought,* iii, 111–17.
17. John Bates Clark, "The Society of the Future," in *Democracy and the Gospel of Wealth,* pp. 77–80; Paul T. Homan, *Contemporary Economic Thought,* New York: Harpers, 1928, pp. 21–31, 73–103; Dorfman, *Economic Mind in American Civilization,* iii, 188–205.
18. See William G. Sumner, *What Social Classes Owe to Each Other,* New York: Harpers, 1883; William G. Sumner, *Folkways,* Boston: Ginn, 1940.
19. Dorfman, *Economic Mind in American Civilization,* iii, 207.
20. Henry George, *Progress and Poverty,* New York: Robert Schalkenbach Foundation, 1956, pp. 454–56.

21. Edward Bellamy, *Looking Backward*, Boston: Houghton Mifflin, 1917.
22. James Bryce, *The American Commonwealth*, New York: Macmillan, 1924, p. 593.
23. Arthur M. Schlesinger, *The Rise of Modern America*, 4th ed., New York: Macmillan, 1951, p. 68.
24. Quoted in Parrington, *Main Currents in American Thought*, ii, 257.
25. Henry Demarest Lloyd, *Wealth Against Commonwealth*, New York: Harpers, 1894, p. 1.
26. Quoted in Dorfman, *Economic Mind in American Civilization*, iii, 335.
27. Emerson, *Emerson*, ed. Lindeman, p. 162.
28. "Friendly Visiting," in *Proceedings of the National Conference of Charities and Correction*, Buffalo, 1907, Boston: G. Ellis, 1907, pp. 308–09.
29. Whitman, "Democratic Vistas," in *Democracy and the Gospel of Wealth*, p. 21.
30. Commager, *American Mind*, p. 177.
31. *Jane Addams, A Centennial Reader*, New York: Macmillan, 1960, pp. 10–14.
32. Ibid., p. 202.
33. Jane Addams, "The Settlement as a Factor in the Labor Movement," *Hull House Maps and Papers*, Boston: Crowell, 1895, pp. 186–87.
34. Jane Addams, *The Second Twenty Years of Hull House*, New York: Macmillan, 1930, p. 288.
35. Emerson, *Emerson*, ed. Lindeman, p. 152.
36. Lester F. Ward, *Dynamic Sociology*, New York: Appleton, 1911.
37. Quoted in Hofstadter, *Social Darwinism*, p. 79.

Chapter 13

1. Joseph Dorfman, *The Economic Mind in American Civilization*, New York: Viking, 1946 ii, 637; Louis Hacker, *The Shaping of the American Tradition*, New York: Columbia U. Press, 1947, i, 336–37.
2. Dorfman, *Economic Mind in American Civilization*, ii, 661–71.
3. Selig Perlman and Philip Taft, *History of Labor in the United States*, iv, New York: Macmillan, 1935, 150.
4. Edward C. Kirkland, *A History of American Economic Life*, 3d. ed., New York: Appleton-Century-Crofts, 1951, pp. 501–05.
5. Robert H. Bremner, *From the Depths*, New York: New York U. Press, 1956, pp. 5 ff.
6. Quoted in Vernon L. Parrington, *Main Currents in American Thought*, New York: Harcourt, Brace, 1930, ii, 256.
7. Quoted in Frank D. Watson, *Charity Organization Movement in the United States*, New York: Macmillan, 1922, p. 85.
8. "One Means of Preventing Pauperism," in *Proceedings of the National Conference of Charities and Correction* [*NCCC*], Chicago, 1879, Boston: G. Ellis, 1879, p. 193.
9. Charles D. Kellogg, "Charity Organization in the United States," in *Proceedings, NCCC*, Chicago, 1893, p. 79.

10. Quoted in Bremner, *From the Depths,* p. 47.
11. Graham Taylor, "Organized Charity and Organized Labor," *Proceedings, NCCC,* Portland, Ore., 1905, pp. 458-62.
12. Mary Richmond, *The Long View,* New York: Russell Sage Foundation, 1930, p. 46.
13. *Jane Addams, A Centennial Reader,* New York: Macmillan, 1960, p. 21.
14. David M. Schneider and Albert Deutsch, *The History of Public Welfare in New York State,* Chicago: U. of Chicago Press, 1938, II, 202.
15. Philip S. Foner, *History of the Labor Movement in the United States,* New York: International Publishers, 1947, pp. 446–47.
16. Dorfman, *Economic Mind in American Civilization,* III, 43.
17. Quoted in Leah H. Feder, *Unemployment Relief in Periods of Depression,* New York: Russell Sage Foundation, 1936.
18. Don D. Lescohier and Elizabeth Brandeis, *History of Labor in the United States,* III, New York: Macmillan, 1935, 316–21.
19. Fred H. Wines, "Causes of Pauperism and Crime," in *Proceedings, NCCC,* St. Paul, 1886, pp. 207–14.
20. *The Heritage of American Social Work,* ed. Ralph E. and Muriel W. Pumphrey, New York: Columbia U. Press, 1961, pp. 244–51.
21. Ibid., p. 245.
22. *Proceedings, NCCC,* Boston, 1881, pp. 115–16.
23. Hal C. Wyman, "The Michigan Poor in Almshouses," in *Proceedings, NCCC,* San Francisco, 1889, p. 204.
24. R. E. and M. W. Pumphrey, ed., *The Heritage of American Social Work,* p. 246.
25. Amos G. Warner, Stuart A. Queen, and Ernest B. Harper, *American Charities and Social Work,* 4th ed., New York: T. Y. Crowell, 1930, pp. 53–55.
26. Dr. Luther, "Causes and Prevention of Pauperism," in *Proceedings, NCCC,* Cleveland, 1880, p. 242.
27. Edmond J. Butler, "Causes of Poverty," in *Proceedings, NCCC,* Atlanta, 1903, pp. 272–83.
28. W. H. McClain, "Relations Existing Between Defective Character and Dependence," in *Proceedings, NCCC,* Minneapolis, 1907, pp. 347–54.
29. Edward T. Devine, *The Principles of Relief,* New York: Macmillan, 1905, p. 151.
30. Quoted in Lescohier and Brandeis, *History of Labor in the U. S.* III, 129.
31. Quoted in ibid., III, 130.
32. Quoted in Feder, *Unemployment Relief,* p. 87.
33. Charles H. Cooley, "Nature versus Nurture in the Making of Social Careers," in *Proceedings, NCCC,* Grand Rapids, 1896, p. 404.
34. *Proceedings, NCCC,* Boston, 1911, p. 294.
35. See Bremner, *From the Depths,* pp. 124–33.

Chapter 14

1. David M. Schneider and Albert Deutsch, *The History of Public Welfare in New York State,* Chicago: U. of Chicago Press, 1938, II, pp. 107–10.

2. Leah H. Feder, *Unemployment Relief in Periods of Depression,* New York: Russell Sage Foundation, 1936, pp. 74–85.
3. "Indoor and Outdoor Relief," in *Proceedings of the National Conference of Charities and Correction,* [*NCCC*], Baltimore, 1890, Boston: G. Ellis, 1890, p. 77.
4. Schneider and Deutsch, *Public Welfare in New York State,* ii, 53–54.
5. Feder, *Unemployment Relief,* pp. 154–67.
6. Frederic Almy, "Public and Private Outdoor Relief," in *Proceedings, NCCC,* Topeka, 1900, p. 138.
7. Edward T. Devine, *The Principles of Relief,* New York: Macmillan, 1905, pp. 303–04.
8. Quoted in Frank D. Watson, *Charity Organization Movement in the United States,* New York: Macmillan, 1922, p. 325.
9. Mary E. Richmond, *Social Diagnosis,* New York: Russell Sage Foundation, 1917, p. 27.
10. Mary E. Richmond, *The Long View,* New York: Russell Sage Foundation, 1930, p. 151.
11. W. Alexander Johnson, "The Dangers Attending Almsgiving by Charity Organization Societies," in *Proceedings, NCCC,* St. Louis, 1884, p. 77.
12. Mrs. Charles Russell Lowell, "The Economic and Moral Effects of Public Outdoor Relief," in *Proceedings, NCCC,* Baltimore, 1890, p. 89.
13. Ibid., p. 91.
14. Richmond, *Social Diagnosis,* p. 32.
15. Rev. S. Humphreys Gurteen, *A Handbook of Charity Organization,* Buffalo: privately printed, 1882, pp. 30–32.
16. Charles D. Kellogg, "Report of the Committee on the Organization of Charities," in *Proceedings, NCCC,* Omaha, 1887, p. 130.
17. "The Problem of Pauperism in the Cities of Brooklyn and New York," in *Proceedings, NCCC,* Chicago, 1879, p. 201.
18. Richmond, *Social Diagnosis,* pp. 237–38.
19. Joseph Dorfman, *The Economic Mind in American Civilization,* New York: Viking, 1946, iii, 281.
20. Devine, *Principles of Relief,* Ch. 2; Leo A. Frankel, "The Uses of Material Relief," in *Proceedings, NCCC,* Atlanta, 1903, pp. 317–28.
21. Devine, *Principles of Relief,* Ch. 2.
22. Almy, "Adequate Relief," in *Proceedings, NCCC,* Boston, 1911, pp. 281–91.
23. *Proceedings, NCCC,* Boston, 1911, p. 295.
24. Thomas M. Mulry, "Private Relief Societies and Needy Families," in *Proceedings, NCCC,* Atlanta, 1903, p. 289.
25. "Social Settlements," in *Proceedings, NCCC,* Toronto, 1897, p. 345.
26. Ibid., p. 339.
27. Julia C. Lathrop. "The Cook County Charities," in Jane Addams, *Hull House Maps and Papers,* Boston: Crowell, 1895, p. 144.
28. James Bryce, *The American Commonwealth,* New York: Macmillan, 1924, p. 592.
29. *Proceedings, NCCC,* Cincinnati, 1878, p. 78.
30. *Proceedings, NCCC,* Chicago, 1879, p. 39.
31. "Outdoor Public Relief in Massachusetts," in *Proceedings, NCCC,* New Haven, 1895, p. 62.

32. Amos G. Warner, Stuart A. Queen, and Ernest B. Harper, *American Charities and Social Work,* 3d ed., New York: T. Y. Crowell, 1908, pp. 374–76.
33. Quoted in Feder, *Unemployment Relief,* p. 132.
34. Quoted in *The Heritage of American Social Work,* ed. Ralph E. and Muriel W. Pumphrey, New York: Columbia U. Press, 1961, pp. 145–46.
35. Feder, *Unemployment Relief* pp. 132–33.
36. "Report of the Committee on State Supervision and Administration," in *Proceedings, NCCC,* Portland, Ore., 1905, p. 420.
37. See "diagram of forces with which the social worker may cooperate," Watson, *Charity Organization Movement in the U. S.,* p. 137.
38. Richmond, *Long View,* p. 135.
39. Watson, *Charity Organization Movement in the U. S.,* p. 200.
40. Richmond, *Long View,* p. 134.
41. Quoted in R. E. and M. W. Pumphrey, ed., *Heritage of American Social Work,* p. 177.
42. Alfred O. Crozier, "Organized and Unorganized Charity," in *Proceedings, NCCC,* Toronto, 1897, p. 162.
43. A. W. McDougall, "The Relief of Needy Families," in *Proceedings, NCCC,* Detroit, 1902, p. 287.
44. David I. Green, "Treatment of Needy Families in Their Homes by Public Agencies," in *Proceedings, NCCC,* Atlanta, 1903, p. 293.
45. Richmond, *Long View,* p. 41.
46. *Proceedings, NCCC,* Detroit, 1902, p. 296.
47. "Charity Organization in the U. S.," in *Proceedings, NCCC,* Chicago, 1893, p. 84.
48. "The Use of Volunteers by Public Aid Officials," in *Proceedings, NCCC,* Portland, Me., 1904, p. 120.
49. See Watson, *Charity Organization Movement in the U. S.,* pp. 103, 275, 336.
50. Devine, *Principles of Relief,* pp. 310–13.
51. *Proceedings, NCCC,* Indianapolis, 1891, p. 35.
52. Isaac P. Wright, "The Recipients of Outdoor Relief," in *Proceedings, NCCC,* Baltimore, 1890, p. 93.
53. Lowell, "The Economic and Moral Effects of Public Outdoor Relief," p. 85.
54. *Proceedings, NCCC,* Cincinnati, 1899, pp. 116–17.
55. Don D. Lescohier and Elizabeth Brandeis, *History of Labor in the United States,* New York: Macmillan, 1935, iii, 164; Feder, *Unemployment Relief,* p. 172.
56. Quoted in Feder, *Unemployment Relief,* p. 69.
57. Philip W. Ayres, "Is Emergency Relief by Work Wise?" in *Proceedings, NCCC,* New Haven, 1895, p. 100.
58. *Jane Addams, A Centennial Reader,* New York: Macmillan, 1960, p. 28.
59. Quoted in Lescohier and Brandeis, *History of Labor in the U. S.,* iii, 169.
60. Ayres, "Is Emergency Relief by Work Wise?" p. 100.
61. Warner, Queen, and Harper, *American Charities,* p. 262.
62. See Robert H. Bremner, *From the Depths,* New York: New York U. Press, 1956, Ch. 8.
63. Quoted in Schneider and Deutsch, *Public Welfare in New York State,* ii, 204–05.

64. *Proceedings, NCCC,* Cleveland, 1912, p. 91.
65. Devine, *Principles of Relief,* pp. 334–36.
66. Schneider and Deutsch, *Public Welfare in New York State,* II, 204–05.
67. Lescohier and Brandeis, *History of Labor in the U. S.,* III, 129.
68. Quoted in Schneider and Deutsch, *Public Welfare in New York State,* II, 39–40.
69. Lescohier and Brandeis, *History of Labor in the U. S.,* III, 170.
70. Ibid., pp. 171–72.
71. Ibid., pp. 117–21.
72. Ibid., p. 671.
73. "Minimum Wage Boards," in *Proceedings, NCCC,* Cleveland, 1912, pp. 395–96.
74. Ibid., p. 403.
75. See *Proceedings, NCCC,* Cleveland, 1912, pp. 468–98.
76. Frederick L. Hoffman, "The Problem of Poverty and Pensions in Old Age," *Proceedings, NCCC,* Richmond, 1908, pp. 219–34.
77. Bremner, *From the Depths,* p. 250.
78. Quoted in R. E. and M. W. Pumphrey, eds., *Heritage of American Social Work,* p. 334.
79. Jane Addams, "Child Labor and Pauperism," in *Proceedings, NCCC,* Atlanta, 1903, pp. 114–21.
80. Quoted in Grace Abbott, *The Child and The State,* Chicago: U. of Chicago Press, 1938, II, 232.
81. *Proceedings, NCCC,* Cleveland, 1912, p. 492.
82. Lescohier and Brandeis, *History of Labor in the U. S.,* III, 356.
83. Warner, Queen, and Harper, *American Charities,* p. 350.
84. Lescohier and Brandeis, *History of Labor in the U. S.,* III, 386–87.
85. Ibid., pp. 259–62.
86. See E. A. Vanderlip, "Insurance from the Employers' Standpoint," *Proceedings, NCCC,* Philadelphia, 1906, pp. 462–63.
87. Louis D. Brandeis, "Workingmen's Insurance—The Road to Social Efficiency," in *Proceedings, NCCC,* Boston, 1911, pp. 157–58.
88. Frederick L. Hoffman, "American Problems in Social Insurance," in *Proceedings, NCCC,* Memphis, 1914, pp. 349–50.
89. Arthur M. Schlesinger, *The Rise of Modern America,* 4th ed., New York: Macmillan, 1951, pp. 79–80, 154–55.

PART III

Chapter 15

1. See Alfred H. Conrad, "Income Growth and Structural Change," in *American Economic History,* ed. Seymour E. Harris, New York: McGraw-Hill, 1961, p. 58; Karl Polanyi, *The Great Transformation,* Boston: Beacon Press, 1944, pp. 200–58.
2. See Richard M. Titmuss, "War and Social Policy," in *Essays on 'The Welfare State,'* 1st ed., New Haven: Yale U. Press, 1959, pp. 75–87; also *Problems of Social Policy,* London: HMSO, 1950.

3. Titmuss, *Problems of Social Policy*, p. 506.
4. Alfred M. Skolnik, "Growth of Employee-Benefit Plans, 1945–1961," *Social Security Bull.* xxvi, 4 (April 1963) 4–6; Bureau of Labor Statistics, *Labor Mobility and Private Pension Plans*, Bull. No. 1407, Washington, D. C.: USGPO (June 1964), pp. 4–7.
5. Bureau of Labor Statistics, *Health, Insurance, and Pension Plans in Union Contracts*, Bull. No. 1187, Washington, D. C.: USGPO, (October 1955), p. 4; Skolnik, "Growth of Employee-Benefit Plans."
6. J. Wiseman, "Occupational Pension Schemes," in *Fringe Benefits, Labour Costs, and Social Security*, ed. G. L. Reid and D. J. Robertson, London: Allen & Unwin, 1965, pp. 170, 184; A. E. Homans, "Fringe Benefits in the United States," in *Fringe Benefits, Labour Costs, and Social Security*, p. 143; see also Richard M. Titmuss, *Income Distribution and Social Change*, London: Allen & Unwin, 1962, pp. 155, 150; G.D.H. Cole, *The Post-War Condition of Britain*, New York: Praeger, 1957, p. 316; Brian Abel-Smith and Peter Townsend, *New Pensions for Old*, London. Fabian Publications, 1955.
7. International Labour Office, *The Cost of Social Security, 1949–1957*, Geneva: International Labour Office, 1961, p. 209. While these figures represent rough comparisons at best, there has been a consistent difference of between two and three times greater proportion of national income spent by the United Kingdom from 1950.
8. United Nations, *Demographic Yearbook 1963*, New York, 1964, pp. 190, 220; Bureau of the Census, *Historical Statistics of the United States, Colonial Times to 1957*, Washington, D. C.: USGPO, 1960, p. 10; Central Statistical Office, *Annual Abstract of Statistics*, No. 90, London: HMSO, 1953, p. 8; Political and Economic Planning, *Growth in the British Economy*, London: Allen & Unwin, 1960, p. 35. The data above are not completely in harmony because of differences in census periods. The 1963 comparisons cover data of 1963 for the United States and 1962 for the United Kingdom. The 1940 comparisons cover data for 1940 for the United States and 1939 for the United Kingdom.
9. National Economic Development Council, *Growth of the United Kingdom Economy 1961–1966*, London: HMSO, 1963, pp. 22–26; PEP, *Growth in the British Economy*, p. 36.
10. PEP, *Growth in the British Economy*, p. 31.
11. Ibid., p. 31.
12. Joint Economic Committee, *Report on the 1963 Economic Report of the President*, 88th Congress, 1st sess., Report No. 78, Washington, D. C.: USGPO, 1963, pp. 1–2.
13. See ibid., and National Economic Development Council, *Growth of the United Kingdom Economy 1961–1966,*; see also *Economic Report of the President*, January 1963, and *Economic Report of the President*, January 1964, Washington, D. C.: USGPO.
14. U. S. Bureau of the Census, *Historical Statistics of the United States, Colonial Times to 1957*, p. 73; Health, Education, and Welfare *Indicators*, Washington, D. C.: USGPO (January 1965), p. 20.
15. G.D.N. Worswick, "The British Economy 1950–1959," in *The British Econ-*

omy in the Nineteen-Fifties, ed. G.D.N. Worswick and P. H. Ady, Oxford: Clarendon Press, 1962, pp. 22–24.

16. William Beveridge, *Social Insurance and Allied Services*, New York: Macmillan, 1942, par. 441, p. 164; William Beveridge, *Full Employment in a Free Society*, New York: Norton, 1945, p. 21.
17. Ibid., p. 21; U. S. Bureau of the Census, *Historical Statistics of the U. S.*, p. 73.
18. U. S. Congress, Committee on Long-Range Work and Relief Policies, *Security, Work, and Relief Policies*, 78th Congress, 1st sess., House Document No. 128, Pt. 3, Washington, D. C.: USGPO, 1943, p. 7.
19. U. S. Bureau of the Census, *Historical Statistics of the U. S.*, p. 139.
20. Sidney Pollard, *The Development of the British Economy 1914–1950*, London: Edward Arnold, 1962, p. 290.
21. Ibid., pp. 290–96.
22. U. S. Bureau of the Census, *Historical Statistics of the U. S.*, p. 14.
23. Ibid., p. 74.
24. Central Statistical Office, *Annual Abstract of Statistics*, No 90, 1953, London: HMSO, 1953, p. 15.
25. Ibid., p. 13.
26. U. S. Bureau of the Census, *Historical Statistics of the U. S.*, p. 74.
27. Central Statistical Office, *Annual Abstract of Statistics*, No. 90, 1953, p. 15.
28. See Cole, *Post-War Condition of Britain*, pp. 25–44.

Chapter 16

1. For a trenchant discussion of the issues here, see Isaiah Berlin, *Two Concepts of Liberty*, London: Oxford U. Press, 1958, particularly pp. 16–19.
2. Harold Macmillan, *The Middle Way*, London: Macmillan, 1938, p. 26.
3. T. E. Utley, *Essays in Conservatism*, London: Conservative Political Centre, 1949, pp. 11–12.
4. Elliott Dodds, "Liberty and Welfare," in *The Unservile State*, ed. George Watson, New York: Macmillan, 1957, p. 16.
5. Walter Lippmann, *The Good Society*, New York: Grosset & Dunlap, 1943.
6. Ibid., pp. 184–92.
7. Talcott Parsons et al., eds., *Theories of Society*, New York: Free Press, 1961, I, 37.
8. For an interesting discussion of the influence of different norms on consumer behavior according to Keynesian theory, see Harry G. Johnson; "The Macro-Economics of Income Redistribution," in *Income Redistribution and Social Policy*, ed. Alan T. Peacock, London: Jonathan Cape, 1954, pp. 19–40.
9. Lawrence K. Frank, *Society as the Patient*, New Brunswick: Rutgers U. Press, 1949, pp. 7–9.
10. John Herman Randall, *The Making of the Modern Mind*, rev. ed., Cambridge, Mass.: Riverside Press, 1946, pp. 517–18.
11. U. S. Supreme Court in Cudahy Packing v. Parramore, 44 Sup. Ct., 153 (1924).
12. Ernst Freund, *Standards of American Legislation*, Chicago: U. of Chicago Press, 1917.
13. I. M. Rubinow states in regard to workman's compensation: "And thus far

a measure of social welfare—call it social insurance if you will—must differ from ordinary insurance which remains a purely business transaction. Compensation obviously fails in its primary social purpose unless it enables the sufferer and his dependents to tide over the period of disability without physical or moral deterioration, without undue suffering and without appeal to public or private charity." *(The Quest for Security,* New York: Henry Holt, 1934, p. 100).

14. Adolf A. Berle. *The American Economic Republic.* New York: Harcourt, Brace, & World, 1963, p. 35.

15. John Kenneth Galbraith, *The Affluent Society,* New York: Mentor, 1958, p. 257.

16. Ibid., p. 198.

17. Ray L. Wilbur and Arthur M. Hyde, *The Hoover Policies,* New York: Scribner's, 1937, pp. 6–8. For a general discussion of the adherence to laissez-faire, see Lippmann, *The Good Society,* pp. 183–202.

18. "Factors That Contribute to Insecurity of Workers," *The Annals of the American Academy of Political and Social Science,* CLIV, March 1931, 57; also 89–91 and 73–77.

19. Quoted in Rubinow, *The Quest for Security,* p. 541.

20. Robert Moats Miller, *American Protestantism and Social Issues.* Chapel Hill: U. of North Carolina Press, 1958, pp. 17–30.

21. Joseph Dorfman, *The Economic Mind in American Civilization,* New York: Viking, 1949, v, 492–515.

22. See Joan Robinson, *Economic Philosophy,* Chicago: Aldine, 1963, Ch. 4; W. T. Foster and W. Catchings, *The Road to Plenty,* Houghton: Pollak Foundation, 1928.

23. J. M. Clark, *Economic Reconstruction,* Report of the Columbia U. Commission, New York: Columbia U. Press, 1934, pp. 122–23.

24. Berle, *American Economic Republic,* pp. 78–81.

25. Adolf A. Berle and Gardiner C. Means, *The Modern Corporation and Private Property,* New York: Macmillan, 1933.

26. Berle, *American Economic Republic,* p. 84.

27. Lippmann, *Good Society,* p. 182.

28. Roscoe Pound, *An Introduction to the Philosophy of Law,* New Haven: Yale U. Press, 1922, p. 99.

29. Mary P. Follett, *The New State,* New York: Longmans, Green, 1918.

30. Dodds, "Liberty and Welfare," in *Unservile State* p. 17.

31. Macmillan, *Middle Way,* p. 27.

32. F. D. Roosevelt, Message to Congress, June 8, 1934, 73rd Congress, 2d. sess., Washington, D. C.: USGPO, 1934, p. 10,770.

33. Ibid.

34. For a thorough discussion of this position, see A. Delafield Smith, *The Right to Life,* Chapel Hill: U. of North Carolina Press, 1955, Chs. 2 and 3.

35. J. M. Clark, *Economic Institutions and Human Welfare,* 1st ed., New York: Knopf, 1957, p. 68.

36. Alan T. Peacock, "Welfare in the Liberal State," in *Unservile State,* p. 130.

37. Edward Hallett Carr, *The New Society,* Boston: Beacon Press, 1957, p. 58.

38. Ibid., p. 59.

39. Ibid., p. 67.
40. Milton Friedman, *Capitalism and Freedom,* Chicago: U. of Chicago Press, 1962, pp. 85-107, 182-89.
41. Arthur Seldon, *Pensions for Prosperity,* London: Institute of Economic Affairs, 1960, pp. 7-8.
42. See Charles Cooraw, "Forward from Beveridge," *Crossbow,* IV, 15 (Autumn 1960), 25-26; Authur Seldon, "Pensions and Prosperity," *Crossbow,* III, 11 (Spring 1960), 38; Daniel Lees, "A Social Security System for Today," *Crossbow,* VI, 23 (April-June 1963), 21-28; Jack Wiseman, "The Political Economy of Social Services," *The Listener* (October 7, 1965), 515-17; John MacGregor, "A New Strategy for Social Security," *Crossbow,* VII, 28 (July-September 1964), 29-33.
43. *Putting Britain Right Ahead,* London: Conservative and Unionist Central Office, October 1965.
44. Brian Abel-Smith and Peter Townsend, *The Poor and the Poorest,* London: G. Bell, 1965; Dorothy Cole Wedderburn, "Poverty in Britain Today—The Evidence," *Sociological Rev.,* X, n.s. (November 1962), 257-82; Richard M. Titmuss, "The Irresponsible Society," in *Essays on 'The Welfare State',* 2d ed., London: Allen & Unwin, 1963, pp. 241-43; also Seldon, *Pensions and Prosperity,* pp. 38-40.
45. Tony Lynes, "Pension Rights and Wrongs," Fabian Tract No. 348, September 1963.
46. Philip Ashworth, "Can the Tories Afford to Relinquish Planning?" *Crossbow,* IX, 34 (January-March 1966), 26-29; Titmuss, "The Irresponsible Society," in *Essays on 'The Welfare State,'* 2d ed., pp. 231-40.
47. Ralph Harris and Arthur Seldon, *Choice in Welfare, 1965,* London: Institute of Economic Affairs, 1965.
48. Joan Barnes, "Paying for Welfare," *Crossbow* IV, 15 (Spring 1961), 23-2
49. Ashworth, "Can the Tories Afford to Relinquish Planning?"
50. Titmuss, "The Irresponsible Society," in *Essays on 'The Welfare State,'* 2d ed., p. 229.
51. Richard M. Titmuss, "The Role of Redistribution in Social Policy," *Social Security Bull.,* XXVIII, 6 (June 1965), 20.
52. *New Frontiers for Social Security,* London: The Labour Party, 1963, pp. 18-19.
53. Titmuss, *Essays on 'The Welfare State,'* 2d ed., pp. 23-28.
54. François Lafitte, *Social Policy in a Free Society,* Birmingham, England: U. of Birmingham, 1962, p. 14.
55. Brian Abel-Smith, "Freedom in the Welfare State," Fabian Tract No. 353, March 1964, p. 15.
56. See R.H.S. Crossman, *Planning for Freedom,* London: Hamish Hamilton, 1965.
57. See Karl Polanyi, *The Great Transformation,* Boston: Beacon Press, 1944.
58. Dorfman, *Economic Mind in American Civilization,* III, 352 ff.
59. Aaron I. Abell, *American Catholicism and Social Action,* New York: Doubleday, 1960, pp. 189-263.
60. John A. Ryan, *A Better Economic Order,* New York: Harper, 1935, pp. 148-90.

61. Paul A. Carter, *The Decline and Revival of the Social Gospel*, Ithaca: Cornell U. Press, 1956, pp. 175–78; Charles C. Morrison, *The Social Gospel and the Christian Cultus*, New York: Harper, 1933, pp. 15–19; Miller, *American Protestantism and Social Issues*, pp. 63–112.
62. Reinhold Niebuhr, *Moral Man and Immoral Society*, New York: Scribner's, 1932.
63. Utley, *Conservatism*, pp. 28–30.
64. Abell, *American Catholicism and Social Action*, p. 263.
65. Dorfman, *Economic Mind in American Civilization*, v, 634.
66. See Broadus Mitchell, *Depression Decade*, New York: Rinehart, 1947, pp. 228–58.
67. A. J. Youngson, *The British Economy, 1920–1957*, Cambridge: Harvard U. Press, 1960, pp. 219–29.
68. For a discussion and criticism of cultural lag, see R. M. MacIver, *Society*, New York: Farrar and Rinehart, 1937, pp. 438–73.
69. A. C. Pigou, *The Economics of Welfare*, London: Macmillan, 1920, pp. 112–13.
70. Macmillan, *Middle Way*, p. 43.
71. David C. Marsh, *The Future of the Welfare State*, London: Penguin, 1964, pp. 29–30.
72. Geoffrey Howe, "Can Conservatives Plan?" *Crossbow* iv, 16 (Summer 1961), 19–24.
73. Simon N. Patten, *The Theory of Prosperity*, New York: Macmillan, 1902.
74. John Dewey, *Human Nature and Conduct*, New York: Henry Holt, 1922; John Dewey, *The Public and Its Problems*, New York: Henry Holt, 1927; John Dewey, *Individualism Old and New*, New York: Minton, Balch, 1930; John Dewey, *Liberalism and Social Action*, New York: Putnam's, 1935.
75. Charles A. Beard, *Whither Mankind*, New York: Longmans, Green, 1928; Charles A. Beard, *Toward Civilization*, New York: Longmans, Green, 1930.
76. Rexford G. Tugwell, *Industry's Coming of Age*, New York: Harcourt Brace, 1927; Rexford G. Tugwell, *The Industrial Discipline and the Governmental Arts*, New York: Columbia U. Press, 1933.
77. George Henry Soule, *A Planned Society*, New York: Macmillan, 1932.
78. James Tobin, "How Planned Is Our Economy," *The New York Times Magazine*, October 13, 1963, pp. 18 ff.; J.C.R. Dow, *The Management of the British Economy*, Cambridge: Cambridge U. Press, 1964, pp. 11–12; George A. Steiner, *Government's Role in Economic Life*, New York: McGraw-Hill, 1953, pp. 17–18.
79. G. D. N. Worswick, "The British Economy," in *The British Economy in the Nineteen-Fifties*, ed. G.D.N. Worswick and P. H. Ady, Oxford: Clarendon Press, 1962 pp. 73–74; Youngson, *The British Economy, 1920–1957*, pp. 264–65.
80. Gunnar Myrdal, *Beyond the Welfare State*, New Haven: Yale U. Press, 1960, pp. 9–13.

Chapter 17

1. Royal Commission on the Poor Laws, *Minority Report*, London: HMSO, 1909, pp. 1195–98.

2. Leo Wolman, "Stabilization or Insurance," in *Essentials for Prosperity*, CLXV of *The Annals of the American Academy of Political and Social Science*, January 1933, p. 22.
3. Ray L. Wilbur and Arthur M. Hyde, *The Hoover Policies*, New York: Scribner's 1937, pp. 49–50.
4. *United States Statutes at Large*, Public Law 304, 79th Congress, 2d sess., sec. 4, LX, Pt. I, Washington, D. C.: USGPO, 1947.
5. See Letter of Transmittal, *Economic Report of the President*, Washington, D. C.: USGPO, January 1954.
6. See J.C.R. Dow, *The Management of the British Economy*, Cambridge: Cambridge U. Press, 1964.
7. Wolman, "Stabilization or Insurance," pp. 22–23; The Rockefeller Panel Reports, *Prospect for America*, New York: Doubleday, 1961, p. 310.
8. A. C. Pigou, *The Economics of Welfare*, London: Macmillan, 1920, pp. 67–68.
9. Abraham Epstein, *Insecurity, A Challenge to America*, rev. ed., New York: Random House, 1936, p. 197.
10. J. M. Keynes, *The General Theory of Employment Interest and Money*, London: Macmillan, 1936, p. 28.
11. See U. S. Bureau of the Census, *Historical Statistics of the United States, Colonial Times to 1957*, Washington, D. C.: USGPO, 1960, pp. 67–69; William Beveridge, *Full Employment in a Free Society*, New York: Norton, 1945, pp. 328–37; John H. G. Pierson, *Insuring Full Employment*, New York: Viking, 1964, pp. 267–68; U. S. Senate, Special Committee on Unemployment Problems, 86th Congress, 2d sess., *Studies in Unemployment*, Washington, D. C.: USGPO, 1960, pp. 17–36.
12. Ibid., pp. 303–488.
13. See Emile Benoit-Smullyan, "On the Meaning of Full Employment," *Rev. of Economics and Statistics*, xxx (1948), 127–34.
14. Beveridge, *Full Employment*, p. 21.
15. Benoit-Smullyan, "On the Meaning of Full Employment," p. 131.
16. Beveridge, *Full Employment* p. 21; Pierson, *Insuring Full Employment*, p. 108.
17. John Kenneth Galbraith, *The Affluent Society*, New York: Mentor, 1958, p. 289.
18. See Edward E. Schwartz, "A Way to End the Means Test," *Social Work*, IX, 3 (July 1964), 3–11, 97.
19. Pierson, *Insuring Full Employment*, pp. 115–16.
20. National Economic Development Council, *Growth of the United Kingdom Economy, 1961–1965*, pp. 19–25.
21. *Economic Report of the President*, Washington, D. C.: USGPO, January 1963, p. xxviii.
22. See Maurice Bruce, *The Coming of the Welfare State*, London: B. T. Batsford, 1961, pp. 232–34.
23. *Men Without Work* (A Report made to the Pilgrim Trust), Cambridge: Cambridge U. Press, 1938.
24. E. Wight Bakke, *Citizens Without Work*, New Haven: Yale U. Press, 1940; also, *The Unemployed Man*, New York: Dutton, 1934; Mirra Komarovsky,

The Unemployed Man and His Family, New York: Institute of Social Research, 1940; Eli Ginzberg, *The Unemployed,* New York: Harper, 1943.

25. U. S. Congress, Committee on Long-Range Work and Relief Policies, *Security, Work, and Relief Policies,* p. 491.

26. Quoted in Pierson, *Insuring Full Employment,* p. 151.

27. Gunnar Myrdal, *Challenge to Affluence,* New York: Pantheon, 1962, pp. 40–41; Margaret Mead, "The Pattern of Leisure in Contemporary Culture," in *Recreation in the Age of Automation,* cccxiii of *The Annals of the American Academy of Political and Social Science,* September 1957.

28. Hallowell Pope, "Economic Deprivation and Social Participation in a Group of 'Middle Class' Factory Workers," *Social Problems,* xi, 3, (Winter 1964), 290–300.

29. See Ely Chinoy, *Automobile Workers and the American Dream,* New York: Doubleday, 1955; Herbert H. Hyman, "The Value Systems of Different Classes," in *Social Perspectives on Behavior,* ed. Herman D. Stein and Richard A. Cloward, Glencoe: Free Press, 1958, pp. 315–30.

30. Beveridge, *Full Employment in a Free Society,* p. 20.

31. See J. A. Hobson, *Work and Wealth,* London: Allen & Unwin, 1933.

32. Nancy C. Morse, and R. S. Weiss, "The Function and Meaning of Work and the Job," in *Man, Work, and Society,* ed., Sigmund Nosow and William H. Form, New York: Basic Books, 1962, pp. 29–35; E. A. Friedmann, and R. J. Havighurst, "Work and Retirement," in *Man, Work, and Society,* pp. 41–45.

33. Galbraith, *Affluent Society,* p. 259–69.

34. William Beveridge, *Social Insurance and Allied Services,* New York: Macmillan, 1942, par. 440, p. 163.

35. See Joseph A. Schumpeter, *History of Economic Analysis,* New York: Oxford U. Press, 1954, pp. 1057–59.

36. Thorstein Veblen, *The Theory of the Leisure Class,* New York: Modern Library, 1934; Ruth Benedict, *Patterns of Culture,* Boston: Houghton Mifflin, 1961.

37. Galbraith, *Affluent Society,* pp. 101–23.

38. Leon H. Keyserling, *Progress or Poverty,* Washington, D. C.: Conference on Economic Progress, 1964.

39. *Economic Report of the President,* Washington, D. C.: USGPO, January 1964, p. 3.

40. Ibid., p. 17.

41. G.D.N. Worswick, "The British Economy 1950–1959," in *The British Economy in the Nineteen-Fifties,* ed. G.D.N. Worswick and P. H. Ady, Oxford: Clarendon Press, 1962, pp. 22–24.

42. *Growth of the United Kingdom Economy to 1966,* p. viii. (1963)

43. *The Growth of the Economy,* London: HMSO, March 1964, par. 14.

44. Galbraith, *Affluent Society,* p. 99.

45. Keyserling, *Progress or Poverty,* p. 90.

46. Economic Report of the President, Washington, D. C.: USGPO, January 1964, p. 15.

47. Beveridge, *Social Insurance and Allied Services,* par. 449, p. 167; Keyserling, *Progress or Poverty,* p. 89.

48. Julius Gould, "Full Employment—A Discussion of Some Recent Literature," *British Journal of Sociology*, III (1952), 178–82.
49. Quoted in Wilbur and Hyde, *Hoover Policies*, p. 2.
50. Sidney and Beatrice Webb, *The Prevention of Destitution*, London: Longmans, Green, 1912, p. 297.
51. "Economic Opportunity Act of 1964," Health, Education, and Welfare *Indicators*, Washington, D. C.: USGPO, September 1964, p. vii.
52. Quoted in Robert E. Sherwood, *Roosevelt and Hopkins*, New York: Harper, 1948, p. 84.
53. See, for example, Conference on Economic Progress, *Poverty and Deprivation in the United States*, Washington, D. C.: USGPO, 1962; Michael Harrington, *The Other America: Poverty in the United States*, New York: Macmillan, 1962; Herman P. Miller, "New Definition of Our 'Poor,'" *The New York Times Magazine* (April 21, 1963), pp. 11 ff.; James N. Morgan, et al., *Income and Welfare in the United States*, New York: McGraw-Hill, 1962.
54. There is an extensive literature; see Herman P. Miller, *Rich Man, Poor Man*, New York: T. Y. Crowell, 1964; Mollie Orshansky, "Counting the Poor: Another Look at the Poverty Profile," *Social Security Bull.*, XXVIII, 1, (January 1965), p. 3; Conference on Economic Progress, *Poverty and Deprivation*.
55. Frank Riessman, *The Culturally Deprived Child*, 1st ed., New York: Harper, 1962; Albert K. Cohen, *Delinquent Boys*, Glencoe: Free Press, 1955.
56. Morgan, et al., *Income and Welfare* pp. 348–424.
57. J. B. Lansing, T. Lorimer, and C. Moriguchi, *How People Pay for College*, Ann Arbor: U. of Michigan Press, 1960.
58. Robert E. Iffert, "Retention and Withdrawal of College Students," *Office of Education Bull.*, No. 1, Washington, D. C.: 1958.
59. August B. Hollingshead, *Elmtown's Youth*, New York: Science Editions, 1961.
60. Patricia Cayo Sexton, *Education and Income*, New York: Viking, 1961.
61. Kenneth Eells, et al., *Intelligence and Cultural Differences*, Chicago: U. of Chicago Press, 1951.
62. Alvin L. Schorr, *Slums and Social Insecurity*, Washington, D. C.: USGPO, pp. 98–99; U. S. Department of Agriculture, *Dietary Levels of Households in the United States*, Household Food Consumption Survey, 1955, Report No. 6, Washington, D. C.: USGPO, 1957.
63. Leo Srole, et. al., *Mental Health in the Metropolis*, New York: McGraw-Hill, 1962, I, Ch. 12.
64. U. S. Public Health Service, *Children and Youth: Selected Health Characteristics, United States, July 1957-June 1958*, Health Statistics from the U. S. National Health Survey, No. C-1, Washington, D. C., October 1959, pp. 35, 42.
65. Brian Abel-Smith and R. M. Titmuss, *The Cost of the National Health Service*, Cambridge: Cambridge U. Press, 1956, pp. 148–52.
66. See Richard M. Titmuss, "The Irresponsible Society," *The Listener*, August 11, 1960, pp. 207–09.
67. Pigou, *Economics of Welfare*, pp. 101–06.
68. Epstein, *Insecurity*, p. 18.

69. See Galbraith, *Affluent Society*, pp. 252 ff.
70. Keynes, *Employment, Interest, and Money*, p. 16.
71. I. M. Rubinow, *The Quest for Security*, New York: Henry Holt, 1934, p. 314.
72. Keyserling, *Progress or Poverty*, p. 89.
73. See Myrdal, *Challenge to Affluence*, particularly Ch. 2.
74. J. M. Clark, *Economic Institutions and Human Welfare*, New York: Knopf, 1957, p. 63.
75. Karl Mannheim, *Man and Society in an Age of Reconstruction*, London: Kegan Paul, Trench, Trubner, 1946, p. 322.
76. Roy Lubove, *The Professional Altruist*, Cambridge: Harvard U. Press, 1965, Ch. 2.
77. Clark, *Economic Institutions and Human Welfare*, pp. 65–66.
78. Edwin E. Witte, "The Development of the Social Security Act," in *Social Security Perspectives*, ed. Robert J. Lampman, Madison: U. of Wisconsin Press, 1962, p. 61.
79. Ibid., p. 62.
80. U. S. Congress, Committee on Long-Range Work and Relief Policies, *Security, Work and Relief Policies*, p. 449.
81. B. Seebohm Rowntree, *Poverty and Progress*, London: Longmans, Green, 1941, p. 35.
82. Conference on Economic Progress, *Poverty and Deprivation*, pp. 14–15.
83. Morgan, et al., *Income and Welfare*, pp. 188 ff.
84. Orshansky, "Counting the Poor: Another Look at the Poverty Profile," p. 3.
85. Robert J. Lampman, "The Low Income Population and Economic Growth," U. S. Congress, Joint Economic Committee, Study Paper No. 12, Washington, D. C.: USGPO, 1959, p. 35.
86. Miller, "New Definition of Our 'Poor,'" p. 11.
87. Ibid.
88. Brian Abel-Smith and Peter Townsend, *The Poor and the Poorest*, London: G. Bell, 1965, pp. 39–49.
89. Galbraith, *Affluent Society*, Ch. 7.
90. I. M. Rubinow, "Poverty," *Encyclopedia of the Social Sciences*, New York: Macmillan, 1934, XII, 285; C.A.R. Crosland, *The Conservative Enemy*, New York: Schocken Books, 1962, pp. 97–98.
91. Pigou, *Economics of Welfare*, pp. 787–96.
92. Harold J. Laski, *Liberty in the Modern State*, New York: Harper, 1930, p. 218.
93. Crosland, *Conservative Enemy*, pp. 97–98.
94. Pigou, *Economics of Welfare*, pp. 691–700, 107.
95. Keynes, *Employment, Interest, and Money*, pp. 372–84.
96. For a full discussion, see I.M.D. Little, *Critique of Welfare Economics* 2d ed., London: Oxford U. Press, 1957.
97. Harry G. Johnson, "The Macro-Economics of Income Redistribution," in *Income Redistribution and Social Policy*, ed. Alan T. Peacock, London: Jonathan Cape, 1954, pp. 38–40.
98. Jacob Viner, *The Long View and the Short*, Glencoe: Free Press, 1958, pp. 177–212.
99. Adolf A. Berle, *The American Economic Republic*, New York: Harcourt, Brace & World, 1963, p. 51; Crosland, *Conservative Enemy*, pp. 28–29.

100. Thus, for example, C.A.R. Crosland's statement: "Moreover, the inequality is unjust in that it often reflects disparities not in natural talent, but in childhood opportunities for developing natural talent. It fosters social resentment, and it perpetuates the deep divisions in our society, the sense of 'we' and 'they,' the underprivileged and the privileged. We want a more equal distribution of wealth, not because redistribution today will make all the workers rich, but to help create a more just, united and humane community." (*Conservative Enemy*, p. 28.)

101. Richard M. Titmuss, *Income Distribution and Social Change*, London: Allen & Unwin, 1962.

102. Robert J. Lampman, "Changes in the Share of Wealth Held by Top Wealthholders, 1922–1956," *Rev. of Economics and Statistics*, XLI, 4 (November 1959), 379–92.

103. Simon Kuznets, *Shares of Upper Income Groups in Income and Savings*, New York: National Bureau of Economic Research, 1953.

104. Selma Goldsmith, et al., "Size Distribution of Income Since the Mid-Thirties," *Rev. of Economics and Statistics*, XXXVI, 1 (February 1954), I.

105. Herman P. Miller, *Income of the American People*, New York: Wiley, 1955, pp. 104–05.

106. See Bertrand de Jouvenel, *The Ethics of Redistribution*, London: Cambridge U. Press, 1951; R. Lewis and A. Maude, *The English Middle Classes*, New York: Knopf, 1949; and *Professional People in England*, Cambridge: Harvard U. Press, 1953; B. S. Rowntree and G. R. Lavers, *Poverty and the Welfare State*, New York: Longmans, Green, 1951; E. Powell, *Saving in a Free Society*, Hutchinson, 1960.

107. Titmuss, *Income Distribution and Social Change*.

108. Peter Wiles, "Property and Equality," in *The Unservile State*, ed. George Watson, New York: Macmillan, 1957, p. 91.

109. H. F. Lydall and D. G. Tipping, "The Distribution of Personal Wealth in Britain," *Bull. of the Oxford U. Institute of Statistics*, February, 1961.

110. Crosland, *Conservative Enemy*, pp. 37–38.

111. Richard M. Titmuss, "The Social Division of Welfare: Some Reflections on the Search for Equity," in *Essays on 'The Welfare State,'* New Haven: Yale U. Press, 1959, pp. 34–55.

112. Lampman, "The Low Income Population and Economic Growth," p. 35; Morgan, et al., *Income and Welfare* p. 217.

113. Tony Lynes, "Pension Rights and Wrongs," Fabian Tract 348, September 1963.

114. Allan M. Cartter, *Redistribution of Income in Postwar Britain*, New Haven: Yale. U. Press, 1955, pp. 91–92.

115. I. M. D. Little, "Fiscal Policy," *British Economy in the 1950's*, p. 289.

116. Sidney Pollard, *The Development of the British Economy, 1914–1950*, London: Edward Arnold, 1962, p. 207.

PART IV

Chapter 18

1. Arthur F. Burns, *Prosperity Without Inflation,* New York: Fordham U. Press, 1957, p. 18.
2. G.D.H. Cole, *The Post-War Condition of Britain,* New York: Praeger, 1957, p. 232.
3. See Milton Friedman, *Capitalism and Freedom,* Chicago: U. of Chicago Press, 1962; Robert Theobald, *Free Men and Free Markets,* New York: Clarkson Potter, 1963; Lady Juliet Rhys-Williams, *Something to Look Forward To,* London: MacDonald, 1943. For an interesting discussion of the whole issue, see Edward E. Schwartz, "A Way to End the Means Test," *Social Work,* IX, 3, (July 1964), 3–13.
4. I. M. Rubinow, "Poverty," *Encyclopedia of the Social Sciences,* New York: Macmillan, 1934, XII, p. 285.
5. B. Seebohm Rowntree, *Poverty and Progress,* London: Longmans, Green, 1941, p. 214.
6. A. C. Pigou, *The Economics of Welfare,* London: Macmillan, 1920, pp. 752–60.
7. William Beveridge, *Social Insurance and Allied Services,* New York: Macmillan, 1942, p. 14.
8. Ibid., pp. 6–7, par. 9.
9. Edwin E. Witte, *Social Security Perspectives,* ed. Robert J. Lampman, Madison: U. of Wisconsin Press, 1962, p. 103.
10. I. M. Rubinow, *The Quest for Security,* New York: Henry Holt, 1934, pp. 169, 180.
11. Lewis Meriam, *Relief and Social Security,* Washington, D. C.: Brookings Institute, 1946, p. 588.
12. Ibid., p. 615.
13. U. S. Congress, Committee on Long-Range Work and Relief Policies, *Security, Work and Relief Policies,* 78th Congress, 1st sess., House Document No. 128, Pt. 3, Washington, D. C.: USGPO, 1943, pp. 492–93.
14. Report of the Committee on the Economic and Financial Problems of the Provision for Old Age (Cmd. 9333), 1954, Table XIV, p. 41.
15. Rubinow, *Quest for Security,* Ch. 3.
16. Abraham Epstein, *Insecurity, A Challenge to America,* rev. ed., New York: Random House, 1936, Ch. 8.
17. Lenore A. Epstein, "Income of the Aged in 1962: First Findings of the 1963 Survey of the Aged," *Social Security Bull.,* XXVII, 3 (March 1964), 14.
18. Ibid., p. 11.
19. Dorothy Cole Wedderburn, "Poverty in Britain Today—The Evidence," *Sociological Rev.* x, n. s. (November 1962), p. 27.
20. Ibid., pp. 15–16, 13; M. Penelope Hall, *Social Services of Modern England,* p. 35; Cole, *Post-War Condition of Britain,* pp. 325–26.
21. "New Graduated Retirement Benefits in Great Britain," *Social Security Bull.* XXII, 9 (September 1959), 4–9.
22. Ministry of Pensions and National Insurance, *Earnings-related Short-term*

Benefits and Other Proposed Changes in the National Insurance Schemes, Cmnd. 2887, London: HMSO, January 1966.

23. Joseph Krislov, "Employee-Benefit Plans, 1954–62," *Social Security Bull.*, xxvii, 4 (April 1964), 4–21.

24. Joan Robinson, *Essays in the Theory of Employment,* New York: Macmillan, 1937, p. 101.

25. For example, see E. Wight Bakke, *The Unemployed Worker,* New Haven: Yale U. Press, 1940; also J. Wilbur Cohen, William Haber, and Eva Mueller, "The Impact of Unemployment in the 1958 Recession," 86th Congress, 2d sess., Washington, D. C.: USGPO, 1960; Mary B. Gilson, *Unemployment Insurance in Great Britain,* New York: Industrial Relations Counselors, 1931.

26. John Kenneth Galbraith, *The Affluent Society,* New York: Mentor, 1958, p. 17.

27. Ibid., p. 234.

28. Ibid., p. 230.

29. Williams, *Something to Look Forward To,* pp. 166–67.

30. Friedman, *Capitalism and Freedom,* p. 192.

31. Theobald, *Free Men and Free Markets,* pp. 197–201.

32. Friedman, *Capitalism and Freedom,* p. 192.

33. Theobald, *Free Men and Free Markets,* pp. 166–68.

34. Jack Wiseman, "The Political Economy of Social Services," *The Listener,* Oct. 7, 1965, p. 516; Dennis Lees, "A Social Security System for Today," *Crossbow,* vi, 23 (April-June 1963), 24.

35. John MacGregor, "A New Strategy for Social Security," *Crossbow* vii, 28 (July-September 1964), 29–33.

36. Wiseman, "The Political Economy of Social Services," p. 516.

37. Eveline M. Burns, "Social Security in Evolution: Towards What?" Paper presented at the Seventh Annual Meeting of the Industrial Relations Research Association, Chicago, 1964.

38. Ibid.

39. Ray L. Wilbur and Arthur M. Hyde, *The Hoover Policies,* New York: Scribner's, 1937, p. 45.

40. Matthew Woll, "The Economic Policy Proposed by American Labor," *The Annals of the American Academy of Political and Social Science,* cliv, 88 (March 1931).

41. Rubinow, *Quest for Security,* pp. 345–46.

42. Epstein, *Insecurity,* p. 164.

43. Ida C. Merriam, "Social Welfare Expenditure, 1963–64," *Social Security Bull.* xxvii, 10 (October 1964), 14.

44. Bureau of Public Assistance, *Characteristics of General Assistance in the United States,* Public Assistance Report No. 39, Washington, D. C.: USGPO, 1959.

45. See for example, H. R. bill 6675, 89th Congress, 1st sess., where in regard to medical assistance programs, appropriations to a state require that there be no "residence requirement which excludes any individual who resides in the State" (sec. 1902 (b) 3).

46. "Report of the Advisory Council on Social Security," *Social Security Bull.,* xxviii, 3 (March 1965), 9.

47. For a general discussion of the issues, see Eveline M. Burns, *Social Security and Public Policy,* New York: McGraw-Hill, 1956, Ch. 10.
48. I. C. Merriam, "Social Welfare Expenditures, 1963–64," p. 14.
49. Krislov, "Employee-Benefit Plans, 1954–62," *Social Security Bull.,* xxvii, 9.
50. Ibid., p. 4.
51. Sumner Hubert Slichter, *The Turnover of Factory Labor,* New York: D. Appleton, 1919.
52. *Economic Report of the President,* January 1964, Washington, D. C.: USGPO, 1964, pp. 73–77.
53. See Karl Mannheim, *Man and Society in an Age of Reconstruction,* London: Kegan Paul, Trench, Trubner, 1946, p. 322.
54. Abraham Epstein, *Insecurity: A Challenge to America,* rev. ed., New York: Random House, 1936, pp. 719–20; William H. Beveridge, *Insurance for All and Everything, the New Way,* Series vii, London: Daily News Ltd., 1924, pp. 6–7; also *Unemployment: A Problem of Industry,* New York: Longmans, Green, 1909, p. 234.
55. Epstein, *Insecurity* p. 719.
56. Jane M. Hoey, "The Significance of the Money Payment in Public Assistance," in *Social Security Bull.,* vii, 9 (September 1944), 3–5.
57. Hall, *Social Services of Modern England,* p. 37.
58. I. C. Merriam, "Social Welfare Expenditures, 1963–64," pp. 5, 9.
59. Ibid., pp. 6, 7.
60. United Kingdom Central Statistical Office, *Annual Abstract of Statistics,* No. 101, 1964, London: HMSO, 1964, pp. 44–47, Table 38.
61. *Child Care,* vii, 1 (January 1953), 26; See Alan Keith-Lucas, *Decisions about People in Need,* Chapel Hill: U. of North Carolina Press, 1957.
62. See Abel-Smith, "Freedom in the Welfare State," Fabian Tract No. 353, March 1964.
63. U. S. Congress, *Should the Federal Government Establish A National Program of Public Work for the Unemployed?* 88th Congress, 2d sess., House Document No. 363, Public Law 88–246, Washington, D. C.: USGPO, 1964, p. 75.
64. U. S. Congress, Committee on Long-Range Work and Relief Policies, *Security, Work, and Relief Policies,* p. 27.
65. For a recent review, see Sherwin D. Smith, "Boondoggle that Helped 38 Million People," *The New York Times Magazine* (May 2, 1965), pp. 37 ff.
66. See U. S. Congress, *Should the Federal Government Establish a National Program of Public Work for the Unemployed?,* pp. 116–90.
67. For an insightful discussion of the issues, see Nathan Glazer, "A Sociologist's View of Poverty," unpublished manuscript.
68. Hall, *Social Services of Modern England,* pp. 241–51.
69. *Working for Prosperity,* London: HMSO, 1965, pp. 12–13.
70. Royal Commission on the Poor Laws, 1909, *Minority Report;* Beveridge, *Unemployment.*
71. Beveridge, *Social Insurance and Allied Services,* par. 441, p. 164.
72. Ibid., par. 326, p. 128.
73. Hall, *Social Services of Modern England,* p. 44.
74. Ministry of Pensions and National Insurance, *Earnings-related Short-term*

Benefits and Other Proposed Changes in the National Insurance Schemes, Cmnd. 2887, London: HMSO, January 1966, p. 3.
75. Health, Education, and Welfare *Indicators,* Washington, D. C.: USGPO (September 1964), p. vi.
76. Health, Education, and Welfare *Indicators* (August 1962), p. v.
77. See Perry Levinson, "Chronic Dependency: A Conceptual Analysis," *Social Service Rev.* XXXVIII, 4 (December 1964), 371–81.
78. See Samuel Mencher, "Perspectives on Recent Welfare Legislation," *Social Work* VIII (July 1963), 59–65.
79. Hall, *Social Services of Modern England,* pp. 54–55.
80. *Report of the National Assistance Board, 1949,* Cmnd. 8030, London: HMSO, 1950, p. 16.
81. Ibid., pp. 16–17.
82. Barbara Wootten, *Social Science and Social Pathology,* London: Allen & Unwin, 1959, p. 54.
83. *Putting Britain Right Ahead,* London: Conservative and Unionist Central Office, October 1965, pp. 13–14.
84. See Gladys M. Kammerer, *British and American Child Welfare Services,* Detroit: Wayne State U. Press, 1962; Gordon Hamilton, "Editor's Page," *Social Work,* VII, 1 (January 1962); Eveline M. Burns, "What's Wrong with Public Welfare?," *Social Service Rev.,* XXXVI, 2 (June 1962); Mencher, "Perspectives on Recent Welfare Legislation," pp. 63–64.
85. *Report of the National Assistance Board, 1964,* Cmnd. 2674, London: HMSO, 1965, pp. 40–45.
86. Ibid., p. 58.
87. See Karl de Schweinitz, *People and Process in Social Security,* Washington, D. C.: American Council on Education, 1948; also Alfred J. Kahn, "Social Services in Relation to Income Security: Introductory Notes," *Social Service Rev.* XXXIX, 4 (December 1965), 381–89.
88. National Assistance Act, 1948, secs. 10, 16, 2; *Report of the National Assistance Board, 1964,* pp. 43–45.
89. Hall, *Social Services of Modern England,* pp. 56–57.
90. Ibid., pp. 122–23.
91. 470 H. C. Debs, 5s, 2486–87, 2466; *Child Neglect and the Social Services,* London: National Association for Maternity and Child Welfare, 1953, p. 10.
92. Glazer, "A Sociologist's View of Poverty," p. 15.

Conclusion

1. For a thorough discussion of this issue, see Calvin Woodward, "Reality and Social Reform: The Transition from Laissez-faire to the Welfare State," *The Yale Law Journal,* LXXII, 2 (December 1962) 286–328.
2. See Morris Ginsberg, "The Growth of Social Responsibility," *Law and Opinion in England in the Twentieth Century,* ed. Morris Ginsberg, Berkeley: U. of California Press, 1959, pp. 3–26.

INDEX

Index